The
Mac® OS X Book

Mark R. Bell

The Mac® OS X Book

Copyright © 2001 The Coriolis Group, LLC. All rights reserved.

Limits of Liability and Disclaimer of Warranty

Trademarks

The Coriolis Group, LLC
14455 N. Hayden Road
Suite 220
Scottsdale, Arizona 85260

(480)483-0192
FAX (480)483-0193
www.coriolis.com

Library of Congress Cataloging-in-Publication Data
Bell, Mark R.
    The Mac OS X book / by Mark R. Bell
        p.   cm.
    Includes index.
    ISBN 1-57610-605-5
    1. Mac OS.   2. Operating systems (Computers).   3. Macintosh
(Computer) -- Programming.   I. Title.
QA76.76.O63 B4497 2001
005.4'469--dc21   2001032383

Publisher
Steve Sayre

Acquisitions Editor
Charlotte Carpentier

Product Marketing
Manager
Tracy Rooney

Project Editor
Toni Zuccarini Ackley

Technical Reviewer
James Thomson

Production Coordinator
Peggy Cantrell

Cover Designer
Jesse Dunn

Layout Designer
April E. Nielsen

CD-ROM Developer
Chris Nusbaum

Printed in the United States of America
10 9 8 7 6 5 4 3 2 1

CORIOLIS

Look for these related books from The Coriolis Group:

Mac OS X Little Black Book
by Gene Steinberg

Mac OS X Black Book
by Mark R. Bell and Debrah D. Suggs

The iMac Book, 2nd Edition
by Don Rittner

The Mac OS 9 Book
by Mark R. Bell

Mac OS 9.1 Black Book
by Mark R. Bell and Debrah D. Suggs

Windows 2000 Mac Support Little Black Book
by Gene Steinberg

Also published by Coriolis Technology Press:

Game Architecture and Design
by Andrew Rollings and Dave Morris

Java 2 Black Book
by Steven Holzner

HTML Black Book
by Steven Holzner

To Virginia . . .
And now good morrow to our waking souls,
Which watch not one another out of fear;
For love, all love of other sights controls,
And makes one little room, an everywhere.
— John Donne, "The Good-Morrow"

About the Author

Mark R. Bell is a best-selling author of over 22 computer books, articles, and software manuals, including *The Mac Web Server Book*, *The Mac OS 8 Book*, *Mac OS 8.5 Black Book*, *The Mac OS 8.6 Book*, *The Mac OS 9 Book*, and *Mac OS 9.1 Black Book*. He is also a technical editor and contributing author, and has spoken at several conventions and workshops, including Mactivity/Web and Macworld Expo.

Mark holds a bachelor's degree with a triple-major (English, history, and political science) from MTSU, and a master's degree in theology from Duke University. He and his wife, Virginia D. Smith, live in Chapel Hill, North Carolina, where they are surrounded by a network of Macs and a small herd of Cocker Spaniels. He is currently at work on a book about Mac OS X for advanced users, as well as a book about the theology of *Star Trek*.

Acknowledgments

Writing computer books is a group effort, and I'd like to acknowledge the many people with whom I've worked to complete this book. Coriolis has many dedicated staff who have been essential to this project, chief among whom is Toni Zuccarini Ackley, who has served as the Project Editor and is also the Managing Editor for the Technology Press group. Toni has been assisted by many others at Coriolis, including Peggy Cantrell (Production Coordinator), April Nielsen (Layout Designer), Jesse Dunn (Cover Designer), Chris Nusbaum (CD-ROM Developer), and Charlotte Carpentier (Acquisitions Editor). The Coriolis team is dedicated to producing the best Mac books on the market, and I appreciate being part of their efforts.

There is another fantastic group of people that I work with every step along the way who contributed so much to this book, I should ask for their names to be on the cover, too. My wife Virginia Smith served as Copy Editor and keeps me from making a fool of myself in the English language on a daily basis; Mary Catherine Bunn again served as the eagle-eyed Proofreader, catching mistakes even Bill Shakespeare would have let pass; Debrah D. Suggs, my long-time coauthor, assisted in writing the appendices; and Rob Terrell recruited me into the business as coauthor on my first Mac book. I am lucky to have James Thomson (author of DragThing) serve as the Technical Editor for this book because of his intimate knowledge of, and programming skills in, Mac OS X. I look forward to working with this group in the future!

Finally, I'd like to extend my thanks to the 74 software authors and companies who have graciously allowed us to include their software on the companion CD-ROM for this book. The success of Mac OS X depends on people like this, and I think we're off to a great start. :-)

Contents at a Glance

Table of Contents

Introduction

I first used the Mac OS when I was sweating bullets over my first graduate research project at Duke University. I had been using a PC in a public cluster of computers in the library back in the days of DOS, so you can just imagine my level of frustration in trying to remember the correct combination of Shift, Alt, and Function keys to insert the cursor in a line of text. I was rescued—and spontaneously converted to the Mac OS—by Blake Leyerle, a fellow student working on her dissertation on the Macintosh side of the cluster.

Blake asked if I would like to see how to use a program called MacWrite on a Macintosh SE, which had dual floppy drives and no hard drive. A diskette with the application went into the top drive, and a floppy for storing my documents went in the bottom. This new computer used something called System 6, which featured a graphical user interface and mouse instead of a blue background with white text. Within five minutes, I wasn't *learning* how to use the Macintosh, I was *using* the Macintosh, and I never looked back.

That was in the 1980s, and now Mac OS X—the latest version of Apple's operating system—includes, strangely enough, a command-line interface buried deep beneath a stunningly beautiful interface called Aqua. Mac OS X is a dramatic change from previous versions of the operating system because of Darwin, its industrial-strength core operating system. However, Mac OS X retains a tremendous level of backward-compatibility with earlier, "Classic" versions of the Mac OS and advances its powerful leverage of the Internet further than ever. Like its predecessors, Mac OS X is easy enough to use. As Blake did for me, I hope to introduce you to all the features of the Mac OS so you can be productive sooner than you thought.

Who Needs This Book?

This book is for anyone who is new to Mac OS X, such as a new G4 owner, or anyone who has used a previous version of the Mac OS and recently upgraded to a G3 or G4 and needs to know what's new in Mac OS X. Of course, some of you who are experienced users will already know much of what lies ahead in this book, such as managing aliases, switching among multiple applications, or customizing your Desktop. An equal number of you who are experienced users will be surprised to learn a thing or two about such tricks as customizing the Dock, typing commands in the Terminal application, and Web Sharing using the built-in Apache Web server. So, this book is for the earliest beginner, as well as the experienced user.

Hardware Requirements

Mac OS X will run on any Macintosh with a G3 or G4 processor, except the original G3 PowerBook. Specifically, Mac OS X also requires:

- 128MB of RAM

- 1.5GB of free disk space

- An internal monitor connection, or a video card from IXMicro, ATI, or Nvidia that was installed by Apple

The list of supported machines includes all Power Mac G4, Power Macintosh G3, iMac, iBook, and G3 or G4 PowerBooks except the very first G3 PowerBook.

And although Mac OS X uses a sophisticated and persistent form of virtual memory, experience tells me that you will be happier with the performance of your computer if it has at least 256MB of RAM.

What's Inside

Here is a chapter-by-chapter rundown of what you will find in this book:

- *Chapter 1, Getting to Know Mac OS X*—Provides an overview of tasks performed by the Mac OS, looks at its various components, and explains how to use its basic features and how to configure the basic preferences.

- *Chapter 2, Configuring Classic*—Explores how to best configure Mac OS 9.1 to run in the Classic environment under Mac OS X, or boot directly into Mac OS 9.1.

- *Chapter 3, Working with Classic*—Explains the differences between working with Classic versus Carbon and Cocoa applications, including memory management and using multiple applications.

- *Chapter 4, Working with the Finder and Desktop*—Explores the various drop-down menus in the Finder and how to use them; how to manipulate Finder windows; advanced Finder and Desktop features; and how to use the new Trash and Info windows.

- *Chapter 5, Customizing Mac OS X*—Explores how to customize the Mac OS using built-in features and third-party utilities, as well as how to create user accounts to make sharing your computer easier and safer than ever.

- *Chapter 6, Organizing Your Data*—Looks at the various ways you can manage the new file structure and the contents of your hard drives using aliases and comments, as well as how to search for information using Sherlock and how to encrypt files for security purposes.

- *Chapter 7, Take X (on the Road)*—Explains issues that mobile users are likely to encounter, including power, performance, display, remote access, and security.

- *Chapter 8, Working with Applications*—Addresses the various levels of compatibility between the three types of Mac OS X applications, as well as how to launch your applications and use stationery documents, layered windows, and attached sheets.

- *Chapter 9, Managing Fonts and Printers*—Describes the new Quartz imaging model, various types of fonts that may be used in Mac OS X, how to use the new Fonts panel and a few third-party utilities, and how to configure ColorSync to manage color matching more efficiently.

- *Chapter 10, Exploring Multimedia*—Shows off the impressive multimedia capabilities and utilities in Mac OS X, including QuickTime 5, QuickTime VR, Preview, speech capabilities, and the latest about listening to MP3s using iTunes and creating your own movies with iMovie.

- *Chapter 11, Scripting Mac OS X*—Explains the basics of AppleScript and how you can use scripts to automate tasks.

- *Chapter 12, Using Java*—Shows how you can run Java applets on your Mac using your Web browser or the Applet Launcher, as well as how Java applets can take on the look and feel of other operating systems.

- *Chapter 13, Troubleshooting Mac OS X*—Explains the various errors you might encounter, what to do about them, and the best tools for fixing problems.

- *Chapter 14, File and Web Sharing*—Demonstrates how you can use the built-in File Sharing and Web Sharing features to share your files, folders, and documents over a local area network or the Internet.

- *Chapter 15, Collaborating on a Network*—Explores how to use the new Connect To Server command to access remote servers and volumes, as well as how to use FTP and SSH to access your iDisk and other computers, and how to store passwords in the Keychain.

- *Chapter 16, Connecting to the Internet*—Explains the different types of Internet access and how to configure ports and protocols, switch among Internet locations, and connect to a dial-up ISP using the Internet Connect application.

- *Chapter 17, Mastering Internet Applications and Utilities*—Provides an overview of the Internet configuration features, applications, and utilities installed by Mac OS X, as well as a handful of essential applications and utilities from third-party developers.

- *Appendix A, Getting Help*—Shows you the various ways you can get online help.

- *Appendix B, Shortcuts*—Lists the keyboard shortcuts available in Mac OS X.

- *Appendix C, Learning Unix Shell Commands*—Introduces the basics of using the Terminal application to execute commands.

- *Appendix D, Mac OS 9.1 and Mac OS X Feature Comparison*—Gives a brief overview of the differences in features between Mac OS 9.1 and Mac OS X.

- *Appendix E, Installing and Updating Mac OS 9.1 and Mac OS X*—Explains how to use the installation CDs to install, reinstall, add, and remove Mac OS 9.1 and Mac OS X components, as well as how to use the Software Update feature to update the Mac OS over the Internet.

- *Appendix F, Additional Resources on the Web*—Lists several categories of Web sites for additional information about Apple and the Mac OS.

Contacting the Author

Finally, the publisher and I welcome your input on how to make this book even better. If you have any suggestions, rants, or raves, please send them my way. You can find my contact information, as well as errata and other information, on the official Web site for this book at **www.MacOSBook.com**. Or you can email The Coriolis Group at **ctp@coriolis.com**. Happy reading!

Part I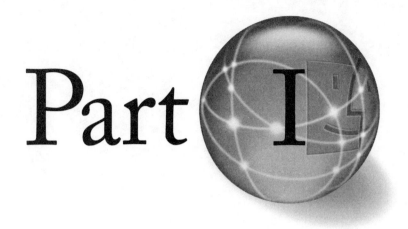

The Operating System

Getting to Know Mac OS X

Computer operating systems make it easy for you to perform complex tasks without having to navigate the intricate maze of computer code that controls everyday actions. An operating system enables you to accomplish these tasks by way of symbolic gestures such as clicking on an icon to open a document, dragging a file to the Trash to delete it, and clicking on a URL to access a Web site. Mac OS X is an operating system designed to give you the power to execute unwieldy commands with the grace and style that have always been synonymous with the Macintosh. Mac OS X distills complex, industrial-strength tasks down to a few elegant steps—a click of the mouse here, a press of the keyboard there. Don't be fooled by Mac OS X's deceptively simple appearance, however—underneath it all lies a weapons-grade operating system! OS X offers more flexibility than previous versions of the Mac OS, especially in the areas of ease of use and Internet access. To understand how to make the most of the expanded capabilities of the OS, you need to understand how the OS works. This chapter introduces and defines the functions of Mac OS X and offers a quick tour of Macintosh basics as well as some of the more common commands and features provided by the new OS.

This tour is designed for readers who are using the Mac OS for the first time, as well as Mac OS 8 and 9 users who are upgrading to Mac OS X. Because Mac OS X is a significant departure from previous versions of the Mac OS, I suggest reading this chapter before diving into the details of Mac OS X's features in subsequent chapters. If you're comfortable using Mac OS X, you can probably skim the sections entitled "What Tasks Does the Operating System Perform?" and "Using the Mac OS" before moving on to Chapter 2.

What Tasks Does the Operating System Perform?

What makes the Macintosh smile when you turn it on? Why does the CD-ROM icon appear on the Desktop when you insert an audio CD? How can you access the Internet and check your email? How are fonts shared among all your applications?

The answer to these questions is an easy one: The operating system does it for you. The operating system (abbreviated OS, which computer geeks rhyme with *boss*) has three main responsibilities: it controls the hardware built into your computer (and any peripherals you have connected to it); it provides common elements and features to all your software applications; and it helps you manage your disks, files, and directories. Let's briefly look at each of these areas:

- *Hardware control*—In order for your Mac to work, its random access memory (RAM), disk drives, video monitor, keyboard, mouse, printer, and digital versatile disc (DVD) drive (or other peripherals) must be collectively managed. Saving files to disk, drawing images on the screen, and printing are examples of hardware control managed by the OS.

- *Common software elements*—Every Mac OS software application has common elements such as menus, windows, and fonts. These common elements are perpetuated by application programmers who follow Apple's suggested human interface design principles. Apple provides these elements and conventions to software developers for their use.

- *Disk and file management*—The Finder provides a graphical user interface (GUI) that employs icons and windows to represent the complex operations necessary to manage your disks and files. It enables you to navigate disks and remote file servers; allows you to find, copy, move, rename, and delete files; and displays icon- and text-based information about disks and files. The Finder also allows you to launch applications and acts as the "home base" from which you start up or quit applications.

Mac OS X is also remarkable for its backward compatibility with earlier versions of the OS. This feature's history dates back to Apple's transition from the old Motorola 68000 series of microprocessors to the PowerPC processor. The Mac OS allowed PowerPC processors (such as the G3 and G4 processors), which are Reduced Instruction Set Computing (RISC) microprocessors, to run programs and software libraries written for the much older Complex Instruction Set Computing (CISC) microprocessors—albeit more slowly than software written specifically for the Power Macintosh.

Mac OS X is also compatible with applications written for earlier versions of the Mac OS. Under Mac OS X, programs can be executed in five distinct types of application environments:

- *Classic*—For applications written for Mac OS 9.1 and much earlier versions of the Mac OS, including System 6, System 7, and Mac OS 8. To run in Mac OS X, Classic applications require that a copy of Mac OS 9.1 be installed on your computer. Classic applications written for 68K or PowerPC processors will run in the Classic environ-ment but cannot take advantage of the advanced features of Mac OS X. See Chapters 2 and 3 for detailed information regarding running Classic applications.

- *Carbon*—For applications written for Mac OS 8 and 9 that have been "tuned up" for Mac OS X and take advantage of all its advanced features (see the "Mac OS X Components" section for more information).

- *Cocoa*—For applications that take full advantage of Mac OS X's advanced features and user interface.

- *Java*—For applications written for the Java programming language. This is not so much an application environment as an execution environment. Mac OS X includes a Java Virtual Machine (VM) that allows Java applets to be executed without modification.

- *Berkeley System Distribution (BSD) commands*—For executing command-line instructions from within the Terminal application. Anyone with Unix experience will find a host of familiar commands to execute here.

By coordinating these application environments, Mac OS X allows you to access your old applications. Mac OS X's consistent user interface provides continuity from one application to the next and allows software developers to focus on creating unique and sophisticated programs while leaving the complexities of the modern OS to Apple. Figure 1.1 illustrates the central roles played by Mac OS X—using icons as symbols of the various application environments, file and network management, and user inter-face standards.

Figure 1.1
Mac OS X provides the central link between various application environments and user interface metaphors.

Mac OS X Components

Unlike its predecessors, Mac OS X is not extensible through the addition of third-party modifications such as Extensions and Control Panels. At first this may sound like a limitation, but it's actually a good thing—these modifications to the Mac OS often caused it to be unstable or slow. Furthermore, many of the programming elements of the Mac OS that enabled extensibility also prevented it from being able to implement advanced features that Mac OS X is now fully capable of, such as:

- *Preemptive multitasking*—The OS's ability to ensure that processing time is shared appropriately between the OS and running applications. Cooperative multitasking, used by Mac OS 9, relies on applications to "play well" with one another and is a far less efficient method for dividing processor resources.

- *Protected memory*—Dedicated RAM space that other applications cannot invade or disturb. Users have become all too familiar with the memory errors associated with previous versions of the Mac OS that do not have protected memory.

- *Persistent virtual memory (VM)*—An advanced virtual memory system that is managed by the Mac OS and cannot be disabled. Earlier versions of the Mac OS have user-configurable virtual memory options that are accessible through the Memory Control Panel.

- *Symmetric multiprocessing (SMP)*—The ability to use two or more processors in unison. Despite Apple's tinkering with multiprocessor support in previous versions, the OS was never capable of using more than one processor.

These improvements are only the tip of the iceberg, however. To really begin to appreciate the radical differences between Mac OS X and its predecessors, let's take a look at how the components of Mac OS X work.

Foundation Layer

Darwin, the foundation layer upon which the rest of Mac OS X depends, is based on *open source* software. This means that (under the Apple Public Source License) Darwin's core belongs in the public domain. Developers are encouraged to improve upon Darwin, the idea being that their input will eventually make the OS stronger and better-suited to the real-life environments in which Macs are used. Darwin was named after Charles Darwin, the English naturalist who developed the modern theory of evolution. Figure 1.2 illustrates Darwin and all the other layers of Mac OS X.

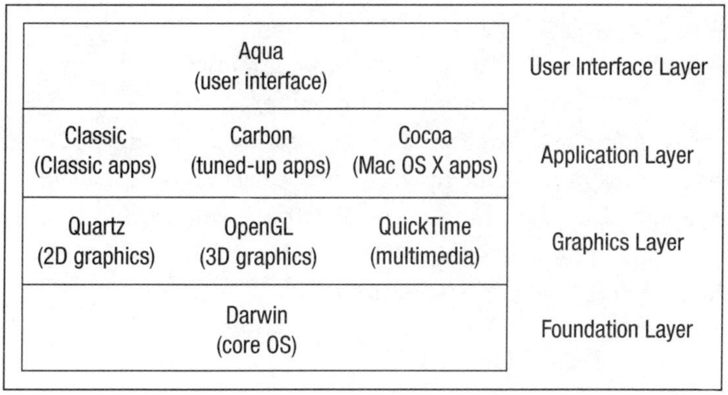

Aqua (user interface)			User Interface Layer
Classic (Classic apps)	Carbon (tuned-up apps)	Cocoa (Mac OS X apps)	Application Layer
Quartz (2D graphics)	OpenGL (3D graphics)	QuickTime (multimedia)	Graphics Layer
Darwin (core OS)			Foundation Layer

Figure 1.2
You can think of Mac OS X as a series of layers built on top of Darwin, an open source operating system.

Darwin provides the low-level operating services, such as pre-emptive multitasking and symmetric multiprocessing, that allow Mac OS X to be as rock-solid as any operating system available today. Darwin is actually a collection of technologies woven together to provide the foundation upon which everything else sits. It includes:

■ *Mach kernel*—The central portion of Darwin that connects the Mac OS to the computer's hardware.

■ *Berkeley Software Distribution (BSD)*—Also an open source Unix operating system, this version of BSD provides file system and networking services for Mac OS X.

■ *I/O Kit*—A customized device driver support that allows for fast plug-and-play access to external hardware such as scanners, cameras, and storage drives.

■ *Network Kernel Extensions (NKEs)*—Extensions to Darwin that allow you to add and configure third-party networking features to the OS.

■ *Virtual File System (VFS)*—Darwin's VFS allows the Mac OS to access hard drives and file server volumes in several formats, including Hierarchical File System (HFS), Hierarchical File System Plus (HFS+), Unix File System (UFS), Universal Disk Format (UDF) for DVD discs, and International Standards Organization (ISO) 9660 for CD-ROMs. VFS allows for file names up to 255 characters (up from 32 in Mac OS 9.1) as well as access to hard drives via the Apple File Sharing Protocol (AFP) and Network File Service (NFS) protocol.

As operating systems go, Darwin is about as sophisticated as they come—it pulls off the feat of tying legacy Mac OS 9.1 services into the new OS without burdening users with its underlying complexity. All we see is a crisp, colorful, and intuitive graphical interface!

Graphics Layer

The graphics layer that sits on top of Darwin is composed of one new and two familiar technologies. These three components control all of Mac OS X's visual effects, including icons, windows, 2D and 3D graphics, multimedia, and printing. In fact, some of the most obvious improvements over previous versions of the OS can be seen in the Aqua theme interface, with its larger icons, drop shadows, and sharply drawn windows. For example, Figure 1.3 shows the contents of the same hard drive viewed in Mac OS X (top) and Mac OS 9.1 (bottom).

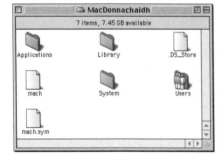

Figure 1.3
The 2D and 3D graphics capabilities of Mac OS X are more impressive than ever!

Like the foundation layer of the OS, the graphics layer consists of several technologies that work together behind the scenes and present a unified front:

- *Quartz*—Handles screen drawing, cursor manipulation, antialiasing of fonts and graphics, and 2D graphics acceleration. Because the default screen and document format is based on the Portable Document Format (PDF) standard, all documents can be manipulated and saved in PDF format with crisp colors and special effects such as vector graphics and drop shadows. Carbon-based applications can still take advantage of QuickDraw, the graphics standard for Mac OS 9.1.

■ *OpenGL*—Allows OS X to run games and a variety of applications (including modeling, animation, video, and scientific) that render 3D objects. Open GL, produced by Silicon Graphics, is the industry standard for 3D graphics rendering.

■ *QuickTime*—Powers the movie and MP3 capabilities of Mac OS X and allows users to view movies, sounds, and images in dozens of formats. QuickTime is the long-time multimedia standard for the Mac OS.

Application Layer

Like the foundation and graphics layers, the application layer consists of several components. The application execution environments mentioned earlier in this chapter are the components that make up the application layer. These environments allow different types of applications to run simultaneously under Mac OS X for maximum backward compatibility with Mac OS 9.1. The main application environments include:

■ *Classic*—For unmodified Mac OS 9.1 (and earlier) applications. The Classic environment allows these applications to run in conjunction with Mac OS X.

■ *Carbon*—For Mac OS 8 and 9 applications that have been modified to take advantage of Mac OS X's advanced features and Aqua interface. Carbon applications are based on approximately 70 percent of the same programming code as Mac OS 9.1 (i.e., Classic) applications. The remaining code base, which prevents applications from using advanced features like pre-emptive multitasking, is stripped out of Carbon applications and replaced with Application Programming Interfaces (APIs) that enable the new features. Figure 1.4 shows an example of Microsoft Internet Explorer, a Carbon application.

■ *Cocoa*—For applications written specifically for Mac OS X. In other words, Cocoa applications contain no *legacy code* from earlier versions of the Mac OS.

Aqua

The topmost layer of Mac OS X is the Aqua interface. Aqua is only the third major interface change in the history of the Macintosh, after the original (System 6 and earlier) and the Platinum (Mac OS 8 and 9) interfaces. Aqua is a fairly radical departure because it incorporates dramatic changes from previous OSs, including:

■ Color interface elements

■ Pulsating buttons

■ Greater depth of color

■ Larger icons

Figure 1.4
Microsoft Internet Explorer, an example of a Carbon application.

■ Translucence

■ Drop shadows

■ Animated windows

■ "Attached Sheet" dialog windows

■ Column views

■ Dock

For example, Figure 1.5 shows many of the new features, including the column list, Dock, larger icons, and color interface elements.

The design principal for the new Aqua interface is to provide a fluid and deep interface that mimics Apple's new line of hardware, including the Titanium PowerBook and the Cube. Some graphic designers may find the colors of the new interface distracting, so Apple includes an Appearance theme called Graphite that uses gray buttons in place of the red, yellow, green, and blue buttons of the Aqua theme. Most users, however, will be happy to discover that Aqua provides more interactivity and more opportunities for customization, and does so more intuitively than previous interfaces. We'll explore the basic features of Aqua in the next section, and learn in detail how to customize the user interface in Chapter 5.

Figure 1.5
The new Aqua interface is a radical departure from earlier versions of the Mac OS.

Using the Mac OS

The Mac OS is loaded from the hard drive when the computer is turned on, and remains in use until the computer is turned off. Any additions, deletions, or modifications you make to the OS are saved back to the hard drive; when you choose Restart or Shut Down from the Apple menu and the Mac OS is loaded again, your changes are ready for use. To further help you understand the role of the Mac OS, let's take a look at a few of the essential tasks it controls:

- *Start-up*—Almost immediately after the power is turned on, the Mac OS takes control of the start-up process, verifies that your hardware is functioning properly, and loads the Desktop and Finder.

- *File management*—When you manipulate windows and icons in the Finder and on the Desktop, your actions are translated from the onscreen graphical display into actual code changes to the files on disk. As you know, files aren't stored on disk as cute little icons—they're actually strings of 1s and 0s. The OS transforms them into meaningful text, beautiful graphics, stirring sounds, and moving images.

- *Application launching*—When you run a software program, the OS accesses the computer and ensures that the correct portions of the file are read from disk, that the available memory is properly managed, and that data files (and sometimes temporary work files) are created and maintained on disk.

- *Font usage*—Every time a font—whether it's bitmapped, Type 1, TrueType, or OpenType—is used on the Macintosh, the OS supplies information about the font, including the way it should look in any particular size and style. This ensures that the font is displayed on screen or printed properly.

- *Windows and dialog boxes*—The Mac OS provides the basic format for all windows and dialog boxes used on the Macintosh. For the Open and Save As dialog boxes, the Mac OS now supplies programmers with the ability to use a drop-down sheet attached to the document in question. This window replaces the old modal dialog boxes that often stopped everything on your computer until the document was saved or closed. Apple publishes a complex set of documentation called the "Apple Human Interface Guidelines" to help software programmers create consistent window elements and dialog boxes.

- *Printing*—An application must pass its data through one of the OS's printer drivers in order to convert it into a format that the printer can understand. After this has been taken care of, the OS communicates the file to the printer and, in some cases, receives feedback from the printer during output.

- *Screen display*—The OS is responsible for producing the display that appears on your computer's screen. Applications communicate the display information to the OS using Quartz, which converts this information and draws it on the screen.

- *Networking*—Nearly every aspect of communication between the Mac and its peripherals is controlled by the OS. This includes data transfer from the disk to the Internet or other networked service; the timing of network communications while other software is being run onscreen; two-way communications with sophisticated printers, modems, and storage drives; and cabling.

As you can see, almost every task you perform on your Macintosh—from the smallest mouse click to the largest data transfer—relies on the OS. Although it isn't necessary to understand the technical intricacies of how the OS performs these tasks in order to use your Macintosh, an appreciation for the range and depth of the OS's functions is useful, nonetheless.

Basic Mac OS Operations

Let's turn from technical descriptions of the Mac OS to the easiest and most fundamental aspects of using the OS. This section looks at the things you need to know in order to use Mac OS X efficiently, and defines terms you'll encounter throughout the book. This information is intended primarily for readers who are using Mac OS X in their first experience on the Macintosh.

The Graphical User Interface

The first and most fundamental requirement for using the Mac OS is understanding its graphical user interface. Instead of communicating your commands in words, you select pictures—or icons—that represent Macintosh hardware and software functions and features. The mouse cursor also plays an important role in communicating with the Macintosh. (Yes, you'll use the keyboard too, but I'll assume you've already mastered that device.)

Let's look at each of the elements of the graphical user interface.

Icons

Icons are small graphics (pictures) that appear on the Macintosh screen; they represent items such as disks and folders and, in fact, they actually look like a hard drive or folder, as shown previously in Figure 1.5. Different icons are used to represent the various types of files stored on your disks. Figure 1.6 shows examples of an application icon and a document icon for the application Preview (a PDF and image viewing program).

Figure 1.6
An example of an application icon (left) and a document icon (right) used by the application.

Most applications and their associated documents use application-specific icons. All document icons are in the shape of a dog-eared page, but a custom document icon also contains a small version of the application's icon. If an application or document doesn't have a custom icon, Mac OS X assigns a generic icon instead.

Windows

When a file, folder, or disk is opened, its contents are displayed in a window. The most common type of window, which looks like the one shown in Figure 1.7, usually includes a title bar at the top and scroll bars on the right and bottom edges. Because many windows are customizable under Mac OS X, they may not look exactly like the one shown here. You can move a window around (by dragging its title bar), close a window (by clicking the close button), increase the size of the window (by clicking the zoom button), change the size of a window (by dragging the resize tab), or minimize

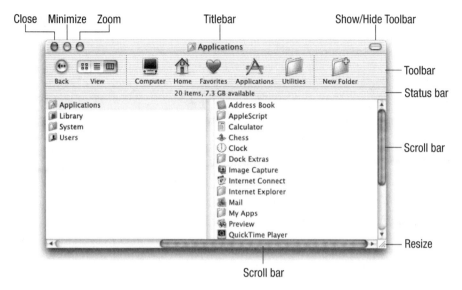

Figure 1.7
A sample Finder window.

the window (by double-clicking on the titlebar or clicking on the minimize button). Minimized windows are placed in the Dock at the bottom of the screen.

Mac OS X features other types of windows as well, including application-specific windows that have fewer (or additional) window elements than shown in Figure 1.7. You won't see as many dialog boxes as in previous versions of the OS—Apple recommends replacing them with the drop-down windows called *attached sheets* mentioned earlier. These small, specialized windows usually present a set of options that allow you to Save or Save As. Unlike the old modal dialog boxes, you can switch to another application or the Finder while the window is open without the Mac OS coming to a screeching halt. Figure 1.8 illustrates the way in which one of the new windows is "attached" to its document.

An alert window, another new type of window, simply provides information—usually feedback concerning a command or action you're engaged in or a message from one of your hardware devices. Along with this information, an alert window usually has an OK button and nothing else. An example of an alert window is displayed in Figure 1.9.

Finally, a floating palette is yet another type of window used in some software applications. Palettes "float" on top of the active document windows and the Desktop and cannot be obscured by them. Unlike an ordinary window, which disappears after you've selected options or closed it, a palette may remain open for the duration of a work session (although it may also become invisible when the application is minimized). A

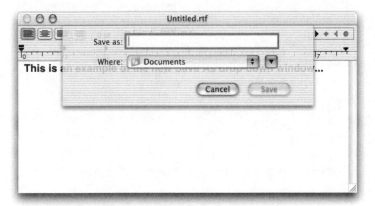

Figure 1.8
A drop-down sheet often replaces the old Save As dialog box.

Figure 1.9
A standard alert window in Mac OS X.

floating palette displays a collection of icons that represent the tools that are available to you, in much the same way that an artist's palette displays her paints. Sometimes a palette presents a text list of commands or options for you to choose from. Figure 1.10 shows several types of palette windows.

Menus

In Mac OS applications, most commands are presented in the menu bar at the top of the screen. Commands are usually grouped logically and have names befitting their functions. The menu bar is one of the most distinctive elements of the Mac OS. The familiar fonts Chicago and Charcoal, specifically designed for the purpose of attractive screen display on the original Macintosh, have been replaced in Mac OS X by Lucida Grande.

 In Mac OS X, menus drop down and stay open until you make a menu selection or click somewhere else on the screen. (They're sometimes referred to as "sticky" menus.) Drop-down menus relieve you from holding down the mouse button while navigating the menu.

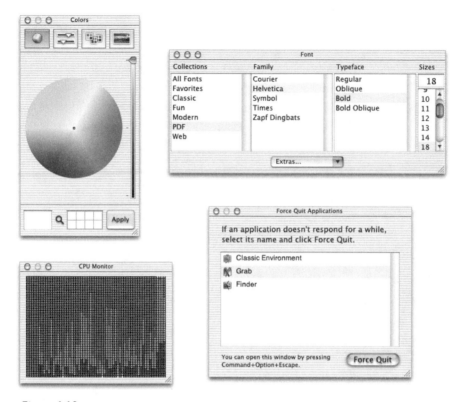

Figure 1.10
A sampling of floating palettes.

When you click on the menu name, the menu drops down and stays down until you make a selection or click somewhere else on the screen (this feature was introduced in Mac OS 8, but was previously available only when using third-party utilities). As you drag the mouse along the menu while holding the mouse button, each command is highlighted as the mouse cursor passes over it. If you release the mouse while a particular command is highlighted, that command will be executed; the selected command flashes once to confirm that it has been executed successfully. (Using the mouse will be covered more fully later in this chapter.) In Mac OS X, activated menus, which are translucent, do not time out as they did in Mac OS 9.

The Mac OS employs four basic types of menu commands. Some commands execute as soon as they're selected. Others act as a toggle to turn a feature on and off. Command names that end with ellipses (...) bring up a dialog box of related options. A fourth type of menu command offers you a hierarchical submenu of commands. To select an item from one of these normal, toggling, or elliptical menus, click the item once. Figure 1.11 shows an example of a hierarchical, translucent menu.

Figure 1.11
Mac OS X adds several new features to drop-down menus, including translucence and staying open an unlimited amount of time if not dismissed.

The Mouse and Cursors

Each of the graphical elements we've discussed so far interacts with the Mac OS via mouse manipulation. Operating the mouse is simple enough: You move the mouse on your mouse pad, and the cursor moves onscreen accordingly. Only the motion of the cursor on your Desktop produces a change in cursor position, making the mouse a relative pointing device. (Some devices like graphics tablets are absolute pointing devices, meaning that each point on their surface maps to a point on your screen.) The type of cursor that appears at any given time depends on many variables, including the item you're pointing to, the software you're using, the commands you've chosen, and the keys you've pressed.

Arrow cursors appear whenever you're pointing to the menu bar, regardless of the application in use. When you're working in the Finder, the mouse cursor will be a left-pointing arrow. Macintosh applications also use the arrow cursor to select and manipulate objects. Custom cursors are employed by applications to indicate the specific tool being used or the type of operation being performed by an application. For example, a cursor in the shape of a pencil could represent the ability to draw freehand in a graphics application. Similarly, a cursor in the shape of a magnifying glass might be used to indicate that you can zoom in or out on a document in a painting program.

You can perform five common actions with the cursor. These actions manipulate icons, invoke commands, and control application tools:

- *Pointing*—Positioning the cursor over a particular icon, object, or window element. When the cursor takes the form of an arrow, the arrow's tip marks the exact spot you're pointing to. Other cursor styles have their own "hot spots," or specific points of action.

- *Clicking*—Quickly pressing and releasing the mouse button. In most cases, the click executes when the button is fully released, not while it's being pressed. Mouse clicks select objects, including icons, buttons, and dialog box options.

- *Double-clicking*—Pressing and releasing the mouse button twice in rapid succession. Most beginners don't double-click fast enough to prevent the Mac OS from inter-preting two single clicks instead of one double-click. Double-clicking controls many Macintosh actions, such as opening icons to display their windows. The sensitivity with which the OS responds to double-clicking can be changed in the Mouse System Preferences pane.

- *Pressing*—Holding down the mouse button while a command or action is completed.

- *Dragging*—Moving the mouse—and therefore the cursor—while holding down (pressing) the mouse button. This action usually moves an item or employs the active cursor tool (such as when you're drawing a line with a pencil tool).

Files and Folders

Now that you understand icons and windows and are comfortable working with your mouse, you're ready to put all that knowledge and skill to work. Manipulating files on the Desktop is one of the most important tasks you'll undertake.

Files come in many different types—applications, data documents, OS files, utilities, fonts, and dictionaries. You can keep all these files organized by putting them into folders. The File menu's New Folder command enables you to create folders to hold any type of file. You can also create folders inside other folders to establish a hierarchical arrangement of files and folders, the importance of which will be explained in Chapter 6.

Mac OS X replaces Mac OS 9.1's button view with the column view, a new way of viewing the contents of your files and folders (see Figure 1.12). Although the new column view takes some getting used to, it's really helpful when browsing through multiple layers of folders.

To reposition files or folders (that is, to add them to a folder or copy them to another disk or hard drive), point to the icon of the file or folder you want to manipulate, click and hold the mouse button, drag the file onto the destination icon, and release the mouse button. If you drag files to a different folder on the same disk, the files are moved and will appear in the new location only. If you drag files to a different disk, or to a folder on a different disk, they're copied rather than moved, and therefore exist in both the new and old locations.

Figure 1.12
A hierarchical view of a collection of related files and folders viewed in the new column view.

Popular Macintosh Utilities

When working with Mac OS X, you'll frequently use several utilities to access files and folders, customize the user interface, and locate information. Mac OS X has a few new ways to perform these tasks, which are routine for experienced Mac users. Let's take a quick look at a few of these innovations.

Using the Dock

The Dock is one of the most interesting additions to the Mac OS—even though some people may think of it as a replacement of the old Application menu rather than an entirely new feature. The Dock, shown in Figure 1.13, displays the running applications just as the old Application menu did, but it also stores shortcuts to minimized windows as well as frequently used files, folders, disks, and URLs.

The Dock has many customizable features, including the order, size, and visibility of its contents. For detailed instructions on how to customize the Dock, as well as information on third-party alternatives such as DragThing, see Chapter 5.

Browsing the New Apple Menu

The Apple menu, one of the most familiar elements of the Mac OS interface, has undergone some serious changes under Mac OS X. Not only are familiar utilities such as Calculator, Scrapbook, and Stickies missing, the new Apple menu is not

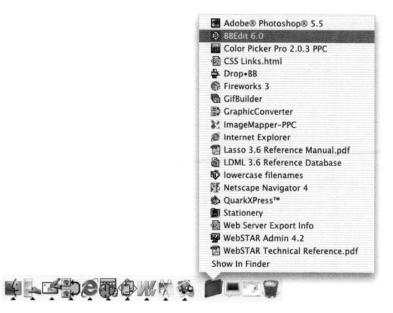

Figure 1.13
The new Dock replaces the functionality of the Application and Apple menus, and is far more customizable.

customizable through the Apple Menu Items folder. The Apple menu now contains many of the commands previously found in the old Special menu, including Sleep, Restart, and Shutdown. Figure 1.14 shows an example of the new Apple menu, including the Recent Items submenu.

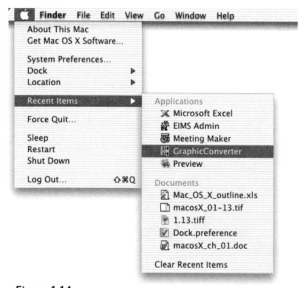

Figure 1.14
Although the new Apple menu preserves some aspects of the old menu, such as the Recent Items submenu, it is fundamentally different.

Configuring System Preferences

One of the guiding principals of Mac OS X is the consolidation of like features into a central location for easier access. Mac OS 9.1 did this to some degree, for example, by placing all the Control Panels into a folder called—you guessed it—Control Panels. However, each Control Panel was an individual item that had to be opened separately and had its own interface design. Mac OS X changes this with System Preferences, a single utility for system-wide configuration. System Preferences is accessible from the Apple menu or the Dock (in its default configuration). The following sections of the System Preferences control several elements of the Mac OS user experience, most of which should be familiar to long-time Mac users:

■ The General System Preferences pane allows you to configure the overall appearance of the Mac OS. You can choose the Blue (Aqua) or Graphite (grayscale) Appearance options, as well as the color of highlighted items in the Finder. This is also your opportunity to determine what happens when you click in the scroll bar of any window, as illustrated in Figure 1.15. The options found in the old General Controls Panel, including cursor blinking, Desktop show/hide, Launcher, improper shutdown warnings, and default document locations, are no longer applicable under Mac OS X.

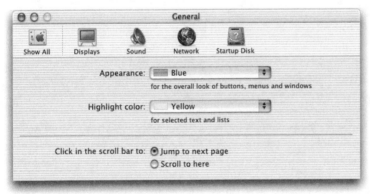

Figure 1.15
The General System Preferences.

■ The Date & Time System Preferences pane is used to set the date and time, time zone, and network time server information. In this pane, you can set the Mac OS's internal clock, which determines the date and time that appear in your menu bar as well as the creation and modification times of files. Many applications, including the Clock application itself, refer to the Date & Time System Preferences pane when performing. Figure 1.16 shows the Date & Time System Preferences pane with the translucent, digital version of the Clock application hovering over the right side of the pane. You normally set the date and time parameters once; then an internal battery runs the clock under its own power. If your Mac isn't keeping time accurately, your battery may be low.

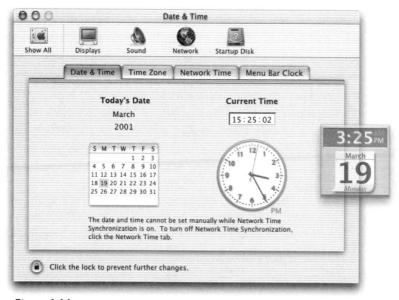

Figure 1.16
The Date & Time System Preferences pane controls most of the same tasks as its predecessor, the Date & Time Control Panel.

■ The Displays System Preferences pane defines your monitor's display of colors, refresh rate, and resolution (if you have a multiresolution monitor). You can also set the relative position of each monitor if you have more than one connected to your Macintosh. ColorSync preferences are now accessible through the ColorSync System Preferences pane instead of the Displays pane.

■ The Sound System Preferences pane determines the volume of your system and alert sounds, as well as speaker balance preferences. These sound functions were previously controlled through the Monitors & Sound (and later just Sound) Control Panel.

■ The Mouse System Preferences pane allows you to adjust the speed of your onscreen cursor relative to the speed with which you move the mouse. This pane also gives you the opportunity to set the delay interval between clicks. The double-click speed setting determines if two clicks will be interpreted as two separate clicks instead of one double-click. A PowerBook- and iBook-specific pane lets you make similar adjustments to the Track Pad, the equivalent of a mouse on portable Macintoshes.

■ The International System Preferences pane replaces the old Text and Numbers Control Panels. This pane supports language, text, and number formats. The Languages section offers three simple options: Language (such as English or Nederlands), Script (the method of writing characters, such as left to right for Latin languages or right to left for Hebrew or Arabic), and Behaviors (which specifies character sets, such as English versus German case sorting). In the Date, Time, and

Numbers sections of the International System Preferences pane, you can specify
how information that falls under these categories is displayed in the Finder and in
applications. You can also choose to display the Keyboard menu to the left of the
Help menu in the Finder by selecting additional keyboard layouts in the Keyboard
Menu section, as shown in Figure 1.17. This is a useful feature for users who
frequently switch between keyboard layouts.

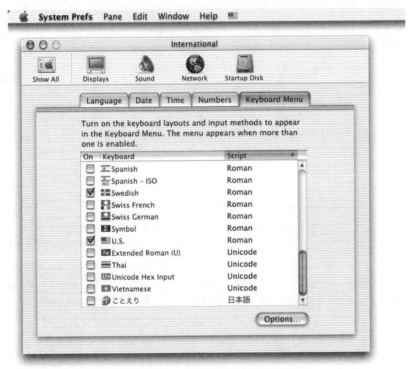

Figure 1.17
The International System Preferences pane consolidates all of the configuration options for language
localization.

■ The Login System Preferences pane allows you to determine the items that will be
  launched at startup, as well as the default user (if any) for your computer. Whereas
  earlier versions of the Mac OS supported multiple users as an option, Mac OS X is
  based on the concept of multiple users—and therefore the login options are especially important for security purposes. Figure 1.18 shows the settings that will
  permit a user to log in automatically at startup without having to enter a username
  or password (I'll discuss this in Chapter 5).

Figure 1.18
The new Login System Preferences pane.

Launching Classic Applications

Launching Classic applications is another task that you're likely to encounter on a regular basis. We'll cover Classic in great detail in the next two chapters; for now, all you need to know is that once you've told Mac OS X the location of a valid installation of Mac OS 9.1 on your computer, your Classic applications can be launched by double-clicking on the application's icon or alias. Classic will launch automatically; Mac OS 9.1 will be loaded into the Classic application environment; and your application will launch pretty much as usual. Or, if you prefer, you can have Classic and Mac OS 9.1 start up automatically when you boot your computer into Mac OS X, including any Classic applications in the System Folder's Startup Items folder. In other words, Mac OS X will start up Classic automatically, and then Classic will start up your favorite Mac OS 9.1 applications automatically. How's that for a smooth transition between operating systems!

Connecting to Printers and Servers

Under Mac OS X, the Chooser is no longer the main way to connect to printers and file servers. The Chooser and the Network Browser have been replaced with the Print Center utility and the Connect To Server command (Command+K from within the Finder). Any printer connected via Universal Serial Bus (USB) will be recognized automatically at startup; you'll be prompted if the Mac OS cannot find the appropriate USB driver for the printer. We'll discuss printing in more detail in Chapter 9.

Mounting Removable Media

Removable media such as CD-ROM, DVD-ROM, DVD-RAM, Zip, Jaz, and even floppy disks are mounted and accessed in Mac OS X just as they were in the past—but with one important exception. In the Finder Preferences (Finder|Preferences), you can choose to hide disks, including removable media, on the Desktop. You may still access and eject removable media from within a Finder window, however. This option, which is another example of Apple's principle of "less screen clutter is better," is bound to be useful for a lot of people.

Searching with Sherlock

If you're anything like me and have more than 50,000 files on your computer, you'll need Sherlock to find what you're looking for. Mac OS 9.1 users will recognize all of the features of Sherlock, including the ability to search for files and folders by name, full-text searches of documents indexed by Sherlock, as well as searching the Internet for general reference information, shopping resources, or personal contact information. Sherlock, an example of which is shown in Figure 1.19, is discussed in Chapter 6.

Figure 1.19

Sherlock is now a Mac OS X–native application.

Transferring Data

The Clipboard is the Mac OS's built-in method for transferring text, sounds, graphical elements, and even movies from one location to another. You can use the Clipboard to move items within a document or from one document to another—even if the documents were created by different software applications. The metaphor of the Clipboard is continued in the commands used to manipulate it—Cut, Copy, and Paste—each of which can be found in the Edit menu.

Because you never see the information being transferred, it's easy to make mistakes with Clipboard operations. Even when you're careful and check the contents of the Clipboard using the Show Clipboard command, Clipboard transfers are at least a two-step operation; checking the Clipboard for content adds a third step.

Drag and drop is a more direct method for moving information in Mac OS X, even among application environments (Classic, Carbon, and Cocoa). With drag and drop, you click and drag information to other locations on your Desktop, hard drive, or in other applications. You'll be glad to know that the Dock is fully drag-and-drop compliant as well.

Using drag and drop, you can even move data to the Desktop in the form of clipping objects—text as text clippings, graphics as picture clippings, sound as sound clippings, video as video clippings, and Internet addresses and URLs as one of eight different types of Internet clippings. Many types of applications are capable of creating clippings—just drag and drop them to the Desktop or to any open Finder window. Applications written for Mac OS 8 or higher most likely include drag-and-drop support. You can also use this method to start processes such as opening files (by dragging and dropping a file onto an application icon). We'll pay particular attention to drag and drop as we proceed through the book.

Cut and Paste: Using the Clipboard

You rarely access the Clipboard directly; instead, you manipulate the contents of the Clipboard using the Cut, Copy, and Paste commands. In fact, you'll use these commands so frequently that it's a good idea to remember their keystroke equivalents: Command+X for Cut, Command+C for Copy, and Command+V for Paste. These commands provide you with the following capabilities:

- *Cut*—Removes the selected objects from their current location and places them on the Clipboard, overwriting the previous Clipboard contents. (The Clipboard can contain only the result of the most recent Cut or Copy command.)

1

- *Copy*—Places the selected objects on the Clipboard, but leaves them in their current location as well. The copied objects replace the previous contents of the Clipboard.

- *Paste*—Places a copy of the objects now on the Clipboard into the current document at the cursor location. Using the Paste command does not remove items from the Clipboard; you can paste the same item repeatedly.

Although there are many uses for the Clipboard, the most common is moving an element such as a paragraph or graphical item from one place to another within the same document. To do so, select the element, choose the Cut command, position the cursor at the new location, and choose the Paste command.

The Clipboard is also used to move elements—even elements created by different applications—between different documents. For example, to move a chart from a file you created with your spreadsheet into a word processor document, follow this procedure:

1. Open the spreadsheet and select the chart. Use the Copy command, rather than Cut, to ensure that the chart remains in the spreadsheet even after it has been moved to the word processor.

2. Open the word processor, or switch to it if it's already open. Open the document that will receive the copied chart. You can quit the spreadsheet if you like, but it's not required.

3. Position the cursor at the point in the word processor document where you want the chart placed. Choose the Paste command.

Chances are that if you can select some information, you can copy it to the Clipboard and move it around. In addition to simple ASCII text, the Clipboard supports stylized text and various graphics formats. The Clipboard even supports sound and QuickTime video clippings. Because the Clipboard can hold only one item at a time and is not saved out to a file, it is overwritten whenever it is modified.

 If you want to remove selected items without involving the Clipboard, use the Clear command or the Delete key.

It's easy to forget the contents of your Clipboard. Some applications have a menu item called Show Clipboard; its location varies. In the Finder, this command is found in the Edit menu. Microsoft Word 2001 has its own special Clipboard menu, the Office Clipboard, which holds multiple clippings and can float above your Word documents. Other programs place the Show Clipboard command in a View menu. In the Finder, the Show Clipboard command opens a window that shows you the Clipboard's contents and tells you what kind of data it contains. Figure 1.20 shows an example of the contents of the Clipboard (a frame from a QuickTime movie).

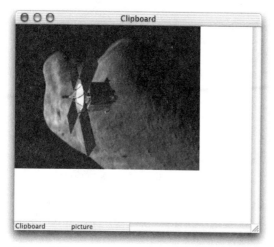

Figure 1.20
Use the Show Clipboard command in the Finder to reveal the contents of the Clipboard.

Macintosh Drag and Drop

Drag and drop is a technique for sharing data among documents, files, and applications. Various aspects of drag-and-drop behavior are familiar. In some versions of System 7, it was possible to open a file by dragging the file's icon onto an application—assuming the application was capable of opening and translating that type of file.

Drag and drop, which has a long history as a core feature of the Macintosh OS, is a terrific method for data exchange because it is intuitive. If you've used drag and drop in other applications (such as Microsoft Word), then you're familiar with the basics: Simply select the data, drag it to a new location, and drop it. Figure 1.21 shows an example of moving text within a document.

Mac OS X also allows you to drag and drop selections to the Desktop. The resulting objects are called *clippings* and are given a default file name, such as "text clipping," to indicate the data type. You can edit the file name using standard Macintosh editing techniques. Click once on the file name, type a new name, and press the Return key to change the name. If you're working in an application that was written to take advantage of Mac OS 9 or higher, the clipping may be automatically named using the first 18 or so characters of the clipping contents (if it is a text clipping). Figure 1.22 contains some clippings from Microsoft Word and Internet Explorer that use this naming feature.

1

Figure 1.21
An example of drag and drop.

www.macnn.com/   Untitled clipping

One very co...e clipping   Drag and d... clipping

Figure 1.22
Several examples of Desktop clippings.

To use a clipping, simply drag it to the desired location within another file. Clippings are a convenient way to transfer logos or headers to documents or to other items you might have stored for future reference. Consolidating your clippings within a single folder in your Documents folder helps reduce clutter.

Stickies

Mac OS X has a handy little application called Stickies, located in the Applications folder. With Stickies, you can create windows of text that float on your Desktop, as shown in Figure 1.23. They resemble the paper notes found in most offices and homes that are stuck to desks, lamps, doors, and refrigerators as reminders. You can scroll the text of Stickies using the arrow keys and collapse the windows to a single bar.

Figure 1.23
The new Stickies application, rewritten for Mac OS X.

The Stickies accessory supports Cut, Copy, and Paste and can import and export text. It even supports formatted text and images. You can vary the colors of notes and make them any rectangular size down to a single line. When you're done with a note, you can close it and save it to a file, or simply delete it.

Wrapping Up

The OS is the core of what we think of as the Macintosh, and the core of Mac OS X, Darwin, is the foundation upon which many layers are built. The Mac OS makes it possible for you to interact with the computer; enables the computer to communicate with your applications; and allows you and the computer to connect to the Internet and access peripheral hardware such as printers, scanners, and storage devices.

Some of the features of Mac OS X include:

- Icons, windows, and dialog boxes instead of endless lines of computer code and obscure syntax
- Mouse controls and menus instead of just keystrokes
- Windows and palettes
- Configurable System Preferences
- The Clipboard
- Drag-and-drop capabilities

In Chapter 2, I'll examine Mac OS X's ability to run your older Classic applications. You'll learn how to configure Classic and Mac OS 9.1 to best suit your needs.

Configuring Classic

The Classic application environment allows Mac OS X to run Mac OS 9.1 and just about any "legacy" application written for versions of the Mac OS as far back as Mac OS 8. To keep our terminology straight, however, I'll use *Classic* to refer to both Mac OS 9.1 (the last version of the classic Mac OS) as well as to pre-Carbon or pre-Cocoa applications (classic apps). When discussing components or features of Mac OS 9.1 that are not available while in Classic mode within Mac OS X, I'll make a distinction about booting the computer directly into Mac OS 9.1. When Mac OS X was released in March 2001, fewer than 500 Carbon or Cocoa applications—compared to over 10,000 Classic applications—were available. So it's probably safe to assume that Classic support won't be disappearing from Mac OS X altogether (at least not anytime soon).

In this chapter I'll cover how to configure Mac OS 9.1, as well as how to configure Mac OS X to run the Classic environment to best suit your needs. Since Mac OS 9.1 is actually a self-contained operating system into which you can boot your computer, I'll also cover the basics of working with Mac OS 9.1, paying special attention to the role of the Mac OS 9.1 System Folder. The next chapter covers what you need to know to run your favorite Classic applications, including Classic application memory management and a few tips on troubleshooting Classic.

Configuring Mac OS 9.1

To run Classic on your computer, you must have Mac OS 9.1 or later installed on your computer. If you don't have Mac OS 9.1 installed or just need to update an earlier version of the Mac OS to version 9.1, refer to Appendix E for detailed instructions. For now, I'll assume you have Mac OS 9.1 installed and are ready to go.

Hard Drive Options

Mac OS X doesn't load Classic by default. However, if you try to launch a Classic application, OS X will look for a valid installation of Mac OS 9.1 on your computer and then launch the Classic application. Mac OS X first searches for Mac OS 9.1 on the same hard drive on which OS X resides. Then, if Mac OS 9.1 cannot be found there, OS X searches any other hard drives connected to your computer.

If Mac OS 9.1 cannot be located, the Classic environment cannot load and the application will not launch. If you intend to use Classic applications on a regular basis, or if you have multiple Mac OS 9.1 System Folders on your computer, you should tell Mac OS X on which drive Mac OS 9.1 is located. The following section contains instructions for doing this.

The two main options for placing the Mac OS on your hard drives are illustrated in Figure 2.1, which shows two versions of the operating system on one hard drive versus each operating system on its own drive. I have several Macs with each configuration, and I prefer to have Mac OS X on one drive and Mac OS 9.1 on another; however, both will function properly on the same drive. Having two drives makes it a little easier to repair disk errors because you can boot from one drive and repair the other.

Other drive setup options, such as dividing a drive into multiple partitions and installing two versions of the OS into different partitions, will be discussed in Appendix E.

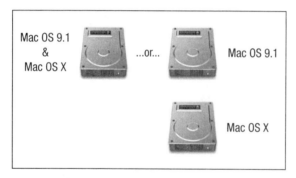

Figure 2.1
The two main installation options for Mac OS X and Mac OS 9.1.

Booting into Mac OS 9.1

Occasionally, you may find that you really need to boot directly into Mac OS 9.1 rather than use your Mac OS 9.1 applications from within the Classic environment of Mac OS X. For example, when I need to defragment my Mac OS X hard drive, I boot into Mac OS 9.1 and run Norton SystemWorks or TechTool Pro. Until more disk repair or optimization utilities are available for Mac OS X, it's OS 9.1 to the rescue. Fortunately, booting directly into Mac OS 9.1 is no big deal because Apple has made this an easy operation to perform.

You can force most modern Macs to boot into Mac OS 9.1 by holding down the Option key when starting or restarting the computer and selecting the drive containing

Mac OS 9.1 from the list of drives found by the built-in drive selection utility. If your computer doesn't respond to this procedure, you'll have to select the drive by following these steps:

1. Choose System Preferences from the Apple menu.

2. Select Startup Disk from the list of icons or from the Pane menu.

3. Choose a drive containing Mac OS 9.1, an example of which is shown in Figure 2.2.

Figure 2.2
Choosing a startup drive containing Mac OS 9.1.

If you have Mac OS X and Mac OS 9.1 installed on the same drive, choose the icon containing the Mac OS 9.1 logo.

Booting into Mac OS X

Booting back into Mac OS X is very similar to booting into Mac OS 9.1. In earlier versions of the Mac OS, the Startup Disk utility could only identify one System Folder per drive; an additional utility such as System Picker was required to identify which version of the OS was to be used to boot. Starting with Mac OS 9.1, however, the Mac OS can identify multiple System Folders and allows you to choose which is to be "blessed" (i.e., authorized) for booting. To boot back into Mac OS X:

1. Choose Control Panels from the Apple menu.

2. Choose Startup Disk from the list of Control Panels.

3. Choose a drive containing Mac OS X, an example of which is shown in Figure 2.3.

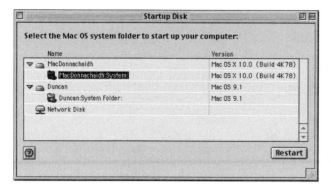

Figure 2.3
Choosing a startup disk containing Mac OS X.

The Startup Disk utility displays a hierarchical view of disks and System Folders. Therefore, if you have multiple System Folders on one disk, you'll need to expand the view to see all of them.

Configuring Classic System Preferences

The Classic environment has a few configuration options that enable you to customize Classic and Mac OS 9.1 on your computer. For example, configuring Classic to start up automatically can save time for users who want to access their Classic applications on a regular basis. On the other hand, this configuration can add to the time it takes for your computer to boot up. Fortunately, Mac OS X makes it easy for you to sort out your Classic configuration options by putting them all in one place, the Classic pane of the System Preferences. To access the Classic configuration options:

1. Choose System Preferences from the Apple menu.

2. Select the Classic pane from the list of icons or from the Pane menu.

First, you'll see a brief description of how Classic applications are launched, followed by Classic's current status, as shown in Figure 2.4.

The following list describes the options found in the Start/Stop and Advanced sections of the Classic System Preferences pane:

■ *Select A Startup Volume For Classic*—Allows you to identify a specific drive from which Mac OS 9.1 should be launched, similar to how the Startup Disk System Preferences and Control Panels work in Mac OS X and Mac OS 9.1. Only drives with a valid Mac OS 9.1 System Folder will appear as selectable options in this area.

■ *Start Up Classic On Login To This Computer*—Enables Classic to start automatically for some users, but not for others. Mac OS X has another System Preferences pane

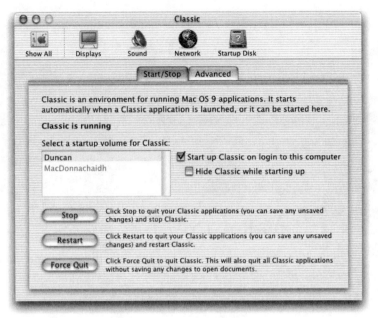

Figure 2.4
The Classic System Preferences pane in Mac OS X.

called Login that allows you to configure items such as applications, utilities, documents, folders, or hard drives to also start up automatically when a designated user logs in; however, Classic is configured as a login item in the Classic pane instead because it is composed of multiple startup configuration items that cannot be configured through the Login pane.

■ *Hide Classic While Starting Up*—Tells Mac OS X to hide the Mac OS 9.1 startup window in the background. If this option is not selected, you can see the startup process in a collapsed or full view; an example of the full view is shown in Figure 2.5. The value of seeing the full view is that you can monitor the loading of Extensions and Control Panels, as well as any messages generated by the Mac OS.

■ *Stop*—Stops (quits) the Classic environment. If you have any open documents, you'll be given an opportunity to save your work before Classic is unloaded.

■ *Restart*—Stops and then restarts Classic, allowing you to save any open documents.

■ *Force Quit*—Stops Classic without saving open documents. Mac OS X gives you a warning dialog before carrying out the command to force quit, however.

The following commands, which are found under the Advanced section of the Classic System Preferences pane, give you a little more control over the startup process of the

Figure 2.5
An expanded view of Classic and Mac OS 9.1 starting up from within Mac OS X.

Classic application environment and Mac OS 9.1. Figure 2.6 shows the Advanced section while Classic is running; when Classic is not running, the Restart Classic button will read Start Classic instead:

- *Startup Options*—When starting or restarting Classic using the Start/Restart Classic button, the following options are possible:

  - *Turn Off Extensions*—Turns off Extensions and Control Panels when Mac OS 9.1 starts up, as if the Shift key were held down.

  - *Open Extension Manager*—Forces the Extension Manager to open at startup.

- *Use Key Combination*—Programs a key combination to be virtually pressed (initiated by the OS) when Classic starts up. You can program a combination of up to five keys, which is useful for certain applications that look for such a key combination at startup. If you have selected the Hide Classic While Starting Up option, how would

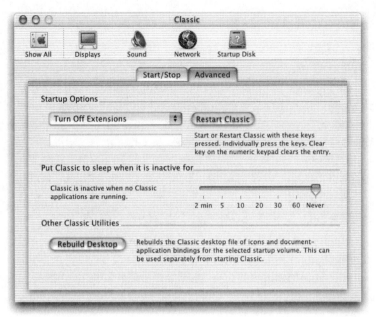

Figure 2.6
The Advanced section of the Classic System Preferences pane.

you know when to press such a key combination? This option presses the keys for you automatically at just the right time.

■ *Put Classic To Sleep When It Is Inactive For*—Tells Classic when to go to sleep if no Classic applications are running. All computer processes require system resources, and this option lets you redirect processing power for other purposes when Classic is not being used. You can configure Classic to sleep after as little as 2 or as many as 60 minutes of inactivity, or to never sleep at all. If you do allow Classic to sleep, it will take several seconds for it to "wake up" from sleep when you're ready to use a Classic application.

■ *Rebuild Desktop*—Rebuilds the Desktop database of the Mac OS 9.1 startup disk. The Desktop database keeps track of information about the files on your Classic startup disk, including the icon and application associated with each file (such as word processing applications and their associated documents). You can rebuild the Desktop using this option at any time, but only on the volume identified in the Start/Stop tab of the Classic System Preferences pane.

These options allow you to customize the way that Classic and Mac OS 9.1 are started and stopped. Now let's take a quick look at how you can work with Mac OS 9.1 from within the Classic application environment.

Working with Mac OS 9.1

Because Mac OS X requires a fully functional version of Mac OS 9.1 in order to run Classic applications, you are essentially responsible for maintaining two operating systems. If Mac OS X is installed on a hard drive or partition other than the one where OS 9.1 resides, maintaining the operating system will be a more manageable task. System files, applications, and utilities are less likely to intermingle and cause problems (system files are very particular about where they like to be stored). This section covers what you need to know to keep Mac OS 9.1 happy and functioning well, whereas Chapter 6 discusses the organization of Mac OS X's files and folders.

Exploring the Mac OS 9.1 System Folder

Every Macintosh has one folder that's distinct from all the others—the System Folder, home of the operating system and many other important files. The System Folder requires special treatment from the operating system, other software applications, and you, the Mac OS user.

Because of the fundamental role that software in the System Folder plays in the operation of the classic Mac OS (i.e., all versions prior to Mac OS X), your freedom to change the organization of the System Folder is limited. However, the Mac OS hasn't always been organized the way it is in Mac OS 9.1—an important concept to keep in mind as you consider the role of Mac OS 9.1 and the Classic application environment.

In Mac OS 9.1, the System Folder includes a number of predefined subfolders, each designed to hold a specific type of file. This organizational system, which is created when Mac OS 9.1 is installed, greatly reduces the potential for clutter. The actual number of items in the System Folder depends on the components chosen for installation and the type of Mac. (Appendix E provides more detailed information on the options available for installation with Mac OS 9.1, as well as Mac OS X.) Depending on which components you install in addition to the OS, your Mac OS 9.1 System Folder will include many items, including the following:

- Appearance
- Apple Menu Items
- Application Support
- Clipboard
- ColorSync Profiles
- Contextual Menu Items

2

- Control Panels
- Control Strip Modules
- Desk Accessories
- Extensions
- Favorites
- Finder
- Fonts
- Help
- Internet Plug-Ins
- Internet Search Sites
- Language & Region Support
- Launcher Items
- Login
- MS Preference Panels
- Mac OS ROM
- MacTCP DNR
- Panels
- Preferences
- PrintMonitor Documents
- Scrapbook File
- Scripting Additions
- Scripts
- Servers
- Shutdown Items
- Startup Items
- System
- System Resources
- Text Encodings

Once you launch the Extension Manager Control Panel to turn off or on Extensions—either from within Mac OS 9.1 or using the Open Extensions Manager option from within the Classic System Preferences pane—you'll see the following subfolders in the System Folder as well:

■ Control Panels (Disabled)

■ Extensions (Disabled)

■ Shutdown Items (Disabled)

■ Startup Items (Disabled)

■ System Extensions (Disabled)

These folders are created "on the fly" (computer-speak for automatically) by the Extensions Manager program; the types of folders that are created depend on what portions of the Mac OS you disable. This is an example of one of the ways in which the System Folder in Mac OS 9.1 is more complex than in previous versions of the Mac OS. Fortunately, as we'll see, Apple has built in an "invisible hand" to help make sure that System Folder files are always located correctly.

When you start Classic for the first time, Mac OS X adds a few more items to the System Folder to enable interoperability between the two operating systems. They include the following subfolders:

■ Classic

■ Classic Support

■ Classic Support UI

■ ProxyApp

If any of these items is moved, renamed, or deleted from the System Folder, Mac OS X will detect the change and ask for permission to reinstall the missing component.

Because the System Folder and subfolders are so important to the operation of your computer, it's important to understand what type of files should be placed in each subfolder. The following section describes the subfolders and provides some basic tips for organizing and using them.

Appearance

The Appearance folder serves as a storage area for many of the elements you use to customize the aesthetics of your computer. Desktop pictures, sound sets, and themes are all stored here in individual folders. The Mac OS will automatically direct to the

Appearance folder all images, sound sets, and theme files dropped onto the System Folder. This feature is designed to help keep files where they belong within the System Folder (which is good for the overall stability of the OS) and helps users by reducing the number of operations needed to store files correctly. Figure 2.7 shows a typical alert dialog box that appears when a JPEG image file is dropped onto the System Folder.

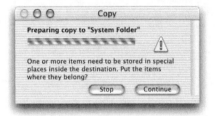

Figure 2.7
The Mac OS X is aware that certain Mac OS 9.1 files should be stored in certain locations, such as the Desktop Pictures folder.

The Apple Menu Folder

Accessibility—from inside any application via the Apple menu—is one of the best features of the many utilities and small applications that come with Mac OS 9.1. Although Mac OS X also has an Apple menu, its traditional functionality is now in the hands of the Dock. However, the Classic Apple menu is independent of Mac OS X and is fully functional in the Classic environment or if you're booting directly into Mac OS 9.1.

Many of the Apple menu programs were known as desk accessories in earlier versions of the Mac OS. In System 7, the convenience of the Apple menu was extended to include access to applications, documents, folders, and even aliases to volumes (hard drives or hard drive partitions mounted on your desktop). And best of all, this power-ful new Apple menu was completely customizable. When Mac OS 9.1 is installed, however, most of the following items are automatically placed in the Apple Menu Items folder:

■ Apple DVD Player

■ Apple System Profiler

■ Calculator

■ Chooser

■ Control Panels

- Favorites

- Key Caps

- Network Browser

- Remote Access Status

- Scrapbook

- Sherlock 2

- Speakable Items

- Stickies

Some of these items, such as the Apple System Profiler and Sherlock 2, are applications, but others are desk accessories, folders, or aliases to other files and folders.

 An alias is like a shortcut to an original file or folder; you can always tell an alias from the original when viewing it in a Mac OS 9.1 Finder window because its name is italicized and often contains the word *alias* at the end. In Mac OS X, however, the alias name is not italicized and the word *alias* is no longer added.

Long-time Macintosh users will note the loss of the venerable Alarm Clock desk accessory from the Apple menu. The Alarm Clock was the preferred method for changing the system date and time in several whole-number versions of system software. Prior to System 7.5, you could also change the date and time from within the General Controls Panel. The Alarm Clock was replaced by the Date & Time Control Panel in Mac OS 8, and is easily accessible in OS 9.1 through the Control Panels submenu of the Apple menu.

 Some people prefer to rearrange the Apple menu items to make them easier to work with. To modify the contents of the Apple menu, add or remove files or aliases to the Apple Menu Items folder. The Apple menu is updated immediately and alphabetically displays the first 50 items contained in the top level of the Apple Menu Items folder. The only item you can't remove is the About This Computer option, which is always the first choice in the Apple menu when the Finder is the active application.

To make frequently used folders and applications more easily accessible, add their aliases to the Apple Menu Items folder. For example, you can add the aliases of applications, documents, folders, and volumes. Each item will be much easier to access from the Apple menu than by using traditional double-click methods. Choosing an item from the Apple menu is equivalent to double-clicking on the item's icon—the selected application or Control Panel will run, or the selected folder or volume will open.

Most of the files added to the Apple Menu Items folder should be aliases rather than original files so that you avoid moving the file, folder, or volume icon from its original location. In the Apple Menu Items folder, the alias file name is displayed in italics, but it appears in standard font in the Apple menu. You can't tell by looking at the Apple menu that the file in the Apple Menu Items folder is an alias.

Because the Apple menu displays files alphabetically, you can reorder the menu items by modifying their names with numerical or alphabetical prefixes. A list of some of the available prefixes appears in Table 2.1, where a blank space ( ) forces an item to be listed first in the Apple menu, and the tilde (~) forces an item to be listed last. Figure 2.8 illustrates how a customized Apple menu might appear using a small sample of prefixes from Table 2.1.

 Prefixing the contents of the Apple menu using the suggestions in Figure 2.8 will not work for some non-American English keyboard layouts.

Table 2.1 Custom prefixes for the contents of the Apple menu.

Prefix	Keyboard Entry	Prefix	Keyboard Entry	Prefix	Keyboard Entry
0	0	1	1	2	2
3	3	4	4	5	5
6	6	7	7	8	8
9	9	–	Option+-		space bar
)	Shift+0	!	Shift+1	@	Shift+2
#	Shift+3	$	Shift+4	%	Shift+5
^	Shift+6	&	Shift+7	*	Shift+8
(	Shift+9	[	[	{	Shift+[
\	\	|	Shift+\	]	]
}	Shift+]	°	Option+0	i	Option+1
™	Option+2	£	Option+3	¢	Option+4
∞	Option+5	§	Option+6	¶	Option+7
•	Option+8	ª	Option+9	`	Option+]
"	Option+[	«	Option+\	≠	Option++

Figure 2.8
A customized Apple menu.

Application Support

The Application Support folder is created by the Mac OS for the benefit of other applications, such as Adobe Acrobat, Aladdin StuffIt Deluxe, and Norton AntiVirus, that are designed to store important files and folders for their own use. By default, this folder is empty, and it cannot be renamed.

Clipboard

Under Mac OS 9.1, the Clipboard is a file that holds information (text, pictures, sounds, and so on) that has been cut or copied using the Cut (Command+X) or Copy (Command+C) commands found under the Edit menu of most applications. It can hold only one piece of information at a time, although several utilities that allow users to have multiple clipboards now exist for Mac OS 9.1 as well as Mac OS X.

ColorSync Profiles

ColorSync is a system created by Apple to assist in the conversion and management of colors used in documents that were created on computers and with printers. Because monitors and printers use different methods of interpreting color values, a standard method of describing color was created to ensure consistency across the board. ColorSync creates documents called *profiles* for computers, which define colors using red, green, and blue (RGB), and printers, which use cyan, magenta, yellow, and black (CMYK). It then attaches these profiles to a document. The ColorSync folder in the System Folder stores profiles for most models of Apple monitors, as well as custom profiles you create with ColorSync (which is also supported in Mac OS X). Figure 2.9 illustrates the similarities in the ColorSync Control Panel (Classic) and the System Preferences pane (Mac OS X).

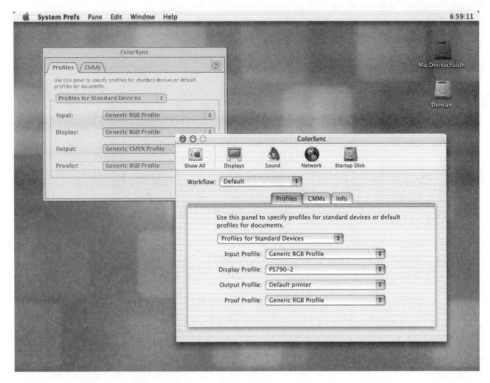

Figure 2.9
ColorSync configuration options for Mac OS 9.1 and Mac OS X.

Contextual Menu Items

Contextual menus are accessible in the Finder when booting directly into Mac OS 9.1 and in most Mac OS 8-savvy applications by clicking the mouse while holding down the Control key. The Contextual Menu Items folder contains several contextual menu plug-ins that are automatically installed by the Mac OS, as well as any others installed by third-party applications. Figure 2.10 shows an example of a contextual menu in Microsoft Word 2001.

The Control Panels Folder

Control Panels, a familiar concept to most Mac users, have undergone a dramatic transformation under Mac OS X. They are now consolidated into a single application called the *System Preferences*. Under Mac OS 9.1, however, Control Panels still work as they have for many years: as individual applications that are launched, have menu options, and are exited by quitting. Figure 2.11 shows a typical Control Panels folder.

The individual files for each Control Panel are stored in the Control Panels folder, which is stored inside the System Folder—mainly because Control Panels often

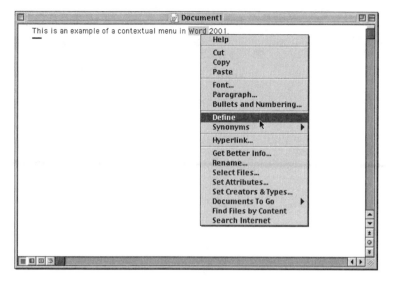

Figure 2.10
The Contextual Menu Items folder contains plug-ins that provide contextual menus for the Mac OS 9.1
Finder as well as many applications, such as Microsoft Word.

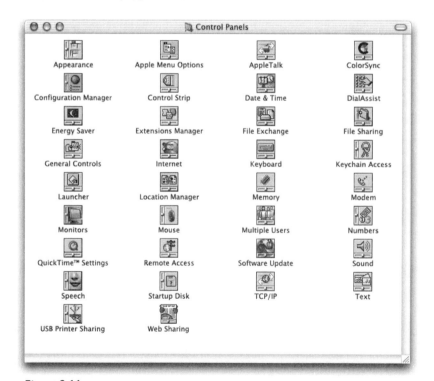

Figure 2.11
Classic Control Panels can be launched and configured as long as the Classic environment is running under
Mac OS X.

contain special resources (like Extensions) that must be run during startup. If the Extensions portion of the Control Panel isn't loaded when Classic is activated, the Control Panel may not function properly. For example, the Location Manager and Control Strip Control Panels both rely on corresponding Extensions to function.

The contents of your Control Panels folder will depend on the components of the Mac OS that you've installed. Moreover, different models of computers will contain different Control Panels, which is most obvious when you compare the contents of the Control Panels folders of desktop and PowerBook computers. However, most Macs with Mac OS 9.1 will have the following Control Panels in common:

- Appearance
- Apple Menu Options
- AppleTalk
- ColorSync
- Configuration Manager
- Control Strip
- Date & Time
- DialAssist
- Energy Saver
- Extensions Manager
- File Exchange
- File Sharing
- General Controls
- Internet
- Keyboard
- Keychain Access
- Launcher
- Location Manager
- Memory
- Modem

■ Monitors

■ Mouse

■ Multiple Users

■ Numbers

■ QuickTime™ Settings

■ Remote Access

■ Software Update

■ Sound

■ Speech

■ Startup Disk

■ TCP/IP

■ Text

■ USB Printer Sharing

■ Web Sharing

If you want to keep a copy of any Control Panel in another location, create an alias and move the alias to your preferred location. You could, for example, store aliases of frequently used Control Panels in the Apple Menu Items folder or in a folder containing other utility applications.

You should be aware, however, that not all Control Panels are functional when running in Classic mode. In fact, a few of them do not work at all, whereas others are partially disabled because the function they perform is handled by Mac OS X instead. For example, the Control Strip and Location Manager are not supported at all. The General Controls Control Panel, on the other hand, is only partially functional, as illustrated in Figure 2.12. Note that the Show Desktop When In Background and Check Disk If Computer Was Shut Down Improperly options are disabled.

Control Strip Modules

The Control Strip was originally designed to provide quick (to save time) and easy (because of the small screen) access to frequently used commands for PowerBook users, who until recently had small displays and limited processing power. Both the Control Strip Modules folder and the Contextual Menu Items folder contain items installed by the Mac OS as well as modules installed by other applications. Although

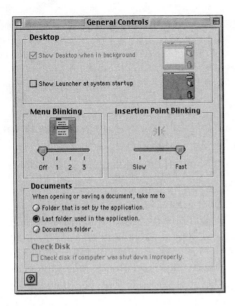

Figure 2.12
Several Control Panels are disabled while in Classic mode; others are only partially functional.

the Control Strip is not functional under Mac OS 9.1 when in Classic mode, it is available when booting directly into Mac OS 9.1.

The Extensions Folder

As mentioned previously, Extensions, printer drivers, and network drivers are major contributors to System Folder overcrowding. These files, which invaded System Folders in epidemic proportions since the introduction of System 6, have found a home in the new Extensions folder since System 7. Your Extensions folder may still become quite crowded, depending on how many of your Classic applications add files and subfolders to the Extensions folder. Most Extensions add features to the Mac OS, thereby extending its capabilities—hence the name Extensions. Drivers extend system software capabilities in a less dramatic, albeit important, way.

During startup, the Mac OS looks in the Extensions folder and loads all its contents. Extensions and Control Panels that aren't stored in the Extensions or Control Panels folders will not execute at startup, nor will they operate properly, until they're correctly positioned and Classic is restarted. The icons of some (but not all) Extensions will appear at the bottom of your screen during startup, as will the icons of some Control Panels (refer back to Figure 2.5 for an example).

Because Extensions and Control Panels modify or enhance the Mac OS at startup, a newly installed Extension or Control Panel may cause your Macintosh to crash when booting directly into Mac OS 9.1. If you are starting up Classic and a conflict occurs, only Classic will terminate; the rest of Mac OS X will not be affected. Crashes can occur if the item is incompatible with the operating system, another Extension or Control Panel, a certain combination of Extensions and Control Panels, or even an application.

If you experience a compatibility problem, such as sudden or unexplained freezes or crashes, suspect an Extension conflict first. To test the theory, try turning off your Extensions by using the Turn Off Extension command in the Advanced section of the Classic System Preferences (described earlier in this chapter). This will disable all but the most essential system Extensions and allow you to remove the incompatible file from the System Folder. When you restart or start up with Extensions off, the words "Extensions Off" will appear under "Welcome to Mac OS" during startup.

Various third-party utilities were introduced to automate the process of turning Extensions on and off, changing the loading order, or creating Extension worksets. The best-known of these products is Cassidy & Green's Conflict Catcher, which you should purchase if you're having a significant startup problem or otherwise suspect an Extension conflict. If the problem is particularly bad, change the Startup Disk option in the System Preferences to boot from the hard drive containing Mac OS 9.1. You may find it easier to resolve an Extension conflict directly, and not while in Mac OS X.

 The Mac OS loads Extensions first, then Control Panels, then the contents (if any) of the Startup Items folder. All items are loaded alphabetically.

In Mac OS 9.1, the number of Extensions was so overwhelming that Apple expanded the capabilities of the Extensions Manager Control Panel, shown in Figure 2.13. Click the checkmark off to remove an Extension, System Extension (one found in the System Folder, not the Extension folder), Control Panel, or Startup item. Disabled items are placed in one of the following folders:

- Control Panels (Disabled)

- Extensions (Disabled)

- Shutdown Items (Disabled)

- Startup Items (Disabled)

- System Extensions (Disabled)

You can create sets of enabled and disabled Extensions or get information about a particular item by selecting an item such as the AppleShare Extension in Figure 2.13.

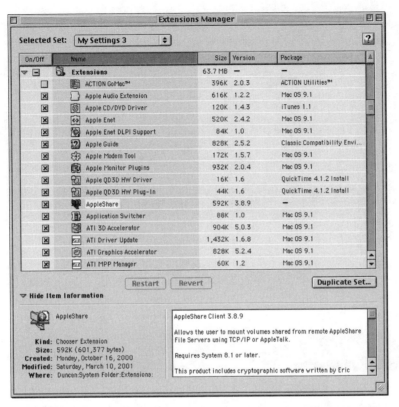

Figure 2.13
Use the Extensions Manager to enable or disable elements of Mac OS 9.1's System Folder.

You'll still need to reboot your Macintosh to effect the new system configuration when booting into Mac OS 9.1. If you are in Classic mode, just restart Classic as outlined earlier in the chapter.

Favorites

In Mac OS 9.1, the Favorites folder serves as a storage bin for shortcuts to your favorite documents, applications, folders, disks, file servers, and Internet location documents, just as it does in Mac OS X. You can add items to the Favorites folder from within Mac OS 9-savvy applications (such as the Network Browser) by selecting an item in the Finder and choosing File|Add To Favorites, or by activating the contextual menu (Control+click) and choosing Add To Favorites. The contents of the Favorites folder are either aliases to files, folders, servers, applications, or Internet location documents; however, you can manually add these types of items by dragging them into the Favorites folder. Mac OS X continues the inclusion of a Favorites folder for each user—Figure 2.14 shows the contents of the Favorites folders in Mac OS X (bottom) and Mac OS 9.1 (top).

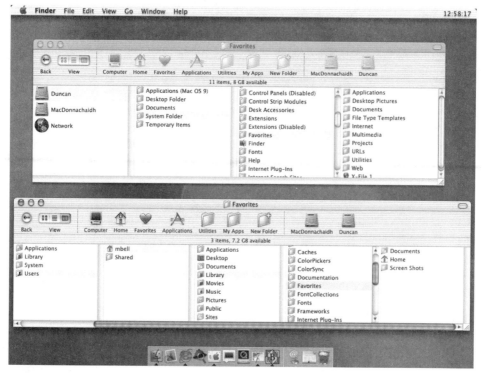

Figure 2.14
The Favorites folder contains shortcuts to frequently accessed files, folders, applications, documents, and Internet location documents.

Finder

The role of the Classic Finder is usurped by the Finder in Mac OS X, although the roles of the two Finders are similar. In fact, if you are working in a Classic application and switch to the Finder from the Application menu, as shown in Figure 2.15, the Mac OS X Finder will be activated. The role of the Finder is explored in great detail in Chapter 4.

Fonts

Support for a wide range of typefaces continues to be an important characteristic of the Macintosh. Apple uses different locations for storing fonts in Mac OS 9.1 and Mac OS X. Each version of the OS uses a Fonts folder, but because Mac OS X is a multiuser operating system, it is possible to store fonts for specific users. Chapter 9 covers fonts and printing in Mac OS X.

Figure 2.15
Switching to the Finder from within a Classic application takes you to the Mac OS X Finder.

Help

The Help folder contains the Help Viewer application and its associated HTML-style Help documents. The Help folder also contains sample AppleScripts and Balloon Help files, none of which you'll probably ever need to access except through the Help Viewer application. Although Mac OS X provides tool tips, it doesn't support Balloon Help; this feature will continue to work for Classic applications for which it has been enabled. Refer to Appendix A for a detailed explanation of how to use the Help Viewer application.

Internet Search Sites

Mac OS 9.1 and Mac OS X both include a search engine called Sherlock, which takes the place of the old Find command. You can activate both Sherlock and the Find command by selecting File|Find or by pressing Command+F.

Sherlock allows you to search the Internet as well as your hard drive. The Internet Search Sites folder is used to store the resources needed by Sherlock to search particular Internet sites, such as AltaVista or Apple's Tech Info Library. The contents of the Internet Search Sites folder is organized into several subfolders, such as Files, News, and Shopping, for easier searching of your favorite categories. Because Sherlock is available as a Carbonized application under Mac OS X, you might consider just using this version rather than updating the Internet Search Sites folder in Mac OS 9.1.

Language & Region Support

The Language & Region Support folder contains files required to provide support for languages such as Chinese, Nederlander, Finnish, and Swedish. The Mac OS is extremely flexible in terms of language support; see Appendix E for information about installing additional language support for Mac OS 9.1 and Mac OS X.

Launcher Items

The Launcher Items folder contains aliases and folders used by the Launcher Control Panel to assist with the organization of frequently used items. The functionality of the Launcher has been taken over by the Dock in Mac OS X and is itself a holdover from previous versions of the Mac OS; nevertheless, it is still utilized by many users. Figure 2.16 shows the contents of a customized Launcher Items folder as well as the Launcher itself.

Note: Items beginning with a bullet (Option+8) become subcategories in the Launcher window.

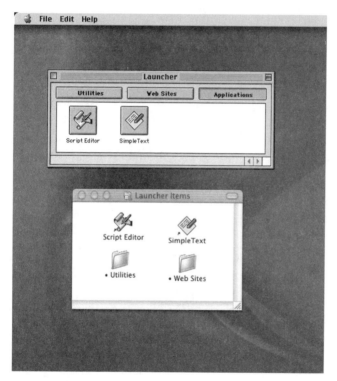

Figure 2.16
The Launcher Items folder can be customized to suit your needs.

Login

The Login file, used by the Multiple Users feature in Mac OS 9.1, is not supported in the Classic environment because of the true multiuser capabilities of Mac OS X. See Chapter 5 for more information about customizing your computer to work with multiple users.

MacTCP DNR

The MacTCP DNR file is a holdover from the days when MacTCP (instead of Open Transport) was the primary networking software for the Mac. Its presence ensures backward compatibility with applications that require MacTCP. Although you'll never need to worry about what it does or about the fact that you'll never need to use it, don't delete it—doing so could cause problems down the road.

MS Preferences Panels

Microsoft Internet Explorer (IE) is installed as part of the default installation of Mac OS 9.1. The MS Preferences Panels folder contains 20 or so files that are used by IE to configure such things as downloading options, security, and user passwords.

Note Pad File

Although similar to the Scrapbook, the Note Pad File can hold only textual data, not sounds or pictures. Mac OS X offers no counterpart to the Note Pad, but several software developers have come forward with data management utilities that greatly exceed the abilities of Note Pad. These products include iOrganize (**www.brunoblondeau.com**), OmniOutliner (**www.omnigroup.com**), and Sticky Brain (**chronos.iserver.net**).

Panels

The Panels file, part of the Multiple Users feature, presents users with a panel-style interface instead of the traditional Desktop. Much of the Multiple Users interface is derived from At Ease, Apple's popular security application.

Preferences

Under System 6, preferences files created by applications became important contributors to System Folder growth. Since System 7, these files have been stored in the Preferences folder; Mac OS 9.1 and the Classic application environment also store preferences here for Classic applications. As a user, you shouldn't have to do anything to the Preferences folder or its files. Your applications should create and maintain these files automatically.

PrintMonitor Documents

The PrintMonitor application is used to handle printing tasks in the background; the PrintMonitor Documents folder serves as a temporary storage area for documents that are to be printed (sometimes referred to as *print jobs*). Once a document has been printed by the PrintMonitor, it will be deleted from this folder.

Scrapbook File

The Scrapbook File is capable of storing various types of data, including text, images, and sounds, that are accessible via the Scrapbook utility. Mac OS 9.1 installs samples of the various types of data that may be stored in the Scrapbook. You can easily modify the contents of the Scrapbook using the Cut and Paste commands.

Scripting Additions and Scripts

The Scripting Additions folder contains several files that AppleScript uses to enable certain Classic operations, such as providing scripting for File Sharing. Other applications may install items in this folder in order to enable close collaboration with AppleScript. As with other special folders in the System Folder, a scripting addition that is dropped onto the closed System Folder (when you have booted the computer directly into Mac OS 9.1) will be automatically placed in the Scripting Additions folder by the Mac OS.

The Scripts folder, a relatively new addition to the Mac OS, stores AppleScripts in a central location. In earlier versions of the Mac OS, scripts could be stored wherever you liked. The addition of the Scripts folder has proved to be a great help in organizing various scripts. See Chapter 11 for more information about AppleScript in Mac OS X and how your scripts may or may not be used in Mac OS 9.1.

Shutdown and Startup Items

The contents of the Shutdown Items folder are executed as the last step when you tell the Mac OS to restart or shut down the Classic environment. This is especially helpful if you want to sweep your hard drive for viruses prior to restarting or shutting down. For example, if you have an application that can quickly scan your hard drive for viruses, just make an alias to that application and place it in the Shutdown Items folder.

Applications, documents, folders, and volumes in the Startup Items folder are automatically run (or opened) each time Classic is started or restarted. As with the Apple Menu Items folder, most of the icons in the Startup Items folder will probably be aliases, as shown in Figure 2.17. If you rely on several Classic applications on a regular basis and want them to be launched automatically whenever Classic is activated, just add their aliases to the Startup Items folder.

System Suitcase and System Resources

The System file (technically it's a suitcase) is one of the most critical elements in the Mac OS 9.1 System Folder. The System suitcase oversees all basic Mac OS activities and assists every application and utility that runs on the Macintosh. The System Resources file is a second critical file that contains data that is utilized by various

Figure 2.17
The Startup Items folder, the contents of which will be opened every time Classic is started or the computer is booted into Mac OS 9.1.

elements of the Finder, System suitcase, and Mac OS in general. As a user, you can remain blissfully ignorant of most of the work performed by the System suitcase. However, you should understand that the System suitcase's traditional role as home to sounds and keyboard resources does require user interaction; now, however, it is only accessible when you boot into Mac OS 9.1 directly and not from within the Classic environment. Most other types of data stored in the System suitcase are hidden from view and are inaccessible to the user.

In the days before System 7, a single System file stuffed with these items could grow to 600KB or larger—often much larger. This overload often resulted in an unstable System file that would easily and frequently become corrupt, necessitating the annoying and time-consuming task of deleting and rebuilding the System file. In Mac OS 9.1, the System file is between 8MB and 10MB in size.

The System Resources file, a critical part of Mac OS 9.1, is required to boot the computer into Classic mode or directly into Mac OS 9.1.

Text Encodings

The Text Encodings folder stores conversion files used by the Mac OS to translate data among languages such as Chinese, Hebrew, and Korean. You won't need to interact with the contents of this folder yourself, but certain applications may not work if the proper translator isn't located in this folder.

Modifying the System Folder

The System Folder and its subfolders are created by the Installer when you first install Mac OS 9.1. At that time, all system software files are placed in their proper locations. The System Folder is constantly modified, however, as you install other software applications and perform common tasks on your Macintosh.

After the initial installation, several types of files are added to the System Folder. These files include fonts and sounds, system Extensions (which add functionality to the Mac OS, applications, and utilities), and miscellaneous files that enable other software applications to function properly.

Several features, including Extensions, Control Panels, and printer or network drivers, allow you to modify the way the system software works and extend the features it provides. Default Folder and ACTION Utilities are among the most popular of the hundreds of examples of Extensions and drivers that modify your system software. You've probably already added files of this type to your System Folder.

Many applications store miscellaneous files—files that don't interact directly with the system software—in the System Folder. They're placed in the System Folder for the following reasons:

- *Reliability*—The System Folder is the only "common ground" on a hard drive that applications can rely on in every configuration.

- *Simplicity*—The Macintosh operating system can easily find the System Folder, regardless of what it's called and where it's located. This gives applications quick access to files stored in the System Folder.

- *Security*—The System Folder is a safe place for applications to store files because most users are not likely to disturb files in their System Folder.

Some of the many application-related files (or folders) that use your System Folder as a safe storage place are Microsoft Word's temporary (temp) files, PageMaker and StuffIt's encryption engines, translators, Claris translators, and viewers.

Printer font files are also in this category. Printer fonts are placed in the Fonts folder to ensure their availability when needed for automatic downloading to a PostScript printer and for Adobe Type Manager. They can also be located in the System file, but it's best to keep them in the Fonts folder. Printer font files are usually the most space-consuming files—30KB to 50KB each—in the System Folder (when loading in the System file). Although utilities such as Suitcase II and MasterJuggler make it possible to store printer and screen fonts in other locations, many people choose to keep them in the System Folder anyway. It's the preferred location when you have a static set of fonts that you normally work with.

Adding Files to the System Folder

After Mac OS 9.1 has been installed or upgraded, files may be added to the System Folder in several ways:

- *By the Mac OS Installer*—To add printer drivers, network drivers, or keyboards, you can run the Mac OS Installer application at any time after booting directly into Mac OS 9.1, but not from within Classic. The Installer installs the selected files to your System Folder and places them in the proper subfolders.

- *By application software installers*—Many software applications use installation programs that copy the software and its associated files to your hard drive. Installers that have been specifically written or updated for compatibility with Mac OS 9.1 can place files correctly into the System Folder or its subfolders.

  Older installer applications often place all files directly in the root level of the System Folder, ignoring the subfolder structure. In these cases, the application may require that the files remain as positioned by the installer. However, most Extensions belong in the Extensions folder, and Control Panels belong in the Control Panels folder—regardless of how they were originally positioned. Remember, only properly located files in the System Folder will be loaded at startup.

- *By software applications*—Many software applications read and write temporary and preferences files to the System Folder. Others use the System Folder for dictionaries and other ancillary files. Some applications, such as Microsoft Internet Explorer and Microsoft Office, even reinstall missing portions of the application if they're accidentally deleted. My experience has been that most applications, including Office 2001, are not confused about how to add required files to the System Folder when in Classic mode.

  Older applications not updated for Mac OS 9.1 may not use the proper subfolders found in the System Folder, such as the Scripting Additions and Scripts folders. Files placed directly in the System Folder may not be accessed properly and may cause problems for your system software or other programs.

- *By you, the Macintosh user*—Because some programs and utilities don't use installer applications, many files must be placed into the System Folder manually. These files can be dragged onto the System Folder icon or into an open System Folder window from within Classic mode or while booting from Mac OS 9.1.

Earlier, Figure 2.7 illustrated how files dragged onto the closed System Folder icon are placed automatically in the correct subfolder, such as the Control Panels or Extensions folder. This helps you add files to the System Folder correctly, even if you know nothing about the System Folder structure. After booting directly into Mac OS 9.1, the OS informs you that it's at work and tells you how it's positioning your files, as shown in Figure 2.18. This works only when files are dragged onto the System Folder icon when it is closed, and not when you're working in Classic mode.

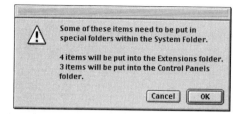

Figure 2.18
When booting directly into Mac OS 9.1, the OS gives you detailed information about the placement of system files.

If you are in Classic, you will not get a detailed summary of which files will be placed where. Instead, you'll only see a generic message like the one shown earlier in Figure 2.7. However, once files are in the System Folder, you can reposition them freely. The "helping hand" feature of the Mac OS will not affect the repositioning of files moved from within the System Folder.

Deleting Files from the System Folder

For the most part, files in the System Folder can be deleted just like any other file—by dragging them into the Trash or by selecting the files and the selecting File|Move To Trash. However, some files cannot be deleted because they're "in use." These files include the System file, the Finder, any Extensions or Control Panels that were loaded at startup, fonts, open Control Panels, and any temporary or preferences files used by open applications.

To delete the System file or Finder (but you wouldn't ever want to do this, would you?), you must restart the Macintosh using another boot disk. To delete an in-use Extension or Control Panel, move the file out of the Extensions or Control Panels folder, restart the Mac, and then delete the file. To delete open Control Panels or temporary or preferences files of open applications, simply close the Control Panel or application and drag the file to the Trash.

Updating Mac OS 9.1

Like Mac OS X, Mac OS 9.1 has the ability to update the operating system automatically over the Internet via the Software Update feature—but not from within Classic. Because the Mac OS is modular, various components of the OS may be upgraded independently of the Mac OS as a whole. This is a real timesaver, considering how long upgrading the entire OS over the Internet would take! You don't have to update

2

the Mac OS, but you would be wise to check the Apple Web site (**www.apple.com**) often for a new version of the OS that may potentially add new features, increase the speed of the OS, or fix a bug or incompatibility issue.

You can manually check for software updates, or configure the Software Update Control Panel to check automatically. To check manually for new versions of Mac OS components:

1. Boot into Mac OS 9.1.

2. Open the Software Update Control Panel, shown in Figure 2.19.

3. Click the Update Now button.

4. A dialog box will appear asking you for permission to proceed.

Figure 2.19
The Software Update feature of Mac OS 9.1.

If no updates are found for your particular model or versions of installed Mac OS components, another dialog box will appear informing you that no updates are necessary.

You can also check for updates on a schedule that is convenient for you, which frees you from having to remember to do it manually. To configure an automated update after booting into Mac OS 9.1:

1. Open the Software Update Control Panel.

2. Check the Update Software Automatically checkbox.

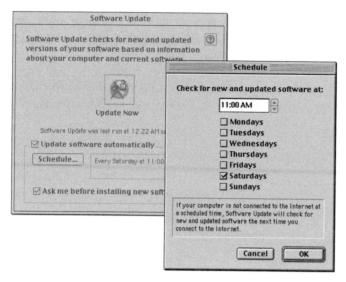

Figure 2.20
Setting the schedule for an automated update of the Mac OS.

3. Click on the Schedule button and choose a schedule for the update, as in Figure 2.20.

4. Decide whether you want to be asked by the Mac OS before downloading the updates, and then check (or not, depending on your preference) the option entitled Ask Me Before Downloading New Software.

5. Close the Software Update Control Panel.

6. Click on OK and then Agree when presented with the Apple Software License Agreement.

At the appropriate time, the Software Update Control Panel will automatically launch itself and begin searching for updated versions of the Mac OS. If no updates are found, then nothing will be installed. If an update is found, you will be presented with an option similar to the one shown in Figure 2.21. In this example, several components for Mac OS 9.1 are available for updating.

If you select a software package to update, you may be required to restart your computer to complete the updating process. Also, keep in mind that some update packages may be several megabytes in size and could take more than an hour to download, depending on the speed of your Internet access.

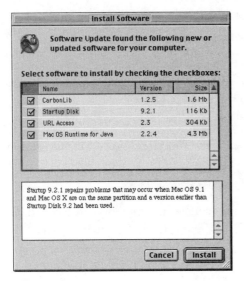

Figure 2.21
Selecting software to update in Mac OS 9.1.

Wrapping Up

Mac OS X offers a new approach to working with Mac OS 9.1 by allowing you to run it in Classic mode from within Mac OS X or boot directly into Mac OS 9.1. For the most part, you'll interact less with the contents of the System Folder when in Classic mode because several features are disabled. You'll probably want to work with Carbon and Cocoa applications as much as possible anyway because of the advanced features provided by Mac OS X when using non-Classic applications. When booting directly into Mac OS 9.1, however, keep in mind that the operating system is very particular about the location of its files, so don't muck around too much. The items contained in the System Folder that are especially useful include:

- *The Apple Menu Items folder*—Enables you to customize your Apple menu.

- *The Control Panels folder*—Houses special "mini-applications" that set preferences for system software features, utilities, and even hardware peripherals. Not all Control Panels work under Classic, however.

- *The Extensions folder*—Contains all the Extensions and drivers that add features to Mac OS 9.1.

- *The Favorites folder*—Holds shortcuts and aliases to your favorite files, folders, applications, file servers, and Internet addresses.

- *The System suitcase*—Contains keyboard mappings, sounds, and critical portions of the Mac OS that are responsible for a wide variety of functions (and are invisible to the user).

- *The Startup and Shutdown Items folders*—Allows you to determine which files and applications are opened or launched each time Mac OS 9.1 or Classic is started, restarted, or shut down.

In addition to learning about the components and functions of the Mac OS, you have also learned how to keep your OS up to date by way of manual or automated, scheduled updates.

In Chapter 3, we'll look at a few special issues concerning memory allocation in Mac OS 9.1 and how to best work with your Classic applications from within Mac OS X.

Working with Classic

Until your favorite programs are available as Carbon or Cocoa applications for Mac OS X, you have two options for using them—running them in Classic mode or booting directly into Mac OS 9.1. When your computer is booted directly into Mac OS 9.1, Classic applications are no different from any other applications. You can launch them, use them, and quit them just as you have for years and years. But when you're running these applications in Classic mode under Mac OS X, they require a little more attention to make sure they run smoothly. With Mac OS X, the amount of RAM installed in your Mac, although still important, is no longer the total measure of memory or the only important memory issue.

This chapter looks at the differences between running Classic applications when booting directly into Mac OS 9.1 and in Classic mode under Mac OS X, including memory issues, the About This Mac and About This Computer windows, ways you can configure applications to use memory most efficiently in Mac OS 9.1, and a few tools to help you better monitor your Mac's memory usage.

Memory vs. Storage

Before we jump into Mac OS X's new memory options and their implications, let's clarify the difference between random access memory (RAM)—frequently termed plain old "memory"—and storage (disk space). This distinction may be clear to experienced Macintosh users; however, if you're not sure of the difference, please read this section carefully.

In the simplest terms, memory consists of the chips in your computer where data is *temporarily* stored while it is being used by the Macintosh. This is in contrast to your hard disk, floppy disks, and other storage devices where data is *permanently* stored when it's not being used by your Macintosh.

Although both RAM and storage hold data, including applications, system software, and data files, the similarities end there. Because RAM stores data electronically on a set of chips, these chips "forget" their contents as soon as the flow of electricity is interrupted (when the Mac is turned off or restarted). Storage devices such as hard drives and floppy disks, which operate magnetically or by optical technology, are not affected by changes in the power supply. They "forget" information only if it's intentionally erased or becomes corrupted during the writing process. In other words, information stored in RAM is short-lived, whereas information saved to a storage device can hang around for years.

Furthermore, the Macintosh can only work with data stored in RAM; it cannot directly manipulate data on any storage device. Therefore, in order to open an application or file, the data must be read from storage and written into memory. Once the data is in memory, the application can be executed or the file can be modified. To make these changes permanent, however, the information in RAM must be written back out to the storage device—this is what happens when you choose the Save command.

How the Mac OS Controls Memory

One of the realities Macintosh users must face is the finite amount of memory available in their computers. Today's software seems to have an insatiable appetite for RAM, and technologies—including multitasking, 24-bit color and sound, and particularly the Web and Web browsers—intensify the problem. The quest for additional memory has always been subject to certain roadblocks: the OS's limited ability to address the need for large amounts of memory, the computer's physical limitations, and the high price of memory chips.

One of the most significant differences between Mac OS X and Mac OS 9.1, however, is in the use of virtual memory, which is the use of hard disk space to emulate RAM. For much of the history of the Mac OS prior to Mac OS X, users could enable, adjust, or disable virtual memory by way of the Memory Control Panel. In Mac OS X, however, virtual memory is "always on" and cannot be otherwise adjusted. In fact, when you open the Memory Control Panel from within Classic, you'll find that most of the options are disabled (see Figure 3.1).

As far as Mac OS 9.1 knows, virtual memory is turned off when in Classic mode and the total amount of memory installed on your computer is also the same amount of memory available to your Classic applications. In general, virtual memory issues are pretty much non-existent in Mac OS X and Mac OS 9.1 in Classic mode.

On the other hand, when booting directly into Mac OS 9.1, virtual memory issues are important because of the configuration options you'll have to consider in order to

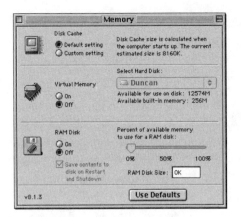
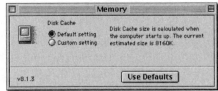

Figure 3.1
The Memory Control Panel in Mac OS 9.1 (left) and from within Classic (right).

optimize the performance of your Classic applications. In previous versions of the Mac OS, the appearance of the Memory Control Panel differed according to which model of Macintosh (or Macintosh clone) you owned. With Mac OS 9.1, however, each model of computer has the same three sections in the Memory Control Panel:

- Disk Cache

- Virtual Memory

- RAM Disk

Under Classic mode, Mac OS 9.1 will not allow you to configure any of these options. Although it appears you may modify the first of these three options, the feature is actually disabled. All three options are discussed in the following sections.

Disk Cache

The disk cache is a small section of RAM set aside to store a copy of the most recent data read from disk (or volume) into memory. Most operating systems, including Mac OS 9.1 and Mac OS X, have a disk cache. Most hard drives also have a RAM chip installed within the drive enclosure; the proximity of the RAM chip decreases the time it takes to access frequently used information. A good hard drive will have at least 2MB of cache—some have as much as 4MB. In addition to caching documents and applications, portions of the Mac OS such as menus are also cached so that they are displayed immediately whenever one of them is pulled down. Because menu performance varies with CPU speed, this difference will be most apparent to users with slower machines.

The disk cache portion of the Memory Control Panel was reworked in Mac OS 8.5 to provide two types of cache settings, both of which exist in Mac OS 9.1 as well:

- Default setting
- Custom setting

The Mac OS uses roughly 32KB of cache for every 1MB of RAM installed in your computer. If you have 128MB of RAM, for example, then the default cache setting would be 4,096KB. Clicking the Default button will allow the OS to select the setting that is best for most users according to this formula. Don't reduce the cache below its default setting unless you have specific memory limitations—the small amount of memory the cache consumes delivers a big return by significantly improving your computer's performance.

Conversely, it's usually a bad idea to increase the size of your cache too much. Settings greater than 32KB per 1MB of installed RAM should be used only in very specific situations in which large cache allocations aid performance; your software's documentation should advise you on how to handle this. For example, Adobe's Type Manager can use large cache allocations when it's rendering several fonts for a document. Most applications use their own internal memory caching scheme, however, rather than relying on the system software's cache for performance enhancement.

To use a custom cache setting (i.e., one that is smaller or larger than the default) after booting into Mac OS 9.1:

1. Open the Memory Control Panel and click the Custom button to reveal an information/warning dialog box, and then select the Custom button within this dialog box.

2. Increase or decrease the cache size. The minimum size is 128K, and the maximum size allowed by Mac OS 9.1 is 32,736K.

The perfect disk cache size is a matter of great debate even among the most technically knowledgeable Macintosh users. Because variables such as your Macintosh hardware and software configurations and the way you use your Mac significantly influence your optimal setting, trial and error is really the only way to find what works best for you. For example, Figure 3.2 shows a custom disk cache set to almost 16MB.

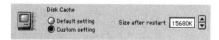

Figure 3.2
Custom disk cache setting for Mac OS 9.1.

The Disk Cache option is always on; you may adjust its size downward or upward, but you cannot turn it off.

Virtual Memory

As mentioned earlier, virtual memory is actually a hardware trick. It uses space on your hard drive to "fool" the Mac OS into thinking that the available amount of physical memory is greater than it really is. Using virtual memory, a Mac with only 128MB of physical RAM can operate similarly to one that has 129MB or more. In fact, virtual memory can provide your Mac with almost 1GB (990MB, to be precise) of memory when booted directly into Mac OS 9.1. Because virtual memory substitutes hard disk space for RAM, and hard drive space is generally much less expensive than actual RAM, virtual memory offers an obvious financial benefit. Furthermore, virtual memory can provide access to more memory than is possible with RAM chips alone.

However, using virtual memory has two main drawbacks. First, performance is slower than with real RAM because the mechanical actions required of your hard drive are no match for the electronic speed of RAM chips, which have no moving parts. Second, virtual memory appropriates hard disk space normally available for other activities. If you have a fast drive (7,200 to 10,000 RPM), you'll probably notice a difference in overall speed while using virtual memory. Drives with an onboard hard drive disk cache (RAM installed on the hard drive itself, discussed earlier in this section) can greatly improve virtual memory performance.

Enabling Virtual Memory

To enable virtual memory, go to the Virtual Memory section of the Memory Control Panel after booting into Mac OS 9.1 and follow these steps:

1. Select the On button, at which time the Select Hard Disk option becomes available. From the pop-up menu, choose the hard disk volume on which the virtual memory file will be created and stored. If you have only one hard drive, the menu will offer only one option.

2. Indicate the total amount of memory you want to have after the computer has been restarted.

The amount of available space on the selected hard disk is displayed below the hard disk pop-up menu where it says Available For Use On Disk. The amount of free space available partially determines the amount of virtual memory that can be configured. The second determining factor is the maximum amount of memory Mac OS 9.1 will allow, which is 990MB. A virtual memory storage file equal to the total amount of

---

memory available while using virtual memory will be placed on the selected disk. In other words, if your Macintosh has 128MB of actual RAM, and you want to reach 512MB by using an additional 384MB of virtual memory, a 512MB virtual memory storage file must be created on the selected volume. Here's another example: You have 128B of RAM, and you want to turn virtual memory on but use as little disk space as possible for this purpose. In this case, you would add 1MB of additional memory for a total of 129MB, thereby creating an invisible 129MB storage file called VM Storage on the selected volume.

Below the Available For Use On Disk option is the Available Built-in Memory field, which tells you how much physical RAM is installed and recognized by the Mac OS. If you increase the amount of virtual memory to be used, a field labeled After Restart will appear. The After Restart option indicates the amount of memory specified, including actual RAM and virtual memory. Click on the arrows to modify this specification. If the After Restart option is not visible, click one of the arrows until it appears. Figure 3.3 illustrates the differences in the Virtual Memory section of the Memory Control Panel before (top) and after (bottom) virtual memory has been enabled under Mac OS 9.1.

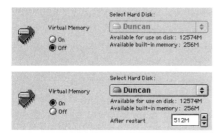

Figure 3.3
Configuring virtual memory under Mac OS 9.1.

Any changes made to the Virtual Memory option will not take effect until you restart your computer. To verify that virtual memory is on, choose the About This Computer command to display the current memory status. (You'll find more information on the About This Computer and the About This Mac windows in the "About This Computer/About This Mac" section, later in this chapter.)

 It's possible to have more RAM installed than is recognized by your computer. The RAM that is not recognized is either installed improperly or is not the right type of chip for your particular model of Macintosh. Consult your computer's documentation for the correct specifications.

Virtual Memory Performance in Mac OS 9.1

Virtual memory works by moving information between a disk-based swap file and the RAM inside the computer; even when virtual memory is being used, the Mac OS communicates only with the real RAM. This movement of data between hard disk and RAM, technically known as paging, causes the Macintosh to perform slower than it does when using actual RAM alone.

The amount of paging slowdown depends on how much actual RAM is available and how virtual memory is being used. The more available RAM, the less paging interference. The activity called for also affects paging—activities such as working on multimegabyte data files and frequent switching between open applications usually require more paging and therefore decrease performance. Problems with virtual memory show up as poor performance in animation, video, and sound. Games and multimedia content that require manipulation of large amounts of data are the first to suffer. Frequent hard disk activity associated with virtual memory is a prime energy drain for PowerBooks and iBooks because of the electricity required to keep the disk drive spinning.

A good rule of thumb in determining your own RAM/virtual memory mix is that you should have enough actual RAM to cover your normal memory needs and enough supplemental virtual memory to handle occasional, abnormally large requirements. If you find that approximately 128MB of RAM lets you work comfortably in the three or four open applications you use regularly, but you occasionally need another 128MB to open additional applications or work with large data files, then 128MB of real RAM and a combined total of 256MB of RAM and virtual memory would probably be adequate. However, if you don't need an additional 128MB of virtual memory on top of your 128MB of physical memory, use just one additional megabyte of virtual memory instead. This will help speed up things a bit and, as with using any amount of virtual memory, your applications won't ask for as much RAM.

Why is this, you ask? The presence of virtual memory allows only the PowerPC-native code necessary for an application to launch to be read into memory upon launch. The remaining code used by an application is loaded only when needed. This allows for a quicker launch; however, when you actually use the program, it may be slower to operate than if you weren't using virtual memory because all the code was loaded in the beginning. This trade-off is inherent to using virtual memory: Applications launch faster, but any speed gained in the beginning may very well be lost as you continue to use the application. This is only true for PowerPC-native applications, however. Applications written for the older Motorola 68K family of processors do not behave in this way.

Similar to the disk cache debate, the appropriate ratio of real to virtual memory has long been the subject of speculation. Ultimately, this question will fade into the past because Mac OS X uses persistent virtual memory; it cannot be turned off, one benefit of which is that you will never get an "out of memory" error message like in previous versions of the Mac OS. However, the answer for Classic Mac OS users is to use as much virtual memory as is practical and efficacious. Physical RAM is fairly cheap these days (about $1/megabyte), and you must have at least 128MB to run Mac OS X. Bear in mind that most entry-level Macs ship with 128MB now—and some ship with 512MB of RAM—but some entry-level iMacs only have 64MB of RAM, so you'll have to purchase at least 64MB of additional RAM to run Mac OS X. My personal preference is to have no less than 256MB of RAM and not to use virtual memory at all when booting into Mac OS 9.1. With this amount of physical RAM, the disk cache defaults to the maximum of 8,160K, which is adequate for all my needs.

Virtual Memory Advantages in Mac OS 9.1

I've discussed how PowerPC-native applications may be partially loaded into memory at startup if virtual memory is turned on. But what about the effect virtual memory has on the memory requirements of an application? Figure 3.4 gives you an idea of how this works. On the left side of the figure is the memory section of the Get Info window for BBEdit with virtual memory turned on, which is the default setting for Mac OS 9.1. Observe that the Note section points out the application may require 4,110K of additional memory to run if virtual memory is turned off.

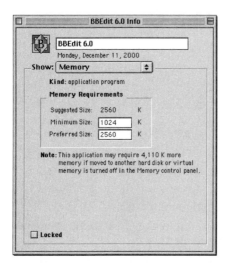 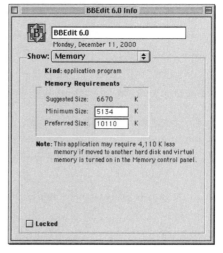

Figure 3.4
A comparison of memory requirements with virtual memory turned on (left) and off (right) for the same application while in Mac OS 9.1.

The right side of the figure shows the same dialog box once the computer has been restarted with virtual memory turned off. The reverse is now true: The Note section says the application may require 4,110KB less memory if virtual memory is turned on.

Another benefit to using virtual memory (in addition to a quicker launch time for applications) is that you'll have more room to launch additional applications simply by turning on virtual memory. The amount of virtual memory your computer is using doesn't matter, however; the changes in memory requirements for an application will never vary in proportion to how much virtual memory is in use. It will only change if it is in use at all.

Disabling Virtual Memory

Virtual memory can be disabled by clicking the Off button in the Virtual Memory area of the Memory Control Panel and restarting your computer directly into Mac OS 9.1. After disabling virtual memory, the invisible virtual memory storage file (VM Storage) is deleted from your hard drive automatically, and the space it occupied is returned to the Mac OS for use by other programs. The Mac OS is said to launch applications more slowly with virtual memory disabled, whereas the overall speed of an application is said to increase without virtual memory.

Memory Control Panel Tips

Here are a few tips to keep in mind when configuring the Mac OS to use both physical and virtual memory in Mac OS 9.1:

■ *Use at least the minimum recommended disk cache as defined by the Default setting.* Because the disk cache speeds up operation, you should set it to at least 32KB for every megabyte of RAM installed in your Mac (that means 4,096KB for 128MB of RAM).

■ *Install enough physical RAM in your Macintosh.* Real RAM chips should provide enough memory to cover your normal daily memory needs—at least 128MB, and in most cases, up to 512MB. Although virtual memory can provide inexpensive additional memory, 80 percent of your memory needs should be covered by real RAM. The relatively small amount of money saved does not justify the performance drawbacks of relying too heavily on virtual memory.

■ *Extend your available memory with virtual memory.* Once you've installed enough RAM to satisfy your everyday needs, use the virtual memory when special situations (such as working with large color images, animation, or more than the usual number of simultaneously open programs) demand extra memory.

■ *Some applications, especially multimedia games, movies, and audio programs, just don't like virtual memory.* If these types of programs don't behave properly, check with their instructions for information about possible virtual memory incompatibilities.

 Turn off virtual memory when you experience performance problems. Some programs, such as games and graphics programs, execute considerable data input/output. Virtual memory can degrade performance, and rapid paging can lead to system crashes.

RAM Disk

A RAM disk is a chunk of RAM set aside to emulate a hard disk. When running in Classic mode within Mac OS X, the RAM disk feature is not available; when you boot directly into Mac OS 9.1, however, you can set aside a certain amount of memory to use as a RAM disk, which functions just like a hard disk in many respects. You can add, delete, edit, and save files on a RAM disk. The chief advantage of using a RAM disk is speed: Unlike a hard drive, a RAM disk has no moving parts, which makes working with large files on a RAM disk significantly faster. The chief drawback, however, is that the amount of RAM set aside as a RAM disk is not available to the rest of the Mac OS or your applications.

To create a RAM disk, open the Memory Control Panel; select the On button in the RAM Disk section, and then select the amount of RAM to set aside as a RAM disk. When you reboot the computer into Mac OS 9.1, the RAM disk will appear on the Desktop. To remove the RAM disk, select the Off button in the Memory Control Panel and reboot.

Controlling Memory for Classic Applications

After you have determined how much memory you need and made it available to Mac OS 9.1 (by installing RAM and by using virtual memory), you'll want to manage that memory wisely and use it economically. Managing your Mac's memory ensures that each application has enough RAM to operate properly and that enough total memory is available to open as many different applications as necessary. This is possible for Classic applications under Mac OS 9.1 because they are allocated memory on an application-by-application basis that is determined by preferences set by the software programmer and your own preferences. Carbon and Cocoa applications do not allow such changes because Mac OS X handles all aspects of memory management.

The Classic environment provides two excellent tools for memory management—the About This Computer command and the Get Info window. In this section, we'll look at both of these tools in conjunction with their Mac OS X counterparts, the About This Mac command and the Show Info window.

About This Computer/About This Mac

Starting with Mac OS 8, the familiar About This Macintosh command was changed to About This Computer, and the dialog box associated with it was improved. The About This Computer window provides information about the Macintosh you're using, including the system software version, installed and available memory, and the amount of memory used by each open application. Figure 3.5 shows an example of the About This Computer window in Mac OS 9.1 with multiple applications open.

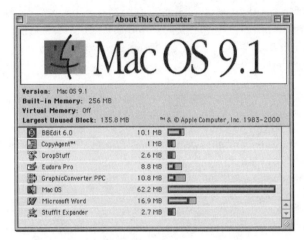

Figure 3.5
The result of executing the About This Computer command.

The upper section of the window shown in Figure 3.5 gives the version of the operating system that is currently in use as well as the following data regarding the available memory:

- *Built-in Memory—256MB*. Displays the amount of physical RAM installed in this particular Macintosh, exclusive of virtual memory.

- *Virtual Memory—Off*. States the total memory available in your Macintosh, including installed RAM plus available virtual memory, if enabled. The name of the hard disk storing the virtual memory file and the amount of hard drive space being used are listed to the right of the Virtual Memory field. Virtual memory and hard drive designations are set via the Memory Control Panel, described earlier in this chapter.

- *Largest Unused Block—135.8MB*. Calculates the largest contiguous section of memory currently not being used by open software applications. This number is important because it determines both the number and size of additional software applications you can open. In some cases, the largest unused block will not equal the amount of total memory available minus the size of all open applications. This is the result of memory fragmentation—the formation of gaps between sections of memory that are used and those that are available. To defragment your memory and create larger unused blocks, quit all open applications and then relaunch them. As they're relaunched, applications will use available memory sequentially, leaving the largest possible unused block.

Each application requires a particular amount of memory in order to be opened successfully. The amount of memory is documented and can be controlled in the Memory section of the Get Info window, as described later in this chapter. When a program is launched, it cannot be opened if its memory requirement is larger than the largest unused block. Therefore, it's important to know approximately how much memory an application needs.

If you get an out-of-memory alert box when plenty of memory should be available, you could have a fragmented memory situation. This occurs when you launch and quit programs repeatedly. You can avoid this problem by leaving open programs you'll most likely use again instead of quitting them as soon as you've finished using them. If you have a fragmented memory problem, first try quitting programs in the sequence that is the reverse of the order in which they were launched. If that doesn't do the trick, you'll have to restart to flush your computer's memory.

The lower portion of the About This Computer window displays information about the memory used by the Mac OS as well as information about each open application:

- *Application icon and name*—Each open application, preceded by a small version of its icon, is listed in alphabetical order.

- *Amount of memory used*—In most cases, only a portion of an application's total allocated memory is used immediately upon opening it. Usually, some of the memory is used by the application itself, some is used to hold open document files, and some is left over for use by the software's commands and features. Only the memory currently being used appears as the filled-in percentage of the memory allocation bar.

- *Amount of memory allocated*—The total amount of memory that was allocated to that program when it was opened is displayed in a bar graph that shows the allocated amount in relation to amounts used by other open applications. The entire bar represents total allocated memory; the filled portion of the bar represents the portion of allocated memory currently in use.

Double-clicking on the name of an application in the About This Computer window will bring that application to the foreground.

Holding down the Option key when choosing the About This Computer command changes the command into About The Finder. Choosing About The Finder brings up a copyright screen that first appeared in Finder 1.0 in 1984 (if you wait a bit, you'll see a message about the Finder scrolling across the screen).

Under Mac OS X, the command has been changed to About This Mac, two examples of which are shown in Figure 3.6. Since memory usage is not as big an issue in Mac OS X as it is in Classic, About This Mac does not offer you as many details regarding memory allocation. However, it still provides information about:

- The operating system version (including the *build* number, which refers to a specific compilation of the entire operating system)

- The amount of RAM

- The type of processor

Figure 3.6
The About This Mac command for two different computers.

Additional information about running applications can be obtained by other utilities, which are discussed in Chapter 8.

Get Info/Show Info

All visible files, folders, and applications have information properties that can be viewed using a simple command called Get Info (in Mac OS 9.1) or Show Info (in Mac OS X). The Memory section of the Get Info window allows you to take charge of your Macintosh's memory consumption (additional information about which is provided in the About This Computer window discussed earlier in this chapter). To minimize problems related to memory shortages, or to better allocate your available

RAM to the different applications you want to open simultaneously, you can adjust the amount of memory each program uses.

Because the memory-related options of the Get Info window differ among older versions of the operating system (such as System 7) and Mac OS 9.1, we'll examine each of them separately.

Get Info in Earlier Versions of the Mac OS

Versions of the Mac OS prior to OS 9.1 provided fewer options for memory management than does Mac OS 9.1. The Memory option has only two parts:

- *Suggested Size*—Displays the amount of RAM (as recommended by the developer) necessary to properly run the application. Although you can't change this option, it's very valuable as a reminder of the original Current Size setting.

- *Current Size*—Specifies the actual amount of RAM that the application will request when it's launched. (By default, the Current Size is equal to the Suggested Size.) You can change the amount of memory that will be allocated by entering a new value in this option and then closing the Get Info window.

When an application is launched, the program requests the amount of memory specified in the Current Size option. If this amount is available in an unused block, the memory is allocated and the program is opened. You can check the size of the largest available block in the About This Computer window, as described earlier.

If the amount of memory requested is larger than the largest available unused block, a dialog box will appear stating that not enough memory is available, asking if you want to try to run the application using less memory, or suggesting that you quit an open application to create enough free memory.

Memory Section of Get Info/Show Info

Mac OS 9.1 adds a third option in the Memory section of the Get Info window to provide greater control over how your applications use memory. The Get Info window's options in Mac OS 9.1 (as in System 7.6 and later) also eliminate the need to change settings for different memory situations; they allow you to set options that determine how much memory will be used depending on the amount of memory available at launch time. Now, however, these memory requirements are set in the Memory section of the Get Info window, which is activated by follow-ing these steps:

1. From the Finder, navigate to an application icon such as Microsoft Internet Explorer and select the icon by clicking on it once.

2. Press Command+I or choose File|Get Info (Mac OS 9.1) or File|Show Info (Mac OS X).

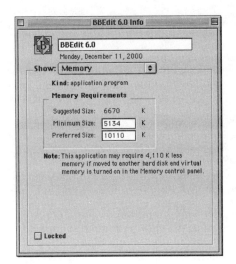 

Figure 3.7
BBEdit's memory settings in the Get Info (left) and Show Info (right) windows.

3. Select the Memory section of the Get Info/Show Info window, examples of which are shown in Figure 3.7.

In Mac OS 9.1, the Memory option here includes four main parts—Suggested Size, Minimum Size, Preferred Size, and Note:

- *Suggested Size*—Lists the amount of RAM needed to properly run the application. This option cannot be modified; however, it serves as a reminder of the memory requirements as defined by the application developer.

- *Minimum Size*—Designates the smallest amount of RAM required for the application to run properly. Although you can change this option by entering a new value, your application may become unstable as a result.

- *Preferred Size*—Specifies the actual amount of RAM that the application will request when it's launched. You can change the amount of memory that will be allocated by entering a new value in this option and then closing the Get Info window.

- *Note*—Informs you of how much additional memory may be required if virtual memory is turned on.

In Mac OS X, the Show Info window only has three parts. Although each part is also found in Mac OS 9.1's Get Info window, the order differs. The Show Info window includes:

- *Suggested Size*—Lists the amount of RAM, as recommended by the developer, needed to properly run the application.

- *Preferred Size*—Specifies the actual amount of RAM that the application will request when it's launched.

- *Minimum Size*—Designates the smallest amount of RAM required for the application to run properly.

This may be a little confusing because you can actually view and change memory allocation for Classic applications from within Mac OS X, and to top it off, your choices are different! The effect of the changes is the same, however. When an application is launched, the program requests the amount of memory specified in the Preferred Size option. If this amount is available in a contiguous, unused memory block, the memory is allocated and the program is opened. You can check the size of the largest available block in the About This Computer/About This Mac window, as described earlier.

If the amount of memory requested by the Preferred Size option is not available, but more memory is available than the Minimum Size option, the application will launch using all available memory. If the amount of RAM specified in the Minimum Size option is unavailable, and you have booted directly into Mac OS 9.1, a dialog box will appear offering advice on quitting other applications to free enough memory to complete the launch. If you are running the application while in Classic mode from within Mac OS X, the application will not launch and you are unlikely to receive an error message.

Setting Memory Options for Classic Applications

Although you can modify a Classic application's memory parameters from either Mac OS 9.1 or Mac OS X, you can determine how active applications are using memory usage only in Mac OS 9.1's About This Computer window, which I discussed earlier. Optimally, 15 to 25 percent of the space in the memory allocation bar (displayed next to an application name in the About This Computer window) should remain open (or unused) while the application is running. (As explained earlier, the bar illustrates total allocated RAM in gray and the portion of memory actually being used in blue.)

Some applications do not use all of their allocated memory at all times—usage may vary as commands and features are executed. Other applications, however, automatically grab all of their allocated memory. Therefore, if you want to determine the actual, average, and maximum amount of memory used, keep the About This Computer window open while you work so that you can monitor the changes in memory used by your applications in the lower half of the screen, as illustrated in Figure 3.8.

Given that 15 to 25 percent unused space is the goal, watching the amount of actual memory used will tell you if the current memory allocation is too low, too high, or about right. You may discover that you need to increase a program's memory allocation, or you may be able to decrease it. Either of these modifications is made via the Size options.

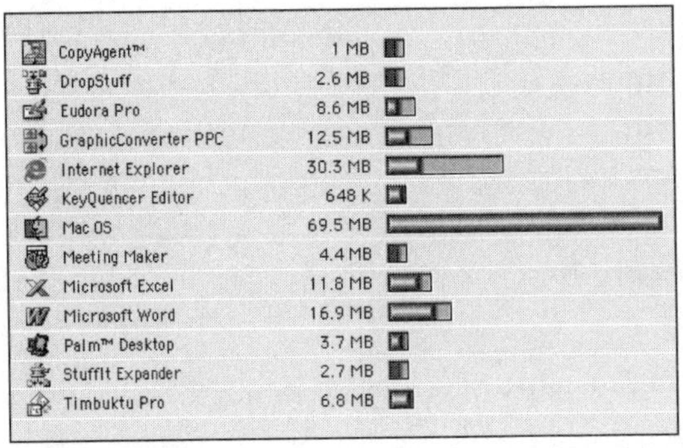

Figure 3.8
Application memory use is documented in the About This Computer window.

Increasing memory allocation provides additional memory that, in many cases, can improve application performance, allow larger and more complete document files to be opened, and reduce or eliminate the possibility of memory-related crashes. For example, I often open numerous large HTML documents in BBEdit, and I often change its memory requirements to accomplish a specific set of tasks. These benefits are hardly surprising when you consider how an application uses its allocated memory: It must control and manage its own code, in addition to data from any open document files and all data manipulations performed by its commands and features. And it must do all this with an allocated memory that's less than the total size of the application program and its data files, let alone what it needs to manipulate its data. As a result, software must constantly shift parts of its own code and data from open documents back and forth between disk-storage memory and real memory. Providing additional memory minimizes this activity and allows the program to concentrate on operating efficiently.

For most programs, increasing the Current Size or Preferred Size option by 20 to 25 percent is optimal. If you experience frequent "out of memory" errors in any software application, however, continue increasing the amount of memory until these errors are eliminated. Increasing the amount of memory will sometimes fix problems associated with launching applications even though a specific error is not presented by the Mac OS.

Decreasing memory allocation allows you to successfully launch applications with less memory and run more programs simultaneously. Although this practice is generally not recommended, in many cases software will operate successfully using less RAM than suggested by the developer.

The true minimum, although it will rarely be more than 20 percent smaller than the suggested size, cannot easily be determined. Don't be afraid to try, however—just be sure to test the application in this configuration before working on important data, and save frequently once you begin working. Start by reducing the Current or Minimum Size option by just 5 to 10 percent; if you find that the About This Computer window shows large amounts of unused space, you may be able to reduce the allocation even more.

With the low price of RAM and the availability of virtual memory, the need for most Macintosh users to reduce these sizes should become less common. Even if you have only 128MB of RAM installed, using virtual memory is preferable to reducing the Current or Minimum Size options when you boot directly into Mac OS 9.1. You're less likely to experience crashes or loss of data with virtual memory than with a reduced Current Size. (See the discussion of virtual memory earlier in this chapter.) Of course, the best long-range solution is to add enough RAM to your Macintosh so you won't have to depend on either virtual memory or Memory Requirements reductions.

Memory-Related Utilities for Mac OS 9.1

Several great utilities that are either freeware (meaning they don't cost you anything), shareware (they may cost a few bucks), or commercial software (lots of bucks) are out there to help you analyze or test your Mac's memory when booting into Mac OS 9.1. Of course, the About This Computer command is free, but it only gives you rudimentary information about your memory situation. Here are some of the best tools for a more thorough job.

Memory Mapper

If you want to know more details on your computer's memory usage when not in Classic mode, check out Bob Fronabarger's great utility called Memory Mapper (see **www.jintek.com/freeware.html**). Memory Mapper provides you with a detailed list of applications, extensions, and background processes that are currently loaded into memory on your Mac. Equally as important, Memory Mapper also tells you about virtual memory usage and in what order items have been loaded into memory. This is important because you should always try to quit applications in the order opposite to the order in which they were launched to prevent memory fragmentation.

Figure 3.9 shows an example of Memory Mapper with 40 entries for the Mac OS, applications, and free memory blocks. When the Mac OS is loaded into memory, it's loaded into the top portion of the memory area (called the High Memory area) as well as the bottom portion, which is occupied by portions of the Mac OS called the

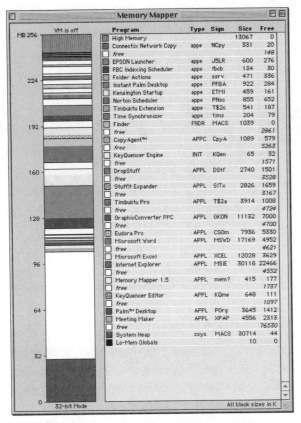

Figure 3.9
Memory Mapper provides detailed information on how much memory is used by Mac OS 9.1, applications, and background processes.

System Heap and the Lo-Mem Globals. All applications and the remaining elements of the Mac OS, such as the Finder, are loaded between the top and bottom portions of the memory area, in a zone referred to as the *application pool.*

Items are loaded from top to bottom in the application pool; when all the memory has been used, you'll get an error message that says something like, "This cannot be completed because not enough memory is available." Not all errors are the result of an actual memory shortage. The System Heap (at the bottom of the memory pool) grows and shrinks dynamically as applications are launched and quit. Some applications, like Microsoft Internet Explorer, grab all the available memory in the System Heap. If the System Heap is full and no memory is available to an application that requests it, the Mac OS may return an error stating that no memory is available to launch the application—even though plenty of memory is available in the application pool.

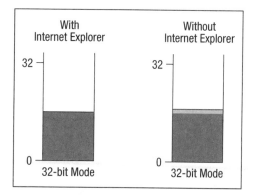

Figure 3.10
A detailed view of Memory Mapper, showing how a single application can consume the System Heap in Mac OS 9.1.

Figure 3.10 illustrates how one application can hog the System Heap. The image on the left is a detailed view of Memory Mapper while Internet Explorer is running with no open windows. The image on the right shows the same detail after the application was quit, which freed up over 1MB in the System Heap.

When compared to Mac OS 9.1, Mac OS X changes the memory-usage landscape for the better. Who has time to worry about so many details of memory usage and allocation?

Mac OS Purge

Mac OS Purge by Kenji Takeuchi (**www.macinsearch.com**) is a simple, faceless utility for Classic Mac OS that does two things. First, it purges the areas of memory occupied by stale data that was not automatically purged by an application, extension, or the Mac OS itself. This predicament occurs after you have launched and then quit applications that rely on large extensions or that, having written data to the System Heap, have not properly returned the memory to it or the application pool. Second, after the program has run (and because it's faceless, you won't actually interact with it) and quit, it will automatically open the About This Computer window.

To try this out, launch several applications and use them for a few minutes each, then quit them all. Then open the About This Computer window and take note of how much memory is used by the Mac OS. Finally, launch Mac OS Purge and then use the About This Computer command to compare how much memory is used by the Mac OS. For example, Figure 3.11 shows a before (top) and after (bottom) comparison of the results of this exercise. Notice that the Mac OS uses about 200KB less memory after Mac OS Purge has been launched, and the largest unused block is 500KB larger.

Figure 3.11
Use Mac OS Purge to free up memory no longer in use by the Mac OS or your applications.

Memory Implications for Mac OS 9.1 Multitasking

Everything has its price. Macintosh users know this well (especially experienced Macintosh users). Multitasking is no exception—its price is memory. Put simply, you can run only as many applications at once as your available Macintosh memory can handle. A predefined amount of memory must be dedicated to the application while it's open. Running multiple applications simultaneously requires enough memory to satisfy the cumulative amounts defined by those applications. Your total amount of available memory includes what's supplied by the RAM chips installed on your computer's logic board or on an expansion card (for PowerBooks), plus any virtual memory created with the Memory Control Panel.

When you first turn on a Macintosh running Mac OS 9.1, some of your memory is taken up immediately by the system software and the Finder. This amount varies depending on how many fonts and sounds you've installed, your disk cache setting, the extensions you're using, and whether you're using File Sharing. In some circumstances, as much as 25 to 33 percent of your Mac's available memory may be consumed by the system software itself. Your Macintosh's memory usage is documented in the About

This Computer window. To reduce the amount of memory your system software consumes, remove unused fonts or sounds, reduce the size of your RAM disk, and turn off File Sharing.

Each time you launch an application, it requests the amount of memory that it needs in order to run. If enough memory is available, the application is launched. On the other hand, if the available memory is insufficient, one of several dialog boxes will appear warning you of the situation or offering a suggestion about how to make more memory available.

If available memory is insufficient to launch an application, quit one or more of the open applications to free up additional memory. Then try again to launch the application you want. If this doesn't do the trick, quit additional open applications and retry the launch until you're successful. If all else fails, restart the computer.

Managing Classic Applications

Mac users have had multitasking—the ability to run multiple applications at the same time—for many years. Mac OS 9.1 features cooperative multitasking, a type of multitasking that requires individual application programmers to request and yield the computer's processor cooperatively. Without cooperative multitasking, for example, Program A is allowed to hog the processor, forcing other applications to suffer until Programs A quits. Cooperative multitasking has been the standard way to work with multiple applications for desktop operating systems such as Mac OS 9.1, Windows 98, and Windows ME.

Multitasking in Mac OS 9.1

Multitasking allows you to run your word processor, Web browser, and graphics package at the same time and switch among them freely. In fact, one application can continue processing information while you're using another application. Cooperative multitasking is actually an old feature that Macintosh users have been using for more than 10 years that allows you to:

■ Run multiple applications simultaneously

■ Switch among open applications as necessary

■ Leave one program working while you switch to another

■ Copy multiple items concurrently and return to the Finder or another application while the items are being copied in the background

Figure 3.12 shows six applications running simultaneously in addition to the Mac OS. Only three (Internet Explorer, Microsoft Word, and iTunes) are running as visible

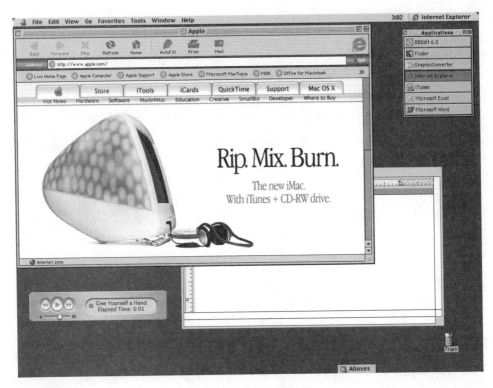

Figure 3.12
Mac OS 9.1 running several applications.

applications, however—the others have all been hidden by the Hide command in the Application menu.

Because it allows you to use both time and resources with maximum efficiency, Multitasking is a fantastic productivity booster. Here's an example: You're working in your word processor when you receive a telephone call from your mother. She wants to know whether she should invest the $10,000 she just won playing bingo in a 10-year CD paying 8.25 percent or sink it into T-bills paying 6.15 percent tax-free. To help her solve this dilemma, you need access to a spreadsheet. You quit your word processor, launch your spreadsheet, perform the necessary calculations, offer your advice, quit the spreadsheet, launch the word processor, reload your file, and say good-bye to Mom.

Taking this approach is fine—of course you want to help your mother—but multi-tasking could have saved you some time by enabling you to run your spreadsheet without quitting your word processor.

The most obvious benefit of multitasking is that it enables you to use two or more applications together to complete a single project. To prepare a mail merge, for example, you can export data from your database manager, prepare the merge lists, and then execute the merge into a word processing document. In most cases, the raw data exported from your database will require some cleaning up before it's ready to be merged, and often you'll encounter a minor data formatting problem that requires you to repeat the whole export and data cleanup process. By using multitasking, however, you avoid the delay and frustration of quitting the word processor to return to the database and then quitting the database to return to the word processor.

Suppose you need to read reports and view database or spreadsheet data while preparing presentation graphics, update graphic illustrations in a drawing package before importing them into a page layout, or use an optical character recognition package to scan in articles for storage in a database. In situations like these, switching from one application to another and using the Cut, Copy, and Paste commands makes it possible to transfer information between applications that otherwise could not share data.

Another benefit of multitasking is the one that yields the greatest productivity gains: Multitasking supports background processing. This means that an open application can continue to process data even when you switch away from that application to work in another. Tasks that tie up your computer, such as printing, downloading files from the Internet, making large spreadsheet calculations, and generating database reports, are likely to benefit from background processing. Examples of background processing and techniques for taking advantage of it are discussed later in this chapter in the section entitled "Background Processing."

The ability to keep multiple programs in memory and recall them from the background to the foreground has been part of Macintosh system software since before MultiFinder, and it persists in Mac OS X as well. This kind of behavior is called *context switching*. An application in the background is suspended at its last point of execution. Context switching is not multitasking because only one process is running at a time. In technical parlance, your Macintosh stores the different threads of execution—but only a single thread in one application can execute.

Multitasking and Classic Applications in Mac OS X

Mac OS X introduces *preemptive multitasking* and is one of the first desktop operating systems to provide such an advanced feature. With preemptive multitasking, the Mach portion of Mac OS X plays the role of traffic cop, allowing each program to have as much processor time as needed without denying other programs or the operating system itself the processor time they require. "Balance and share" is the motto of preemptive multitasking. As far as access to multiple applications is concerned, multitasking in Mac OS X is no different from multitasking in Mac OS 9.1. However, Mac OS X does a much better job of sharing processor time among all applications and dividing up requests for processor time among multiple processors, if available. If you run Mac OS 9.1 applications in Classic mode instead of booting directly into Mac OS 9.1, you get the best of both worlds.

In Mac OS X, each Carbon or Cocoa application that is launched has a main thread (or process); other subthreads may be spawned by the application. These threads are managed preemptively because they are written for Mac OS X, but they may also be managed cooperatively as well. On the other hand, when Mac OS 9.1 is running in Classic mode within Mac OS X, it too is considered a thread, and Classic applications are processes within this thread. If you boot directly into Mac OS 9.1, all applications are managed cooperatively instead of preemptively and therefore are still vulnerable to processor hogging and cascading failure that can bring down the whole system. But because Classic is running as an application environment within Mac OS X, if an application were to crash, the worst-case scenario is that only the main Classic thread will crash, and Mac OS X and all your Carbon and Cocoa applications will survive unscathed.

To summarize, although Classic applications still rely on cooperative multitasking even when in Classic mode, the entire computer will not crash if a Classic application misbehaves. For example, Figure 3.13 shows the same Classic applications found in Figure 3.12, but running in Classic mode. If one of them was to drastically misbehave,

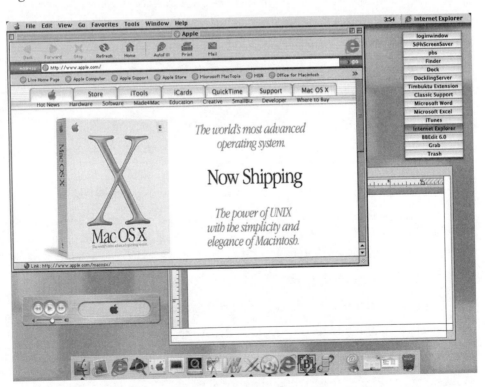

Figure 3.13
Applications in Classic mode still behave in a cooperative fashion, but within the Classic application environment.

the worst scenario is that the Classic environment would terminate without interrupting Mac OS X.

Managing Multiple Applications

When you first start using multiple applications simultaneously, the sight of several windows open at the same time may be a little disconcerting. As you learn to arrange and manipulate these windows and enjoy the benefits of multiple open applications, you'll soon find yourself wondering how you ever got along using just one program at a time. The number of applications you can launch simultaneously is practically unlimited in Mac OS X, but under Mac OS 9.1 the number of applications is limited by the amount of memory available to your computer.

Foreground and Background Applications

Although more than one program can be open at once, only one program can be active at any one time. This is true for applications in Mac OS 9.1, Classic mode, and Mac OS X. The active program is known as the *foreground application*; other open but inactive applications are called *background applications*, even if you can see portions of their windows or if they're simultaneously processing tasks. For example, Figures 3.12 and 3.13 show multiple applications, but Internet Explorer is the sole active application in both examples.

Under Mac OS X, you can identify the currently active program in several ways:

■ The menu bar displays the menu commands of the active program.

■ The title of the application is shown in the menu bar.

■ The icon is displayed with a small triangle in the Dock (although the Dock doesn't indicate which is the frontmost application).

■ The active program window overlaps other visible windows or elements.

■ The active program window's close, minimize, and zoom buttons are displayed in color (although you can change them all to shades of gray in the Appearance section of the General System Preferences pane).

Mac OS 9.1 offers additional ways to identify foreground applications, including:

■ The active program's icon appears at the top of the Application menu.

■ The active program name is checked in the Application menu.

■ The Apple menu's About This Computer says About Program A.

■ The Application Switcher will highlight the most active application.

Switching Among Classic and Carbon/Cocoa Applications

Because only one program can be in the foreground, it's important to be able to switch quickly and easily from one program to another. Switching between applications is commonly referred to as "sending to the back" and "bringing to the front." You can switch between open applications in at least five ways, several of which are illustrated in Figure 3.14:

■ *Use the Dock*—Located in the bottom of the screen, the Dock lists the icons of all applications currently running with a small triangle underneath the icon, as well as bookmarked files, folders, and applications. Select the icon of the application you want to switch to, and its menu bar and windows will be brought to the front.

■ *Use the keyboard shortcut*—Press Command+Tab to cycle through the open applications one at a time, whether in Mac OS 9.1 or Mac OS X. Press Shift+Command+Tab to cycle in reverse.

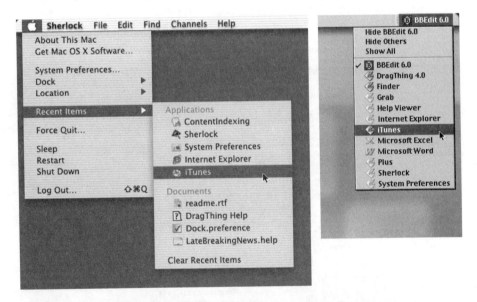

Figure 3.14
Examples of ways to switch between applications.

■ *Click any visible window*—Clicking any visible element of the application brings the application to the front. For example, while working in your word processor, if you can still see the icons on the Desktop, clicking one of them will bring the Finder to the front, making it the current application. You can then return to the word processor by clicking in its window.

■ *Use the Recent Items/Applications menu*—Select an application by name from the Recent Items submenu of the Apple menu (Mac OS X) or the Recent Applications submenu (Mac OS 9.1).

In Chapter 5, we'll look at multiple applications and utilities from third-party developers that track foreground and background applications and enhance many other facets of the user experience.

Finally, you can layer Classic, Carbon, and Cocoa application windows and easily switch among them by clicking on the appropriate window. For example, Figure 3.15 shows three Classic applications and two Carbon applications intermingled with one another.

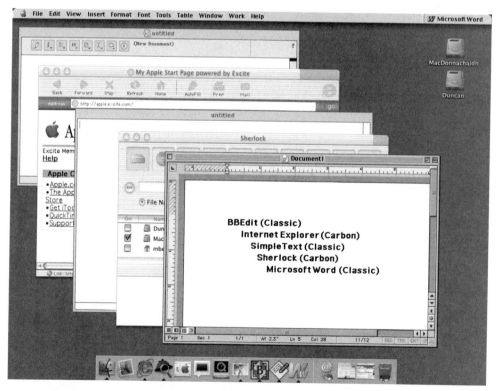

Figure 3.15
Application windows from multiple application environments.

Background Processing

You can bring any application to the foreground, thereby sending any other applications to the background, at any time—except when dialog boxes that are not Navigational Services-savvy are open in Mac OS 9.1. Classic Mac OS applications that have the new Navigational Services (i.e., Open and Save) dialog boxes open can be moved safely into the background even if one of those dialog boxes is active. In fact, you can have multiple Navigational Services windows open for different Classic applications, even if they are intermingled with Carbon and Cocoa applications windows. However, you should be aware that many Classic programs do not implement Navigational Services; when an Open or Save dialog box for such an application is open, you may not be able to continue working with any of your open Classic applications until you have dismissed the window. These types of windows are often referred to as *modal* windows. The new Aqua interface eliminates modal dialog boxes, enabling you to continue working even if an Open or Save window is open for a Carbon or Cocoa application.

You can send most applications to the background while they're processing data, and they will continue to calculate or process in the background. Background processing brings to light an entirely new dimension of using multiple open applications simultaneously.

If you could use multiple open applications only sequentially (one after the other), the increase in productivity would be limited to the time you saved by avoiding repeated opening and quitting of applications. Background processing, however, lets you print a newsletter, calculate a spreadsheet, and download files from the Internet at the same time. This capacity is the ultimate in computer productivity, but keep this in mind: The efficiency of background processing depends on your Macintosh's power and the number and requirements of the background tasks being performed. Classic applications will suffer the most because they share system resources cooperatively; Carbon and Cocoa applications will benefit from preemptive multitasking.

 Using virtual memory can emphasize slowness when switching between applications while in Mac OS 9.1.

The Mac OS will notify you if your attention is needed for a task running in the background, or when a task has been completed.

Hiding Applications

Running several applications concurrently can result in an onscreen clutter of windows. To alleviate this problem, the Mac OS lets you "hide" open application windows and the Desktop, thus removing them from the screen without changing their status or the background work they're doing. Hiding applications instead of quitting them is an important point to remember because of the way the Mac OS allocates memory, as discussed earlier in this chapter. If you've booted directly into Mac OS 9.1 and decide to quit an application out of the sequence in which it was launched, you can potentially cause problems down the road. The memory used by that application may not be reclaimed until you reboot the computer, and this delay could lead to memory fragmentation and pollution of the System Heap. So, when working with multiple applications, leave them open until you are either ready to quit all the applications or reboot. In fact, I recommend adding aliases for each of the frequently used applications to your Startup Items folder so that they will launch automatically. Quit these applications only when you are ready to shut down the computer; in the meantime, just hide them. Your system, whether in Mac OS 9.1 or Classic mode, will be more stable, and you won't have to relaunch the applications.

You can hide an application at the time you leave it to switch to another application, or while it's running in the background. Figure 3.16 shows how your Desktop can become cluttered when running multiple applications simultaneously. Hiding some programs while continuing to operate other programs can help clear things up a bit, as shown in Figure 3.17.

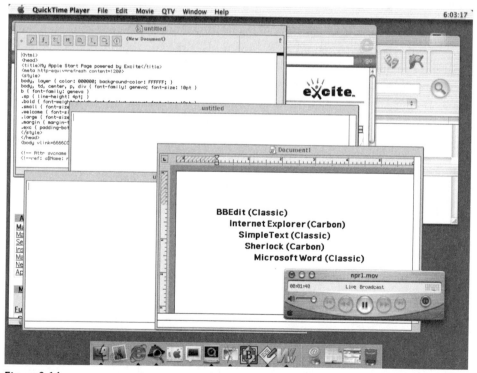

Figure 3.16
Running multiple applications without hiding some of them can result in Desktop chaos.

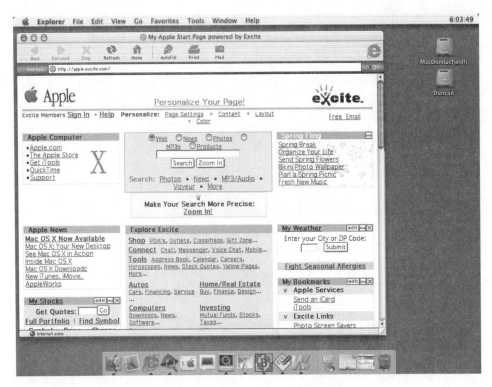

Figure 3.17
Hiding—rather than quitting—unused applications can help you focus on an application.

Mac OS 9.1 and the Classic application environment feature commands that can also be used to hide and show applications. Mac OS 9.1 provides three commands in the Application menu (at the upper-right corner of your screen) for these purposes, and Mac OS X places the same commands in the application menu for each program (between the Apple and File menus in the upper left corner of your screen). The commands are Hide *Current Application* (*Current Application* being the name of the current foreground application), Hide Others, and Show All:

- *Hide Current Application*—Removes all windows of the current application from the screen. The next-most recently used application is brought to the front when this command is selected. The icon of a hidden application is dimmed in the Application or Application Switcher menu (in Mac OS 9.1) to signify that it has been hidden. Unfortunately, the Dock cannot distinguish between hidden and unhidden applications. To unhide the application, select its name from the Application menu, Application Switcher menu, or Dock, or choose the Show All command.

- *Hide Others*—Removes all windows from the screen except those of the currently active application. This is useful when onscreen clutter is bothersome, or if you're accidentally clicking the windows of background applications and bringing them forward. After the Hide Others command has been used, the icons of all open applications—except those of the foreground application—are dimmed in the Application menu as a visual reminder that these applications are hidden.

- *Show All*—Makes all current applications visible. When you choose the Show All command, the current foreground application remains in the foreground and the windows of hidden background applications become visible.

Figure 3.18 illustrates the similarities between Mac OS X (left) and Mac OS 9.1 while in Classic mode (right).

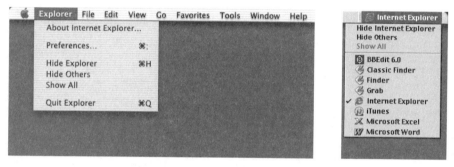

Figure 3.18
Note the similarities in the Hide and Show commands between Mac OS X and Mac OS 9.1.

While an application is hidden, it continues to operate exactly the same as it would if it were running as a visible background application. If an application normally performs tasks in the background, hiding the application will not interfere with its ability to perform these tasks. In fact, because of the effort saved by not having to upgrade the screen display, the background operation of some tasks is faster when their parent application is hidden.

To hide the current foreground application completely when you send it to the background, hold down the Option key while clicking on the Desktop or bringing another application forward (either by choosing its name from the Application menu, Applica-tion Switcher menu, the Dock, or by clicking the mouse in one of its windows). You can retrieve applications hidden in this manner by using the Show All command or by selecting their dimmed icons from the Application menu or Application Switcher menu.

Hiding the Desktop in Mac OS 9.1

A potential problem lies in wait for novices who are working with multiple applications at the same time. If you inadvertently click the Desktop, you switch into the Finder and out of your current program. Suddenly you've lost your place, and the menus have changed. Because the old Performa series was built for the home market (and for novices), Apple included in System 7.0.1P and 7.1P a feature called Finder hiding that prevented users from switching to the Finder by inadvertently clicking on the desktop.

 Some users simply close all of an application's windows and mistakenly believe that the application has therefore been quit. Some applications will automatically quit after the last window has been closed, but most will continue to run until "Quit" has been selected from the File menu.

Voluntary Desktop hiding first appeared in System 7.5 and continues to be a useful option in Mac OS 9.1. A modified form of this feature can be replicated in Mac OS X as well. With Desktop hiding, when you switch into an application other than the Finder, the Desktop disappears (not unlike the way things worked before System 7—the difference is that this hiding is by choice). You can't click in the background and switch out of your application. You turn on Desktop hiding by disabling the Show Desktop When In Background checkbox in the General Controls Control Panel. Therefore, if you're working in an application and you can't see your hard disk, Trash, or file and folder icons, blame Desktop hiding. Figure 3.19 shows an example of iTunes with the Desktop hidden.

Figure 3.19
Using iTunes with the Desktop hidden in Mac OS 9.1.

For the ultimate way to focus on a single application, hide the Desktop and all other applications to reduce the number of visual distractions on your screen.

Hiding the Desktop in Mac OS X

Mac OS X allows you to mimic the Hide Desktop feature of Mac OS 9.1 through the Finder Preferences instead of System Preferences. To hide disk icons for file servers, hard drives, CD-ROMs, and other removable media:

1. Open the Finder Preferences by choosing Finder Preferences from the Application menu.

2. Uncheck the Disks option, as shown in Figure 3.20.

3. Close the Finder Preferences.

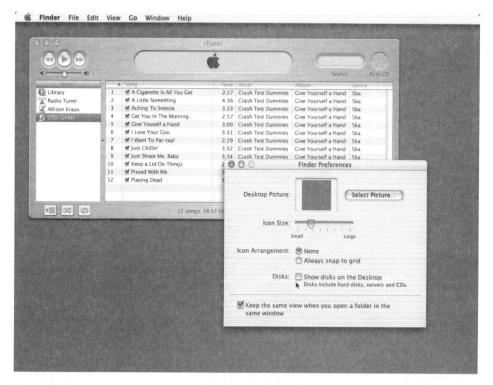

Figure 3.20
You can remove disk and server icons from the Desktop using the Disks option in the Finder Preferences.

To completely mimic the Hide Desktop feature of Mac OS 9.1, you'll also need to manually relocate other items on the Desktop such as aliases, files, folders, applications, and Internet downloads. Unlike Mac OS 9.1, however, you can still launch a new Finder window by pressing Command+N (or choose File|New Finder

Window) and browse the contents of your computer or networked server without the assistance of a third-party utility such as Greg's Browser (**www.kaleidoscope.net/ greg/browser.html**).

Classic Multitasking Tips

When you start using the Hide commands to reduce screen clutter, you should be comfortable working with multiple open applications. The following tips can help:

■ *Saving before switching*—Before bringing another application to the foreground, save your work in the application you're using in Classic mode; if Classic crashes, you won't lose your work.

■ *Resuming after crashing*—If an application crashes in Mac OS 9.1 while in Classic mode, you can usually force the Mac to close that application (referred to as a force quit) and regain access to your other Classic applications by pressing Command+ Option+Escape. Figure 3.21 shows the new Force Quit commands in Mac OS X (top) compared to the old command in Mac OS 9.1 (bottom).

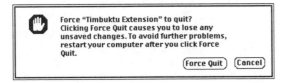

Figure 3.21
The Force Quit dialog box.

Note that after this kind of crash, the Classic environment may be unstable and prone to additional crashes. Using this option is a bit like driving a nail with a sledgehammer—it works but is likely to do some damage. You should save any work you've done in other open applications and immediately restart Classic, just to be safe.

■ *Shutting down or restarting*—Selecting the Shut Down or Restart commands from the Apple menu while multiple Classic, Carbon, or Cocoa applications are open will cause all open applications to quit (even if an application hasn't been properly programmed to accept the Quit command using Apple Events). If any Classic documents contain changes that haven't been saved, the parent application will be brought to the foreground and you'll be asked whether you want to save those changes before the Classic environment is terminated.

■ *Maintaining efficiency for background applications*—Remember that because Classic applications rely on cooperative multithreading while in Classic mode, processor-hungry applications in the foreground will slow down other Classic applications considerably. Try hiding these applications when not in use.

Wrapping Up

Working with Classic applications is slightly different when booting directly into Mac OS 9.1 than when in Classic mode under Mac OS X, especially in the areas of memory management and switching between applications. The amount of memory available on your Macintosh determines, in large measure, what you can do with your computer. As we've seen in this chapter, Mac OS X introduces dramatic changes in memory management, although most of the old ways of managing memory are still alive and well thanks to the Classic environment. These improvements were designed to give you much more control over memory availability and how that memory is utilized. This chapter has covered many aspects relating to working with Classic applications, including:

■ Virtual memory lets you "create" memory by using space on your hard drive as if it were RAM. In Mac OS 9.1 it is optional; in Mac OS X it is always on.

■ The About This Computer and About This Mac windows provide useful information about what's happening with your Mac's memory.

■ Utilities like Memory Mapper and Mac OS Purge can help you manage your memory usage in Mac OS 9.1.

■ The Memory section of the Get Info window helps you control the amount of memory an application uses while in Mac OS 9.1 or Classic mode.

■ You can launch as many different applications as your available memory permits.

■ Many applications can continue to process data while they're running in the background.

■ Hiding open applications reduces onscreen clutter without affecting the operation of the applications.

■ Remember to quit Classic applications in the reverse order in which they were launched to avoid memory fragmentation, or just leave them running until you're ready to shut down the computer.

Because Classic is probably going to be around for several years as developers port their applications to Mac OS X, it's a good idea to have an adequate understanding of how Mac OS 9.1 and Mac OS X interact. In Chapter 4, I'll explore the Finder and the Desktop, two important aspects of the OS that provide the interface and tools you use to control your disks and files on the Macintosh.

3

Working with the Finder and Desktop

Just like your word processor, spreadsheet, or Web browser, the Finder is an application—even though most people don't think of it that way. Whereas each of those other applications is dedicated to creating and manipulating one specific type of data, the Finder focuses on helping you manage your disks and files.

The new Mac OS X Finder provides you with features that make navigating your disks and drives easier than ever. These include the distinctive Macintosh Desktop, where icons represent files, folders, disks, and servers; the Dock; the indispensable Finder menus; and the new column view option. Through the Finder, you can view and modify the contents of your disks and drives in many different ways, and launch other applications or System Preferences.

In Mac OS X, the Finder has been enhanced to give you more information about your disks and files, more consistency in commands and features, and additional customizing capabilities. These benefits come with the most significant change in the Finder's interface in the history of the Mac OS. However, if you were comfortable working in earlier versions of the OS, including Mac OS 8 through OS 9.1, you'll have few problems taking advantage of the Finder's expanded capabilities in Mac OS X.

This chapter starts by examining the Finder's menu commands and then looks at Finder windows. Advanced features such as customizing the Finder toolbar, column views, the Dock, and icon proxies are covered along with other familiar features in the Finder, such as Mac Help, the Trash, and the Show Info window.

This chapter is not, however, the only place in this book where you'll read about new Finder and Desktop capabilities. Several of the new Finder features were introduced in Chapter 1, and will be elaborated upon where the context is more appropriate. For example, customizing the Dock, windows, and the Desktop are covered in Chapter 5, and aliasing and Sherlock are discussed in Chapter 6.

Finder Menus and Commands

To gain some perspective on the changes in the Finder and Desktop, consider for a moment the dramatic changes in the Finder and Desktop between System 7 and Mac OS 9.1. Figure 4.1 shows a few Finder windows in System 7.0.1.

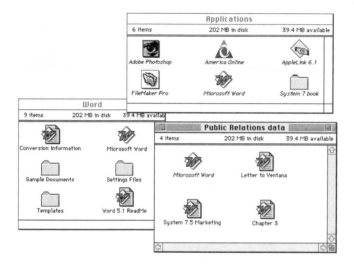

Figure 4.1
A few sample Finder windows in System 7.0.1.

Now take a look at Figure 4.2, which shows the Finder and Desktop in Mac OS 9.1. You may notice a few new elements, including:

■ A revised Help menu

■ The removal of the Label menu

■ Tabbed folders (examples of which can be seen at the bottom of the screen)

■ The new Window menu

In addition to these features, the most obvious and basic change is in the overall appearance of the interface. The original Mac OS draws windows without depth and with a twig-like simplicity (which was cutting edge at the time!), whereas Mac OS 9.1 draws windows using a more appealing 3D look called the Platinum appearance. Folders are more accessible, icons are richer in appearance, and menus are more intuitive.

As discussed in Chapter 1, the Mac OS X Finder and Desktop represent both radical change (the new Aqua appearance theme) and sophisticated refinement (the Finder menus) of the most basic of all Mac OS elements. However, I believe that you can

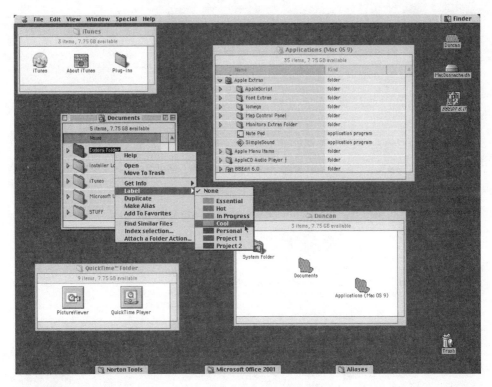

Figure 4.2
The Finder and Desktop in Mac OS 9.1.

adequately grasp the fundamentals of just about any operating system—no matter how novel—by learning how to open, close, and minimize windows, navigate the file system, and operate menus. Let's use this approach to start learning about the Mac OS X Finder and Desktop. For starters, take a look at Figure 4.3, which shows the Finder menus and commands as they appear when Mac OS X is first installed.

Although Mac OS X has enhanced a few of the Finder menus, many (if not most) of the Finder commands should be familiar to anyone who has used previous versions of the Mac OS. The following sections focus on the menus found in the Mac OS X Finder.

Apple Menu

The Apple menu is a compilation of Apple and Special menu items from previous versions of the Mac OS, plus a few new commands:

■ *About This Mac*—Opens a window that displays information about your computer, such as available memory and facts about your Mac's processor. (Chapter 3 contains

Figure 4.3
The new Finder menus in Mac OS X.

a more detailed description of this window.) This menu choice was previously called About This Macintosh or About This Computer.

■ *Get Mac OS X Software*—Launches a Web browser and then opens the page on the Apple Web site that contains information about applications for Mac OS X, as well as download links to many categories of software.

■ *System Preferences*—Opens the System Preferences application, where you can customize many aspects of Mac OS X.

■ *Dock*—Reveals three quick options to help you configure the Dock: Turn Magnification On/Off, Turn Hiding On/Off, and Dock Preferences. I'll discuss using the Dock later in this chapter; customizing the Dock is covered in Chapter 5.

■ *Location*—Reveals a shortcut to open the Network Preferences System Preferences pane, where you can add, delete, and modify network locations (which are discussed in Section III of this book).

■ *Recent Items*—Makes it easier to open a recently used document or application. Figure 4.4 shows an example of the new Recent Items menu option, a tremendous time-saver that you're likely to use frequently.

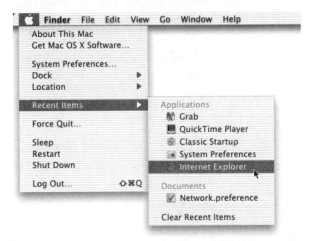

Figure 4.4
The new Recent Items menu option provides access to recently used applications and documents.

■ *Force Quit*—Brings up a command that allows you to force an application (including Classic applications) to quit. See Chapter 13 for information on how and when to use the Force Quit command.

■ *Sleep*—Places your computer in energy-saving mode. Press any key or jiggle the mouse to wake your computer from sleep.

■ *Restart*—Commands your Mac to close any open documents, quit all open applications, and then restart the computer. If you have any unsaved documents or applications that are in the middle of performing operations, you'll be prompted to attend to the documents and applications.

■ *Shut Down*—Commands your computer to log out the current user, close any open documents, quit all open applications, and then turn itself off. If you have any unsaved documents or applications that are in the middle of performing operations, you'll be asked to attend to the documents and applications (just like with the Restart command).

■ *Log Out*—Commands your computer to log out the current user, close any open documents, quit all open applications, and then present the login screen. If you have any unsaved documents or applications that are in the middle of performing operations, you'll be asked to attend to the documents and applications (just like with the Restart command).

Application Menu Items

The Application menu, located next to the Apple menu, contains commands associated with the foremost application (i.e., the one that's operating in the foreground of your screen). The Application menu goes by the name of the foremost application; for example, if BBEdit is the foremost application, you'll see BBEdit in bold lettering next to the Apple menu. The options in this menu will vary depending on the application; the following list describes what you'll see when working in the Finder:

■ *About the Finder*—Displays a small window with information about the version of the Finder, such as "Finder Mac OS X (v10.0)."

■ *Preferences*—Opens the Finder Preferences window, which is shown in Figure 4.5. The Preferences command allows you to configure the way the Desktop displays background images and icons and opens windows. See Chapter 5 for details on how to configure the look and feel of your computer's Desktop.

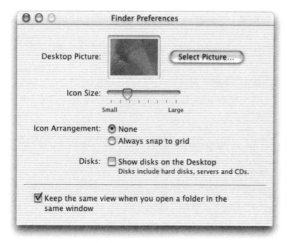

Figure 4.5
The New Finder Preferences.

■ *Empty Trash*—Empties the Trash. In previous versions of the Mac OS, this command was located in the Special menu. If the Trash is already empty, this menu option will be inactive.

■ *Hide Finder*—Moves the Finder into the background, as well as hides all open Finder windows. However, the Finder Preferences and windows are still accessible in the Dock, examples of which is shown in Figure 4.6. If any Finder windows are

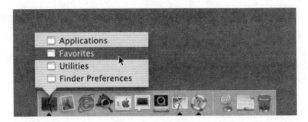

Figure 4.6
Hidden Finder windows are accessible from the Dock.

already minimized when this command is chosen, these windows will also be moved from the right side of the Dock into the Finder Dock proxy icon. You can unhide the Finder by selecting any of the minimized windows from the Dock (click and hold on the icon, or Control+click for an instant listing), or by selecting Show All from the Application menu of the current application (discussed next).

■ *Show All*—Reveals all hidden applications and returns hidden Finder windows that were previously minimized to the right side of the Dock.

File Menu

The File menu is almost a universal constant in the Mac OS cosmos. Virtually all applications have a File menu and the contents are predictable: New, Save, Save As, Page Setup, and Print. In Mac OS X, the only surprise is the relocation of the Quit option from the File menu to the Application menu. The Finder offers the following File menu options:

■ *New Finder Window*—Opens a window in the Finder for browsing the contents of your computer, local area network (LAN), servers, and removable media such as CD-ROMs. This feature, which is new to Mac OS X, is described in detail later in this chapter.

■ *New Folder*—Creates a new folder in the active Finder window or on the Desktop, but not in the root level of the computer (where your computer's hard drives and Network folder are listed).

■ *Open*—Opens the item(s) selected—including files, folders, aliases, or volumes—in a Finder window or on the Desktop, just as in previous versions of the Mac OS.

■ *Close Window*—Closes the foremost window on your screen.

■ *Show Info*—Reveals detailed information about the item selected in the Finder, such as a file, folder, volume, or server. This command retains some of the information found under the Get Info command of Mac OS 9.1 and includes some major differences as well.

- *Duplicate*—Makes a copy of whatever is selected in the Finder, including multiple selected items, just as in earlier versions of the Mac OS.

- *Make Alias*—Creates an alias of the item that is selected in a Finder window or on the Desktop. The concept of aliases is discussed in Chapter 6.

- *Show Original*—Enables you to select an alias and then reveal its original in the Finder. The Show Original menu option is identical to the Reveal Original option of System 7.x and the Show Original command in Mac OS 9.1.

- *Add To Favorites*—Makes an alias of the item selected in the Finder or on the Desktop and places it in the Favorites folder.

- *Move To Trash*—Allows you to throw selected items into the Trash without dragging them to the Trash icon in the Dock. To use this command, select one or more items in the Finder or on the Desktop; then choose the Move To Trash command or use the keyboard equivalent (Command+Delete).

- *Eject*—Ejects the item selected in the Finder or on the Desktop if it is a removable media, such as a CD-ROM, or unmounts nonremovable media, such as a server. The Eject command has the same effect as dragging the item to the Trash icon in the Dock—both cause the Trash icon to turn into the new Eject icon (see Figure 4.7 for an example).

Figure 4.7
Dragging removable media or servers to the Trash icon in the Dock will eject or unmount the item.

- *Find*—Launches Sherlock to help you find files on your computer or information on the Internet. Sherlock can search for files by file name, size, creation date, label, and so on. See Chapter 6 for more information about Sherlock.

Edit Menu

In Mac OS X, the Edit menu is pretty much the same as it is in Mac OS 9.1—except for the Clear command, which is no longer present, and the Preferences command, which has been relocated to the Finder's Application menu (discussed earlier). The Undo command is enhanced in Mac OS X, allowing you to undo Finder commands such as moving an item back to the Desktop after moving it to the Trash, for example. On the whole, the commands in the Edit menu are very straightforward:

■ *Undo/Can't Undo*—Allows you to reverse an action such as changing the name of a file or folder, moving items to the Trash, or relocating a file you've downloaded from the Web to another location on your computer. Not all commands can be undone, however; in those instances, you'll see Can't Undo in the View menu instead of Undo Rename or Undo Move Of "Untitled Folder", as illustrated in Figure 4.8.

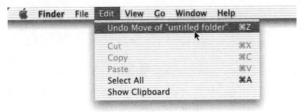

Figure 4.8
The Undo command is enhanced in Mac OS X to undo Finder actions such as renaming files or moving folders.

■ *Cut*—Removes (cuts) the text or image selected in the Finder. Like all the commands in the View menu, the purpose of the Cut command depends on the active application. When you're working in an imaging editing program such as GraphicConverter, for example, the Cut command cuts the selected image data; when you're working in a word processor, on the other hand, the Cut command removes a selected block of text.

■ *Copy*—Makes a duplicate of the selected data and stores it in the Clipboard.

■ *Paste*—Takes the data that is stored in the Clipboard and copies it to the cursor insertion point.

■ *Select All*—Selects all the items on the Desktop or in a Finder window. Like the Cut, Copy, and Paste commands, the Select All command is found in many types of applications such as word processors, HTML editors, and imaging programs.

■ *Show Clipboard*—Displays the contents of the Clipboard in a special type of window in the Finder. Many applications include this command, which opens the Clipboard contents in a window belonging to the active application rather than the Finder.

View Menu

The commands in the View menu relate to how you view the contents of the Desktop and Finder windows. The View menu's purpose in Mac OS X is the same as in Mac OS 8.5 through 9.1; however, the new version replaces the button view with the column view and allows you to configure both your global and window-by-window viewing preferences. In Mac OS 9.1, global preferences were configured in the Edit|Preferences menu. The following options are available in Mac OS X:

- *As Columns*—Configures a Finder window to the new column view. Column, icon, and list views are discussed in great detail later in this chapter.

- *As Icons*—Changes a Finder window to the familiar icon view.

- *As List*—Organizes the contents of a Finder window in the form of a list.

- *Clean Up*—Unclutters the contents of a view-by-icon window so that icons and file names do not overlap and obscure each other. This command only pertains to the Desktop and to Finder windows in the icon view.

- *Arrange By Name*—Alphabetizes the contents of the Desktop and Finder windows in icon views. In previous versions of the Mac OS, the Arrange By Name command could arrange lists by date modified, date created, etc., as well as by name; however, this is not possible in Mac OS X. Refer to the View as List section later in this chapter for list view sorting options.

- *Hide/Show Toolbar*—Shows and hides the toolbar, a major new feature in the Mac OS X Finder. The toolbar is a customizable navigation tool that is extraordinarily useful for maneuvering the contents of computers with large quantities of files, folders, and attached servers. Figure 4.9 illustrates two views of the same window—with the toolbar shown (top) and hidden (bottom). Later in this chapter, the section entitled "Using the Toolbar" will introduce you to working with this new feature.

- *Customize Toolbar*—Allows you to modify the commands and icons in the toolbar, or to restore the default set of commands (also shown in Figure 4.9). Chapter 5 includes instructions on how to configure the toolbar with the Customize Toolbar command and by dragging and dropping files and folders onto the toolbar.

- *Hide/Show Status Bar*—Toggles the display of the status bar off and on. In all previous versions of the Mac OS the status bar could not be hidden. In Mac OS X, it still displays only the number of items in a Finder window and the amount of free space on the disk to which the window belongs. Figure 4.10 shows a Finder window with the status bar shown (top) and hidden (bottom).

- *Show View Options*—Allows you to customize global icon and list view options, including icon size, the arrangement of items in the Finder window, default display of columns, and the use of relative versus exact dates. The Show View Options command also lets you override the global view and select viewing options on a window-by-window basis. In Mac OS X, this command doesn't work for the Desktop, although it did under Mac OS 9.1. The Desktop view options are now configured through the Preferences menu in the Finder. All the options for the Show View Options command are discussed in the next section of this chapter.

Figure 4.9
The new Finder toolbar, which can be toggled on and off, is great for navigating your computer.

Figure 4.10
The status bar can be toggled on and off in Mac OS X.

Go Menu

The Go menu, another new addition to the Mac OS X Finder, contains additional shortcuts to commonly used folders (including the four locations in the default configuration of the toolbar) and services. The Go menu also contains a rather interesting new command that lets you open a folder by typing the path to that folder in the Finder, a command that some Mac purists may find a little odd for an operating system that uses icons and mouse clicks rather than typing to accomplish tasks. You'll find the following entries under the Go menu:

- *Computer*—Opens a Finder window (if no windows are already open) to the root level of the computer, displaying your hard drives, removable media, network folder, and connected servers. If a Finder window is already open, the top-most window will switch to the Computer view.

- *Home*—Takes you to the Home location of the user currently logged in to the computer.

- *iDisk*—Logs into your iDisk account (if you have an iTools account configured in the Network section of the System Preferences) and mounts the iDisk.

- *Favorites*—Displays the contents of the Favorites folder (as in previous versions of the Mac OS), where you can store a shortcut to just about anything. For example, Figure 4.11 shows the Favorites menu with shortcuts to several folders, a hard drive, a server, and the Home folder on the computer. Also note that the Favorites menu includes an option for a keyboard shortcut that opens the Favorites folder in the Finder (Command+Option+F).

- *Applications*—Opens the main Applications folder (not the Applications folder located in each user's home folder) in a Finder window.

- *Recent Folders*—Lists the folders recently opened in the Finder.

- *Go To Folder*—Allows you to type the path of a folder to open it into a new Finder window, but only if no Finder windows are already open; if one is open, the folder will open in the top-most window. The term *path* refers to the location of a file or folder similar to the way you might type a URL of a document on a Web server using forward slashes to separate folder names. For example, you would type "/Duncan/System Folder/" to go to the System Folder on a hard drive named Duncan, or "/MacDonnachaidh/Applications/Utilities/" to go to the Utilities folder on a drive named MacDonnachaidh. Figure 4.12 shows how to use a variation of this command to open the *home folder* for a user named mbell. Every user account in Mac OS X has a home folder where user-specific documents and applications can be stored. To go to your home folder, just type a tilde (~) followed by your login name.

Figure 4.11
The Favorites folder gives you easy access to items you have bookmarked with the Add to Favorites feature.

Figure 4.12
The Go To Folder command allows you to open a folder in the Finder by typing in the folder's path, or by using a tilde (~) shortcut to go to your home folder.

- *Connect To Server*—Replaces the Chooser and Network Browser of previous versions of the operating system as a means of connecting to Macintosh-based file servers (as opposed to Windows, Novell, or other types of file servers). This command is covered in detail in Chapter 15.

Window Menu

The Window menu provides easy access to Finder windows, including minimized (Docked), active, and inactive windows. This menu is similar to the Window menu that was added to Mac OS 9.1, but with a few added features:

- *Minimize Window*—Minimizes the active Finder window and places it in the Dock. When minimized, the window's name will be prefixed with a diamond in the Window menu; the active Finder window will be prefixed with a checkmark. Because only one window can be active in the Finder at any time, only one menu item will have a checkmark. However, multiple Finder windows may be minimized. For examples of these indicators, refer back to Figure 4.3, which shows the Window menu with two minimized windows (Downloads and Duncan), one inactive window (MacDonnachaidh), and one active window (Favorites).

- *Bring All To Front*—Brings all Finder windows to the front of the screen so they are grouped together. Mac OS X uses a layered windowing system that allows you to stagger windows belonging to different applications in an alternating fashion. In earlier versions of the Mac OS, an application's windows were always grouped together on screen—your Web browser's windows were on top of all your word processor's windows, which were in turn on top of all your QuickTime windows. In Mac OS X, the Bring All To Front command allows you to have one window from each application to be shown in successive layers.

Help Menu

Mac Help, the main conduit for providing help to users, sports an HTML-like interface that should be very familiar to anyone who has ever surfed the Web. You may be disappointed to learn that the venerable Apple Guide and Balloon Help are no longer supported by the Mac OS; however, some applications provide tool tips, which are Balloon Help-like displays of information that appear when the cursor hovers over a context-sensitive area of the Finder or application. When in the Finder, the Help menu displays only one option, Mac Help. Figure 4.13 shows the result of choosing this option.

The Help menu is available at all times in most applications, not just in the Finder. The quality and quantity of help content is determined by how the developers of your software chose to implement a Help menu. The options under the Help menu are specific to the application that is active; for example, if you're using QuickTime you'll

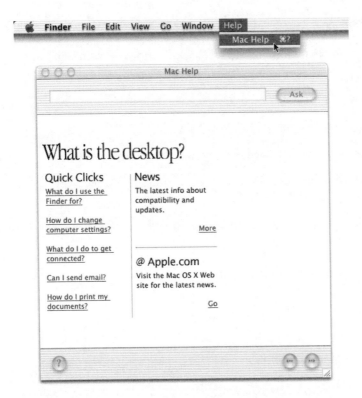

Figure 4.13
The new Help menu in the Finder.

see an option called QuickTime Help, rather than Mac Help. Individual applications may provide additional Help menu options as well.

Menu Bar Clock

The clock is the last item in the Mac OS X Finder's menu bar. The display of the clock is configured in the Date & Time System Preferences pane. The default configuration is to display the clock, which reveals the date when clicked, as illustrated in Figure 4.3.

Finder and Desktop Window Basics

Menu commands are only a small segment of the Finder's overall function as a disk and file management tool. Most of the time, you move, copy, delete, arrange, and open files by using the mouse to directly manipulate icons on the Desktop and in Finder windows. In Mac OS X, your ability to see and manipulate files and folders in windows is dramatically improved compared to the capabilities of all earlier versions of the Mac OS. The basic attributes of Finder windows include:

■ Windows are created each time a volume or folder is opened.

■ Each window has a title bar; close, minimize, and maximize buttons; and an optional toolbar.

■ Windows can be freely positioned by dragging their title bars.

■ Windows can be resized by dragging on the resize tab.

■ The window display is controlled via the View menu.

■ The icon size and type of information displayed in Finder windows can be customized.

■ Keyboard commands enable you to navigate windows and select files without using the mouse.

■ Smart zooming opens windows only enough to display their content, or to the maximum available display area.

■ The contents of any folder or subfolder can be displayed hierarchically in any window.

■ Hierarchical levels allow files in different folders to be manipulated simultaneously.

■ Icon proxies (in the title bar) allow you to move, copy, or alias Finder windows.

■ List view columns may be resized and reordered.

The improvements to the Finder in Mac OS X give you more control over windows, a more consistent user interface, and a wider range of display options:

■ The Dock replaces the functionality of the Application and Apple menus.

■ Finder windows can now display the files and folders for an entire computer; use the Go|Computer menu command and then select the new column view.

■ The toolbar provides customizable shortcuts that allow you to navigate to the contents of the Finder.

■ You can now browse the contents of your computer by way of Finder windows and therefore circumvent the need for hard drive icons on the Desktop.

For a better perspective about the how the Finder has evolved, consider that in the early days of the Mac OS the presentation of text and icons in Finder windows was preset and could not be modified. Text was always shown in 9-point Geneva, and icons appeared only in preset sizes in each icon view. In System 7, the Views Control Panel provided a variety of options that enabled you to control the information and the way it was displayed in Finder windows. In Mac OS 8, the options relating to viewing the contents of a folder or hard drive became even more flexible and customizable, as well as more a part of the core OS rather than a branch of it, such as a Control Panel or Extension add-on. Mac OS 8.6 went even further to allow users to customize more Finder elements, including spring-loaded folders and Finder labels (which are no longer present in Mac OS X). Several elements of the Mac OS X Finder are configurable in the Finder|Preferences menu, as shown earlier in Figure 4.5. Mac OS X separates the preferences for configuring the Finder and Desktop into three categories:

- Finder|Preferences menu
- View|Show View Options menu
- Apple|Dock|Dock Preferences menu

The trend in Mac OS X is to centralize in the Finder the configuration options that were previously scattered in various locations, making them easier to find. Because they have strong ties to Finder configuration options in earlier versions of the Mac OS, let's take a look at the first two configuration options here; the Dock, a new concept for the Mac OS, will be discussed in the next section of this chapter.

The following sections will help you understand the basic configuration options for the Finder, and how to use the different views in Finder windows to get the most out of Mac OS X.

Finder Preferences

The Finder Preferences window provides options that mainly affect the look and feel of the Desktop—the signature feature of the entire line of Macintosh computers. The most noticeable feature, of course, is the Desktop picture, which you can change by following these steps:

1. Open the Finder Preferences by choosing (surprise, surprise!) Finder|Preferences.

2. Click the Select Picture button; this opens a selection window in the Finder (like the one shown in Figure 4.14) in which you can browse the default collection of Desktop images.

3. Select an image from this collection, or navigate through the Finder to any image you'd like to display on the Desktop, provided it is in one of several file formats, including, for example, the Joint Photographic Experts Group (JPEG) or Tagged Information File Format (TIFF) formats.

4. Double-click the image in the Finder window, or single-click the image and then click the Choose button to activate your choice.

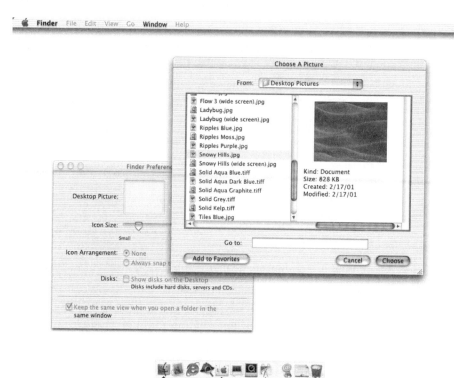

Figure 4.14
Selecting a Desktop image from the default collection of images provided in Mac OS X.

Another striking innovation in Mac OS X is the use of a sliding scale to determine the size of Desktop icons, which frees you from the old limits of just small, medium, and large icons. Moreover, you can choose whether or not to show disk icons on the Desktop at all. (Ironically, the option for selecting the size of the icon precedes the Disks option, which determines the presence or absence of disk icons). Mac OS X also allows for much larger icons (128×128 pixels) at a higher bit depth for stunning clarity. For example, Figure 4.15 shows the largest size of Desktop icons; notice the smaller size of the Finder window icons, which are configured independently of Desktop icons. To hide disk icons on the Desktop, uncheck the Disks checkbox.

You can also arrange Desktop icons with the familiar Snap To Grid option, which forces any repositioned icons on the Desktop to automatically snap to the nearest point on an invisible grid. This is the same invisible grid used by the View|Clean Up command in Finder windows. The concept of always keeping files grid-aligned in this way may sound appealing, but it can be disconcerting when the Finder grabs and relocates files while you're trying to position them precisely. In most cases, it's probably better to leave this option off and use the Clean Up command to correct any icon alignment problems in Finder windows.

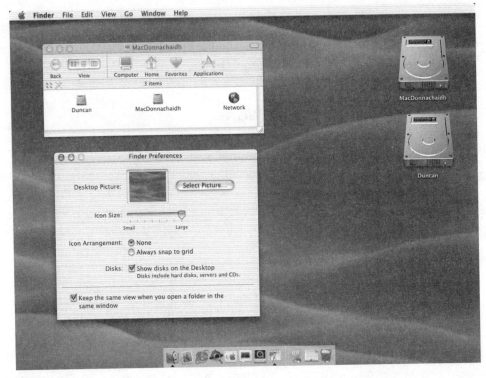

Figure 4.15
Desktop icons can now be as large as 128×128 pixels.

The checkbox at the bottom of the Finder Preference window is new to Mac OS X; it affects the behavior of the Finder window when a folder is opened from within a parent folder. When this option is selected, a folder configured in icon view will beget a folder that is also in icon view. The same is true with folders seen in a list view. To illustrate this point, follow these steps to try out this feature on your computer:

1. Open a new Finder window and select List View from the View menu.

2. Double-click the icon for your hard drive.

3. Double-click the Applications folder.

4. Double-click the AppleScript folder.

Now each folder that you open in the Finder will have a list view. Deselecting this option will result in subsequent folders being opened into the view last used by these folders. Also, windows viewed as columns do not spawn new windows; clicking on a folder while in a column view just advances or retracts the navigation of the columns within the same window, navigating higher or lower in the file system.

You can no longer determine the amount of space between items when viewed by icon or when the Always Snap To Grid option is selected in the Finder Preferences. Previous versions of the Mac OS allow you to choose between tight and wide grid spacing, but Mac OS X defaults to somewhere in between.

Global Window View Options

The View Options command in the View menu controls the global, or default, viewing options for the two types of window views in Mac OS X—icons and lists. Although the Mac OS allows you to select the global view for these types of windows, you can selectively override the global view and customize each folder. I'll look at all the details associated with window views later in this chapter, but for now, here's an overview of the steps you should take to select the global defaults for icon and list views for Finder windows:

1. While in the Finder, choose View|Show View Options, or press Command+J.

2. Select Global Icon or Global List from the View section of the View Options window.

3. Configure the view options to your liking.

Figure 4.16 shows the options for global icon (left) and global list (right) views. These choices go into effect the first time a Finder window is opened—provided that its preferences haven't been overridden.

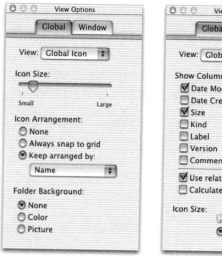 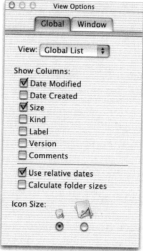

Figure 4.16
Configuring the global icon and list view options.

In the Global Icon view, you can select the size of the icons displayed in Finder windows as well as the style of icon arrangement (by Name, Date Modified, Date Created, Size, Kind, or Label). The Folder Background option, which I'll address in Chapter 5, allows you to select an image to serve as a background for icon views, much like a background image on a Web page. Choosing the Picture option will allow you to activate the same selection tool used for the Desktop image, shown in Figure 4.14.

The global settings for windows viewed as lists should be a familiar affair for Mac users. Just decide on the columns to be displayed in global lists (Date Modified, Date Created, Size, Kind, Label, Version, and Comments), whether or not to use relative dates (such as *yesterday* and *today*), whether or not to calculate the size of folders in the list view, and the size of icons (small or large). List windows have more viewing options than icon windows, and are probably the preferred viewing method these days because users often have tens of thousands of files instead of just a few thousand. List views are easier to manage and quicker to open than icon views.

Individual Window View Options

When viewed as icons or as a list, any Finder window can be customized—or you can just stick with the global values. Mac OS X provides a new column view as well, although most people will want to mix the three views to meet their needs.

Customizing Finder Windows

You can also customize the view of Finder windows on a window-by-window basis. Mac OS X will remember your customized view options for each window; however, if you select the global view by checking the Use Global View Preferences option, shown in Figure 4.17, your customized views will be lost for that window.

Column Views

The main strength of the new column view is not simply viewing the contents of a folder or hard drive, but navigating the file system of your computer or a server for quick access to an item. I like to be able to highly customize certain windows but view others in a way that promotes speedy navigation. For example, I like to keep the root level of my hard drive very lean, using only those folders created by Mac OS X (Applications, Library, System, and Users) and the default folders found in every user's home folder (including Applications, Documents, Movies, Music, and Pictures). The new column view is perfect for navigating a computer organized in this way. However, when I'm working on a project like a Web site, I have to be able to view the contents of a folder using a customized icon or list view in order to work with my files. To navigate using a column view from within the Finder, follow these steps:

Figure 4.17
A highly customized Finder window.

1. Open a new Finder window by selecting Command+N or File|New Finder Window.

2. Choose View|As Columns.

3. Select an item in the window's far-left column to open the contents of that window in the column to the right.

Column views have at least two columns; if you enlarge the window using the grow button in the lower-right corner of the Finder window, the number of columns will increase proportionally—as far as the size of your Desktop will allow. For example, Figure 4.18 shows three versions of a column view with two, three, and four columns.

Of course, you can navigate to a depth that exceeds the number of columns your Desktop is capable of displaying (more than four in this example). The columns will drift to the left of the window as you navigate deeper into a folder hierarchy, which is always to the right. The reverse is true as well—the columns will drift to the right as you go backward in the hierarchy—but you must drag the scroll tab to the left to navigate backward, as illustrated in Figure 4.19.

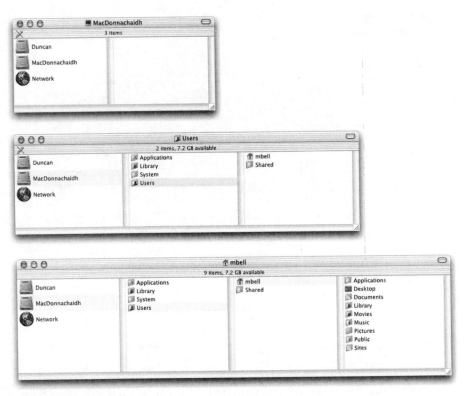

Figure 4.18
You can resize a column window to increase or decrease the number of columns.

Figure 4.19
Use the scroll tab to navigate backward in a column view.

Once you get the hang of it, column views are kind of nifty. However, keep in mind that they are best for navigating because they are customizable only in the number of columns you can display.

Icon Views
The icon view is probably the most flexible of the three Finder window views because you can arrange the contents of a window artistically, using icon placement and

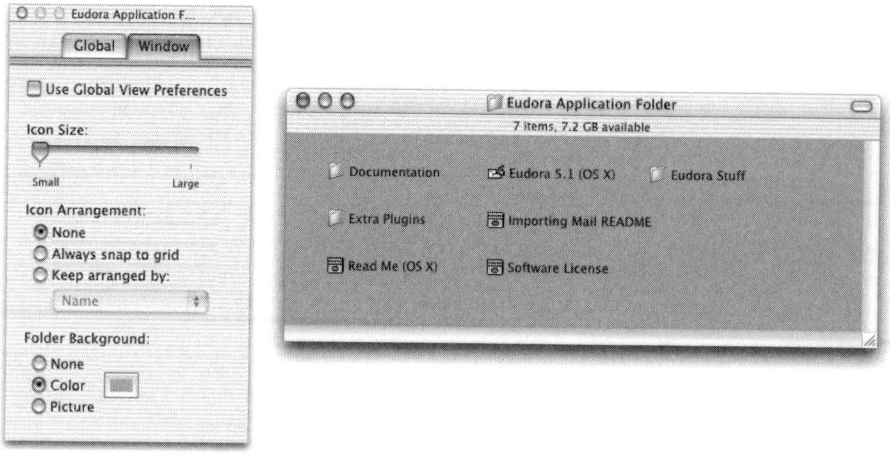

Figure 4.20
The icon view for a Finder window is the most flexible of the three view options, in my opinion.

background colors and images, as well as logically, by sorting the contents using the Icon Arrangement option. For example, Figure 4.20 shows my Eudora (my preferred email client) folder viewed in a highly customized icon view.

If you need to sort the contents of a window when viewing by icon, the following options are available under the Keep Arranged By section of the Icon Arrangement portion of the View|Show View Options menu:

- *By Name*—Sorts files and folders alphabetically (A through Z), from top to bottom.

- *By Date Modified*—Sorts files by the date on which they were last modified, with the most recently updated files at the top of the list. This view is useful when you're looking for files that are much older or much newer than most of the other files in a certain folder.

- *By Date Created*—Sorts files by the date they were created, with the most recently created files at the top of the list. When you copy a file or folder from another source, it will retain its original creation date.

- *By Size*—Sorts files in descending size order. Otherwise, folders are grouped alphabetically at the end of the list. Commonly, the By Size command is used to find files known to be either very large or very small, or to locate large files that could be deleted to free up space.

- *By Kind*—Sorts files alphabetically by a short description based on the *file type*, a designation assigned by the creator of the application. Files associated with a particular application often include the name of that application as the kind. Viewing files by kind is useful if you know the kind of file you're looking for, and if the window containing that file has many different types of files in it.

- *By Label*—Sorts by the label name that you have given the file using the Label command. Labels are used to group files according to some user-defined scheme, although Apple doesn't provide a way to assign labels to elements in the Finder. Perhaps a system update will become available soon to reenable this feature.

List Views

Finally, the List View is a popular way of viewing Finder windows because they are easily sorted. When viewed by name, finding items is easy because most people are accustomed to scanning top to bottom to find items alphabetically. Figure 4.21 shows a customized list view window sorted by name.

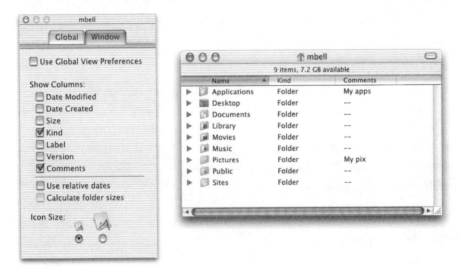

Figure 4.21
A customized list view.

List view options are significantly different from icon and column views because of the following options:

- *Use Relative Dates*—Documents created or modified recently will be listed as Today (*time*) and Yesterday (*time*), and all others will be listed as *Date* (*time*). This is helpful when you have a long list of documents and want to quickly find the ones you've worked on recently.

- *Calculate Folder Sizes*—Checking this option will cause the total number of items in a window's subfolders to be calculated and displayed in the list view. Don't check this option unless you absolutely have to—it may dramatically slow down the performance of your computer if your folders contain numerous files.

- *Show Columns by: Date Modified, Date Created, Size, Kind, Label*—These options work just as they do when viewing the contents of a window as icons.

- *Show Columns by: Version*—Useful only for application files, this command sorts according to the software developer's assigned version number. Ancillary application files (such as dictionaries and references) and data files that you've created usually do not have this type of version number.

- *Show Columns by: Comments*—This command sorts files alphabetically by the text contained in their Show Info window comment fields. Displaying comment text in Finder windows is a handy file management feature, but it's useful only if the first characters of the comment are significant, or if you just want to separate all files that have comments from those that don't. Files without comments are placed at the top of any windows using the View menu's By Comment command.

- *Icon Sizes*—In addition to the small and large icon and button sizes, you can also designate a medium-sized icon when you select View As List.

Viewing Hierarchical Lists

List views may not be the most aesthetically appealing way to look at your files and folders, but most people have so much data on their hard drives that viewing them as lists is the most practical way to find things. List views are also more pragmatic because they can be manipulated more easily than icon or column views. Furthermore, they're more versatile because they can be expanded hierarchically or collapsed back into a single list with great ease. With this feature, you can display the contents of any folder without having to open a new folder window. In older versions of the Mac OS, the only way to view and manipulate folder contents was to open the folder, thereby creating a new window.

In System 7 and all subsequent versions of the Mac OS, the contents of any folder can be displayed by clicking on the small triangle (referred to as a disclosure triangle or button) that appears to the left of the folder icon. A hierarchical view allows you to view several levels of nested folders (folders inside of folders) at one time simply by clicking on the triangle next to the appropriate folder. Folder aliases, which are discussed in Chapter 6, do not have a triangle and cannot be displayed hierarchically.

If you drag hierarchically displayed folders from one list view window to another, however, they will appear as closed, unexpanded folders. You may drag files or folders from a list window to other volumes (copying the files), to other open Finder windows (moving the files), to the Desktop, or to the Trash (deleting the files), just as you would with items selected in icon and column windows. Eliminating clutter is the primary benefit of the hierarchical view—there's no need to open a new Finder window for every folder you want to view, as some people are known to do. In addition, hierarchical views allow you to simultaneously select and manipulate files and folders from different hierarchical levels; this was not possible in some earlier versions of the Mac OS because each time you clicked the mouse in a new window, the selection in the previous window was released.

Figure 4.22 illustrates this capability by showing the selection of three different files, each on a different hierarchical level. The files in this selection can now be copied, moved, deleted, or manipulated as easily as a single file. To select files and folders at multiple levels of the hierarchy at the same time, hold down the Command key while clicking on the file names or icons.

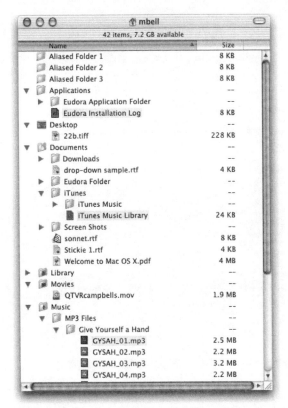

Figure 4.22
In a hierarchical display, you can select files in different folders at the same time using the Command+ click method.

To collapse a folder's hierarchical display, click the triangle next to the folder icon; the enclosed files and folder listing will disappear. When you close a window viewed as a list, the OS will not remember the hierarchical display settings (unlike in Mac OS 9.1).

Of course, you can still open a completely new window for any folder, if you prefer. Simply double-click on the folder icon rather than on the triangle, or select the folder icon and then choose the Open command from the File menu.

Resizing List Columns

Mac OS X enables you to resize the width of a column in a list view. Although the Mac OS no longer limits the length of file names to 32 characters, a practical limit on the width of a column remains a good idea. The lack of space on your display is just one of many possible reasons to shrink a column's width. Figure 4.23 shows an example of a list view before and after the column widths have been manipulated.

To manipulate a column's width, follow these steps:

1. Open a window to a list view.

2. Position the cursor between two column headings, such as Name and Date Modified, until the cursor changes when the mouse is depressed. The cursor will change from the normal pointer cursor into one of three types of cursors, which indicate whether a column may be expanded, expanded or contracted, or contracted, all of which are illustrated in Figure 4.23. The direction of the cursor will indicate the direction(s) in which you can adjust the column width.

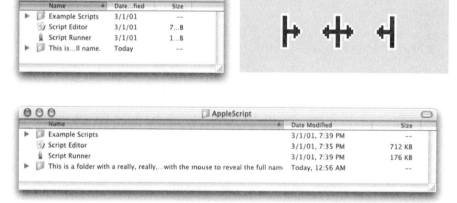

Figure 4.23
Column widths may be expanded or compressed in Mac OS X.

The OS limits the maximum and minimum sizes for columns. Watch for the cursor to change as a visual clue as to how far you are allowed to resize a column.

Reordering List Columns

In Mac OS X, you can reorder any visible column except the Name column, which cannot be reordered or removed from view in the List View Options configuration window. This capability is useful for anyone who wants to sort a list without having to scroll horizontally to bring a particular column into view. Now you can just drag that column closer to the Name column on the left side of the window, as in Figure 4.24.

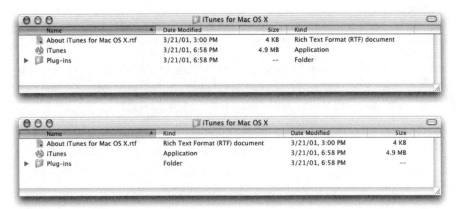

Figure 4.24
Reordering a column's position gives you greater control over how a list is viewed.

To manipulate a column's position in a list window, follow these steps:

1. Open a window to a list view.

2. Place the cursor in the center of a column heading, such as Size; drag it horizontally to a column occupied by another heading; then release it.

Advanced Finder and Desktop Features

Now that I've covered the basics of how windows work and how they can be configured and customized, let's look at a few advanced features for working with the Finder and Desktop.

The Dock

It's easy to get lost when you have a number of windows open on your screen—particularly a problem on PowerBooks or Macs with very small displays. Most applications, including the Finder, have a Window menu to help you out of such a predicament. The Dock incorporates two clutter-management features that are no longer found in the Mac OS: collapsible windows (also called window shades) and pop-up windows. Whereas both features help to temporarily hide windows, the Dock can do even more to manage Finder and application windows. But don't worry if you really, really miss pop-up windows. Chapter 5 shows you how to download and install a handy utility that restores this feature.

The Dock is actually a replacement for other features of previous versions of the Mac OS, in addition to the collapsing and pop-up windows features. It also incorporates elements of the Apple menu, the Application menu, the Application Switcher, and the Control Strip. And if you think it can do even more—you're right. In Chapter 5, I'll cover third-party utilities that significantly enhance the Dock and even replace the features of the Dock with something altogether different.

By default, the Dock is configured to appear at the bottom of your Desktop and to display a standard set of items. As you can see in Figure 4.25, the default version of the Dock includes the following items (shown from left to right):

■ Finder

■ Mail

■ Internet Explorer

■ Sherlock

■ System Preferences

■ Display

■ QuickTime Player

■ Mac OS X home page (URL)

■ Late Breaking News (Help Viewer document)

■ Trash

Figure 4.25
The default Dock items, with the contextual menu for configuring some of the options found in the Display System Preferences pane.

In addition to displaying the default applications, documents, and URLs, the Dock serves as a menu switching utility. A small black triangle appears below the icon for any application that is running in the Mac OS; as the application is being launched, the triangle will blink or the icon will bounce up and down on the Dock. A contextual menu is associated with many of the application icons. For example, the Display icon reveals the resolution and bit depth settings when you click and hold the mouse on the icon or activate the contextual menu (Control+click).

You can also use the Dock as a place to store frequently accessed folders, or even a folder filled with shortcuts to groups of applications and utilities. When activated with a Control+click, the folder reveals its contents in a hierarchical fashion, growing wherever it finds room to grow. For example, Figure 4.26 shows my Favorites folder accessed through the Dock, revealing my Eudora Application Folder several levels deep. Finder windows (column, icon, and list views) can be sent to the Dock using the minimize button or by pressing Command+M, an example of which is also shown in Figure 4.26.

Figure 4.26
You can navigate folders in the Dock.

When adding and deleting items in the Dock, the only rules to remember are these:

■ Applications must go to the left of the divider line.

■ Documents must go to the right of the divider line.

■ The Finder and Trash icons cannot be removed.

■ Everything but the Finder, divider line, and Trash can be repositioned by dragging them to the left or right, as long as you stick to the first two rules.

The Dock has only a few options to configure. You can access them via the Apple menu, the System Preferences, or by Control+clicking on the divider line, the result of which is shown in Figure 4.27. The configuration options include:

■ *Dock Size*—A sliding scale to change the size of the Dock. Clicking on the divider line and dragging the Dock resizer up or down will also accomplish this task.

■ *Magnification*—Increases the size of the icon that is the focus of the cursor when it passes or hovers over it (see Figure 4.27 for an example).

■ *Automatically Hide And Show The Dock*—When selected, this option hides the Dock until the mouse cursor meets the bottom of the Desktop, triggering the Dock to

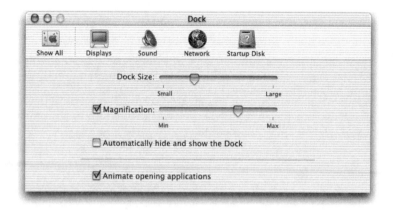

Figure 4.27
The Dock System Preferences pane (top) with an example of magnification (bottom).

pop up. After a Dock item is selected or the focus of the mouse changes, the Dock goes back into hiding.

■ *Animate Opening Applications*—Causes an application icon to bounce up and down and disables the blinking triangle beneath the starting application. To be more precise, there are two forms of animation: subtle (blinking triangle) and overt (bouncing icon). This option really refers to the latter.

Navigating from the Keyboard

Even though the Mac OS relies primarily on its graphical interface and the mouse, keyboard control is, at times, a necessity. A variety of keyboard shortcuts can be used to select files, move between file windows, and manipulate icons. For a complete list of keyboard shortcuts, see Appendix B. The keyboard commands that follow are available in all Finder windows and on the Desktop:

■ *Jump to file name*—Type the first few letters in a file name to select that file. For example, if you want to select a file named Budget, when you type B, the first file name starting with a B is selected. When the u is typed after the B, the selection will be the first file name starting with Bu, and so on. Don't pause between letters, or the Mac will interpret each additional letter as the first letter of a new search. If you don't know an exact file name, type an A to cause the display to scroll to the top of the list, an L to scroll to the middle, or a Z to scroll to the end.

- *Select next alphabetical file name*—Press the Tab key when in an icon view to select the next item. If in a list view, the window will cycle through the visible columns, sorting by each column. For example, if you have a column window with the Name, Kind, and Size columns showing, pressing the Tab key will cause the window to sort by Kind, and then by Size.

- *Select previous alphabetical file name*—Press Shift+Tab when in an icon view to select the previous item. This is useful when you press the Tab key one time too many and need to go back one step in reverse alphabetical order.

- *Select next file*—Use the Down, Left, and Right arrow keys to select the next file or folder icon in the corresponding direction.

- *Open selected folder*—Press Command+down arrow to open the selected file or folder. If the selected file or folder is already open, pressing this key combination brings its window to the front. Command+O will also open your selection.

- *Open selected file or folder and close current window*—Press Command+Option+down arrow. If the selected file or folder is already open, this key combination brings its window to the front and closes the current folder or volume window. Command+Option+O performs the same function.

- *Open parent folder window*—Press Command+up arrow. If the selected file or folder is already open, this key combination brings its window to the front.

- *Open parent folder window, close current window*—Pressing Command+Option+up arrow closes the current window and opens the parent window.

- *Edit file name*—Press Return to enter into editing mode for a window or Desktop item that isn't locked. File names can be made ready for editing by clicking the cursor on the text of the file name twice, with a one-second delay between clicks. You can tell that the name has been selected for editing when its display is highlighted and a box is drawn around the file name. Once the file name is open for editing, the backspace key deletes characters and the right and left arrow keys position the cursor. Pressing Return again saves the file name changes. Items that are locked or whose names are reserved by the Mac OS, such as *Desktop*, cannot be edited.

- *Make Desktop active*—Pressing Command+Shift+up arrow makes the current window inactive and the Finder Desktop active.

- *Throw item into the Trash*—Pressing Command+Delete will move the selected item to the Trash; Shift+Command+Delete will activate the Empty Trash command.

The following keyboard commands are available only when working in Finder windows viewed as lists (By Name, Size, Kind, Version, Label, or Comment):

- *Expand hierarchical display*—Command+right arrow displays the folder contents hierarchically.

- *Expand all hierarchical displays*—Command+Option+right arrow displays the contents of the current folder and all of its enclosed folders hierarchically.

- *Collapse hierarchical display*—Command+left arrow collapses the hierarchical display of the current folder.

- *Collapse all hierarchical displays*—Command+Option+left arrow collapses the hierarchical display of the current folder and all enclosed folders.

Dragging Files between Inactive Windows

Mac OS X allows you to select and move a file from one window to another—even from one inactive window to another. In some earlier versions of the operating system, as soon as an icon was selected in an inactive window, the window containing that icon became the active (and, consequently, the foremost) window. This created a problem when that window overlapped and obscured other folder icons. In the Mac OS X Finder, any visible icon in any window can be selected and dragged to a new location without the source file window becoming active.

 To move a Finder window without making it active, hold down the Command key while dragging the window's title bar.

To copy an item from an inactive Finder window, simply point the mouse over the item to be moved and, while holding the Command key, drag the item to its new location. As long as the mouse button is not released, only a single mouse movement is required to move the file.

This method cannot be used to move more than one file at a time. To move multiple files from one inactive window to another, the window containing the files must be made active.

When you drag items over and into a window, the inside of the window that will contain the item becomes outlined, a feature that first appeared in System 7.1 as a means of telling the user where the item would land if dropped.

Working with Multiple Files

Selecting one item in a Finder window or on the Desktop is easy enough, but you'll often want to select more than one item at a time to duplicate, alias, or move to the Trash. To perform any operation on one or more items in a window or on the

Desktop, first select the file or group of files. Most aspects of selecting files in Mac OS X are the same as in previous versions of the Mac OS:

■ *Immediate marquee selection*—The marquee (selection rectangle), created by clicking the mouse button and dragging with the button pressed while in an icon or list view, selects files as soon as any part of the file name or icon is inside the selection rectangle.

■ *Shift select*—Use the Shift key while drawing a marquee to select noncontiguous sections of any Finder window.

■ *File dragging*—It's still possible to drag files by clicking on their names and moving them while the mouse is depressed. To edit a file name, click on the file name and wait one second for a box to appear around it.

■ *Finder scrolling*—When dragging with a marquee, the Finder window scrolls automatically as soon as the cursor hits one of its edges.

Title Bar Pop-up Menu

Column and list window views make it easy to navigate a folder hierarchy—and with the title bar pop-up menu, you can move up the folder hierarchy of any window, column, icon, or list. You'll find a pop-up menu in the title bar of any window when you hold down the Command key and click on the folder's name in the title bar. For example, Figure 4.28 shows a pop-up menu for the folder named Favorites, which is many layers deep inside the hard drive named MacDonnachaidh.

Selecting a folder or volume name from this pop-up menu opens a new Finder window that displays the folder or volume contents. If a window for the selected folder or volume is already open, that window is brought forward and made active. This feature is a real time-saver when hunting down folders in the Finder.

Icon Proxies

A great advanced Finder feature in Mac OS X is the icon proxy. Each window has a small icon before the name of the window, which serves as a proxy for the folder itself in the Finder. So, you can now move, copy, alias, or delete a folder by manipulating its icon proxy as follows:

1. Click once and hold on the icon proxy until it becomes highlighted.

2. Drag the icon proxy to the Desktop, Trash, or anywhere else.

3. Hold down the Option key to copy the item (Option+drag) or to make an alias of the item (Option+Command+drag). Figure 4.29 demonstrates moving the Applications folder to the Desktop by dragging the icon proxy.

Figure 4.28
You can navigate backward through your hard drive by holding down the Command key while clicking the mouse on the center of the title bar.

Figure 4.29
Use a folder's icon proxy to manipulate the location of the folder.

When I'm working with a group of folders and have to rearrange the folders frequently as my project progresses, icon proxies are especially useful. Manipulating the icon proxy saves several steps each time a change is made.

Resizing Windows

Although windows don't always open up to the size you need, you can resize them using one of several methods. To resize an open window, you can either drag the size tab (also referred to as the size button, although it isn't a button in the way that most people think of buttons) in the lower-right corner of a window or click on the green maximize button in the window's title bar, shown in Figure 4.30. The maximize button expands the window just enough to display the complete file list or all file and folder icons. Clicking on the maximize button while holding the Option key no longer opens the window to the full size of the screen, as in most earlier versions of the Mac OS.

Figure 4.30
Resize your windows using the maximize button (left) and the size tab (right).

Option Key Options

The Option key performs many functions beyond just working with title bar navigation. Holding down the Option key also closes windows in several other situations:

■ *Folders*—While opening a folder by double-clicking on its icon in the Finder, the current folder will close as the new one is opened.

■ *Windows*—While clicking the maximize button in any Finder window, the active window will be opened to its maximum size.

■ *Multiple Windows*—While clicking the close button all open windows will close; also while clicking the minimize button all open windows will minimize.

■ *Applications*—While launching an application, the window in which the application icon appears will close.

Trash and Empty Trash

The Trash has undergone a radical change in Mac OS X in at least two ways. First, there is no icon for the Trash on the Desktop as there has been for as long as anyone can remember. Instead, the Trash has been integrated into the Dock. For me, this makes it harder to discern by looking at the icon whether it is empty or contains unwanted files ready for deleting. The key, of course, is to configure the size of the Dock large enough so you can see the Trash icon more clearly. For example, Figure 4.31 shows an enlarged Trash icon when it is empty (left) and when it contains one or more items (right).

Believe it or not, in really old versions of the Mac OS the Trash was emptied automatically. In Mac OS X, of course, you have to tell the Mac OS to empty the Trash using the Finder|Empty Trash command. And here is the second difference in the new Trash feature: It doesn't provide any feedback relating to the number of files in the Trash or the total amount of disk space the files occupy. It still presents a confirmation message, as shown in Figure 4.32. Compared to the empty Trash command in Mac OS 9.1, however, this version leaves a little to be desired.

Figure 4.31
Two views of the new trash icon in the Dock.

Figure 4.32
The result of the new Empty Trash command.

The Empty Trash command is accessed from the Application menu when in the Finder; by pressing Shift+Command+Delete; or by Control+clicking on the Trash icon and selecting Empty Trash from the contextual menu. I prefer to know how many files are being deleted and how big they are because I've accidentally deleted an entire collection of project files totaling 30MB; what I thought I was throwing away was 30KB of duplicate files, and had I enabled the old "warn me before emptying the Trash" option I would have been saved from my own blunder. In Mac OS X, you know less about what you are deleting than in Mac OS 9.1. Fortunately, you can double-click on the Trash icon in the Dock and have it open a Finder window with the contents of the Trash. Figure 4.33 shows the contextual menu command for deleting the Trash, as well as a manually opened Finder window that reveals the contents of the Trash.

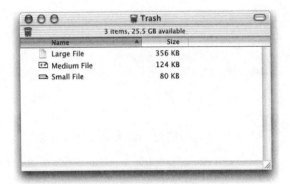

Figure 4.33
To know exactly what you are deleting from the Trash, you have to manually open the Trash in the Finder.

Mac OS X no longer counts the number of files being deleted or calculates how much space they consumed. You'll have to manually open the Trash and see for yourself.

Although using the Trash is straightforward, you'll want to know about several less obvious aspects of this process:

■ *Avoid Trash warnings*—If you hold down the Option key while choosing Empty Trash, the confirmation dialog box will not appear and the Trash will be emptied immediately.

■ *Retrieving Trashed items*—At any time before the Empty Trash command is chosen, items inside the Trash may be recovered and saved from deletion. This is done by double-clicking on the Trash icon and dragging the file icons you want to recover out of the Trash window and back onto the Desktop or any Finder window.

■ *Freeing disk space*—Only when the Trash has been emptied is disk space released. In previous systems, dragging items to the Trash was sufficient to free disk space—although not always immediately.

■ *Trash for removable media*—Although the Trash icon will appear empty, items from removable media such as Zip or Jaz cartridges that have been placed in the Trash will not be deleted when the cartridge is ejected. You must empty the Trash to delete them.

Don't be in too much of a hurry to empty the Trash. Do it every so often when you need to recover disk space, but be sure to give yourself a chance to retrieve mistakenly trashed items first. Once the Trash is emptied, deleted files can often be recovered with the help of a third-party undelete utility such as Symantec's Norton Utilities or MicroMat's Tech Tool Pro, among others.

Displaying Information about Finder Objects

As in previous versions of the Mac OS, you can select any file, folder, or drive icon and get more information about it by choosing a command from the File menu. In Mac OS X, however, there is no contextual pop-up menu for the Show Info command (formerly known as the Get Info command). Basic information and related options are displayed in the Info window for all objects that appear in the Finder, such as files, folders, disks, and mounted server volumes. The Info window for the graphic editing program GraphicConverter, as shown in Figure 4.34, is somewhat different from the Info window in previous Finder versions in that it now has only two levels of information: General and Privileges. Applications that support localization (language support) have a third section, Application Files, that lists the language installed for that application. The Memory section is no longer required for non-Classic applications (discussed in Chapter 3) because the advanced virtual memory feature of Mac OS X does not allow users to manually configure memory requirements for applications.

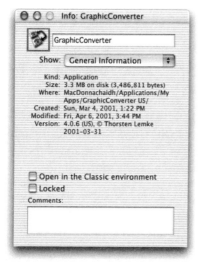

Figure 4.34
The Info window for GraphicConverter.

The Info window is now available in at least six different flavors—one each for files, folders, applications, volumes, the Desktop, and aliases. Options may differ among these types of Finder objects, but the General and Privileges sections will appear in all Finder objects.

General Information

The General Information section of the Info window, shown in the previous figure, reveals some basic information about the selected item:

4

- *Icon*—A small version (32×32 pixels) of the icon associated with the item appears to the left of the file name, providing a visual reference for the file. You can customize the icon of almost any data file, application, or volume by pasting a new icon on top of the existing icon in the Info window. To change an icon, copy any PICT graphic into the Clipboard, select the icon you want to replace in the Info window (a box will appear around the icon, indicating its selection), and choose the Paste command from the Edit menu. If the picture is too large to fit into the icon frame, it will automatically be scaled down. Close the Info window and the new icon will appear in the Finder window or on the Desktop. Likewise, you can copy and paste any icon between Info windows. For example, you can copy a custom icon from one folder to a folder that uses a standard icon using this cut and paste method.

- *File name*—The file name that appears on the Desktop or in a Finder window can be changed from within the Info window, although only the first 36 or so characters will be displayed.

- *Kind*—Provides a brief description of the selected file. For data files, this usually includes the name of the application that created the file.

- *Size*—The amount of disk space the item and its contents (if it's a folder) consumes on a volume.

- *Where*—The location of the selected file, including all folders enclosing it and the volume it's stored on.

- *Created*—The date and time the file was created. The date is reset when a file is copied from one volume to another, or if a new copy is created by holding down the Option key while moving the file into a new folder.

- *Modified*—The date and time the contents of the file were last changed.

- *Version*—Lists the software application's version number. No information on data files, folders, or volumes is provided.

- *Comments*—Any text you would like to add may go here.

Several other options appear in certain Show Info windows:

■ *Locked*—Makes it more difficult to change or delete the selected file. The Locked option appears for data files, applications, and aliases. Locking ensures that unwanted changes are not accidentally made to data files. In most applications, locked data files can be opened but changes cannot be saved unless you use Save As to create a new file.

Locked files are protected from accidental deletion because they must be unlocked before they can be moved to the Trash or have their names modified. If you try to delete a locked file, a dialog box like the one shown in Figure 4.35 appears.

Figure 4.35
The Mac OS will warn you if you attempt to move locked items to the Trash.

■ *Stationery Pad*—Available for data files only, this turns the selected document into a template (a master document on which new documents are based). With this option, a copy of the file is created each time the selected document is opened; any changes or customizations are made to this copy, leaving the original Stationery Pad document available as a master at all times. (A complete discussion of Stationery is provided in Chapter 8.)

Privileges Information

The second portion of the average Info window is the Privileges section (shown for GraphicConverter in Figure 4.36), which replaces the Sharing section of the old Get Info window. Privileges information options configure how an item can be shared among multiple users. These options may differ for applications, documents, and folders. The Privileges section will be covered in Chapter 14 because it really pertains to File Sharing.

Show Info for Aliases

In several ways, the Info window for aliases is a little different from the dialog box used by standard files. First, the version information normally displayed beneath the dates is replaced with the path and file name of the original file. In addition to the path information, you can also associate the alias with a new parent file or folder using

Figure 4.36
The Privileges section of the Info window.

Figure 4.37
The Info window for an alias.

the Select New Original button, an example of which is shown in Figure 4.37. To find the original parent item of an alias, press Command+R (for *reveal*) or choose File|Show Original. This command opens the disk or folder window and selects the original file icon. If the disk or volume containing the original file is not available, a dialog box will ask you to insert the disk containing the original file or to fix the "broken" alias. If the original is located on a network volume, the volume will be mounted once you have entered your username and password. However, Mac OS X no longer uses a contextual pop-up command (Control+click) for the Show Original command.

 The Comments and Locked options are available for aliases, and they behave exactly as they do for any other files. The Stationery Pad option, however, is not available for aliases.

Wrapping Up

The Finder is the most visible part of the Mac OS; as you've seen in this chapter, it gives you powerful and intuitive tools to manage the disks and files you're using with your computer, including:

- The new Finder menus
- Basic Finder operations
- Advanced Finder features such as the Dock and column views
- The many ways you can see and manipulate data in Finder windows
- The Trash and Empty Trash commands
- The new Info window

Next, in Chapter 5, we'll look at the various elements in Mac OS X that you can use to give your computer a more personal look and feel, as well as a few inexpensive third-party utilities that can add a lot of cool features to the Mac OS, as well as restore a few that are missing in Mac OS X!

Customizing Mac OS X

Without a doubt, the fierce loyalty among Mac users is due in large part to the Mac OS's capacity for customization. Mac OS X is just as customizable as earlier versions of the Mac OS—and it has several new features that make it even more flexible. With so many ways to personalize your Mac, you'll never feel locked into using the same computer day after day.

In this chapter, we'll look at Mac OS X's easily customized standard elements, several freeware and shareware utilities for customizing your Mac, and techniques for sharing your computer with multiple users.

Mac OS Customization Features

Mac OS X employs numerous features and System Preferences to allow you to customize the way your Mac looks and functions. You'll probably do a lot of experimenting with the options that affect the way your computer looks before discovering which options work best for you. If you're like most people, your needs change over time; you should be able to change the way your computer displays icons, Desktop, Dock and Finder windows at will. Why not treat yourself to a different interface every day?

Changing the Desktop

Changing the Desktop—ground zero for virtually all interaction with your Mac—is probably the most popular way to customize the look and feel of your Mac. In the old days, you could only modify the Desktop Pattern feature. The minute that Desktop pictures and custom icons were enabled, the race was on to see who could create the wackiest Desktop.

The Finder Preferences window, described in Chapter 4 and shown here in Figure 5.1, is the new home for the two main Desktop configuration options: selecting a Desktop picture and determining the display style for icons that represent hard drives,

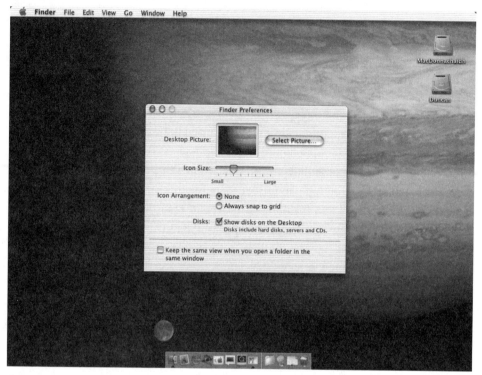

Figure 5.1
Use the Finder Preferences to control the Mac OS Desktop.

servers, removable media, and disk image drives on the Desktop. Many of these features were formerly controlled through the General Controls and the Appearance Control Panels.

To change the appearance of the Desktop picture and icons, select Finder Preferences from the application menu when in the Finder and choose from the following options:

■ *Desktop Picture*—Select a Desktop picture to replace the default Mac OS pattern by clicking the Select Picture button and navigating to the desired image in JPEG or TIFF format. Mac OS X installs several images in *<hard drive>*/Library/Desktop Pictures; you can store your images here, or anywhere on your hard drive, such as the Pictures folder in your home directory. (Every user has a home directory with several default folders for documents, music files, and pictures.)

■ *Icon Size*—Use this sliding scale to increase or decrease the size of the icons displayed on the Desktop.

■ *Icon Arrangement*—Choose Always Snap To Grid if you want your icons to align themselves along an invisible grid, thus preventing overlapping and making them easier to identify and manage. Select None if you prefer no automatic arrangement of Desktop icons.

■ *Disks*—Select this option to show all types of disk icons on the Desktop. If this option is not checked, icons for files, folders, and applications will still appear on the Desktop.

■ *Keep The Same View When You Open A Folder In The Same Window*—Check this option to clone the view options for a window based on the view options of the parent window.

Unlike Mac OS 9.1, Mac OS X does not offer the option of opening a different Desktop picture every time you log into or restart the computer. Furthermore, you cannot drag and drop an image on the preview area of the Desktop Picture preview.

Selecting an Appearance

You can also change the appearance of the Mac OS by selecting one of two appearances in the General Controls pane of the System Preferences, an example of which is shown in Figure 5.2. With Mac OS X, Apple provides only two appearances—Blue and Graphite. They are essentially the same, except that the Graphite appearance uses gray buttons in place of the blue, red, yellow, and green buttons of the Blue appearance. The General Controls pane allows you to configure the following options:

■ *Appearance*—Allows you to choose an appearance that controls the look and feel of buttons, menus, and certain window elements, such as scroll bars. Other means of enhancing the appearance are discussed in the next section of this chapter.

■ *Highlight Color*—Enables you to determine the color used to select items in the Finder, as well as to select blocks of text for drag, drop, cut, copy, and paste

Figure 5.2
Selecting one of two appearances in Mac OS X.

commands. You may only choose from seven colors; in Mac OS 9.1, however, you can select a highlight color using the Color Picker.

■ *Click In The Scroll Bar To*—When working with long documents or windows, allows you to choose whether you want to skip to just the next page, or to the location just clicked in the scroll bar area.

Apple most likely included the Graphite appearance to assuage members of the graphics and desktop publishing communities, many of whom had commented that the colored buttons and other interface features were distracting. The Graphite appearance essentially eliminates all color from all elements of the interface except the tool bar, which can be hidden from view.

Configuring the Dock

The Dock, discussed in detail in the previous chapter, is perhaps the most noticeable addition to the Mac OS. It is highly configurable and replaces the functionality of features found in previous versions of the Mac OS, including the collapsing windows, pop-up windows, Apple menu, Application menu, Application Switcher, and Control Strip. And, as we'll see in the next section, several of the Dock's capabilities become even more usable when enabled via third-party utilities. The default Dock configuration contains shortcuts to several useful items—but why not start from scratch and make the Dock work the way *you* want it to work?

To start customizing the Dock, get rid of all the shortcuts except the Finder and the Trash, which cannot be removed, by dragging each item to the Desktop until you see the trademark "poof" animation (the Mac OS's way of indicating that you have successfully deleted a shortcut from the Dock). When you've successfully completed this task, the icons that remain in the Dock are for the Finder, the Trash, and any running applications (which you cannot remove). For example, Figure 5.3 shows the default Dock (top) and the minimal Dock after deleting everything possible (bottom).

Figure 5.3
The default Dock (top) and the Dock stripped down to the bare essentials (bottom).

No "best" way to configure the Dock or any other aspect of the user interface exists. The ideal configurations enhance your productivity and entertain you, too. I like to use the Dock as a one-stop source for shortcuts to my favorite applications and documents, which I group according to function. For example, because I do a great deal of Web development and network management, my Dock contains folders that I created to house shortcuts to the appropriate applications and documents. Figure 5.4 illustrates a folder called Shortcuts that contains three subfolders, which I located in the Dock by dragging each to the right side of the divider in the Dock. Once in the Dock, each folder can be rearranged by dragging it to the right or left; I keep them in alphabetical order so I know which is which without having to hover the cursor over the folder to reveal the folder name.

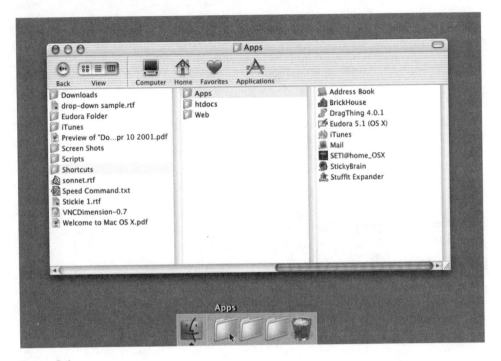

Figure 5.4
A customized version of the Dock.

To remove your customizations and return to the default Dock, delete the Finder preference file from the following location:

`<hard drive>/Users/<username>/Library/Preferences/com.apple.dock.plist`

Then reboot or log out and log back in. The default Dock size and icons view will be restored.

Finally, to hide the Dock from view, press Command+Option+D; to restore the Dock, press this keyboard shortcut again. Alternatively, place the mouse at the bottom center of the screen and the Dock will pop into view. Drag the mouse away from the Dock and it will again be hidden.

Customizing Finder Window Toolbars

Customizing the toolbar for individual Finder windows makes navigating the contents of your hard drive just as easy as using the customized Dock to navigate among applications. For each Finder window, you can show or hide the toolbar; you can also customize the global toolbar in two ways. First, you can include one or more of the shortcuts provided by Apple in your customized global toolbar by following these steps. In this example, I'm customizing the toolbar for the Applications folder:

1. Switch to the Finder by clicking on the Finder icon in the Dock.

2. Open a Finder window by pressing Command+N.

3. Choose View|Customize Toolbar. This opens the window shown in Figure 5.5.

4. Drag and drop one or more shortcuts to the toolbar area.

5. Click the Done button to return to the Finder window, which will contain the new toolbar.

The default set of toolbar shortcuts includes many handy features, including:

- *Back*—Moves back one step in the Finder.

- *Path*—Reveals the path to the current folder.

Figure 5.5
The default set of toolbar shortcuts provided by Mac OS X.

- *View*—Provides buttons to change the view of the current window to icon, list, or column view.

- *Eject*—Ejects the selected removable media or mounted server.

- *Customize*—Activates the Customize Toolbar command.

- *Separator*—Places a vertical separator in the toolbar to help you group shortcuts.

- *New Folder*—Creates a new folder within the current folder.

- *Delete*—Deletes the selected item.

- *Connect*—Opens the Connect To Server window for accessing file servers.

The following default toolbar shortcuts allow you to navigate quickly to the location for which the shortcut is named:

- *Computer*—Root level of your computer's file system

- *Home*—Your Home folder

- *iDisk*—Your iDisk (if configured in the Network System Preferences)

- *Favorites*—Your Favorites folder

- *Applications*—The main Applications folder (not an individual user's Applications folder)

- *Documents*—Your Documents folder

- *Movies*—Your Movies folder

- *Music*—Your Music folder

- *Pictures*—Your Pictures folder

- *Public*—Your Public folder

However, you can always revert to the default toolbar by dragging the Default Set to the toolbar area, which will delete all your custom selections.

 You can customize the toolbar in the System Preferences by dragging the System Preferences shortcuts you like to the toolbar area, just like with a Finder window. To delete a shortcut from the toolbar, drag the icon to the Desktop.

The second method of customizing the toolbar is to populate it with a combination of default shortcuts and applications, documents, files, and even a shortcut to the Trash. For example, I frequently use several of the default shortcuts, but I also like to be able to navigate to certain folders, including my favorite word processing applications, Web development tools, and the Utilities folder, with just one mouse click. In Figure 5.6, I started with the Default Set, added the Path shortcut, and then to the right of the default shortcuts, I added a divider, shortcuts to my three favorite folders, another divider, and the Trash. When I'm working on a particular project that requires a new shortcut, it's just as easy to add it to the toolbar as the Dock.

Figure 5.6
A customized—and personalized—toolbar.

To add a custom shortcut to the toolbar, follow these steps:

1. Open a Finder window.

2. Drag the desired shortcut item to the toolbar area.

The Trash is a little different because it is not among the default shortcuts offered in the Customize Toolbar command. Furthermore, the Trash has no obvious icon that can be added by dragging it to the toolbar of any open window. To add a shortcut to the Trash to the toolbar do the following:

1. Click on the Trash icon in the Dock.

2. Drag the proxy icon for the Trash (located in the center of the menu bar) to the toolbar.

Removing the Trash from the toolbar is a little on the non-standard side as well. To remove the Trash icon:

1. Open a Finder window.

2. Choose View|Customize Toolbar.

3. Drag the Trash icon from the toolbar to the Desktop.

Finally, I recommend that you not create shortcuts or even aliases to servers; the Finder seems to dislike resolving links to servers or server aliases. Server shortcuts tend to work briefly, but then the Finder stops allowing the mounted servers to be dismounted.

Customizing Date & Time Display

Mac OS X contains a clock that is powered by a small battery on the logic board (for times when it is unplugged or if the power is disconnected). It's important to configure the computer's date, time, and time zone settings so that email messages and documents can be tracked according to the date and time they were created or last modified. A file with an incorrect date and time stamp may very well elude you in a search for items created on a particular date. Mac OS X can display the time (and the date, when the time is single-clicked with the mouse) in the menu bar as well as in a small application appropriately named Clock, which is located in the main Applications folder. The settings in the Date & Time System Preferences pane control all of your Mac's time and date features. You can review and configure your date and time settings by following these steps:

1. Open the Date & Time System Preferences pane.

2. Enter the current date and time in the Date & Time tab (see Figure 5.7).

3. Select the appropriate information in the Time Zone tab; Mac OS X automatically configures Daylight Saving Time.

4. In the Network Time section, choose whether you want to use a network time server to automatically set the time on your computer. Refer to **http://time.apple.com** for the address of a time server.

5. Under the Menu Bar Clock tab, you can choose to display the time and date in the menu bar and set several clock display options.

The Clock application, a small clock that has both an analog and a digital interface, can be displayed as a floating window with varying degrees of transparency or in the Dock. Figure 5.8 shows the configuration options for the clock, as well as the clock itself. You can reposition the clock by dragging it to the desired location on the Desktop.

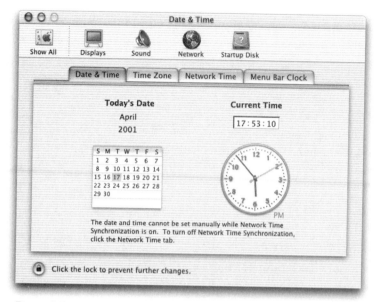

Figure 5.7

The Date & Time System Preferences pane controls the settings for the internal clock, menu bar clock, and Clock application.

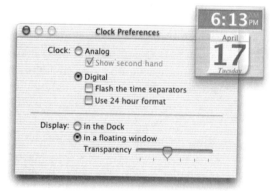

Figure 5.8

The Clock application.

Setting Displays and Sound System Preferences

You can go beyond customizing how your Mac looks by tailoring the way it displays information on your monitor and plays sounds. This flexibility is yet another example of the capacity for individualization that makes the Mac OS so popular. In Mac OS X, the Displays System Preferences pane replaces the old Monitors Control Panel, and the Sound System Preferences pane replaces the Sound Control Panel. Depending on what type of computer and monitor you have, your options may look slightly different from the examples that follow.

Customizing Displays

To customize the style in which your Mac displays information received from the operating system, go to the Displays System Preferences pane, which is shown in Figure 5.9.

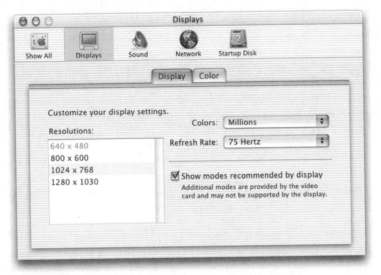

Figure 5.9
The new Displays System Preferences in Mac OS X.

The color depth, or the number of colors your monitor can display, will depend on the amount of video RAM (also called VRAM) and the type of display. Most monitors that ship with new computers are capable of displaying millions of colors; however, if you don't have enough VRAM, you may only be able to display thousands of colors. A good rule of thumb is to set your monitor to display thousands or millions of colors (if it is capable of doing so)—but not 256. If you have a PowerBook or iBook, which I'll talk about more in Chapter 7, additional customization features may apply to the Displays System Preferences.

The amount of VRAM also affects the ability of multiresolution monitors to display multiple resolutions. For example, if your Mac has a monitor that is capable of displaying a maximum resolution of 1024×768 pixels, you'll need 2MB of VRAM. If you only have 1MB of VRAM, however, the higher resolution setting will not be available in the Displays System Preferences pane. A variation on this theme goes like this: If the higher resolution setting is available, the number of colors available to be displayed will decrease. So, to set your monitor's colors and resolution, you'll need to strike a balance between your system's capabilities and the task you're performing. It's unlikely that you'll ever truly come up short, however—the latest PowerMac G4s come with

What's a Good Monitor?

A good CRT (cathode ray tube) monitor has a 17-inch or larger screen and is capable of displaying at multiple resolutions with a good refresh rate and acceptable dot pitch. An LCD (liquid crystal display) monitor should have a 15-inch or larger screen, but usually doesn't have as fine a dot-pitch as a CRT monitor. But what does all this mean and why should you care?

- The size of a monitor is measured diagonally from the top-left of the viewable area to the lower-right, not including the monitor's plastic casing. Early Apple monitors were as small as 8 inches on the diagonal, but the emerging standard these days is 19 inches. A 17-inch monitor is the current standard.

- Resolution refers to the width and height of your display, measured in pixels. For example, 1024×768 pixels is a standard resolution for contemporary monitors, whereas first-generation monitors usually displayed at a fixed resolution of 640×480. A good monitor will display multiple resolutions of 1600×1200 and higher.

- The refresh rate refers to the frequency at which the image displayed on your screen is refreshed or redrawn per second, measured in hertz (abbreviated Hz). The human eye usually can't detect refresh rates higher than 75Hz or so, but if the rate is any lower the image will appear to flicker.

- Dot pitch refers to the size of the tiny elements in a monitor that pass light to the eye, measured in millimeters. Several different technologies, such as shadow mask and invar mask, are used to create these elements—just remember that smaller is better. Look for a monitor with a dot pitch of .26 mm or smaller. The typical range will be from .30 mm (unacceptable) to .22 mm (excellent).

32MB of VRAM, and I've yet to see a monitor capable of exceeding the Mac's ability to provide enough VRAM.

The Color section of the Displays System Preferences pane may be new to many users (we'll cover it in more detail in Chapter 9 when we talk about the font and printing capabilities of Mac OS X). The Color section enables you to select a ColorSync display calibration profile or launch the Display Calibrator Assistant, examples of which are shown in Figure 5.10. The calibration profile affects the display of colors on your screen, as well as how they are transmitted to color printers. In short, ColorSync assists in the color management capabilities of your computer, and the Displays System Preferences pane is the "one-stop shop" for configuration options that determine how your computer manages color.

Customizing Sound

Of all the customizable elements of your Mac's interface, the Sound System Preferences is probably the most familiar—or at least a close second to everybody's favorite, the changeable Desktop picture. Longtime Mac users remember when this feature

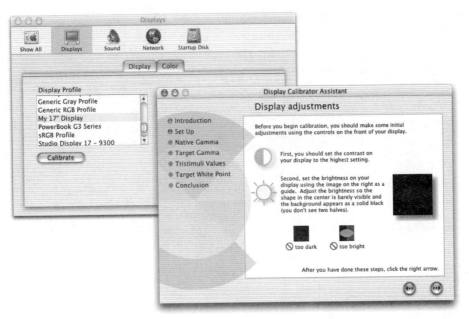

Figure 5.10
The Color configuration portion of the Displays System Preferences, and the Display Calibrator Assistant.

made us say to our friends, "Hey, listen to this. My Mac thinks it's a duck!" Now, of course, you can purchase sample sounds or download them from the Web, so instead of just quacking at you, your computer might have Bart Simpson talk back to you or Captain Janeway beam you aboard.

With Mac OS X, you can choose from many new, high-quality alert sounds—or select the venerable Sosumi, for old time's sake. Although the Sound System Preferences pane allows you to customize the way your Mac plays alert sounds, you cannot record new alert sounds without the assistance of a third-party application. As illustrated in Figure 5.11, you can choose among the following sound-related options:

- *System Volume*—Raises or lowers the volume level for applications and portions of the Mac OS that produce sound (not including alert sounds).

- *Mute*—Mutes all sound output when checked.

- *Balance*—Adjusts the balance between right and left speakers, if you've attached speakers to your Mac. If not, this option is not functional.

- *Alert Volume*—Raises or lowers the volume level for alert sounds only.

- *Alert Sounds*—Selects a sound for the computer to use to alert you to various conditions or warnings.

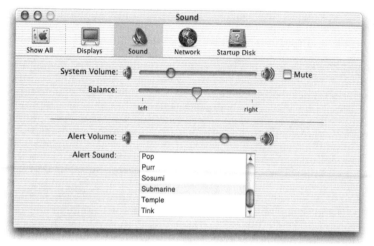

Figure 5.11
The Sound System Preferences.

As with displays, you should customize your sound settings as necessary—and don't be afraid to tinker and explore your computer's options. It's a Mac, after all! To record your own alert sounds, you'll need a sound recording and manipulation application, such as those listed here, and a PlainTalk microphone or other source for sound input, such as a CD-ROM or DVD:

- *Audacity (Dominic Mazzoni, et al.)*—**www.cs.cmu.edu/~music/audacity/ macosx.html**

- *Sound Studio (Felt Tip Software)*—**www.felttip.com/products/soundstudio/**

Be sure to limit the size of your "homemade" alert sound files; large sound files take so long to replay that the system slows down every time an alert is triggered.

Customizing Energy Saver Preferences

Although you may not think of the Energy Saver System Preferences pane as a customization feature, it has a useful purpose, especially for PowerBook and iBook users. (See Chapter 7 for a detailed explanation of Energy Saver features from the perspective of mobile users.) With this feature, you can configure the display and the hard drive to go into energy-conservation mode (i.e., sleep) independently of one another or simultaneously.

As shown in Figure 5.12, the Energy Saver System Preferences pane allows you to tell the Mac OS when the computer should revert to a power-saving mode; however, with Mac OS X, you no longer have the options of telling the computer to shut itself off

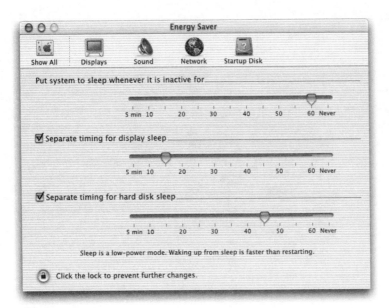

Figure 5.12
Use the Energy Saver System Preferences to configure your Mac to go into sleep mode.

after a specified period of inactivity or start itself up at a certain time and on certain days. Under Mac OS X, your options are limited to stipulating that the entire computer go into sleep mode or that the display and/or hard drive go into sleep mode.

Using Screen Savers

The screen saver, configured via the Screen Saver System Preferences pane, is a new feature in Mac OS X that you're sure to like. The example screen saver modules included with the OS really show off the powerful image rendering capabilities of the Quartz display engine in Mac OS X. These modules gently walk you through still images of beaches (Beach), outer space (Cosmos), and forests (Forest) as if you were actually in the scenes displayed on your monitor. Other screen saver examples include a basic black screen with an Apple logo (Basic), hurling and twirling Mac OS X application icons (Aqua Icons), a collection of familiar Desktop pictures (Abstract), and a module that you can customize yourself by identifying a folder of images to be used as part of the screen saver slide show of images.

To activate the screen saver:

1. Open the System Preferences.

2. Switch to the Screen Saver pane, as shown in Figure 5.13.

3. Select a module in the Screen Savers tab.

Figure 5.13
The new screen saver includes several built-in modules with stunningly beautiful photographic slide shows.

4. Switch to the Activation tab and decide how long the keyboard and mouse should be inactive before the module is activated (5 to 60 minutes, or never) and whether a password is required to dismiss the screen saver.

5. In the Hot Corners tab, select which corners of the display will activate the screen saver whenever the mouse cursor lingers over that area; use a minus sign to identify corners of the screen that should not activate the screen saver if the mouse were to be in that corner.

6. Press the Configure button to change any additional settings for modules that require additional configuration, such as the Aqua Icons module. The Custom Slide Show module asks for the location of a folder of images when the Configure button is selected.

Chapter 7 goes into a little more depth about the screen saver as it relates to battery consumption and using the screen saver password requirement as a security measure. For more Screen Saver modules, visit the following Web sites and check out what they have to offer:

■ *SaverLab (Dozing Cat Software)*—www.dozingcat.com

■ *MacOSXScreenSaver (Epicware)*—www.epicware.com/macosxsavers.html

■ *SETI@home (Search for Extraterrestrial Intelligence)*—http://setiathome.berkeley.edu

Using Third-Party Customization Utilities

When compared to earlier versions of the operating system, Mac OS X is highly customizable—despite the loss of several familiar features, such as the Control Strip, Launcher, and the appearance themes and sounds of the old Appearance Control Panel. Software developers have wasted no time in coming up with new applications and utilities for Mac OS X. They've also been busy adapting tried and true applications such as DragThing and Drop Drawers to work with the new operating system. Because many third-party solutions designed for earlier versions of the Mac OS rely on Control Panels and Extensions to provide functionality, they are not easily "ported" to Mac OS X. At the same time, however, entirely new utilities are being written to fill the gaps or to enable "hidden" features that Apple overlooked, such as the ability to reposition the Dock on the left, top, and right sides of the screen. The following utilities (just a few of my favorites) allow me to customize Mac OS X so that I'm far more productive than before.

5

DragThing
www.dragthing.com

DragThing, created by James Thomson, is the consummate docking utility. Incredibly flexible and very easy to use, DragThing allows you to create several types of docks that you can customize in shape, size, color, location, and functionality. Docks can be minimized or maximized, single- or multilayered, vertical or horizontal, to name only a few of the configuration options. Use the customized docks to store shortcuts to applications, documents, folders, disks, and servers, as well as the Process Dock, which is a special type of dock whose purpose is to display foreground, background, and even hidden processes. You can customize the Process Dock to behave much like the "real" Dock or the old Application Switcher's tear-off menu.

DragThing enables you to create as many docks as you like. For example, Figure 5.14 shows four docks that I'm using for very different purposes in Mac OS X:

■ The Process Dock (upper right) is a floating dock configured to display all non-hidden processes in the order in which they were launched, as well as the Trash; this dock is very similar to the Application Switcher found in previous versions of the OS.

■ A Dock called Utilities (lower right) is a two-layered dock that houses shortcuts to frequently used utilities; one layer is for Mac OS X utilities and the other is for Classic utilities.

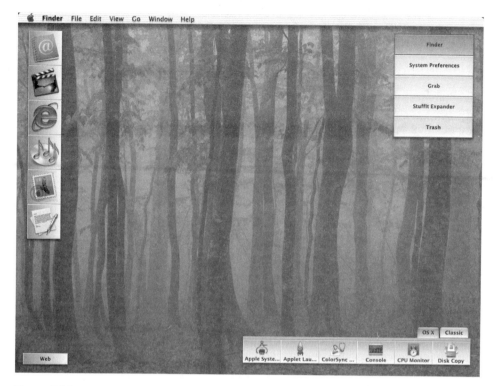

Figure 5.14
A sampling of docks created by DragThing.

■ A minimized dock called Web (lower left) provides quick access to my Web-related utilities, folders, and servers; when clicked, it expands to reveal its contents, and then automatically minimizes itself when not in use.

■ A single-layered dock (upper left) contains icons representing shortcuts to my favorite applications; the icons are arranged alphabetically by name.

DragThing has a set of application-wide preferences that are configured through the main Preferences configuration interface, shown in Figure 5.15, as well as individual preferences for each Dock. The general preferences control many aspects of DragThing's behavior, including Process Dock options; startup options; appearance configuration options such as fonts, color, and sound selections; hot keys to effect application switching and DragThing shortcuts; tool tips; contextual menu support; and dragging behavior.

The flexibility that DragThing lends to the Mac OS X Desktop experience is so expansive that I could easily spend the rest of this chapter just describing its many features and benefits. Try customizing DragThing to see if it can help you organize and navigate Mac OS X.

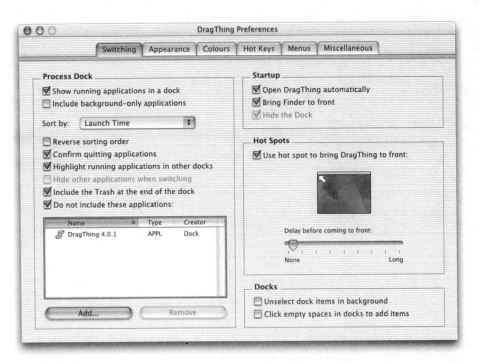

Figure 5.15
DragThing's application-wide preferences.

Docking Maneuvers
http://homepage.mac.com/isleep/

Austin Shoemaker's Docking Maneuvers is a great utility that allows you to customize the behavior of the Dock in several ways. I can only guess why Apple hasn't enabled these features, but thanks to astute programmers like Austin, we can unlock the secrets of the Dock and use it in several new ways. Some of Docking Maneuvers' features include:

- *Orientation*—Places the Dock at the top, left, or right of the screen, in addition to the bottom (default location).

- *Pin*—Determines whether the dock grows from the start, center, or end of the screen as applications/windows are launched or minimized.

To use Docking Maneuvers, just launch it and enable the Dock Orientation and Dock Pinning options; use the contextual menu of the Dock's grow bar to make changes to the Dock's position and orientation. For example, Figure 5.16 shows how I've used Docking Maneuvers to orient the Dock on the left side of the screen; the Dock is pinned to the top so it will "grow" downward as it expands. To return the Dock to the

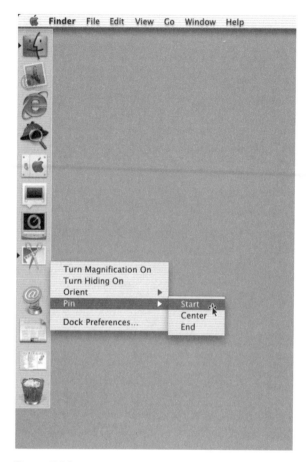

Figure 5.16
You can change the position of the Dock with Docking Maneuvers.

standard position, orient the Dock on the bottom of the screen and pin the Dock to
the center, so it grows equally to the left and right as items are added to the Dock.

Docklets

Several docklets and docklings—modules that can be added to the Dock to enhance
its capabilities—are now available to restore Mac OS 9.1 shortcuts that are not
included in Mac OS X. Docklets appear to be fairly easy to create; in fact, new ones
are popping up all the time, including the following docklets that you may find helpful
for customizing your Dock:

■ *Clocklet*—**www.infinity-to-the-power-of-infinity.com**—Functions as a substitute
clock with several configuration options.

■ *Volume*—**www.on-core.com**—Controls the volume level of system sounds.

- *AudioCD*—www.on-core.com—Provides quick access to controls for playing audio CDs.

- *Everyday Dockling*—**http://homepage.mac.com/everyday/esdock/index.html**— Provides a plug-in architecture for developers to write their own plug-ins, thereby cutting down on the number of docklets.

Figure 5.17 shows all four of these docklets as they appear in the Dock (between the Finder icon and the vertical divider), with the Everyday Dockling activated to reveal several example plug-ins.

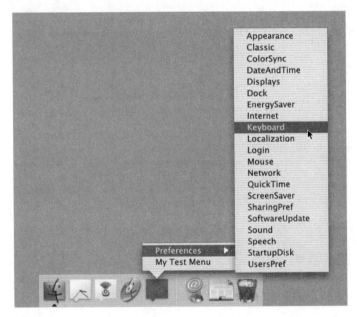

Figure 5.17
Several example docklets, which provide added flexibility to the Dock.

Show Desktop

http://homepage.mac.com/everyday/

Screen clutter is an obstacle for which many solutions have been provided. Some users open so many application windows that locating an item in the Finder or simply focusing attention on one window becomes an exercise in frustration. For example, I use the Desktop as both my general workspace and the download location for my Web browser. Because my Desktop is usually littered with several dozen files and folders (see the next chapter for tips on managing the contents of your hard drive), I often need to hide all open applications in order to reveal the Desktop.

Mac OS X is unable to switch to the Finder and then hide all other applications, thereby revealing the Desktop. Fortunately, Show Desktop from Everyday Software picks up where Mac OS X falls short. When launched, Show Desktop has two simple configuration options and a Dock icon that, when clicked, switches to the Finder and hides all other applications (see Figure 5.18). You even can configure Show Desktop to create a new window, as well, in the event that no Finder window is open.

Figure 5.18
Use Show Desktop to switch to the Finder and hide all other open applications.

TinkerTool and Plus
www.bresink.de/osx/TinkerTool.html
www.orcsoftware.com/~simon/plus/

TinkerTool and Plus provide similar customization capabilities that greatly enhance the Dock's usability. Both utilities allow you to customize the Desktop in the following ways:

- Add two new effects to windows as they are minimized, in addition to the "Genie" effect

- Add a blue triangle to the active application in place of the default black triangle

- Change orientation and pinning of the Desktop (similar to Docking Maneuvers, discussed earlier)

- Make the Dock icons transparent for applications that are hidden

- Enable transparent terminal windows

TinkerTool has several additional Mac OS interface customization features when compared to Plus, including the ability to display hidden system files (which I won't encourage you to do) as well as the Trash icon on the Desktop. Figure 5.19 shows an example of the Dock as customized by TinkerTool and the utility's Desktop configuration tab.

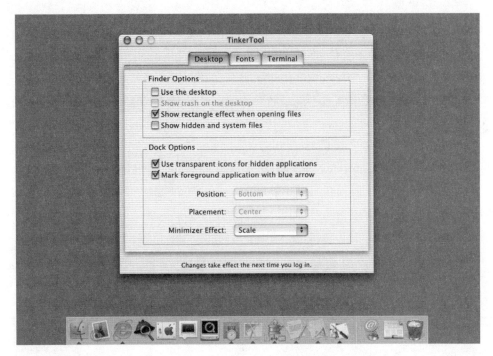

Figure 5.19
Use TinkerTool to customize several Mac OS appearance features, including the Desktop and Dock.

X-Assist

http://members.ozemail.com.au/~pli/x-assist/

X-Assist was created by Peter Li to restore several user interface features found in Mac OS 9.1 that are missing in Mac OS X. The features reenabled by X-Assist include:

■ A Mac OS 9.1-type Application menu

■ A Shortcuts submenu

■ A Recent Applications submenu

■ A user-defined hierarchical submenu

■ A plug-in architecture for developers to add additional features

X-Assist enables a number of Mac OS 9.1-like features. The best of these features is the ability to add multiple subfolders to a special folder in your Favorites folder. For example, I added three folders named Applications, Documents, and Web Development to a folder called X-Assist Items, located in my Favorites folder. X-Assist knows to look in this folder and display its contents hierarchically when the Shortcuts submenu is activated from the application menu, as illustrated in Figure 5.20.

Figure 5.20
X-Assist has no limits to the number of items displayed in its hierarchical menu.

Finally, Mac OS X uses a staggered or layered windowing approach so that an application's windows need not be entirely visible or grouped together on the Desktop. X-Assist provides a shortcut in the Preferences submenu that brings all the windows belonging to a particular application (instead of just the selected window) to the front when any one of the windows is clicked.

Drop Drawers
www.sigsoftware.com

Sig Software's Drop Drawers, a venerable shortcut tool that has been around for quite some time, allows you to create drawers to hold several types of shortcuts and information, including:

- Documents

- Applications

- URLs

- Clippings

Drop Drawers for Mac OS X also includes a process drawer that lists running processes. For example, Figure 5.21 shows several of the drawers created by Drop Drawers, including the process drawer (top) and a text clipping drawer (expanded).

The drawers pop open when the mouse cursor hovers over the drawer's tab and close automatically, making Drop Drawers very unobtrusive.

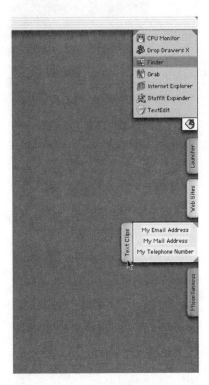

Figure 5.21
Sig Software's Drop Drawers.

Launcher

http://personalpages.tds.net/~brian_hill/launcher.html

For those of you who hate to part with the old Launcher found in many previous versions of the Mac OS, Brian Hill has created a Launcher that is not only faithful to the original, but also uses the advanced features of the Aqua interface to enhance its usability. Shown in Figure 5.22, the new and improved Launcher supports a transparent, color-tinted window as well as an optional system-wide menu in the upper-right area of the screen (the location of the old Application menu).

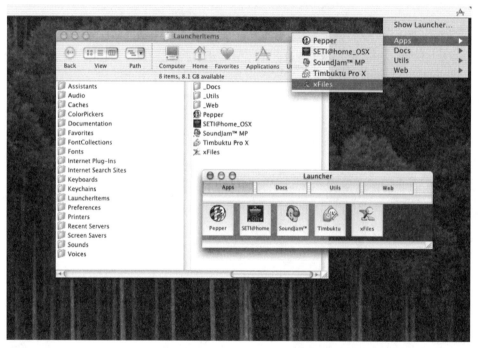

Figure 5.22
The Launcher from Brian Hill.

Like the earlier Launcher, subcategories are supported by creating folders such as _Docs, _Utils, and _Web, as in this example. The Launcher's subfolders are located in your *<username>*/Library/LauncherItems folder.

PopUpX

www.madoverlord.com/projects/popupx.t

The pop-up window, yet another feature that is missing from Mac OS X, has been restored thanks to software developer Robert Woodhead. He has created a Mac OS X version of the pop-up window that behaves very similarly to the Mac OS 9.1 version. Before launching PopUpX, create an alias for the folder you want displayed as a pop-up folder; be sure to place the alias in the same folder that contains the parent application of the alias's original. For example, in Figure 5.23, three folders are aliased: Applications, My Apps, and Utilities.

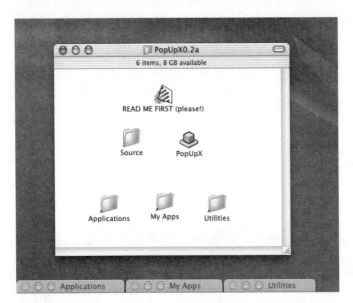

Figure 5.23
PopUpX allows you to customize pop-up folders.

To activate a pop-up folder, nudge the folder upwards or click the maximize button. To dismiss the popped-up window, nudge it downwards or click the maximize button again. Clicking the minimize button will send the pop-up window to the Dock.

Other Utilities

New utilities that allow you to customize Mac OS X to suit your needs are being written almost daily. Many of the utilities mentioned in this chapter focus on restoring or enhancing user interface features that—for whatever reason—were not carried over from previous versions of the Mac OS. Two great Web sites can help you keep track of all the new and revised applications for Mac OS X:

- *VersionTracker*—www.VersionTracker.com/vt_mac_osx.shtml

- *Mac OS X Apps*—**www.macosxapps.com**

Both of these sites are fantastic resources for categorizing and tracking software, as well as providing other services such as bulletin boards, searchable archives, and news relevant to Apple and the Mac OS.

Working with Multiple Users

Mac OS X is a true multiuser operating system because the core operating system was built to support this capability. In previous versions of the OS, however, the Multiple Users feature provided limited options for securely sharing one computer with multiple users. As the "owner" or administrator of your Macintosh, you can create multiple user IDs and assign various levels of privileges to enable other users to customize the Mac OS. Although only one person at a time can use the physical components of your Macintosh—monitor, mouse, and keyboard—services such as file and Web sharing are accessible to other users while you are logged in. You'll use the Users section of the System Preferences, shown in Figure 5.24, to create, edit, and delete user accounts.

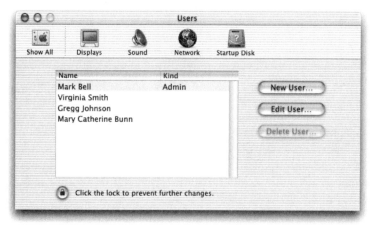

Figure 5.24
Managing user accounts with the Users System Preferences.

Creating User Accounts

When you first used your computer you were asked to create an initial user account with a username and password, among other things. The first account created is given administrative privileges, and the owner of that account may create additional user accounts on the same computer via the New User dialog box, an example of which is shown in Figure 5.25.

To create a new user account on your computer:

1. Open the System Preferences from the Dock or Apple menu.

2. Switch to the Users pane and click the New User button.

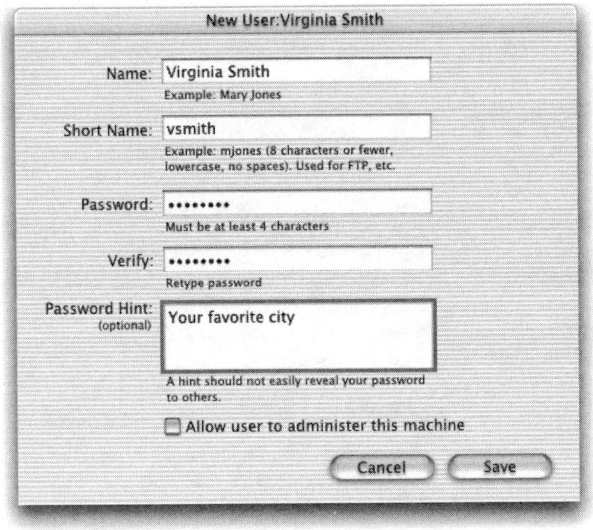

Figure 5.25
The New User dialog box allows you to add user accounts.

3. Enter the appropriate information in the Name, Short Name (username), Password, Verify, and Password Hint fields. A username must be eight or fewer lowercase characters (no spaces), and the password must be at least four characters in length.

4. Click the Save button.

Users should not be granted administrative access to a computer unless you intend to allow that person to have unlimited rights. In Mac OS X, there is no in between—users are either administrators or plain old users. Whenever a non-administrative user logs in, the username and password will be required. As shown in Figure 5.26, administrative users can modify any of the System Preferences, including the option to have the computer automatically log in as that user when started or restarted, which is a useful shortcut if you're the primary user of the computer and if the computer is in a secure location. (You wouldn't want to enable this feature if your computer is located in a public area because of the security risk.) For example, if a user with administrative access entered her username and password and checked the Automatically Log In checkbox, no other user would be able to use the computer unless the administrative user is manually logged out via the Apple menu.

In addition to being restricted from making changes in the System Preferences, non-administrative users are denied access to many areas of the file system, including most of the other users' folders, as illustrated in Figure 5.27. When a user other than mbell

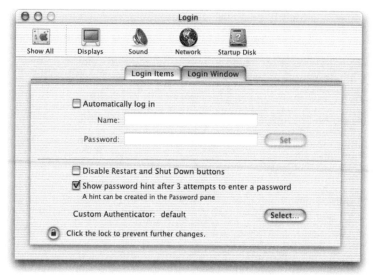

Figure 5.26
Users with administrative access can configure the Users System Preferences to bypass the login screen and automatically log in.

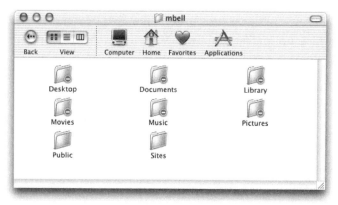

Figure 5.27
Users without administrative access have limited access to a Mac's file system.

is logged in, such as vsmith, for example, restricted folders in the mbell home folder bear a stop-sign–style icon indicating they cannot be opened or deleted.

 You will be logged into Mac OS X automatically until you choose Logout from the Apple menu or create a second account on your computer.

Changing Passwords

If multiple users will be using your computer on a regular basis, someone will inevitably forget their username or password. If you—the owner of the computer—forget your password, you'll need the Mac OS X installation CD-ROM to reset it, which you can accomplish following these steps:

1. Insert the Mac OS X installation CD-ROM.

2. Launch the Install Mac OS X application.

3. From the Installer menu, choose Reset Password.

Once the password has been reset, you will again have full control over the user accounts and configuration capabilities, including software installation.

 See Chapter 14 for additional information about user accounts and access privileges when providing File and Web Sharing services.

Wrapping Up

Using the Mac OS for the first time is kind of like driving someone else's car—when you get behind the wheel, the first thing you do is adjust the mirrors and seat so that you're comfortable. The Mac OS's many and varied opportunities for customizing the user interface have always been among the operating system's greatest attractions. Apple builds much of this capacity right into the interface through:

- Appearance options and Desktop pictures

- Dock configuration options

- Finder window toolbars

- Time, date, display, and sound options

- Windowing options

- Energy Saver features

- Screen savers

- Third-party utilities such as DragThing, Docking Maneuvers, docklets and docklings, Show Desktop, TinkerTool, Plus, X-Assist, Drop Drawers, Launcher, PopUpX, and Web resources for locating additional utilities to customize Mac OS X

- Creating user accounts

In the next chapter, we'll look at the various ways you can manage the many, many files on your hard drive.

Organizing Your Data

As you've seen in Chapter 4, Mac OS X provides several commands and features that help you manage disks and files. Other than a few rules relating to directory permissions for multiple users, Mac OS X does not require that you organize your data in any particular way. It's up to you to decide how to arrange your files, folders, and applications within your home folder or other areas for which you have permission to create files and folders. The challenge of file management is to design a logical arrangement that will allow you to quickly locate the files you need, while striking a balance between the amount of available storage space and the quantity and size of files you need.

Fortunately, Mac OS X provides several data management tools, including the Make Alias command, the Sherlock search engine, and the ability to append comments to items in the Finder. You can use these tools to manage data on removable media, network file servers, or any other removable or remote storage devices—as well as on your hard drive. In this chapter, we'll take a look at these features and how they can help you efficiently organize your data. We'll also look at several third-party utilities designed to help you manage the thousands of files and folders on your computer.

File System Organization

Mac OS X's file structure is radically different from earlier versions of the operating system. What makes it so different? First, the operating system itself, which is completely different from earlier versions of the Mac OS, contains different categories of files that are stored in different places. For example, the System Folder no longer exists, nor do most of its subfolders. Several of the more familiar folders reappear in Mac OS X in different locations, such as the Favorites, however. Second, Mac OS X is a true multiuser operating system. Each user account is created using a standard template of folders not found in earlier versions of the Mac OS (for the most part). The basic components of the new file structure are:

- *Applications*—The default set of user applications installed by Mac OS X, including the Address Book, Internet Explorer, and TextEdit.

- *Library*—Applications and resources used by the Mac OS or shared among multiple applications, including ColorSync, printer resources, and screen savers.

- *System*—The majority of the operating system files. The Mach portion of the operating system, located in the root level of the hard drive, is invisible.

- *Users*—A set of default folders created for each user, including Desktop, Documents, Library, Movies, Music, Pictures, Public (for file sharing), and Sites (for Web sharing).

File storage on the Desktop is also a bit different: Each user has his or her own Desktop, the contents of which are stored in the Desktop folder within the user's home folder (see Figure 6.1).

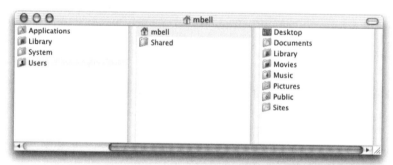

Figure 6.1
The new file structure in Mac OS X.

Working with Aliases

Wouldn't it be nice to be in several places at one time? Imagine, for example, that while you're hard at work earning your paycheck, you could also be lying on a beach enjoying the sun. And if being in two places at once sounds appealing, how would you like to be in any number of places at one time? For example, you could be at work earning a living, at the beach getting a tan, at the library reading a book, and on a plane bound for an exotic destination—all at the same time.

Through a feature called *aliasing*, Mac OS X makes it possible for your electronic files to be in many places at the same time without actually using the amount of space that true duplicates would gobble up. In fact, the Mac OS X takes advantage of aliasing in conjunction with the Favorites folder, as we've seen in earlier chapters. Whenever you add a file, folder, or application using the Favorites menu or toolbar shortcut, you're really just adding that item's alias to the Favorites folder.

Basic Aliasing Concepts

In simple terms, an alias is a special kind of copy of a file, folder, or volume. Unlike copies you create with the Duplicate command, an alias is only a copy of the icon that represents the file, folder, or volume, and not of the item itself.

To understand this distinction, think of an icon as a door; the file represented by the icon is the room behind the door. Each room normally has just one door (just as each file has one icon), and opening that door (the icon) is the only way to enter the room. Creating an alias is like adding an additional door to the room—it presents another entrance to the same place.

The concept of aliasing is not new. Aliasing exists in several earlier versions of the Mac OS as well as in other types of operating systems, including various Unix operating systems, on which they are called *symbolic links*, and Microsoft Windows 3.1 and later operating systems, where they are called *shortcuts*. Because Mac OS X is a Unix-style operating system that can utilize multiple types of file systems, it supports aliases and symbolic links.

Figure 6.2 shows an example in which a folder and the Desktop contain an alias to the same file, index.html. The original file resides in the Sites folder, and the aliases reside in the Favorites folder and on the Desktop.

6

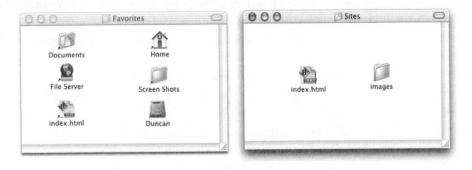

Figure 6.2
Each alias points to the original file (index.html) used to create the alias.

The differences between aliases and symbolic links aren't important for the average user. Most Mac OS X users will utilize the Mac OS Extended (HFS+) file format instead of the Unix File System (UFS) for their hard drives. Symbolic links are used only in UFS volumes, and only advanced users, system administrators, or network servers are likely to employ the UFS format. So, for the purposes of this book, when I refer to an alias I really mean an alias instead of a symbolic link.

An alias can be moved to any folder on the same volume without affecting the relationship between the alias and its original file. In fact, the link between an alias and its original file is maintained even if both files are moved or renamed, feats which would confuse and *break* a symbolic link. The amount of disk space required by an alias is determined by the type and location of the original file, as well as the format of the hard drive. A typical alias is approximately 4KB in size. Aliases can, however, be as large as 50KB.

Details about these and other aspects of aliases are provided later in this chapter. But before getting too far into the technical aspects, let's take a quick look at a few practical ways to use aliases:

- *To launch applications easily*—You can launch an application simply by double-clicking on its alias. For example, if you keep one alias of your word processor on the Desktop and another in a folder full of word processing data files, you could then launch the word processor by double-clicking the alias icon that's most convenient at the moment. Figure 6.3 shows a folder containing aliases to some of my frequently used applications.

- *To organize data files more effectively*—A data file may contain information that's relevant to several different areas of interest. For example, if you keep a spreadsheet file with information on your income taxes in a folder along with all the other

Figure 6.3
Create customized groups of application aliases for easy access to frequently needed applications.

spreadsheets you've created during that year, you may also want to keep alias copies of that same spreadsheet in a personal finance folder, a tax folder, and a general accounting folder.

Storing alias copies in multiple locations makes it easier to locate a file quickly because you can find it in several places. Placing alias files near other files of related content also increases efficiency because you don't have to look in multiple locations to access the applications directly.

■ *To simplify access to files stored on removable media*—Keeping aliases of files from removable storage media (floppy disks, removable hard drives, and CD-ROMs) on your local hard drive allows you to locate those files quickly. For example, clip art collections often have dozens of categories of files, such as business, art, and logos, spread across multiple CD-ROMs. If you create a folder of aliases to the original categories you'll have quick access to them, as well as shortcuts to the archived folders.

■ *To simplify access to files stored on network servers*—Placing aliases of files from network file servers on your local hard drive is another way to promptly locate the files, no matter where they're stored. When an alias of a file stored on the network server is opened, the Finder automatically connects to the server and asks you for the necessary password, if it isn't located in the Keychain (see Chapter 15 for more information on storing passwords in the Keychain).

Creating and Using Aliases

Creating aliases is almost as easy as falling off a log. To create an alias for a file, folder, or volume, switch to the Finder and select the item's icon. Then use one of the following methods to make an alias:

■ Choose the Make Alias command from the File menu.

■ Press Command+L.

■ Press Control while clicking the mouse on the icon; then select Make Alias from the contextual menu.

■ Use Option+Command+drag to move the icon anywhere—even to the same folder or the Desktop.

The first alias created in the same location (whether it's in a folder or on the Desktop) as the original will appear with the same file name and icon as the original. Additional aliases in the same location will append a space and a number to the end of the file name indicating that it is the second, third, or fourth alias to the same file, as shown in Figure 6.4. This is a little different from aliases in Mac OS 9.1, in which the file names of aliases are italicized and followed by a space and the word *alias*.

Figure 6.4
Alias file names that include a number indicate that multiple aliases to the same item exist in the same location.

For the most part, alias icons look and act just like other files, folders, or volumes. You can change the file name of an alias at any time without breaking the link between the alias and its original file. Changing a file name is like changing the sign on a door—it doesn't change the contents of the room behind the door.

Alias icons are differentiated from original icons by a small arrow that points up and to the right (these can be hard to see). The arrow usually appears when aliased files and folders are viewed in Open and Save dialog boxes, and when they're listed in a Finder window. Figure 6.5 shows an example of an application icon that takes full advantage of Mac OS X's ability to display 128×128-pixel, high-definition icons. Although the alias arrow is easy to spot in this example, the arrow isn't as clearly defined in some others.

GraphicConverter

Figure 6.5
A well-designed application icon, such as the one for GraphicConverter, makes it easy to distinguish an alias from the original.

As mentioned earlier, alias icons can be moved to any available folder on the same volume without losing the link they maintain to the original file. This is the magic of aliases and the key to their utility. No matter where files are moved on the volume, the links are maintained.

Original files can also be moved, as long as they remain on the same volume, and they can be renamed without breaking the link with their aliases. When the alias icon is opened, the Mac OS finds and opens the original file.

To illustrate how this automatic linkage is maintained, create an empty folder called *BigFiles* in your home folder. Next, create an alias of this folder, move the alias into the Documents folder, and rename the alias *SmallFiles*.

Later, you decide that this folder will contain only medium-sized files so you change the name of the original folder from *BigFiles* to *MediumFiles* and move the folder to the Desktop. Now, despite renaming and moving both the original folder *and* the alias to the folder, double-clicking on the *SmallFiles* alias in the Documents folder will open the *MediumFiles* folder on the Desktop.

Advanced Aliasing Concepts

So now you understand the basic concepts of aliases. When you begin using aliases, however, questions may arise, such as: How many aliases can one file have? Is it possible to alias an alias? What happens when an alias's original file is deleted? The answers to these and other questions are as follows:

- *Multiple aliases*—You can create an unlimited number of aliases from a single file, folder, or volume.

- *Aliasing aliases*—Although it is possible to create an alias of an alias, you'd be better off creating the second alias directly from the original file or by copying the first alias. Making an alias of an alias results in a chain of pointing references: The third alias points to the second alias, the second alias points to the first alias, and the first alias points to the original. If you do create a chain and one of the aliases in the chain is later deleted, none of the subsequent aliases will be linked to the original file. To illustrate this problem, create an alias to a file called index.html (the parent alias), then make an alias of the alias (the child alias). If you delete the parent alias and then try to open the child alias, you'll get an error message like the one shown in Figure 6.6.

    When a link has been broken and the Mac OS reports an error, a new parent alias to index.html may be re-created and the link to the file index.html will be restored. If you move the parent alias to the Trash, the child alias will not be accessible, whether or not the Trash is emptied.

- *Deleting aliases*—You can delete aliases the same ways you delete normal files:

    - By dragging the alias to the Trash

    - By selecting the alias and pressing Command+Delete, and then choosing the Empty Trash command (or Shift+Command+Delete)

    Deleting an alias has no effect on the original file, folder, or volume. To access the original parent item of the deleted alias, however, you'll have to locate it manually or create another alias.

6

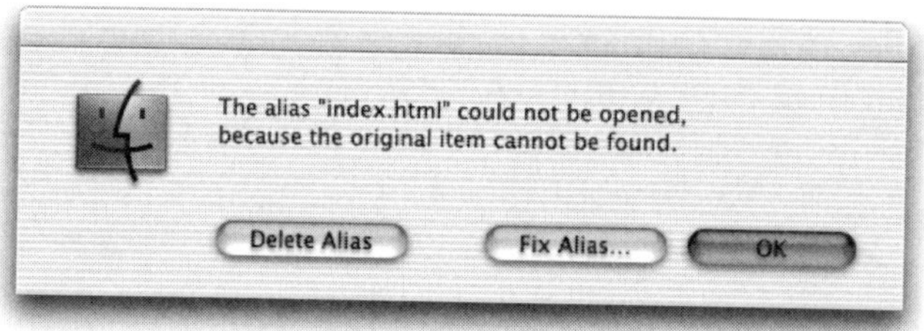

Figure 6.6
Trying to launch an alias that is part of a broken chain of aliases results in an error message.

■ *Moving original files*—Moving an original file within a single volume does not affect the link between that file and its alias. However, copying the original file to a new volume and then deleting that file destroys the link. In other words, you can't transfer the alias link from an original file to a copy of the original file.

If you move a parent file from one volume to another and delete the original file, all aliases created from that file become invalid.

■ *Deleting original files*—Deleting an original file has no immediate effect—you don't even get a warning about breaking the link between the file and its alias. When you try to open an alias of a file that's been deleted, however, a dialog box informs you that the original file cannot be found.

■ *Finding original files*—In order to accomplish tasks such as deleting the original file or copying the original onto a removable disk or cartridge, you'll first need to find the original file. To locate the original file for any alias, select the alias in the Finder and choose one of the following options:

■ Select Show Original from the Finder's File menu.

■ Press Command+R.

■ Press Command+I or select File|Show Info and click the Select New Original button in the General Information section of the Info window. Figure 6.7 shows the path information for an original item—not the alias itself—as seen through the alias's Info window. If the selected item is an alias of an alias, the Mac OS will find the original file, not the alias used to create the current alias.

■ *Replacing alias icons*—As mentioned in Chapter 4, a new icon can be pasted into the Info window for any file, including an aliased file. Replacing the icon of an alias has no effect on the icon of the original file.

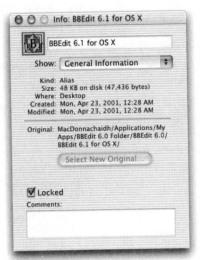

Figure 6.7
The General Information section of the Info window reveals the path to the original of an alias.

Aliasing Folders or Volumes

If you can create aliases for files and applications, you'll have no problem creating aliases for folders and volumes. Folder aliases are created, renamed, repositioned, deleted, and linked to their originals in exactly the same way as the file aliases previously described:

- Aliasing a folder creates a new folder icon with the same name as the original.

- The name of an aliased folder appears with a small arrow when viewed on the Desktop, in a Finder window, or in a dialog box.

- Folder aliases can be renamed at any time, and only one alias can have the same name as an original while in the same folder or on the Desktop.

- Folder aliases can be located inside any other folder.

- When an aliased folder is double-clicked, the original folder is opened in a Finder window. Aliasing a folder does not alias the folder's content. For this reason, the original folder must be available whenever the folder alias is opened. If the original folder is located on a volume that's not currently mounted, the Mac OS will attempt to mount the volume over the network.

- Deleting a folder alias does not delete the original folder or any of its contents.

Folder aliases have a few unique aspects, however:

■ When a folder alias is displayed within a list window, it cannot be opened hierarchically (no triangle appears to its left) because, strictly speaking, the folder alias has no content to display. You can open the folder alias in a new Finder window by double-clicking on it. However, when viewed as a column, an aliased folder displays its contents. Figure 6.8 illustrates the differences between an alias in a list view (top) and a column view (bottom).

■ Anything put into a folder alias—including files, folders, and other aliases—is actually placed into the original folder. The folder alias has no real contents; it's just another "door" to the original folder.

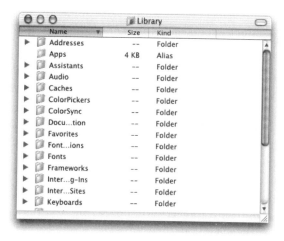

Figure 6.8
Aliased folders displayed in a list view (top) and a column view (bottom).

Volume aliases are similar to file aliases, but have some of the same characteristics as folder aliases:

■ Opening a volume alias mounts the original volume. If the original volume is not already mounted, Mac OS X will attempt to mount it.

■ Opening a volume alias displays the Finder window of the actual volume.

■ Aliasing a volume aliases the *icon* of the volume itself—not the contents of the volume.

Using Aliases

Aliases have a multitude of uses as shortcuts. The following are some of the more interesting possibilities:

■ *Alias applications*—The easiest way to launch an application is to double-click on its icon. Many applications are stored in folders containing a morass of ancillary files, such as dictionaries, color palettes, Help files, and printer descriptions. Amid all this clutter, it's difficult to locate the application icon in order to launch it. The most straightforward way to simplify application launching is to alias each of your applications inside a folder, then drag that folder to the Dock. You can then launch an application by simply choosing its alias from the Dock. For example, Figure 6.9 shows the Apps folder from Figure 6.3 accessed from the Dock. You can also put application aliases, along with groups of documents created with the application, on your Desktop. Because double-clicking on any document will launch the application anyway, this is not really very useful.

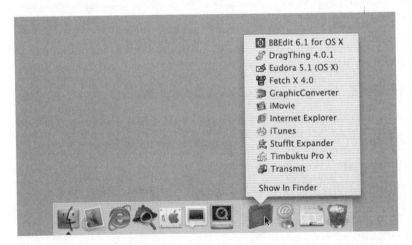

Figure 6.9
A collection of aliases in the Dock provides easy access to your favorite applications, documents, or servers.

- *Multiple data file aliases*—Use aliases to store each data file in as many places as it logically fits—anywhere you might look for the file when you need it later.

- *Removable cartridge maps*—Create a folder for each removable cartridge, drive, or floppy disk. Alias the entire contents of these volumes and store the aliases in the volume's folder. Then you can "browse" these volumes without mounting them. You may also want to keep other aliases of files from these volumes in other locations on your drive.

- *Network file server volume maps*—Create a folder called Servers and place an alias of each remote volume in it. You can then log on to any remote volume by simply double-clicking on the volume alias. This eliminates the need to access the Connect To Server command and locate the file server and volume every time you want to use the volume. Of course, you'll be prompted for any required passwords.

Aliasing Summary

Aliases have many uses and can provide valuable shortcuts, including the following:

- You can alias any file, folder, volume.

- To create an alias, select the desired icon and choose Make Alias from the Finder's File menu, press Command+L, choose Make Alias from the contextual pop-up menu, or drag and drop an icon while holding down the Option and Command keys.

- An alias takes the same name as its original file unless multiple copies of the same target file are created in the same folder on the Desktop.

- Alias names no longer appear in italics, but continue to use a small arrow as a visual clue.

- Aliases can be renamed at any time. The same naming limitations apply to aliases as to files and folders (a maximum of 256 characters).

- Aliases can be moved to any location on the same volume.

- An alias is initially given the same icon as its original. The icon can be changed in the Show Info window.

- An alias requires a very small amount of storage space.

- The link between an alias and its original is maintained even when the original is renamed or repositioned, but not when it is moved to another volume.

- Deleting an alias icon has no effect on its original file, folder, or volume.

- Copying an alias to a new location on the current drive (hold down the Option key while dragging) is the same as creating a new alias of the original file—it does not create an alias of an alias.

- Press Command+R after selecting an alias to locate its original, or choose Show Original from the File menu.

- Opening a folder alias opens the window of the original folder.

- Opening a volume alias opens the window of the original volume.

Working with Sherlock

Regardless of how well organized your electronic filing system is, it's sometimes impossible to remember where specific files are located because many Macs have tens of thousands of files. To solve this problem in the past, Apple provided the Find File desk accessory to enable you to search for files—by file name—on any mounted volume. Find File located the files and listed them in a section of its window. Once a file was found, selecting the file name revealed the path of the file along with other basic file information. Sherlock, introduced in Mac OS 8.5, was a dramatic improvement. In Mac OS X, Sherlock continues to evolve into a more powerful application that allows you to find much more than just files on your hard drive.

Sherlock Basics

Sherlock is accessed via the Find command in the File menu; the program itself is in the Applications menu. Sherlock functions in very much the same way it does in Mac OS 9.1, and allows you to perform three types of searches:

- Finding files on local or networked volumes

- Finding words and phrases in locally indexed volumes (commonly referred to as a full-text search)

- Searching popular Web sites over the Internet using several categories, including general Internet, news, people, reference, and shopping

Sherlock is launched by selecting File|Find or pressing Command+F, which opens a Sherlock window similar to the one in Figure 6.10. Sherlock's default type of search is the traditional search by file name, which I'll discuss in detail a little later.

TIP Sherlock opens the results of each search in the same window instead of a separate window, as with the previous version of Sherlock. Press Command+N or select File|New Window to open a second search window.

Figure 6.10
Sherlock's default search window.

Searching for Files

When the File Names option is selected, Sherlock defaults to a "simple search" window, which allows you to search for files whose names contain the characters in the text entry field. You can ask Sherlock to do a very complex search as well. I'll get into that in just a moment, but for now let's start with the basics. Using the basic File Names option to locate files or folders by name, you can enter the complete name or any portion of the name of the item for which you are searching. Your options include:

■ *Choose a source to search*—Check the sources you would like to search, such as the entire Mac OS X volume, or perhaps just the contents of your home folder. If you want to search just a specific folder, such as your Music folder, open your home folder and drag the Music folder to the section of the Sherlock application window listing the available sources, then check only the Music folder, as in Figure 6.11. You may also select a specific folder using the Find|Add Folder command.

■ *Enter a complete name*—If you know the complete name of the item you're looking for, enter it into the search field. Bear in mind that the correct file may not be found if you make even a slight error in spelling the file name.

Figure 6.11
Drag and drop a specific folder in Sherlock to search that folder.

■ *Enter only the first portion of a name*—Entering the first few characters of the title you're searching for is the most common—and usually the most efficient—file name search method. This locates all files whose names contain the characters you've specified. The exact number of characters you should enter will depend on the circumstances; the goal is to enter enough characters to narrow the search, but not so many that you risk a spelling error and therefore risk missing the file.

For example, if the file you wanted to locate is named *Archaeology Report*, specifying only the letter A would yield a huge number of files to sort through. On the other hand, entering six or seven characters could allow file names with spelling errors, such as Archio or Arhcae, to escape the search. Decide on the number of characters according to how common the first few characters are among your files, and how well you remember the file name. In this example, searching for files starting with Arc would probably be the best strategy.

After specifying the search criteria, click the Search button (with the magnifying glass) to start the search. The search begins with the first source selected and proceeds to search any other sources you specify (more on that in a minute). If the search seems likely to take more than a few seconds, an animated progress bar will appear to let you know that Sherlock is working on the search, and the Items Found section to the left of the status bar will update you every few seconds on how many files it has found thus far. The search results are displayed in the results area of the window, as in Figure 6.12, which shows a search for any item on the boot drive MacDonnachaidh that contains the word *Apple*. Note that the search term is not case sensitive—both *Apple* and *apple* are returned in the results window.

Figure 6.12
Searching for files containing *Apple* using Sherlock.

Note that the results area is divided into two parts. The upper part lists the search results, which may be viewed by name, kind, date modified (but not date created), or size. To change the view, just click on Name, Kind, Date Modified, or Size to sort the search results. You can also resize the columns to make them wider or narrower.

The path to an item is displayed in the lower half of the Items Found section. For example, the first item displayed in Figure 6.12 is a folder named *apple*, which is located in the /MacDonnachaidh/System/Library/Java/com/ path.

To open an item after it has been found by Sherlock, just double-click on it in either the upper or lower portion of the Items Found section of the window or click on the file and press Command+O. To open the item's enclosing folder or volume, press Command+E. See the File menu for additional options.

After you've executed a search, use the File commands and drag-and-drop capabilities of the Mac OS to accomplish various tasks with selections in the Found Items dialog box. These tasks include:

- *Opening the item's window*—Press Command+E to open the item's enclosing folder, or select the Open Enclosing Folder command from the File menu.

- *Moving the file*—Drag the file or folder name to a new location. The item actually moves to where you've dragged it. When you drag the item to another disk, however, it is copied rather than actually relocated.

- *Opening the file*—Double-clicking on a folder, or pressing Command+O with a folder selected, will open the folder. The same actions will open a selected file if the application that created the file is available. You can also drag the file name to an application. If it's not already running—and if it can open this type of file—the application will launch itself and then open the file.

- *Printing the file*—If the item is a file, press the familiar Command+P combination to print the file.

If the selected file is not the one you wanted, or if after modifying the selected file you want to continue searching for the next file that matches the search criteria, choose Command+F to return to the Find File window.

> Once you have completed a search, the Items Found window will remain open until you quit Sherlock, even if you perform an additional search or close the main Sherlock window.

Advanced File Searches

With Sherlock, you can create and save custom searches for a wide variety of criteria. The Custom menu includes several default custom searches, including searches that look on your hard drive for applications, files larger than 1MB, and files that were last modified today or yesterday. You can customize this pop-down menu to include custom searches that best suit your needs. To create your own custom search, select Edit from the Custom pop-down menu or choose Find|More Options. A window such as the one in Figure 6.13 will appear.

To explain all of the possible search variations would take at least five pages, so I'll just summarize the main options:

- File Name Contains, Starts With, Ends With, Is, Is Not, or Doesn't Contain *XYZ*

- Content Includes *XYZ* (more on content searches in a minute)

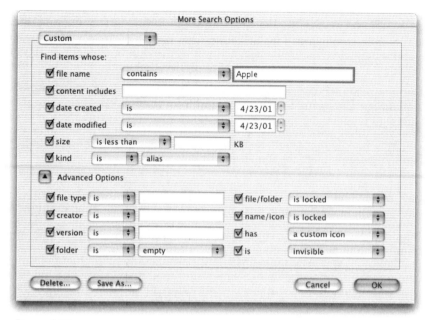

Figure 6.13
Creating a custom search in Sherlock.

■ Date Created Is, Is Before, Is After, or Is Not *XYZ*

■ Date Modified Is, Is Before, Is After, or Is Not *XYZ*

■ Size Is Less Than or Greater Than *XYZ*

■ Kind Is or Is Not Alias, Application, Clipping File, etc.

And if these options aren't enough, Sherlock offers even more advanced custom search options:

■ File Type Is or Is Not *XYZ*

■ Creator Is or Is Not *XYZ*

■ Version Is or Is Not *XYZ*

■ Folder Is or Is Not Empty, Shared, or Mounted

■ File/Folder Is Locked or Unlocked

■ Name/Icon Is Locked or Unlocked

■ Has A Custom Icon or No Custom Icon

■ Is Invisible or Visible

Once you have created a custom search, click on the OK button to execute the search. For example, Figure 6.14 shows the results of a custom search on the Mac OS X startup drive for all items with custom icons.

After completing a custom search, you can save the search criteria in one of two ways. First, you can go to the File menu, choose Save Search Criteria, and save it to a file on your hard drive. The second method is to go back to the Custom search window and then click on the Save button; the search will be saved in the Custom pop-down menu, an example of which is shown in Figure 6.15.

The OS creates a small file when you choose to save the search criteria to disk. Double-clicking on this file causes the search criteria to be automatically entered into a new Sherlock window and executed.

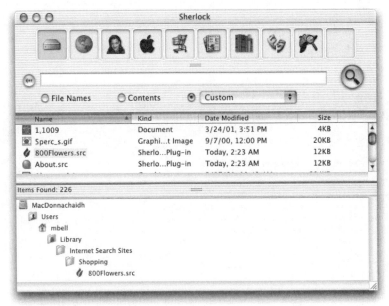

Figure 6.14
The results of a custom search.

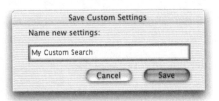

Figure 6.15
Save your custom searches for future reference.

Finding by Content

With Sherlock, you can search a volume for specific words within documents—not just the name of a document itself. This is also commonly referred to as a full-text search, and it's helpful in more ways than you might think. For example, how else could you find a specific piece of information without opening every document on your computer? In order to perform a full-text search, you must first index the contents of the volumes you want to search. This can take a long time on the initial indexing session. Subsequent sessions are fairly quick because Sherlock only reads and indexes documents whose modification dates have changed since the last index was processed. Figure 6.16 shows an example of a search for the word *Macintosh*.

To search for a word or phrase by content, follow these steps:

1. Launch Sherlock from the File menu while in the Finder, or by pressing Command+F.

2. Select the Contents button.

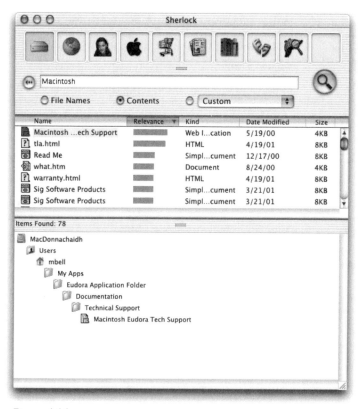

Figure 6.16
An example of a full-text search.

3. Enter a word or phrase in the text entry field.

4. Select the name of the area to search—either an item selected in the Finder or a location that has already been indexed (more on that next).

5. Press the Search button.

The search results are displayed in the results portion of the window, which is similar to that of the File Names search, but with the addition of a Relevance ranking column.

Before you can perform a full-text search, however, you must first index your volumes. Indexing is very easy:

1. Open Sherlock.

2. Check the On box beside an item that has been indexed or is indexable. Note that the Mac OS X startup volume cannot be indexed because it may contain files belonging to other users.

3. Choose Index Now from the Find menu to update the index, if necessary.

4. To automatically index items that are selected with a checkmark in the On column, go to the Sherlock|Preferences menu and choose Automatically Index Items When Sherlock Is Opened, as shown in Figure 6.17.

The initial indexing could take quite a while, depending on how much data is stored on your drives. Reindexing is usually very quick, however, so automatic indexing usually only takes a short time and prevents you from having to manually reindex items.

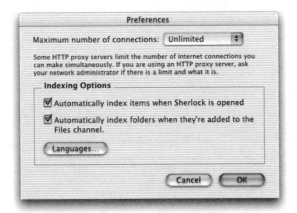

Figure 6.17
Automatic indexing items for content-based (full-text) searches can save you from manually indexing items prior to each search.

To speed up the time it takes to index items using Sherlock, disable the indexing of unnecessary languages in the Sherlock|Preferences menu.

Searching the Internet

The beauty of Sherlock is that it allows you to search multiple Web sites at the same time—directly from your Desktop. You'll still need a Web browser to open the results of your search, however. Mac OS X comes with the ability to search more than two dozen Web sites with several channels of sites, including news, people, reference, and shopping Web sites. As Sherlock's Internet searching capability continues to gain speed, more sites will create the necessary plug-in for Sherlock that enables this type of search. We'll see how this works in just a minute, but for now take a quick look at Figure 6.18, which shows a sample search of the Internet channel for the phrase *Power Macintosh*.

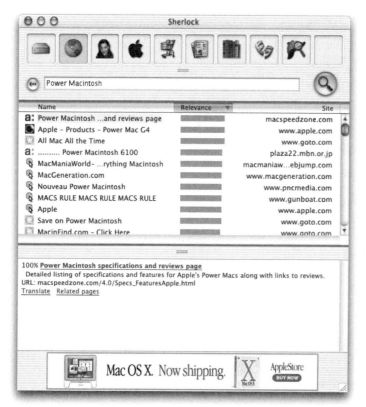

Figure 6.18
Searching the Internet with Sherlock.

To perform an Internet search:

1. Launch Sherlock and select an Internet-related category by clicking on one of the channel icons, such as Internet, People, or Shopping, across the top of the Sherlock window beneath the title bar.

2. Enter some search terms in the text entry field.

3. Click on the Search button.

Although the results window resembles those resulting from Sherlock's other search methods, it lists only the name of the site where the document resides, the relevance of each item returned by the search, and the URL of the site containing the document. In the lower portions of the window Sherlock lists an overview of the document found and any advertisement associated with that page. When you single-click on one of the items, Sherlock will load some basic information about it, such as a banner ad from the site (if it has one), the URL, and the relevance of the item. To go to a particular item using a Web browser, double-click on the item in the Items Found window or single-click on the item in the preview area of the Items Found window.

To enhance the number of Internet-related Web sites Sherlock is capable of searching, visit the Sherlock Plug-In Directory at **www.apple.com/Sherlock/** and follow the directions to locate and download additional plug-ins. You can also add new Internet channels in Sherlock by going to the Channels menu and selecting New Channel, which brings up the window shown in Figure 6.19. Then follow these steps:

1. Give the new channel a name.

2. Choose an icon for the channel.

3. Choose the type of channel from the drop-down menu of predefined channel types.

Figure 6.19
Creating a new channel in Sherlock.

4. Give the channel a description.

5. Click on OK.

6. Download some Sherlock plug-ins from the Internet or choose from the search sites located in the <*home*>/Library/Internet Search Sites/ folder using the Channels|Add Search Site command.

It's OK to have the same search sites in more than one channel. Also, any customizations you make to Sherlock's channels will not affect the Sherlock features of other users on your computer because each user's preferences are saved in that user's directory structure.

Tips for Effective Searches

Here are a few tips to help you create effective searches using Sherlock:

- *You can use Find to locate aliases as well as original items.* Aliases will appear with the small arrow in the Found Items window and will be listed as *alias* in the Kind column.

- *Find also locates folders and volumes.* Like any other file, any folder or volume matching the specified search criteria will be found.

- *Create a custom search to locate all data files created by one specific application or with a particular file extension.* For instance, you can find all your HTML documents by creating a custom search for .html.

- *Use Find to do quick backups.* After you've used Sherlock to locate all files modified after a certain date, you can drag those files to a removable volume for a "quick-and-dirty" backup. Of course, this procedure shouldn't replace a reliable backup utility—but you can never have too many backups.

- *Use a custom search to perform multiple-criteria searches.* For example, the Sherlock search engine can locate all file names beginning with S that are less than 32KB in size and have the Microsoft Word creator type (or any other set of multiple criteria).

- *Use the content search feature to search your computer for detailed information, such as names and addresses of friends or business contacts sent to you by email.* Sherlock will index the data of almost all the popular email clients, such as Mail and Eudora.

- *Use Sherlock to search the Internet instead of opening up a connection to a specific Web search engine site, which limits your search to that engine only.* Leverage Sherlock's capacity for searching multiple sites simultaneously.

Using Comments

A comment is a string of text that you may enter for most items in the Finder using the Show Info command. Earlier versions of the Mac OS allowed users to assign Finder labels as well as comments; because Mac OS X (version 10.0.3) only partially supports labels, comments are the only way for you to categorize files and folders and sort them from within list-style windows using a customized set of criteria. The Comments column option, found in the View|Show View Options preferences, enables you to show or hide comments in list windows. When selected, the comments column will display in Finder windows viewed as lists (but not as icons or columns). Comments can also serve as a notes field in which you can jot down a few words describing the item.

You'll discover a variety of productive ways to apply the comment features. Using comments as cues is one possibility—keywords or phrases can provide information (such as client names, project titles, and names of related documents) beyond what is already included in the standard information about a file (file name, date, kind, and so on). Many shareware developers design their programs to automatically add a comment, including the author's URL, to any file created with their products.

In Mac OS 9.1, for example, I often assign the numbers one through seven to Finder labels so that I can sort the contents of a folder according to my own preferences rather than by the usual options (name, date modified, size, and so on). In Mac OS X, I can assign to each file a comment in the form of the numbers one through seven to achieve the same effect. Figure 6.20 shows a folder containing several HTML and Lasso documents before I've assigned comments (top) and after comments have been added and the list window sorted by comment (bottom).

Using this method, I can easily group certain files together and pick them out of a list at a glance.

Compressing and Encrypting Files

Even with today's multigigibyte hard drives, compressing files is still a necessity because many files must be compressed before they travel over the Internet. This is especially true if you want to send a folder containing several files; sending all of the files in the form of one compressed medium-sized file is more efficient than sending numerous small files. Because files that are stored on Hierarchical File System Plus (HFS+) volumes contain both a data fork and a resource fork, it's easy for the files to get "munged" by alien operating systems that don't know what to do with the resource fork. File compression can help eliminate the issue of a resource fork by encoding your data into a flat file with only one fork.

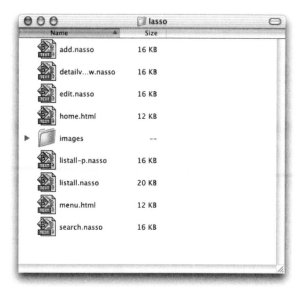

Figure 6.20
A Finder window as it appears before (top) and after (bottom) the comments column is used to create a custom sort of the window.

Like compressing, encrypting files is a valuable skill to possess in today's computing environment. If your Mac is ever connected to the Internet, you will expose yourself to some risk of being hacked.

The initial version of Mac OS X lacks the ability to compress or encrypt files. Fortunately, Aladdin Systems' venerable StuffIt line of tools is ready to fill the void.

DropStuff is an inexpensive utility for encrypting and compressing files into a variety of formats; StuffIt Expander is the freeware decompression utility that is installed automatically as part of Mac OS X. If you want even greater capabilities, you can purchase the complete StuffIt Deluxe package, which includes:

■ StuffIt Deluxe application (compression, decompression, encryption, and so on)

■ DropStuff (compression)

■ StuffIt Expander (decompression)

■ DropZip (compression for Microsoft Windows operating systems)

If you have limited compression needs, you can probably get by with DropStuff and StuffIt Expander. For the intermediate to advanced user, however, StuffIt Deluxe is an essential tool.

Compressing and Encrypting Files with DropStuff

Because DropStuff fully supports drag and drop, you can select items for compression and/or encryption by dropping them onto the DropStuff application or alias. Of course, you can also use the Stuff command from the File menu. Before compressing or encrypting any files it's a good idea to review the DropStuff|Preferences options first. Figure 6.21 illustrates my preferred configuration of DropStuff for everyday use.

The Stuffing section of the DropStuff preferences allows you to select several features, including the option to delete the original after compressing it. This keeps you from ending up with two versions—compressed and uncompressed—of a file or group of files.

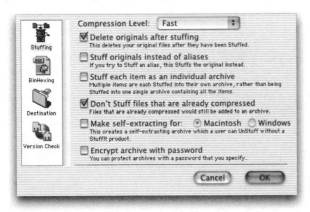

Figure 6.21
Review DropStuff's preferences before using it to compress or encrypt files.

To encrypt a file with a password, check the Encrypt Archive With Password option; the next time you compress a file, a password dialog box will appear. Once you enter or generate a password using the Generate Random button, you will be prompted to reenter the password as a safety measure. Figure 6.22 shows an example of a randomly generated password.

Figure 6.22
Use DropStuff's encryption capabilities to secure important data.

The other preferences for DropStuff allow you to BinHex a file for safe passage across single-forked file systems; specify the location for storing files once they've been compressed and encrypted; and automatically check for new versions of DropStuff.

Decompressing and Decrypting Files with StuffIt Expander

Mac OS X installs StuffIt Expander in the Utilities folder. StuffIt Expander performs the reverse duties of DropStuff, allowing compressed and encrypted files to be expanded and decrypted, resource fork and all. It has several additional preferences that specify what types of files may be processed and how compressed files should be handled. Figure 6.23 shows a few of the many configuration options for StuffIt Expander.

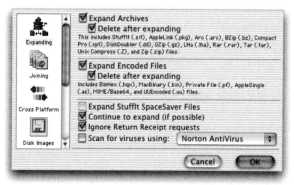

Figure 6.23
A few of StuffIt Expander's many decompression options.

StuffIt Expander, which is capable of decompressing about a zillion file formats, is probably the only decompression tool you'll ever need. In addition to the native StuffIt format files (.sit and .sea), StuffIt Expander is also capable of decompressing the following formats:

■ A to B (.btoa)

■ AppleLink Package (.pkg)

■ AppleSingle (.as)

■ Arc (.arc)

■ BinHex (.hqx)

■ Bzip (.bzip)

■ Compact Pro (.cpt)

■ Disk images (.img and .smi)

■ DiskDoubler (.dd)

■ GZip (.gz and .tgz)

■ LHa (.lha, .lzh)

■ MacBinary (.bin)

■ MIME/Base 64 (.mime)

■ Private File (.pf)

■ RAR (.rar)

■ TAR (.tar)

■ Unix Compress (.z and .taz)

■ UU (.uu, .uue, and .enc)

■ Zip (.zip)

And like DropStuff, StuffIt Expander is capable of checking for updates automatically.

Wrapping Up

We all suffer from info-glut. With so many files, folders, and applications crowding our hard drives, we need all the organization help we can get. To make shortcuts and search and organize our data, Mac OS X has several useful options and features:

- Mac OS X uses a new file structure designed with multiple users in mind.

- Aliases help you locate and launch files, and allow you to access network data quickly and easily.

- The Sherlock search engine will solve your "where is that file?" problem.

- Comments remind you of details about the contents of a particular file or folder, and make it possible to organize your files in highly customizable sorting orders.

- DropStuff and StuffIt Expander enable you to compress and password-encrypt your files.

Next, we'll look at the special software and features available for users who are running Mac OS X on PowerBooks and iBooks.

Take X (on the Road)

Mac OS X is probably the first Unix-based operating system designed to be used equally—and with remarkably few behavioral differences—by workstations, servers, and mobile computers. If you're accustomed to working with Mac OS X on an iMac, for example, you'd be equally comfortable using the same operating system on a Titanium PowerBook. Whereas PowerBook and iBook hardware still differs considerably from desktop hardware in certain respects, the components of the OS itself are pretty much the same from machine to machine. This consistency makes it easier for users of different Mac models to learn the operating system. In fact, as far as mobile users are concerned, the only down side to Mac OS X is the loss of several PowerBook user interface features that were part of previous versions of the OS. Fortunately, numerous Mac OS X software developers have created some useful applications to fill the void.

In the early days of the PowerBook, Apple provided a suite of simple utilities for controlling the PowerBook's basic functions, such as controlling screen display, measuring battery lifetimes, and performing processor cycling. Sensing an opportunity, many vendors rushed in and substantially improved upon Apple's meager offerings with packages like Claris's Power To Go, Connectix's CPU, Norton's Essentials for the PowerBook, and Inline Design's PBTools, to name a few. Some of these improvements, such as the Control Strip, were eventually incorporated into the Mac OS as a standard feature for all Mac users. Whether you have the latest Titanium PowerBook or iBook, you'll certainly be able to get by with the standard features of Mac OS X; however, the addition of several third-party utilities will make your computing life even better.

Mac OS X will run on any PowerBook or iBook introduced after September 1998. See **www.info.apple.com/applespec/applespec.taf** for a database of all Apple hardware that includes information on the date each product was introduced.

What's Missing in Mac OS X?

A few small features of Mac OS 9.1 that were of particular importance for PowerBook and iBook users didn't make it into Mac OS X. These missing features addressed such concerns as conserving battery life and working with a small screen. Although the newer portables continue to close the performance and usability gap between portable and non-portable Macs, the loss of the following features formerly provided by various Control Panels and keyboard shortcuts will be noticeable. In parentheses beside the name of each missing feature is the name of the Control Panel or item that provided the feature:

- Control Strip (Control Strip)
- Separate settings for battery and power adapter (Energy Saver)
- Processor cycling (Energy Saver)
- Reducing processor speed (Energy Saver)
- Remounting servers upon waking (Energy Saver)
- Screen dimming (Energy Saver)
- Turning off power to inactive PCMCIA cards (Energy Saver)
- File synchronization (File Synchronization)
- Infrared networking (Infrared)
- Launcher (Launcher)
- RAM disk (Memory)
- Password protection (Password Security)
- SCSI support (PowerBook SCSI Setup)
- Volume control (keyboard buttons)

Mac OS X provides some new features to make up for the loss of at least a few additional components of earlier versions of the Mac OS. For example, Mac OS 9.1's Location Manager, Modem, and Remote Access Control Panels have been replaced in functionality by the Networking System Preferences pane. The Battery Monitor is now located in the Dock, and the configuration options found in the old Trackpad Control Panel are now in the Mouse System Preferences pane. Workarounds for a few other missing features, such as password protection and the Control Strip, are discussed later in this chapter.

Portability Issues

Beginning with the Apple Portable (1989) and then the Apple PowerBook 100 (1991)—the most successful introduction of any family of portable computers of its time—Apple has had a string of successes with virtually all of its PowerBooks, especially with the Titanium PowerBook. The PowerBook has replaced the desktop machine as the computer of choice for millions of Macintosh users. Over the years, system software support for the PowerBook series has been fortified; now, with the 500MHz Titanium iBook or 500MHz G4 PowerBook, laptop users can enjoy the same benefits from Mac OS X and its enhancements that desktop users do.

Macintosh users who rely on portables have several unique needs that set them apart from users of workstations and servers because of issues relating to mobility and the special features found in their computers. Although Mac OS X is essentially the same on a PowerBook or a G4 workstation, portable users face the following needs:

- *Battery recharging*—Portables can run on AC power or rechargeable batteries. To reduce power consumption and thereby extend use, Mac OS X supports several energy-saving capabilities, including reducing screen brightness, spinning down the hard drive, and putting the entire computer to sleep.

- *Presentation services*—Portables can easily connect to external displays, ranging from monitors to a variety of projectors or presentation devices. A video output port is a standard feature of many models, as is video mirroring.

- *Saving print documents for later printing*—For most Carbon and Cocoa applications, you can save a document as a PDF document for later printing.

- *Supports device input*—Keyboards, trackballs, trackpads, and other input devices are supported, as with any desktop Mac.

Although very few up-to-date books about PowerBooks exist, you can always find plenty of information on the Web at the following URLs:

- Apple Computer's iBook site—**www.apple.com/ibook/**

- Apple Computer's PowerBook site—**www.apple.com/powerbook/**

- Jason O'Grady's PowerPage—**www.go2mac.com**

- PowerBook Army—**www.powerbook.org** (outdated, but good archives)

- The PowerBook Guy—**www.powerbookguy.com**

- The PowerBook Source—**www.pbsource.com**

The PowerBook Source Web site, shown in Figure 7.1, really stands out. Visit this site frequently for the latest scoop on PowerBooks, iBooks, software, and hardware.

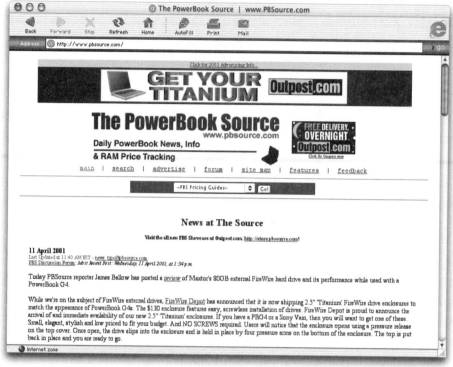

Figure 7.1
The PowerBook Source Web site is popular for PowerBook and iBook users.

Managing Power and Performance

Some models of PowerBooks and iBooks consume more power than others, depending largely on differences in processor speed and the type of display. The power consumption of portable Macs is a major portability issue, particularly for users with CD-ROM and DVD-ROM drives (which consume more battery power). Luckily, Mac OS X employs several techniques to reduce power consumption through the Energy Saver System Preferences pane, shown in Figure 7.2, which is accessed from the Apple menu.

The Energy Saver can't distinguish when your computer is running on battery—which is when energy conservation is most important—and when it is plugged into the AC adapter. However, you can configure the Energy Saver to conserve battery life by sliding the bars to the right or left for the following settings:

■ *Put The System To Sleep When It Is Inactive For*—Puts the entire computer to sleep, including the monitor, hard drive(s), processor, and network interfaces, after it has been inactive for a designated period of time.

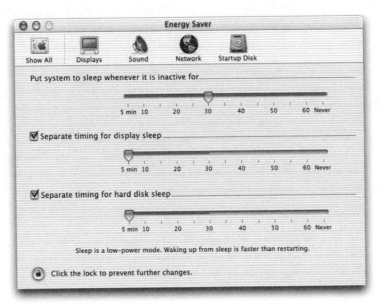

Figure 7.2
The Energy Saver System Preferences.

7

- *Separate Timing For Display Sleep*—Controls the time limit for putting the display to sleep. If this option remains unchecked, the display will go to sleep (turn itself off, instead of dim) at the same time that the computer is set to sleep.

- *Separate Timing For Hard Disk Sleep*—Controls the time limit for putting the hard drive to sleep by stopping it from spinning. The hard disk may also be configured to operate independently from the system and monitor sleep settings.

Although there are no "correct" settings for the Energy Saver configuration options, you may want to keep in mind the following suggestions for optimizing your settings:

- Mac OS X allows a computer in sleep mode to "wake up" very quickly, usually in just a few seconds. My PowerBook wakes up in under three seconds, so it's convenient to put the whole system, and not just the monitor and/or hard disk, to sleep.

- Network connectivity is lost when the entire system goes to sleep, and Mac OS X makes no provision for servers to be remounted upon waking. Perhaps a future version of the Mac OS or a third-party utility will restore this ability.

- Some applications will not function properly if the whole system or parts of the system are in sleep mode. For example, applications (such as calendars) that issue reminders may not work because the internal clock is disabled while asleep. Also, if the monitor is in sleep mode, you will not be able to see any information on screen, although you might hear an alert if the sound is not muted.

- If you have File or Web Sharing enabled, avoid putting the whole system or the disk to sleep. Doing so will disrupt your computer's ability to serve these tasks efficiently.

- Disable speech recognition (in the Speech System Preferences pane) and screen saver (in the Screen Saver System Preferences pane) to further minimize power consumption.

- To prevent any aspect of your computer from going to sleep, configure the Energy Saver System Preferences pane by unchecking all the checkboxes and moving all the sliders over to Never.

Experiment with the various options in the Energy Saver to determine the settings that are best for you. To help gauge your power consumption, you can monitor your battery's performance by viewing the Battery Monitor in the Dock (an example of which is shown in Figure 7.3 when the computer is running on the AC adapter). The Battery Monitor, which provides a general overview of the level of power in your battery, is located in the Dock Extras folder in the main Application folder.

Figure 7.3
The basic view of the Dock's Battery Monitor.

A green icon indicates that the computer is running on battery power. When the mouse hovers over the icon, the Battery Monitor also provides information on the status of the battery. For example, Figure 7.4 shows three views of the Dock with the Battery Monitor recharging and almost full (top), fully charged and running on the AC adapter (middle), and running on battery (bottom).

This system of measuring voltage levels is accurate and reliable—as far as it goes. What voltage measurements don't tell you, though, is how much time your battery has left. For that indicator, you need to know the lowest voltage level your battery will drop to, your instantaneous power consumption, and your history of power consumption. Variables such as which battery you're using, memory effects, and unusual power consumption activities make learning about your battery's life a difficult proposition. So bear in mind that the power warnings only tell you voltage levels, not how much energy remains in a battery or exactly how long you have before you run out of juice. It will only estimate how much time remains.

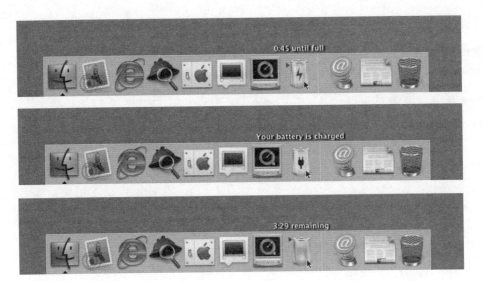

Figure 7.4
The Battery Monitor provides information when the mouse hovers over its icon in the Dock.

Accurate measurement of battery life is so valuable that some batteries contain microprocessors to help calculate performance and give more accurate measurements in the Battery Monitor. The PowerPC processor itself uses about 25 percent of your battery's current. The display is another major power draw; depending on its type, it can consume anywhere from 20 percent to 50 percent of your power supply. Display issues are covered in the next section of this chapter, "Managing Displays."

During sleep, your hard drive spins down, your screen is powered off, and your micro-processor is in a comatose-like state. You can safely transport your portable, or store it for short periods of time, while it is asleep. Depending on the model, your PowerBook or iBook can retain the contents of its short-term memory for two weeks in this state. However, the amount of memory that needs to be refreshed is a major variable in this equation; large amounts of RAM require additional battery power to maintain memory contents during sleep.

In Mac OS X, you have several ways of manually putting your PowerBook or iBook to sleep:

■ Choose the Sleep command from the Apple menu.

■ Set the period of inactivity necessary for automatic hard drive spindown in the Energy Saver System Preferences pane.

■ Press the Power key on the keyboard and click the Sleep button (or press the letter S on the keyboard).

To wake up your Macintosh, press any key other than the Caps Lock key.

Your hard drive consumes, on average, about 15 percent of your battery power. You can improve the hard drive's power consumption with any of the following methods:

■ Use memory-resident (RAM) applications that don't require much I/O.

■ Set the period of inactivity necessary for automatic hard drive spindown in the Energy Saver System Preferences pane.

Don't get too carried away with keeping your hard drive spun down. The energy expended in spinning up a hard drive is equivalent to something like 30 to 60 seconds of the hard drive spinning at its rated speed. For the spin-down feature to be valuable, you would need to be in situations in which you don't access the disk more often than every two or three minutes.

Because AppleTalk perpetually polls the selected port (usually an Ethernet port) for activity, keeping it active while your computer is asleep may also drain power. You can turn AppleTalk on and off in the AppleTalk section of the Network System Preferences pane.

Managing Displays

The capacity for connecting an external monitor is one of the best features of a PowerBook. (Only the latest Titanium iBooks support external video at this time.) In conjunction with LCD projectors, multiple or external monitors are especially useful for making presentations with your PowerBook. Alternatively, you can make your presentation with a larger monitor, often in conjunction with an external mouse and keyboard. Furthermore, you can augment your PowerBook with a "docking" station that allows you to keep an external monitor, keyboard, and mouse plugged into the computer; this option ensures that your computer recognizes the external monitor automatically when you plug the PowerBook into the dock and then boot up.

Most PowerBook models have built-in video, as well as support for video output ports, signified by the TV-like icon on the back of the PowerBook, called S-video; other models may be supplemented by adding video-out through external devices. The latest PowerBooks utilize an SVGA (36-pin) video output port, which is the standard for Windows-based PCs. An SVGA-to-Mac video adapter that will enable you to connect the video output port to an external Apple-style monitor is supplied with some PowerBooks.

You can plug in a monitor during sleep or at shutdown. When you start up your PowerBook, make sure the external monitor is already powered up. After the startup icons appear on your PowerBook, the Desktop should appear on the external monitor as well as the PowerBook's LCD display. If the Desktop does not appear, shut down the computer, restart after connecting the external monitor, and then open the Displays System Preferences pane and make the appropriate selections. When the external monitor is successfully detected, only one of the two displays will contain the Mac OS X menu bar at the top of the screen. Each screen will have its own configuration options, however, because each display will be physically different from the other and have different display characteristics, such as resolution and bit depth capabilities. For example, Figure 7.5 shows the differences in the Display System Preferences pane for a Sony 200ES 17-inch multiscan display (top) and the built-in LCD display of a PowerBook (bottom).

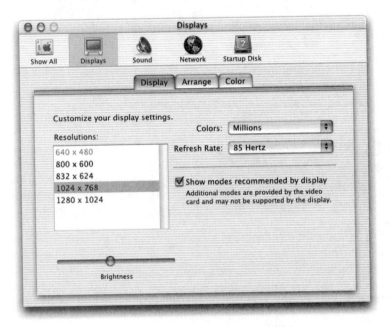

Figure 7.5
The Display settings for an external display (top) and the built-in LCD display for a PowerBook (bottom).

When multiple monitors are in use, only one will have the menu bar. You can decide which display will have the menu bar and serve as the "main" screen by following these steps:

1. Open the System Preferences pane from the Dock or Apple menu.

2. Choose the Displays pane.

3. Select the Arrange tab, as in Figure 7.6.

4. Make any desired changes and quit the System Preferences.

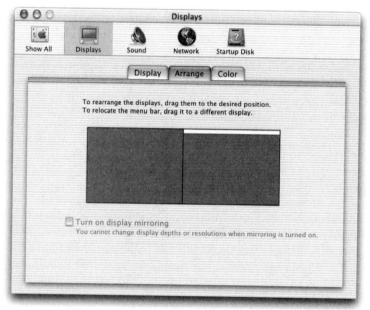

Figure 7.6
Arrange the relative position of an external monitor for a PowerBook using the Arrange tab of the Displays System Preferences pane.

The concept of arranging the two displays is a bit tricky, and even more so to describe here, but let me give it a shot. From your perspective sitting in front of a PowerBook with an external display attached, the two displays can be arranged side-by-side to give the effect of being a single, very wide Desktop on which the mouse can be moved from the far right to the far left. In Figure 7.6, the displays are arranged in this way, with the external monitor's display on the left and the built-in LCD display on the right. The menu bar is positioned on the internal display.

You may reverse the order of the displays by dragging one to the opposite side, or you can even arrange them in a staggered fashion, as in Figure 7.7. The Displays System Preferences pane will not allow you to arrange them as freely as you might like, so

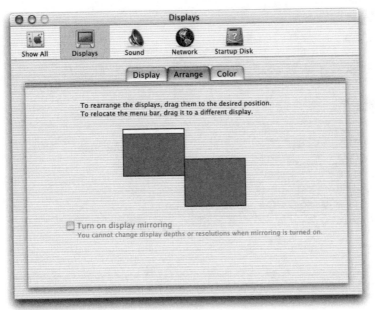

Figure 7.7
Rearrange your displays using the features found in the Arrange tab.

7

you'll have to experiment with repositioning the displays until you come up with a comfortable arrangement.

When working in presentation mode, you may find it convenient to have the display on your external monitor match the one that appears on your PowerBook. This process is called *video mirroring*. To turn on video mirroring:

1. Open the System Preferences from the Dock or Apple menu.

2. Choose the Displays pane.

3. Configure the resolution and bit depth to be the same for each display, such as 1024×768 and thousands of colors.

4. Check the Turn On Video Mirroring option, as shown in Figure 7.8, and quit the System Preferences.

If the Turn On Video Mirroring option is not available, then your PowerBook (or desktop Mac, if a second display card and monitor are available) isn't capable of supporting video mirroring due to a hardware conflict or because the resolution and bit depth are not compatible enough for Mac OS X to support video mirroring.

Finally, you can put your PowerBook into sleep mode when an external monitor is in use only if the external monitor is Energy Star compliant. When the computer is in

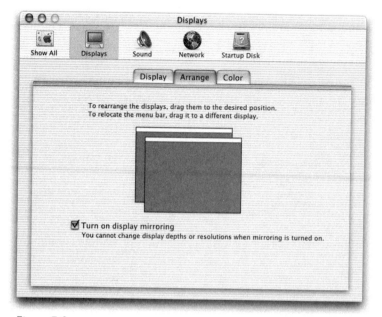

Figure 7.8
Use the video mirroring option to display the same view of the Desktop and Finder on both displays.

sleep mode, the external monitor will go to sleep as well. Monitors that are not compliant will not power down, although the PowerBook's processor and hard drive will.

Changing Locations

As you've noticed, your Mac has a plethora of controls, and many of them change depending on how you are connected to a network. For instance, your office uses an Ethernet-based TCP/IP Internet connection, while at home you use PPP and a dial-up account or TCP/IP and a broadband DSL or cable modem.

Changing all of these settings just to go between office and home can be a major pain, so Apple includes the Locations feature in the Network section of the System Preferences to allow you to easily switch between settings. The Locations feature, the Mac OS X equivalent of the Location Manager in Mac OS 9.1, lets you create a snapshot of only the network settings you use at particular locations, and not for the many other aspects of the Mac OS handled by the old Location Manager, including:

■ AppleTalk & TCP/IP

■ Auto-Open Items

■ Default Printer

- Extension Set

- File Sharing State

- Internet Set

- QuickTime Speed

- Remote Access

- Sound Level

- Time Zone

Even though the Locations features aren't nearly as robust as the old Location Manager, they will allow you to easily switch between locations without requiring a reboot. The Location submenu, found in the Apple menu, is always visible, no matter what application is open at the time. The options under the Location menu (shown in Figure 7.9) allow you to change locations or open the Network System Preferences to edit, add, or delete a location.

7

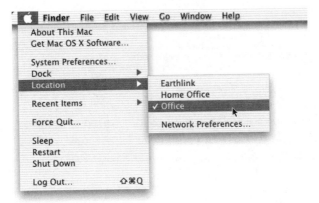

Figure 7.9
Use the Location menu to easily change network locations.

The Location menu also provides a shortcut to the Network System Preferences, where you can edit a location such as a dial-up location for your PowerBook or iBook's internal modem, an example of which is shown in Figure 7.10.

Because most Macs—not just PowerBooks and iBooks—come with an internal modem, please refer to Chapter 16 for information on connecting your laptop or desktop computer to the Internet using the Location feature of the Network System Preferences.

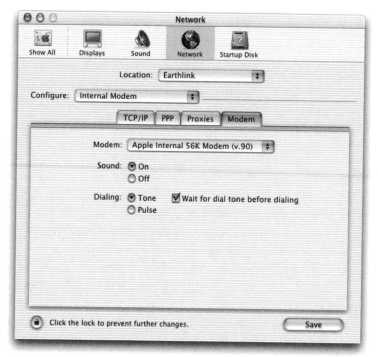

Figure 7.10
Use the Location menu to access your PowerBook or iBook's internal modem settings.

Security

If there's a downside to owning a portable Macintosh, it's that everyone wants to get their grubby paws on yours. Because PowerBooks and iBooks are so fun and cool, it seems that everyone wants to borrow yours—sometimes without asking!

To forestall anyone who tries to boot your computer and poke around, Mac OS X provides a framework around which developers may add authentication services that provide very secure access to network-based lists of users, as well as encryption for passwords traveling across the network. On many corporate and campus networks, for example, the Kerberos authentication method is the preferred way to authenticate users. Mac OS X has a built-in Kerberos module that can be configured to work with most Kerberos-based network environments to match up large lists of usernames and passwords and allow only authorized users to log into a PowerBook, iBook, workstation, or server running Mac OS X.

By disabling a few of the features found in the Login section of the System Preferences (shown in Figure 7.11) and using the password feature of the Screen Saver System Preferences, you can provide a moderate level of protection to your portable

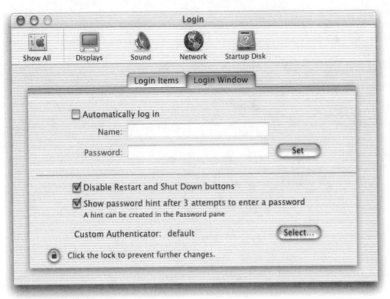

Figure 7.11
Disable automatic login and the restart and shut down options to add additional layers of security to your computer.

7

Mac. Of course, this tip isn't fool-proof if other users have accounts on your computer, or if your PowerBook or iBook has an alternative means of booting, such as a CD-ROM drive or an external FireWire drive. If an additional boot source is present, it is possible to restart the computer and hold down the C key at startup to command the computer to boot from another version of the operating system on the CD-ROM or FireWire drive. Once this is accomplished, all your files are vulnerable to inspection, modification, or deletion.

Because Mac OS X requires a username and password, you can provide some security by following these steps:

1. Open the System Preferences from the Dock or the Apple menu.

2. Switch to the Login pane.

3. Choose the Login Window tab (as in Figure 7.11).

4. Disable the Automatically Log In option.

5. Select the Disable Restart And Shut Down Buttons option.

When your computer is restarted (and until you reenable these options), you will be prompted to enter a username and password at startup, and the Restart and Shut Down buttons will be disabled, as shown in Figure 7.12.

Figure 7.12
Logging into a computer with the Restart and Shut Down buttons disabled.

If you think you may not remember your password, enter a hint in the Password Hint section of your user account information, which is accessed via the Users System Preferences pane. Include only as much information as you're willing to reveal to potential viewers. Avoid hints that are anything like your password—a creative hacker could guess your password based on the hint you have provided.

Finally, you can add an additional layer of security by requiring a password whenever your computer wakes from screen saver mode. Depending on the frequency with which the screen saver is set to activate, this could be irritating for some users. On the other hand, it could help keep prying eyes away from sensitive data. To require a password to unlock the screen saver:

1. Open the System Preferences from the Dock or the Apple menu.

2. Switch to the Screen Saver pane.

3. Choose a screen saver.

4. Choose the Activation tab, shown in Figure 7.13.

5. Select a value from the Time Until Screen Saver Starts section.

6. Choose Use My User Account Password from the section entitled Password To Use When Waking The Screen Saver.

Whenever your computer is in screen saver mode and the mouse, trackpad, or keyboard is moved, the password will be required to exit the screen saver and use the computer. To help conserve battery power, use the Basic screen saver that comes with Mac OS X. It is not graphic-intensive and is therefore not as power-hungry as screen saver images that are read into memory.

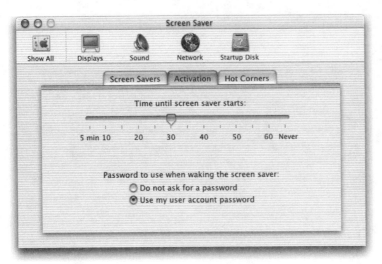

Figure 7.13
Configuring the activation options for the Screen Saver.

Power Shortcuts

Despite the disappearance of several key features like the Control Strip and Launcher, Mac OS X offers a few shortcuts that can make your portable easier to use. As more time passes, software developers are sure to create more utilities with PowerBook and iBook users in mind. My favorites include the trackpad's several clicking features and MenuStrip from **www.MacPowerUser.com**.

Using Trackpad Shortcuts

The PowerBook was one of the very first portable computers to utilize a sensitive electronic surface—the trackpad—in place of a rolling mouse. At first, many users complained about the trackpad—not so much because it was harder to use, but because it was *different*. Now, however, most people accept the trackpad as a vast improvement over the roller ball "technology" of past years. Because the trackpad is an all-electronic solution, it has another added benefit: the ability to act as a clicking device as well as a cursor. Again, some people hate this feature, especially when they sit down to use a PowerBook or iBook without realizing that this feature is enabled.

In addition to moving the cursor around the screen, Mac OS X supports the following three options in the trackpad (shown in Figure 7.14):

■ *Clicking*—Allows a single- or double-tap on the trackpad to emulate single- or double-clicking the mouse.

■ *Dragging*—Allows a selected object to be dragged using the trackpad.

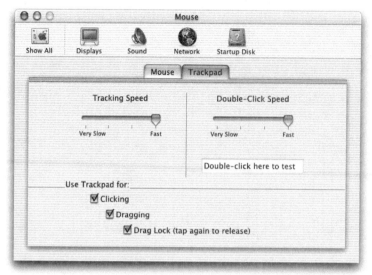

Figure 7.14
Configure the trackpad to do more than just push the cursor around the screen.

■ *Drag Lock*—Allows your finger to be raised and moved again across the trackpad when dragging objects.

Note: For more tips and tricks on customizing Mac OS X's user interface, see Chapter 5.

Using MenuStrip

MenuStrip is a great utility for managing your PowerBook or iBook's Desktop "real estate" by managing windows and providing easy access to a few of the features that disappeared with the old Control Strip. For about $12, MenuStrip is a terrific deal. To download the latest version, visit **www.MacPowerUser.com**. After you have followed the installation instructions for the latest version, follow these steps to take advantage of MenuStrip's shortcuts:

1. Use the Date & Time System Preferences to disable the menu bar clock.

2. Launch the MenuStrip application and check Use MenuStrip's Menu Bar Clock and Set MenuStrip To Automatically Launch On Login. Figure 7.15 shows how these options will appear in the menu bar once the OK button is selected.

From left to right in the menu bar, MenuStrip provides icons for the following features:

■ *Menu Clock*—Displays the time and date, similar to the clock in Mac OS X.

■ *Drag Bar*—Repositions the MenuStrip in the menu bar when dragged to the right or left.

Figure 7.15
MenuStrip provides several handy shortcuts in the menu bar, as well as a more highly configurable clock than the one that is built into Mac OS X.

- *Monitor Settings*—Changes the settings for the display.

- *Volume Control*—Increases, decreases, or mutes the system volume for your computer.

- *Hide All*—Hides all applications other than the Finder.

- *Show All*—Shows all applications (the same as selecting Show All from the Finder application menu).

- *Single App Mode*—Hides all applications except the application in the foreground.

The Hide, Show, and Single App Mode buttons make life with the smaller screen of a portable much more livable. Users of PowerBooks and iBooks will appreciate the ability to focus on the Finder or a single application, thereby clearing the clutter of multiple, layered windows. Whereas the Dock doesn't contain a shortcut to the Sound System Preferences, the shortcut provided by MenuStrip is a welcomed feature. Figure 7.16 shows an example of the Volume Control shortcut.

MenuStrip Prefs, located in the same folder as the MenuStrip application, manages the bulk of MenuStrip's configuration options. To configure its many options, launch MenuStrip Prefs and choose from the options in the following three sections, the first of which is shown in Figure 7.17:

- *Menu Items*—Allows you to selectively enable or disable menu items, including the clock, monitor and sound controls, and the three buttons.

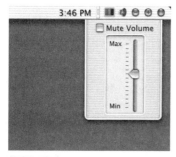

Figure 7.16
The Volume Control button in MenuStrip.

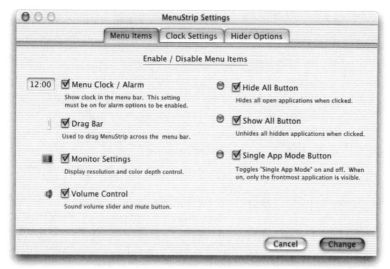

Figure 7.17
You may configure MenuStrip's many options using the MenuStrip Prefs application.

- *Clock Settings*—Enables you to configure the highly functional time and date options for the clock, including alarm clock settings.

- *Hider Options*—Allows you to identify applications that are not to be hidden when the Hide All and Single App Mode buttons are selected.

Give MenuStrip a try on your portable; the shortcuts and enhancements it provides are very well thought out and highly usable.

Wrapping Up

Although mobile computing offers different ways of working with your Macintosh, the freedom of portability comes with a few limitations and risks. In this chapter, you learned:

- What is lacking in Mac OS X in comparison to Mac OS 9.1

- How to make your PowerBook or iBook last longer on a battery charge by configuring the Energy Saver settings

- How to connect an external monitor to your portable computer

- How to configure Internet access in multiple locations

- How to make your computer more secure using login and screen saver passwords

- How to use shortcuts with the trackpad and MenuStrip

This chapter concludes the first part of this book. In the next section, I'll look at the broad issue of applications in Mac OS X. In the first chapter of Part II, I'll examine how the Mac OS works with Carbon and Cocoa applications, and then fonts, printing, and scripting, as well as Java and troubleshooting Mac OS X in the chapters that follow.

7

Part 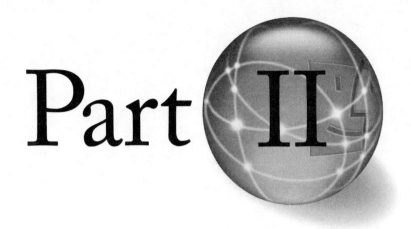 II

Applications

Working with Applications

Thus far, I've discussed the Mac OS X features that change the way you organize and manipulate data files at the OS level. As important as the OS is, however, it's not the reason you use a Macintosh. You use the Mac because its applications—word processors, spreadsheets, databases, graphics programs, and so on—help you accomplish your work effectively.

In this chapter, I'll look at some of the ways that Mac OS X affects applications, beginning with the important issue of compatibility. Then I'll review the standard applications that are installed by Mac OS X, as well as those that have been released by Apple since the debut of Mac OS X. I'll also cover the many ways you can launch your applications, how to create and use stationery documents with some of the more popular applications, and details on two new features of Mac OS X–compatible applications—layered windows and attached sheets. In the remaining chapters of this section of the book, I'll discuss other major changes and enhancements that affect Mac OS X applications, including fonts, printing, multimedia, scripting applications, Java, and troubleshooting applications and Mac OS X.

Mac OS X Compatibility

A new software upgrade is always exciting—it means more features, better performance, and an easier-to-use interface. As seasoned computer users know, however, software upgrades often introduce bugs and incompatibilities along with improvements and solutions. Because Macintosh applications are heavily dependent on the operating system, they're particularly susceptible to upgrade-compatibility problems. Each application must be fine-tuned to function smoothly with the OS. The relationship between the Mac OS and an application is like that of two juggling partners, each throwing balls in the air that the other is expected to catch. When the OS is upgraded, a new partner replaces a familiar one; the routine may stay the same, but there's no time to practice and no room for error.

The introduction of Mac OS X brings the biggest change in Mac OS application programming since the migration from the old 68000 family of microprocessors to the PowerPC family. Although I covered the basics of Classic, Carbon, and Cocoa applications in Chapter 1, the subject bears repeating here because of the importance of the change and because the applications discussed in the following sections are all Carbon or Cocoa—not Classic—applications. To make their existing products Mac OS X compatible, application developers have jettisoned sections of code and reworked the remaining code (commonly referred to as *Carbonizing*). Of course, most applications that are not Mac OS X compatible can still be run in the Classic compatibility environment (described in Chapters 2 and 3). Some Classic applications, such as those that rely on Extensions and/or Control Panels, will function partially—or not at all—when run in the Classic environment. To become Mac OS X compatible, applications such as CopyAgent and Default Folder will have to undergo a major overhaul. And finally, some Carbonized applications, such as GraphicConverter, may also run under Mac OS 9.1 if the CarbonLib Extension is installed.

Mac OS X Applications

The standard installation of Mac OS X includes over three dozen applications and utilities. In fact, so many of the applications are new to the Mac OS that a quick rundown of each one is in order here. Several applications will be discussed in more detail in other chapters, including the Script Editor (Chapter 11), Disk Utility (Chapter 13), and Internet Connect (Chapter 16). By default, the Mac OS creates two folders that house the standard set of applications and utilities: <*hard drive*>/Applications and <*hard drive*>/Applications/Utilities. Each user can store applications in his or her home folder as well, but these applications will not be available to other users on the computer unless the applications are stored in a folder with the proper access privileges. (See Chapter 14 for more information on sharing folders.) The following applications and utilities are available for all users in the Applications and Utilities folders:

- *Address Book*—Application for storing contact information. The Address Book has a customizable toolbar as well as user-defined categories that allow you to group entries. You can also attach an image to an entry, as illustrated in Figure 8.1.

- *Apple System Profiler*—Utility for gathering important information about your computer for use with technical support issues.

- *Applet Launcher*—A utility for launching Java applets without the assistance of a Java-enabled Web browser such as Internet Explorer.

Figure 8.1
The new Address Book application.

■ *Calculator*—A utility for basic mathematical calculations. For complex and scientific calculations, check out DragThing author James Thomson's PCalc (**www.pcalc.com**).

■ *Chess*—An application for playing chess against the computer or watching the computer play against itself.

■ *Clock*—An application for displaying a digital or analog clock on the Desktop or in the Dock. When viewed on the Desktop, you can set the level of transparency from opaque to very transparent.

■ *ColorSync Utility*—A utility for verifying and repairing color profiles used to match color output to screens and printers.

■ *Console*—A utility for displaying highly technical information about both the Mac OS and Mac OS X–compatible applications; used by developers to troubleshoot (debug) programming errors.

■ *CPU Monitor*—A utility for displaying processor activity in one of several graphical formats. On dual-processor machines, the CPU Monitor uses two indicators to show the processor usage levels of each processor, as shown in Figure 8.2.

■ *DigitalColor Meter*—A utility for sampling the color of any pixel that is visible on your display.

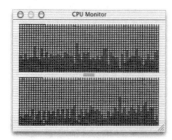

Figure 8.2
The Expanded view of the CPU Monitor utility on a dual-processor computer.

- *Directory Setup*—A utility for configuring directory services using Apple's NetInfo services as well as the Lightweight Directory Access Protocol (LDAP). This utility should be used by system administrators only.

- *Disk Copy*—A utility for mounting and working with disk images. A disk image is a format in which software developers commonly package their applications for downloading over the Web.

- *Disk Utility*—A utility for verifying and repairing disk drive errors.

- *Display Calibrator*—A utility for creating ColorSync color profiles and calibrating monitors, used to more accurately match colors for use in documents on other computers and printers.

- *Grab*—A utility for capturing snapshots of your display (used for many of the images in this book).

- *Image Capture*—An application for downloading images from digital cameras and camcorders.

- *Installer*—A utility used by software developers to assist in the installation of software on your computer.

- *Internet Connect*—An application for connecting to the Internet using a dial-up connection to an Internet Service Provider (ISP). Internet Connect replaces the Remote Access Control Panel in Mac OS 9.1.

- *Internet Explorer*—A very popular application for browsing the Web.

- *Key Caps*—A utility for previewing fonts and using the keyboard.

- *Keychain Access*—A utility for managing passwords to frequently used network resources such as file servers and email accounts.

- *Mail*—An application for sending and receiving email, with integrated support for the Address Book.

- *NetInfo Manager*—A utility for system administrators to manage network resources and root-level access to computers.

- *Network Utility*—A utility for probing and scanning networks, used by system administrators.

- *Preview*—An application for viewing documents in the Portable Document Format (PDF), as well as many popular image file formats. Preview also replaces the functionality of the QuickTime PictureViewer application.

- *Print Center*—A utility for adding, modifying, and deleting printers. Print Center replaces the Chooser found in earlier versions of the Mac OS.

- *ProcessViewer*—A utility for system administrators and computer geeks to monitor various Mac OS components and applications. The ProcessViewer displays technical information about processor usage and memory consumption for assistance in diagnostics and troubleshooting.

- *QuickTime Player*—An application used to view and listen to multimedia broadcasts over the Internet as well as from local sources such as CD-ROMs. The standard version of QuickTime 5 is installed by Mac OS X, but you can upgrade to the professional version to add multiple features. Figure 8.3 shows QuickTime Player used to view the *Rolling Stone* QuickTime TV site.

- *Script Editor*—An application for creating and editing AppleScripts.

- *Script Runner*—An application for managing AppleScripts.

- *SetupAssistant*—A utility used by the Mac OS to initially configure your computer's various settings, such as time, date, and user account.

- *Sherlock*—An application for searching your computer and the Internet.

- *Stickies*—An application for writing notes and brief messages.

- *StuffIt Expander*—A third-party utility from Aladdin Systems for decompressing and/or decrypting files.

- *System Preferences*—An application for configuring various aspects of your computer, such as display, sound, date, and time settings.

- *Terminal*—A utility for displaying information, launching applications, and executing commands using a command-line interface instead of clicking on icons and using a mouse.

- *TextEdit*—An application for creating and editing text documents in Rich Text Format (RTF), plain ASCII, or Unicode.

8

Figure 8.3
Use the QuickTime Player to browse QuickTime-enabled sites such as **www.RollingStone.com**.

Launching

Double-click, double-click, double-click—that's how most Macintosh users launch their applications. Two clicks to open the drive or volume, two to open the application folder, and two on the application icon to launch the software.

This method can quickly grow wearisome when it means clicking through many volumes and folder layers to reach the icon you want. As alternatives, a wide range of application launching utilities—including DragThing and Drop Drawers—have emerged. With these utilities, you can launch applications by selecting their names from a list or button instead of searching through folders for icons. Two- and four-button mice, now available for the Mac OS, allow you to assign button combinations so that a function normally commanded by a double-click can be activated by a single click. And as we've seen, Mac OS X will allow you to place a shortcut to an application in the Dock—and all Dock items are opened with a single click.

Mac OS X offers many ways to open documents or launch applications:

■ *Double-click an application icon*—You can double-click an application icon or its alias to launch that application.

- *Double-click a document icon or its alias*—If you encounter the "file not found" dialog box when trying to open a document, you must either locate the original application or use another application that can open that type of document.

- *Double-click a stationery document or its alias*—A stationery document is a template that automatically creates an untitled new document when opened. (More about stationery documents appears in the section entitled "Working with Stationery Documents," later in this chapter.)

- *Drag a document icon onto an application icon*—This method of launching will work only when the document is dragged onto the icon of the application that created it, or a compatible application. You'll know whether an application is going to launch—its icon will be highlighted when the document icon is dragged above it. Application icons will highlight only when appropriate documents are positioned above them, as shown in Figure 8.4.

Figure 8.4
Application icons are highlighted when you drag compatible documents over them.

8

- *Add applications or documents to the Login Items section of the Startup System Preferences*—To automatically launch an application or open a document and its application at startup, add the application or document to the Startup Items section of the Startup pane of the System Preferences. The application or document will be launched automatically at startup or when you log in to the computer. If someone else logs in, the items will not be opened or launched.

- *Choose an application or document from the Dock*—After you place an application or document in the Dock by dragging the icon to the Dock, the application or document can then be accessed by single-clicking it in the Dock.

- *Choose an application or document name from the Recent Documents or Recent Applications submenus of the Apple|Recent Items menu*—Mac OS X tracks the most recently used documents and applications in the Recent Items menu, a feature that cannot be disabled.

- *Choose an item from the Favorites menu*—Choose an item (file, folder, volume, or application) from the Favorites folder within the Open or Save dialog boxes, or from a Finder window.

The best way to launch applications is the method that works best for you. You'll probably find that a combination approach is the most efficient. Keep the following launching tips in mind:

■ *The Dock*—Add the applications and documents you use most frequently to the Dock. Documents or programs that you use daily will probably stay in the Recent Applications or Recent Documents submenu, so you may not need to put them in the Dock. In any case, consider your work patterns and personal preferences when organizing your Dock.

■ *Folders of aliases*—Assemble groups of application aliases into folders according to application type, then place these folders in the Favorites folder or the Dock. You can choose the item from the Dock via the pop-up list that appears when you click on the docked item, as shown in Figure 8.5.

Figure 8.5
Application aliases are easy to access when they've been organized into folders.

■ *Double-click icons*—When you're browsing in Finder windows to locate specific files, use the tried-and-true double-click method to launch applications, aliases, documents, or stationery icons.

■ *Drag icons onto applications*—If you store documents and applications or their aliases in the same folder, or if you place application icons or aliases on the Desktop, dragging icons onto applications (or drop launching) may prove useful. Drop launching is especially useful for opening multiple documents by dragging a group of documents onto an application.

■ *Favorites folder*—You can add applications, as well as URLs, documents, and volumes, to the Favorites folder and then access these items in Open and Save dialog boxes or via Finder windows.

Working with Stationery Documents

The stationery document is another useful feature supported by Mac OS X. A stationery document allows you to quickly make an existing document into a template. Templates, as you may know, give you a head start in creating new documents by saving you the time otherwise spent creating the basic features of the document from scratch.

For example, the documents in your word processor probably fall into a handful of specific formats—letters, reports, memos, and so on. Rather than start each new document from scratch, you can use, for example, the stationery document for a letter, which provides the date, salutation, paragraph formatting, correct margins, and other basic formatting.

Template support has been available in several Macintosh applications for some time. By adding the stationery documents feature, however, Apple makes templates available in every software package you use to create documents.

Creating Stationery Documents

Stationery documents are supported in different ways, depending on the application. Some applications, such as Microsoft Internet Explorer, have no need for stationery documents. However, for those that do, a stationery document is usually created in three steps:

1. Find an existing example of a document that you create on a regular basis.

2. Modify the example document to make it a good generic representation—take out specific names and dates, for example.

3. Save the document as stationery if possible; if not, select the Stationery option in the file's Show Info window.

For example, create a stationery document for letters by opening an existing letter and modifying it to your liking. Before you save the stationery document, it's a good idea to edit the text in all placeholders, such as greetings, salutations, and dates, with nonsensical data (*greeking*). This ensures that no placeholder elements are accidentally used in finished documents. For example, instead of inserting an actual date and salutation in a stationery document, use 00/00/0000 and Dear Recipient instead.

After you edit the document, use the Save As command to save the template document to disk. Assign a file name that is easily identified in Finder windows and dialog boxes: for example, I like to add the letters *stny* to the end of each stationery file name. Although the Mac doesn't require the use of naming conventions, distinct file names

8

are easier to spot when you're scanning large collections of files for a particular document. For example, Figure 8.6 shows the folder created by Eudora for the specific purpose of storing stationery documents. This example, which contains four stationery documents plus one regular document, shows the difference between a generic icon and the stationery icon.

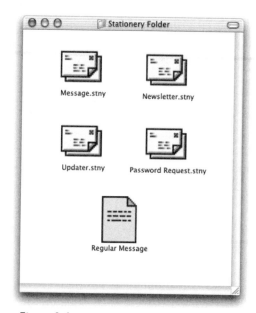

Figure 8.6
A folder containing four Eudora stationery documents and one regular document.

Some applications will not allow you to save documents as stationery, however. To try making a stationery document with this kind of application, follow these steps:

1. Create a document and save it.

2. Go to the Finder and select the document's icon.

3. Choose the Show Info command from the File menu.

4. Refer to the Stationery Pad checkbox in the lower-left corner of the General Information section of the Show Info window to confirm that this is indeed a stationery document, as shown in Figure 8.7. The icon inside the Show Info window may change to show that the document is now a stationery document; however, not all applications support custom icons for stationery documents.

5. After you close the Show Info window, the conversion is complete.

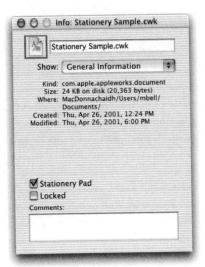

Figure 8.7
Manually configuring a document as a stationery document.

Some applications, such as BBEdit and Apple Works, give you the option of saving your documents in stationery documents format. Saving this way may be simpler than digging up the Show Info window and manually creating a stationery document.

Using Stationery

After you've created a stationery document, you can open it with the appropriate application, just as you would any other document. When you launch a stationery document, it opens in a window that appears to be the original document. It's actually a copy of the stationery, however. The title bar area of the window, which shows the document name as Untitled, Untitled2, Untitled3, and so on, clues you in to the document's true identity as a copy. To save the document as a stationery document, choose the appropriate options in the Save As dialog box.

Stationery Tips

Because using stationery documents may be a new concept to some of you, let's review several tips that may be helpful:

■ *Stationery documents aliases*—An alias of a stationery document accesses the stationery document normally, whether the alias was created before or after the Stationery Documents option was set.

■ *Stationery documents folder*—For easy access to stationery documents, create a stationery or templates folder to house the aliases of all your stationery documents. If you use the aliases frequently, you may want to also put an alias of this folder in the Dock.

■ *Opening stationery documents with the Open command*—When you open stationery documents using the Open command, be sure to assign a new file name using the Save As command—this prevents you from accidentally overwriting your stationery document.

■ *Editing stationery documents*—Unchecking the Stationery Pad option in the General Information section of the Show Info window will turn any stationery document back into a "normal" document. You can then edit the document—think of this as modifying your master template. After editing and saving this document, reselect the Stationery Pad option in the Show Info window to turn the file back into a stationery document.

Working with Multiple Applications

With Mac OS X, you can work with multiple applications simultaneously in many of the same ways you have become accustomed to in Mac OS 9.1 and earlier, including switching between foreground and background applications, hiding applications, and using keyboard shortcuts to cycle between applications. In addition to the Dock, Mac OS X introduces two new concepts for dealing with application windows that need further attention—layered windows and attached sheets.

Managing Layered Windows

Layered windows, a new feature supported by Mac OS X, make it possible for windows to become independent of one another. In previous versions of the Mac OS, all windows belonging to an application were visible on the Desktop at the same time. In Mac OS X, however, you can minimize some of the application's windows (in the Dock) while leaving others visible.

Moreover, Mac OS X allows you to layer an application's windows between the windows of other applications, which makes keeping track of information more challenging at times. This concept is a bit tricky to explain without an example, so I'll give it a try using Figure 8.8. In this example, I have three applications open at the same time: Internet Explorer (multiple windows), BBEdit (one window), and GraphicConverter (one window). Although Internet Explorer is the active application, you can see in this figure that one BBEdit and one GraphicConverter window

8

Figure 8.8
An example of layered application windows for (front to back) Internet Explorer, BBEdit, GraphicConverter, and Internet Explorer again.

are visible between the two Internet Explorer windows. In addition to the two visible Internet Explorer windows, two more Internet Explorer windows, which I've minimized, are in the Dock. You can't see them—or the Dock, for that matter—because I've hidden the Dock. As you can see, layered windows can be a bit tricky to manage.

Mac OS X applications can help you manage the chaotic effects of layered windowing in at least two ways. However, not all applications support these features, and some applications will not allow their windows to be layered among other application windows. For the applications that do allow layered windows, here are a couple of solutions to the chaos:

- *Choose Window|Bring All To Front*—Groups all windows of the selected application in front of windows belonging to other applications.

- *File|Hide Others*—Hides all other applications except the active application.

Attached Sheets

Some (but not all) Mac OS X applications utilize Open and Save dialog boxes that are actually attached to a particular window, instead of existing as standalone dialog boxes. Attached dialog boxes, referred to as attached sheets, allow you to continue working with other documents and applications while the attached sheets are expanded, as illustrated in Figure 8.9.

Some software developers prefer not to implement attached sheets, whereas others may not have enabled this feature in an effort to quickly Carbonize an existing Classic application for use in Mac OS X. Applications that do not employ attached sheets will probably use the secondary form of Open and Save dialog boxes found in Mac OS X that are displayed as floating windows that may or may not allow you to continue working with the application until the window is dismissed.

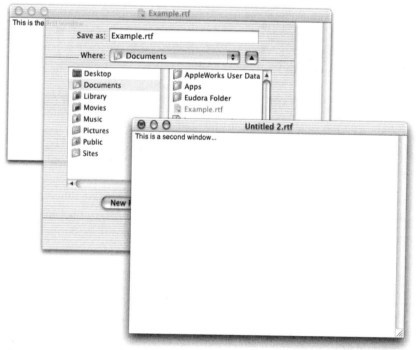

Figure 8.9
An example of how an attached sheet (Example.rtf) can be obscured by other windows without disrupting the application.

Wrapping Up

In many ways, Mac OS X applications are unique compared to applications written for earlier versions of the Mac OS. In this chapter, you've learned about several aspects of Mac OS X applications, including:

- Compatibility of Mac OS X applications

- Application launching methods and strategies

- Applications and utilities automatically installed by Mac OS X

- Creating and using stationery documents

- Layered windows and attached sheets

The innovative use of fonts and thorough support of printing are among the Mac's greatest strengths. In the next chapter, I'll explore what's new in the realm of fonts and printing in Mac OS X.

8

Managing Fonts and Printers

A great measure of the Macintosh's success has been due to its capabilities in the graphics and publishing arena. In fact, you could say that desktop publishing is the Macintosh's heritage. Drawing on years of experience and technological advances, Mac OS X provides the best font and printing technologies that can be found in a personal computer. In this chapter, I'll look at the ways in which Mac OS X displays fonts and images on your screen and handles local and networked printers, paying special attention to fonts and type issues. Here you'll discover what's practical and what's possible.

Imaging Models

The methods, or models, that Mac OS X employs to generate fonts and images differ according to how the fonts and images will be used—on computer screens or by printers. On screen, the Mac OS displays information at a much lower resolution than printers, which are capable of resolutions of 2,400 dpi or higher. This disparity in quality between screen and printer output necessitates the use of different imaging models. Over the last 20 years, Apple has invented several imaging models, including QuickDraw, QuickDraw GX, and QuickDraw 3D. Apple has also licensed OpenGL, the new standard imaging model, as a replacement for some of its own technologies, such as QuickDraw 3D, because of OpenGL's cross-platform appeal. In fact, even the 3D capabilities of Mac OS X rely on OpenGL.

The new imaging model that supplies the 2D, PDF, and font support in Mac OS X is code named Quartz. It plays the same role that QuickDraw held in previous versions of the Mac OS, although many QuickDraw features are still present in Mac OS X. Quartz provides a framework for programmers of Carbon or Cocoa applications to implement several advanced imaging features, including:

- Antialiasing text
- Creating drop shadows around text and windows
- Saving documents in PDF format

The distinctive features of Mac OS X's Aqua interface, including the drop shadows and translucent Finder windows, are the result of Quartz. Aqua is, on the whole, more aesthetically pleasing than the old Platinum interface of Mac OS 9.1. For example, take a look at Figure 9.1, which shows two versions of a BBEdit document in Mac OS X (top) and Mac OS 9.1 (bottom). Note the drop shadow around the window and the overall crispness of the Mac OS X version. Also check out the letter M, which I've blown up to give you a better view of how text is antialiased, thereby presenting an image that is smoother around the edges and easier to read.

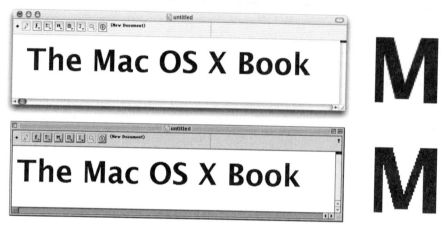

Figure 9.1
The Quartz imaging model allows for antialiased text in Mac OS X applications such as BBEdit.

Quartz enables applications to create cross-platform Adobe Acrobat PDF documents that can be read on any computer that has Adobe Acrobat Reader or a comparable program for reading PDF documents. In Mac OS X, PDF documents created in most Carbon and Cocoa applications can be viewed with the application named Preview.

For most users, the components of the Mac OS that generate images and fonts on screen are not as important as the fonts themselves. Let's move on to the issue of fonts supported by Mac OS X.

Mac OS X Fonts

Mac OS X is a powerful desktop publishing platform that offers improved support for font management as well as maximum backward compatibility for the main types of fonts used in earlier versions of the Mac OS. To some users, backward compatibility may be of little importance. However, if you've ever purchased a set of commercial fonts, you can imagine how much money a graphics or desktop publishing professional must invest in the tools of the trade. In fact, Apple claims to include over $10,000 worth of fonts in Mac OS X.

In addition to a high degree of backward compatibility, Mac OS X also provides a framework for developers to write font management tools into their applications. Users can create and edit groups of fonts for easy reference when working in different types of documents, such as Web documents or word processing documents. Several third-party font utilities, including eBookfaces, FontChecker, and FontExampler, enhance Mac OS X's built-in font management capability for the following types of fonts:

- Bitmapped (fixed-size) fonts

- Type 1 (also called PostScript or variable-size) fonts

- TrueType (variable-size) fonts

- OpenType (variable-size) fonts

Let's look at these types of fonts in detail, paying particularly close attention to TrueType fonts, the most popular type of font for the Mac OS.

Bitmapped Fonts

The original Macintosh fonts (New York, Monaco, Geneva, and Chicago) were fixed-width bitmapped fonts—each character in each font was predefined by the series of dots necessary to create that character at a specific point size. Most bitmapped fonts were produced in 10-, 11-, 12-, and 14-point sizes, and were not scalable (meaning each font was incapable of having a variable width).

The original bitmapped fonts, and the many bitmapped fonts that soon followed, were optimized for display on the Macintosh screen and for printing on the Apple ImageWriter (the only printer available at the time). Limitations to working with these bitmapped fonts included:

- *Dot-matrix bitmapped quality was unacceptable for most business uses.* Although font variety was certainly a welcome improvement, most people still considered the quality of ImageWriter output unacceptable for business use.

- *Font variety was limited.* Although bitmapped fonts proliferated, almost all were novelty styles with little utility beyond advertisements, invitations, and entertainment.

- *The 400KB system disks could hold only a limited selection of fonts.* Because hard drives were not generally available at that time, it was necessary to boot the Macintosh from a 400KB floppy disk. After you squeezed the System folder plus an application or two onto a floppy, only a small amount of room was left for font styles and sizes.

9

■ *Macintosh applications could support only a limited number of fonts at one time.* When too many fonts were installed in the System file, applications acted strangely, often providing only a random subset of the installed fonts.

These problems were solved, after some time, with new releases of system software, application software, and third-party utility programs. The next big change in the Mac font world was not based on software but on the introduction of the Apple LaserWriter printer with its built-in support for the PostScript page description language. Bitmapped fonts are still in use today, but PostScript and other types of fonts are much more popular.

Type 1 Fonts (PostScript)

The introduction of the Apple LaserWriter printer brought a new variety of font to the Macintosh: the Type 1, or PostScript, font. To be more precise, Type 1 fonts are actually a subset of Adobe's PostScript language; they were required in documents created for output to the LaserWriter (and to all later PostScript printers) to ensure that the type could be printed at high resolution. PostScript fonts came to be known by a variety of names, including laser fonts, outline fonts, and Type 1 fonts. Apple traditionally refers to them as PostScript fonts, however.

Each PostScript font consists of two parts: a screen font and a printer font. The screen font is nearly identical to the printer font for a bitmapped font in that it provides different sizes optimized for on-screen use, rather than one font that is viewable at multiple sizes. Other similarities between the two include:

■ Both are provided in different styles and sizes

■ Both appear in the font menu or Font Panel in most Mac OS X applications

Fonts usually have distinctive Finder icons that make identifying and managing them easier when working in the Finder. When viewing the contents of a folder of fonts, you can identify a font's classification by its icon. For example, Figure 9.2 shows the Finder icons for a TrueType font (left) and a Type 1 font (right).

Figure 9.2
When viewed in a Finder window, a font's icon indicates what kind of font it is.

With PostScript fonts, the screen font is only a general representation of the corresponding printer font. The PostScript printer font gives the PostScript printer a mathematical description of each character, as well as other information necessary to create and produce high-resolution output.

Regardless of whether all screen fonts and printer fonts are present in matched pairs, it isn't imperative that you use all the available screen fonts because the Mac OS can simulate a missing screen font. You must, however, always have all printer fonts available to the operating system. In other words, you can *view* Helvetica Bold without installing the Helvetica Bold screen font (by using the Helvetica font and the Bold type style), but you cannot *print* Helvetica Bold without the Helvetica Bold printer font.

For a PostScript font to be printed correctly, the printer font file must be available to the PostScript printer. A font is available when it has been built into the printer's Read Only Memory (ROM) chips, stored on a printer's hard disk, or kept on the Macintosh hard disk and automatically downloaded to the printer. Modern PostScript-enabled printers typically have a hard drive to store fonts and documents sent to the printer, and some have the ability to store additional fonts using software provided by the manufacturer.

PostScript Font Challenges

For a variety of reasons, using PostScript fonts in the real-world Macintosh environment has never been easy. The difficulties are generally related to the fact that the PostScript fonts themselves, as well as the software and hardware environment in which PostScript fonts are utilized, have been perpetually evolving. Most of these problems have been solved through system software upgrades, new font management utilities, or workaround methods that have become well known and commonly accepted.

The following list describes many of the challenges presented by PostScript fonts, along with the corresponding solutions:

- *PostScript fonts versus non-PostScript fonts*—Because PostScript screen fonts are not noticeably different from non-PostScript screen fonts, it's difficult for inexperienced users to distinguish between them when creating documents that will be produced on high-resolution PostScript printers. This problem has been solved, at least partially, by PostScript's dominance in the Macintosh world—most Macintosh users now have access to PostScript printers, and PostScript fonts are now the rule rather than the exception.

- *Screen font availability*—It's a good idea to determine which fonts a document contains in order to ensure the availability of all necessary screen and printer fonts at print time. This isn't always easy to do, however—especially if the person printing the file is not the one who created it. Individual software vendors have developed schemes to help identify the screen fonts in a document: PageMaker displays the dimmed names of used but currently unavailable fonts in its Font menu; both PageMaker and QuarkXPress produce a list of fonts used. Adobe has enabled Illustrator to print files correctly even if the screen fonts used to create the file aren't available at the time of printing. Unfortunately, this solution hasn't caught on with all software vendors.

■ *Printer font availability*—The most fundamental requirement of PostScript fonts is that for each screen font used in a document, a corresponding printer font must be available at print time. This requirement has caused difficulty for Mac users because of the lack of an automated method of tracking the screen font/printer font correlation.

■ *Different fonts with the same names*—As more vendors produced more PostScript fonts, another problem appeared: different versions of the same fonts released by different vendors. This proliferation of fonts caused Macintoshes to become confused about which screen fonts and printer fonts were used in documents. It also made it difficult for service bureaus to know, for instance, if the Garamond specified in a document was the Adobe Garamond, Bitstream Garamond, or some other vendor's version of Garamond. This point was crucial because font substitutions wouldn't work—and even if it did, character width differences played havoc with the output because of the differences in the fonts.

■ *The Type 1 font secret*—Because Adobe Systems developed PostScript, they kept the specifics of the optimized format that came to be known as PostScript Type 1 to themselves. The Type 1 format embedded "hints" in font outlines that made the fonts look better when produced in small type sizes on 300-dpi laser printers.

Because Adobe fonts were compressed and encrypted, other vendors had to reverse-engineer the Type 1 font-hinting scheme to incorporate a comparable feature in their own fonts. Bitstream and others were successful in cloning the functionality of PostScript. Finally, after all the political turmoil surrounding TrueType and the successful cloning of PostScript Type 1 fonts, Adobe unsealed the specifications for the Type 1 font format. Today, most other font vendors have upgraded their fonts to the Type 1 format.

Printing PostScript Fonts

When a document containing PostScript fonts is printed to a PostScript printer, the Mac OS queries the PostScript printer to determine whether the fonts required by the document are resident in the printer. These fonts may be built into a printer's ROM chips, or they may have been previously downloaded into the printer's RAM or onto the printer's hard disk. If the fonts are indeed resident, the document is sent to the printer for output. If the fonts are not resident, the printer driver checks to see whether the printer font files are available on the Macintosh hard disk. If they are, they're temporarily downloaded into the printer's RAM. If they are not available, an error message in the Print Status dialog box alerts you to that fact. This message usually states that Courier is being substituted for the missing font, and your document is then printed.

When the document is printed, the PostScript printer uses the printer font information to create each character. The information from the PostScript screen font is translated into printer font characters. The process of creating the printed characters—*rasterization*—is the most complex part of the PostScript printing process. During rasterization, PostScript uses the printer font file's mathematical character descriptions to select the output device pixels necessary to produce the requested character at the highest possible resolution.

TrueType Fonts

In addition to supporting the same bitmapped and PostScript fonts that Macintosh users have worked with for years, Mac OS X utilizes a preferred font format that was introduced in System 7. TrueType fonts were designed to appear on the Macintosh screen at high resolution at any point size and to print at high resolution on virtually any output device.

TrueType was a fundamental shift from bitmapped and PostScript fonts. Each TrueType font exists as a single file that does the work of both the screen font and the printer font. When used in earlier versions of the Mac OS, TrueType fonts appear smooth and crisp on screen, no matter what the point size. In Mac OS X, the Quartz imaging engine smoothes out everything on screen, including all fonts.

TrueType's font specifications have been published for use by a wide variety of vendors. It is supported by AGFA Compugraphic, Bitstream, International Typeface Corporation, Monotype, and others. Microsoft Windows and even IBM's OS/2 support the TrueType standard, ensuring strong crossplatform compatibility. Both Apple and Microsoft now sell or freely distribute many TrueType fonts. You can buy TrueType font packages from most vendors, with the notable exception of Adobe (because of their historical support for Type 1 fonts, and now their support for OpenType fonts—discussed in the next section).

TrueType Technology

TrueType fonts, like PostScript printer fonts, are outline fonts—each character is described mathematically as opposed to the bit-by-bit description used by older screen fonts. TrueType mathematical descriptions are based on quadratic Bézier curve equations rather than PostScript's standard Bézier curve equations. The difference between these equations is in the number of points used to determine the positions of the lines and curves that make up each character. Apple claims TrueType's method creates better-looking characters in a wider range of output and display resolutions.

Because TrueType uses mathematical descriptions for both on-screen and printer font versions, a single file can serve the display and any output devices. As mentioned previously in this chapter, PostScript requires two files—a screen font file and a printer font file—to display or print at full resolution. Although it's easier to manage one font file than two, Adobe claims that putting its screen fonts and printer fonts in separate files is an asset because either can be updated or enhanced independently at any time without affecting existing documents or printer configurations.

A Word About TrueType GX

TrueType GX, an extension of the TrueType specification, takes advantage of the capabilities found in QuickDraw (and formerly QuickDraw GX), which is now part of the Quartz imaging model. QuickDraw GX and TrueType are adept at handling complex character sets and pictographic languages, traits that make the Macintosh attractive to users of non-Roman languages. In fact, TrueType GX introduced advanced typographical capabilities for fine control over letter forms and intelligent handling of characters in a layout.

TrueType GX and PostScript (Type 1) fonts that follow the QuickDraw GX data structure can store information about justification, optical alignment, optical scaling, hanging punctuation, tracking, and kerning. GX can create precise styling: bold, italic, and expanded or condensed forms along two, three, or four variation axes. Apple defines these axes as weight, width, slant, and optical size (optimal shape of a size).

Because it's possible to adjust letter size and spacing, you can use one TrueType GX font in place of another without changing line and page breaks. QuickDraw GX supplies the conversion that facilitates this substitution.

OpenType Fonts

The OpenType font, the newest arrival on the font scene, is a joint venture from Adobe and Microsoft that provides a crossplatform font for the Mac OS and various Windows operating systems. OpenType uses a single, crossplatform font file to perform all the tasks that require a font, including bitmapping, outlining, display, printing, and multilingual support—no small feat. The font files are also designed to be smaller in size to encourage portability between computers and over the Web.

Choosing a Font Standard

In a laboratory environment, where some Macintoshes used only PostScript fonts and some used only TrueType fonts, and all documents using PostScript fonts were created only on the PostScript machines and those using TrueType fonts were created only on the TrueType machines, the daily use of these systems would be very straightforward from a font-technology perspective.

Unfortunately, none of us live or work in such a laboratory. Most Macintosh computers are likely to be configured with PostScript fonts; TrueType fonts; and non-PostScript, non-TrueType bitmapped fonts. And most people will have some documents that were created with only PostScript fonts, some with only bitmapped fonts, some with only TrueType fonts, and many with mixes of TrueType, PostScript, and bitmapped fonts. So how can all this jumble work in the real world?

The answer is: Easily! The Quartz imaging model takes into account all the advances made in the field of typography—therefore the differences among types of fonts aren't as pronounced as in the days of System 7 and the original Apple LaserWriter. To desktop publishing professionals, this may sound like heresy. As far as the rest of us are concerned, however, use the fonts you like best as long as their on-screen appearance and output meet your standards.

9

Installing Fonts

In the old days of the Mac OS prior to System 7.1, all fonts were stored in the System suitcase (located in the System Folder). The only limitation was that fonts could not be installed while any application other than the Finder was open, and they were installed using a utility called the Font/DA Mover. In System 7.1, a folder called Fonts was introduced to store fonts apart from the System suitcase. The concept of the Fonts folder continues in Mac OS X, but with an interesting twist: As a true multiuser operating system, Mac OS X can access fonts stored in multiple locations—not just the main Fonts folder. This approach makes installing new fonts very easy and allows multiple users to have separate fonts.

When a user logs into Mac OS X, the operating system looks in several places on local and networked file systems for the type of fonts it is capable of using; fonts that are not supported are ignored. Specifically, Mac OS X looks for fonts in the following locations:

- *<Mac OS X Hard Drive>*/Library/Fonts/

- *<Mac OS X Hard Drive>*/Users/*<User Name>*/Library/Fonts/

- *<Mac OS 9.1 Hard Drive>*/System Folder /Fonts/

- *<Network>*/Library/Fonts/

- *<Network>*/Users/*<User Name>*/Library/Fonts

If you don't have Mac OS 9.1 installed on the same computer as Mac OS X, or you are not logged into a Mac OS X Server, no fonts other than those found in the two local Mac OS X folders will be found. If Mac OS 9.1 and Mac OS X are installed on the same computer, all OS 9.1 fonts that are of the correct type will be available for use in Mac OS X as well. When working with any application that allows you to select fonts, all the fonts will be accessible to the application. This is an interesting change since Mac OS 9.1, in which only the contents of the Fonts folder are searched for fonts.

The fonts installed on your Mac in the main Fonts folder include the following, plus Lucida Grande, which is the default system font:

- AmericanTypewriter

- Arial

- Arial Black

- Arial Narrow

- Arial Rounded Bold

- Baskerville

- BigCaslon

- Brush Script

- Comic Sans MS

- Copperplate

- Courier New

- Didot

- Futura

- Georgia

- GillSans

- HelveticaNeue

- Herculanum

- MarkerFelt

- Optima

- Papyrus

- Times New Roman

- Trebuchet MS

- Verdana

- Webdings

- Zapfino

To install additional fonts, just copy or move fonts to one of the Fonts folders mentioned above. You may not be able to add fonts to the Fonts folder when applications other than the Finder are running. Also, when you add fonts to one of the Fonts folders, they will not become available to any applications that are already open until you quit and relaunch those programs. In fact, after installing the fonts, it's best to restart the computer or log out and log back in so that the new fonts will be recognized by the Mac OS. The newly installed fonts will then be available to your Carbon and Cocoa applications.

When you're installing fonts, Mac OS X doesn't display the contents of font suitcases (a family of fonts). Mac OS 9.1, on the other hand, allows you to open font suitcases directly from the Finder by double-clicking them as if they were folders. This action opens a suitcase window that contains individual icons for each screen font in the folder. The icons enable you to distinguish PostScript screen fonts or bitmapped fonts from TrueType fonts. TrueType fonts use an icon with three *A*s, whereas PostScript screen fonts or bitmapped fonts use an icon with a single *A*. Mac OS X doesn't support the telltale icons, which makes managing fonts a little more difficult. For example, Figure 9.3 shows Adobe Garamond viewed in Mac OS X (left), and Arial Narrow (top right) and Adobe Garamond (bottom right) in Mac OS 9.1. Notice that in Mac OS X you cannot open a font suitcase, nor does the Mac OS X Finder icon distinguish between TrueType and bitmapped fonts.

Moreover, double-clicking an individual screen font in Mac OS 9.1 opens a window that contains a brief sample of the font; Mac OS X doesn't offer this option.

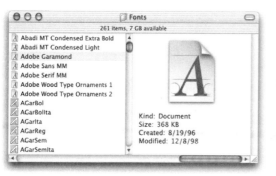

Figure 9.3
Font file icons differ significantly in Mac OS X (left) and Mac OS 9.1 (right).

Removing Fonts

Removing fonts is essentially the same as installing them. First, quit all open applications, then move or delete the selected fonts from the Fonts folder. You cannot move fonts that are in use by the Mac OS itself, such as Lucida Grande. To get rid of these, you'll need to boot from an alternative startup disk such as the Mac OS X installation CD-ROM or a drive containing Mac OS 9.1.

Working with the Font Panel

The portion of the Quartz imaging system that controls the details of fonts is known as the *Apple Type Solution (ATS)*. ATS provides access to all of your fonts through a new feature called the Font Panel (when working with Cocoa applications). The Font Panel, an example of which is shown in Figure 9.4, allows you to group fonts into user-defined categories for easy access from within Font Panel–aware applications such as Mail and TextEdit. (Not all applications provide access to the Font Panel.) This type of coordination is reminiscent of the color picker utility, which provides a similar type of access for color selection in different types of applications.

To access the Font Panel, choose Format|Font|Font Panel (or Command+T) when using TextEdit, or Format|Font|Show Fonts (also Command+T) when using Mail. Both commands open the same Font Panel window.

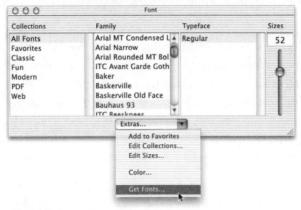

Figure 9.4
The new Font Panel provides a unified method of selecting fonts from within applications such as Mail and TextEdit.

In addition to selecting a font family, such as Bauhaus 93 in Figure 9.4, a typeface such as Regular or Bold, and a font size, click the drop-down menu at the bottom of the Font Panel to reveal the following options:

■ *Add To Favorites*—Adds the selected font to the font category called Favorites.

■ *Edit Collections*—Opens the Font Collections window (shown in Figure 9.5) in which you can edit, add, and delete categories of fonts.

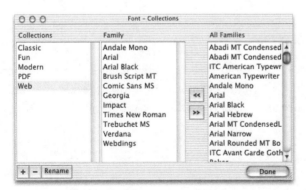

Figure 9.5
Use the Font Panel feature to create collections of fonts.

- *Edit Sizes*—Allows you to set the minimum and maximum font sizes between which the font slider may be moved.

- *Color*—Opens a Mac OS X–style color picker to select the color for a font.

- *Get Fonts*—Opens your default Web browser to an Apple Web page for information on purchasing fonts.

The Font Panel and color picker are actually floating windows that can be resized to suit your needs. They can be made very small or very large, and will float above your TextEdit or Mail documents. To reduce screen clutter, the floating palettes will disappear when Mail or TextEdit is moved into the background by the launching of another application.

Third-Party Font Utilities

Mac OS X is in its infancy, and only a few utilities for managing its fonts are available at this time. Some of the venerable font management utilities, including Font Reserve, are in the process of being Carbonized; for now, let me suggest the following third-party font utilities:

eBookfaces

www.corpus-callosum.com

eBookfaces serves as a utility for viewing large samples of a font at different sizes. The display area is large enough to provide an excellent preview of a particular font, and a tab to the side of the display area allows you to filter certain styles of fonts. For example, Figure 9.6 shows the Monaco font viewed in eBookfaces.

FontChecker

www.wundermoosen.com/wmXFC.htm

FontChecker is a utility for previewing a font and displaying technical information about the decimal, Hex, octal, HTML, and key information for a specific character. In Figure 9.7, for example, FontChecker is displaying the at symbol (Shift+2) in the Copperplate Gothic Bold font.

FontExampler

www.pixits.com

FontExampler is a handy little utility for seeing what a font looks like. It uses a scrolling list that displays the font name on the left and a sample of the font on the

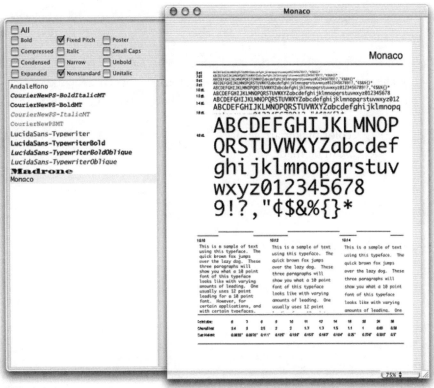

Figure 9.6
eBookfaces allows you to preview and print examples of a font.

9

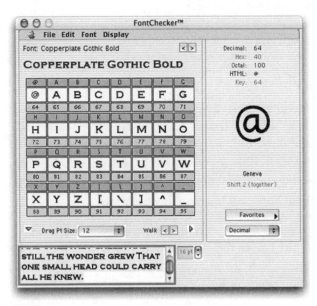

Figure 9.7
FontChecker provides technical information about characters, as well as font types and styles.

right of a window. Figure 9.8 shows an example of how easy it is to browse large numbers of fonts with FontExampler.

Although a few other font utilities are available for Mac OS X, they don't really offer any functionality beyond what eBookfaces, FontChecker, and FontExampler can provide. Keep your eyes peeled for new software to help you manage your fonts.

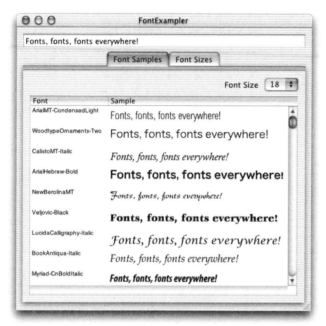

Figure 9.8
FontExampler allows you to preview fonts with a user-defined string of text.

Printing in Mac OS X

Mac OS X introduces a new printing architecture that combines the functionality of the old Chooser with the Desktop printing feature found in earlier versions of the Mac OS. By marshalling these abilities into one application that is independent of the Finder, Mac OS X provides a more flexible framework to help developers incorporate printing capabilities into their programs. To you and me, this means a similar interface to Mac OS 9.1 for printing documents, and fewer problems relating to large or corrupt print files.

With the new printing architecture comes the introduction of several concepts that may be somewhat familiar to many users. To print a document in Mac OS X, you'll eventually encounter the following concepts:

- *Print Center*—A new utility for selecting printers.

- *Page Setup*—The command found in most applications to prepare a document for printing to a specific printer.

- *Print Preview*—A feature found in many applications that enables you to preview a document before sending it to a printer.

- *Save As PDF*—A command that allows you to create a PDF document in any Carbon or Cocoa application that has printing capabilities.

Many people will miss the Desktop printing capability found in previous versions of the operating system. This inconvenience is made up for (at least in my opinion) by the faster and more reliable printing features found in Mac OS X. Let's take a look at the first step—selecting a printer.

Selecting Printers with Print Center

Print Center is the new application you'll use to select, configure, and delete printers in Mac OS X. Its function is similar to that of the old Desktop Printer Utility in that it offers several methods for adding a printer, including:

- AppleTalk

- Directory Services

- Line Printer (LPR), which uses the Transmission Control Protocol/Internet Protocol (TCP/IP)

- Universal Serial Bus (USB)

Most users will access printers via a USB cable directly connected to the printer or over an AppleTalk network. However, because most non-Apple print drivers have yet to be updated for Mac OS X, the number of unsupported printers probably outnumbers those that can be used with Mac OS X at this time.

To connect to a printer connected over an AppleTalk network, follow these steps:

1. Launch Print Center from the Utilities folder. If you haven't already selected a printer, Print Center will remind you of this fact.

2. Choose the Add or Add Printer button.

3. From the pop-up list shown in Figure 9.9, select the protocol through which the printer will be connected.

9

Figure 9.9
When using the Print Center utility to add a printer, select the appropriate protocol in order to locate the printer.

4. If the printer is an AppleTalk-enabled printer, it should appear in a list along with other AppleTalk-enabled printers (provided that AppleTalk is properly enabled in the Network System Preferences pane). Select the printer from the list and click the Add button.

Once the printer has been added to your list of printers, it will remain in the Printer List until you delete it by selecting the printer and choosing the Delete button.

 PostScript printers rely upon PostScript Printer Description (PPD) files to enable the Mac OS to print. These files contain printer-specific information on such things as the number of trays, printer resolution, and color matching. PPDs are stored deep in the /System/ Library/ folder hierarchy.

Line Printer (LPR) is Unix-speak for a network-enabled printer that uses TCP/IP to communicate with host computers such as your Macintosh, a Windows-based computer, or a variety of computers that can print via LPR. Generally speaking, before you can connect to an LPR you need to know the printer's make, model, and most importantly, its IP address. To connect to an LPR, follow these steps:

1. Launch Print Center.

2. Choose the Add or Add Printer button.

3. Select LPR Printers Using IP from the pop-up selection list.

4. Provide an IP address or domain name for the printer in the LPR Printer's Address field, an example of which is shown in Figure 9.10.

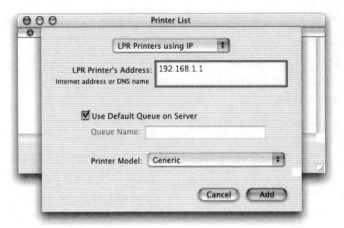

Figure 9.10
Adding an LPR.

5. Do not check Use Default Queue On Server unless a network administrator gives you the name of an alternative queue to use in place of the default.

6. Select the type of printer from the Printer Model drop-down list.

7. Click the Add button to add the printer to the Printer List.

Mac OS X automatically recognizes printers connected via USB when your computer is started up. However, you can manually add a printer that is connected via USB but not recognized by Mac OS X by following these steps:

1. Launch Print Center.

2. Choose the Add or Add Printer button.

3. Select USB from the pop-up list.

4. Select the printer from the list of available printers.

5. Click the Add button to add the printer to the Printer List.

Finally, Directory Services refers to any printer available over a network, including printers networked via AppleTalk, TCP/IP (using LPR), or other protocols yet to be incorporated into Mac OS X. To select a printer using Directory Services:

1. Launch Print Center.

2. Choose the Add button.

3. Select the printer from the list of available printers in the Directory Services menu, which is the default menu option chosen when Print Center is launched.

4. Click the Add button to add the printer to the Printer List.

Printers that have been added using Print Center will be available to any Carbon or Cocoa application whose printing capability was programmed with the Mac OS X printing Application Programming Interface (API). See the "Using Page Setup" and "Working with the Print Dialog Box" sections later in this chapter for instructions on changing printers from within a document.

Using Page Setup

The Mac OS X implementation of the Page Setup command, which should be very familiar to any Mac user who has ever printed, is very similar to the same command found in previous versions of the Mac OS. In Mac OS X, the Page Setup window may look different from application to application because software developers are able to customize it to suit their products. For the sake of continuity, however, Apple strives to make the basics of Page Setup the same for every application.

In Mac OS X, as in previous versions of the OS, the Page Setup command is usually found under the File menu. In some applications, the Page Setup window is presented in the form of an attached sheet (described in several earlier chapters), and in others it resembles a free-floating modal dialog box that must be dismissed before you can use any of the application's other features. For example, Figure 9.11 shows the Page Setup window for the TextEdit application; it is identical to the Page Setup window in AppleWorks, except the latter uses a free-floating window instead of an attached sheet. The following options are found in most implementations of the Page Setup window:

- *Settings*—Select from Page Attributes or Summary. The Summary option just provides an overview of the options that are available in the Page Attributes section.

- *Format For*—Select a printer using the Print Center utility.

Figure 9.11
The new Page Setup command in Mac OS X.

- *Paper Size*—The size of the paper on which the document will be printed.

- *Orientation*—The orientation of the document, either portrait (the default), landscape right-to-left, or landscape left-to-right.

- *Scale*—The scale at which the document is to be printed.

To configure a document for printing, open the Page Setup window, make your selections, and then click on the OK button. Your choices will be saved until you use Page Setup to change them.

Previewing and Saving Documents as PDFs

The new printing architecture in Mac OS X is designed so that any document created in a Carbon or Cocoa application can be previewed before printing. The OS converts the document to PDF format and then opens a temporary version of it in the Preview application. Converting the document to PDF results in excellent display and print quality as well as a very high level of crossplatform compatibility. Any document that can be previewed can most likely be saved as a PDF document—a great option, when you consider that PDF is the preferred document format for Web and business use.

Most Carbon or Cocoa applications will allow you to preview a document by following steps such as these, which describe how to preview a document created using TextEdit:

1. Launch TextEdit and create a document.

2. Choose File|Page Setup; confirm the paper size and orientation, then click the OK button.

3. Choose File|Print and click the Print Preview button.

When previewed, the document will be converted into a PDF file and automatically opened in the Preview application. For example, Figure 9.12 shows how the PDF document (right) looks compared to the original TextEdit document (left).

After a document has been converted to PDF format and is open in the Print Preview feature, you have two additional options at your disposal. You can save the document in PDF format or as a Tagged Image File Format (TIFF) image file, a format commonly used in the graphics and publishing industries. With the aid of an image manipulation application such as GraphicConverter, you could go on to convert the TIFF image to just about any image format you desire, including Graphics Interchange Format (GIF) or Joint Photographic Experts Group (JPEG) for use on the Web.

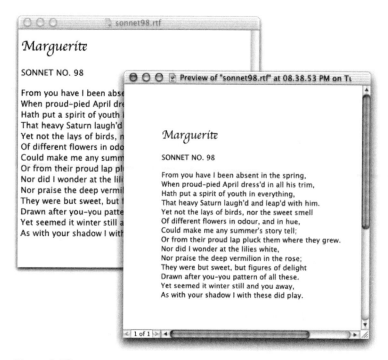

Figure 9.12
Previewing a TextEdit document in PDF format using the Print Preview command.

Working with the Print Dialog Box

Now that you've selected a printer and confirmed your basic options using the Page Setup command, printing a document is just a few clicks away. In most applications, the Print command is located in the File menu and also can be accessed through the Command+P shortcut, which produces a print dialog box like the one shown in Figure 9.13.

The configuration options for a specific print job are easily identified here, but take note of a hidden catch: Each application may have additional settings that apply to only that specific application, as is the case with the HTML and text-editing power-house BBEdit. Figure 9.14 shows the BBEdit-specific settings in the Print dialog box; these settings offer users the opportunity to select a different set of font and tab settings for printing documents, as opposed to font and tab options for viewing documents. To determine whether an application has additional printing options, click on the drop-down menu whose default selection is entitled Copies & Pages (see Figure 9.13) for any available options. Otherwise, just enter any necessary information about the printer to which the document should be sent, the number of copies, and so on.

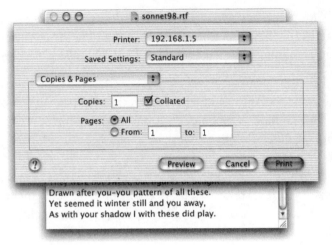

Figure 9.13
A sample print dialog box for TextEdit.

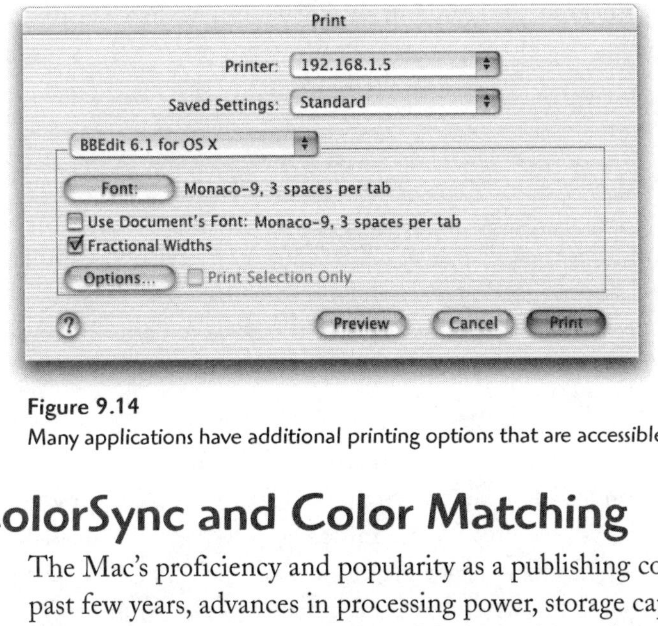

Figure 9.14
Many applications have additional printing options that are accessible via the Print dialog box.

ColorSync and Color Matching

The Mac's proficiency and popularity as a publishing computer is well known. In the past few years, advances in processing power, storage capacities, scanning, and output technology have earned the Mac OS the leading role in even the most demanding high-quality color publishing situations. Publications from *The New Yorker* to *People* are now produced fully or partially on the Macintosh. Mac OS X continues to support this effort with the latest version of ColorSync.

Despite the overall improvements in color publishing technology, one aspect of color publishing has remained a challenge: matching the colors that appear onscreen to

9

those that are printed on color proofing devices and, finally, to the colors of the finished product, which are usually based on film output. Maintaining the consistency of colors as they move from an onscreen display to different output devices has been difficult for two basic reasons.

First, computer monitors produce colors by adding together differing percentages of red, green, and blue light. This method of mixing light from original sources is called *additive color*. Output devices, on the other hand, work by applying color to a page that will selectively absorb light waves when the document is illuminated via an external white light (such as that from light bulbs or the sun). This method of creating colors is called *subtractive color*. Additive and subtractive colors produce fundamentally different ranges of colors. For this reason, onscreen color (additive) offers bright, highly saturated colors that invariably appear darker when printed (subtractive) on paper or other materials.

Second, variations among printers, monitors, and presses make it impossible for each of them to produce exactly the same range and quality of colors. An inexpensive ink-jet printer has one set of printable colors, a color laser printer another, a dye sublimation printer yet another, a web press another, and a high-quality sheet-fed press another still.

Differences in the color models and technical characteristics of color devices result in each device having its own specific gamut, or range, of colors. To achieve consistent color across different devices, the trick is to map colors from one device to another so that when a file is displayed or produced on each device, the differences between the devices' gamuts are accounted and compensated for and the color remains as consistent as possible.

Apple's ColorSync performs this task using a system of device-specific profiles. When ColorSync is installed, colors are converted from their original definitions into a device-independent definition based on the international CIE XYZ color standard or color space. (A color space is a three-dimensional mapping of a range of possible colors.) This conversion is done using a device profile, a small file that tells ColorSync about the color characteristics and capabilities of the input device or monitor. Once a color is defined in CIE XYZ, it is then translated by utilizing a set of color matching method (CMM) algorithms for output using the device profile of the output device. Figure 9.15 shows the ColorSync System Preferences pane, where you'll configure your computer to use ColorSync.

Apple furnishes device profiles for its own monitors, scanners, and color printers, but the success of ColorSync will be dependent upon third-party developers producing

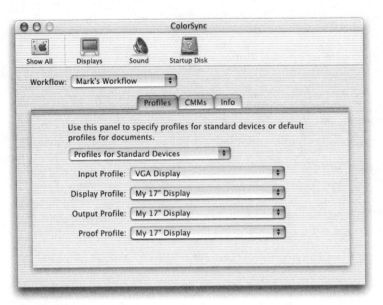

Figure 9.15
The ColorSync System Preferences pane.

and distributing device profiles for their scanners, monitors, and printers. To use ColorSync effectively, you must have device profiles for each of the specific scanners, monitors, and printers you're using for any given project.

When ColorSync translates colors into or out of the CIE XYZ color model, it does so with the goal of providing the best possible match between the original color and the final color. Differences in devices sometimes make an exact match impossible, as explained earlier. The algorithm ColorSync uses to perform this translation was designed for optimum results, but it was also designed to use a small amount of memory and provide good performance. Other companies, such as EFI and Kodak, have developed their own conversion methods—based on look-up tables rather than algorithms—that produce superior results. However, for each input and output device, these methods require far more memory, information, and expertise. Finally, these methods are compatible with ColorSync and can be put to good use by anyone working in high-quality color who desires improved results.

By providing an automated color-matching system, Apple has taken the uncertainty out of using color. What was once tedious work is now handled for you by hardware vendors and software programmers. The quality of this translation will no doubt improve over time.

Wrapping Up

Fonts, printing, and color matching continue to be exciting parts of the Macintosh experience, and as shown in this chapter, font technology remains a source of innovation and complexity. In this chapter, I hope you have learned more about:

■ *The Quartz imaging model*—How Apple's system-level page description language for graphics and type allows for easy development of sophisticated applications.

■ *Fonts*—How to select, install, and work with bitmapped, Type 1 (PostScript), TrueType, and OpenType fonts.

■ *The Font Panel*—How to use the Font Panel to easily change font options from within Carbon and Cocoa applications.

■ *Font utilities*—How to use several third-party font utilities.

■ *Color matching*—How ColorSync helps match colors.

In Chapter 10, you'll learn about how Mac OS X supports the latest multimedia applications.

Exploring Multimedia

10

The definition of multimedia varies from person to person and era to era. When QuickTime was first released by Apple (10 years ago), it helped introduce and popularize the concept of watching movies on your computer—the latest in multimedia technology at the time. Today, on the other hand, watching videos with a Web browser and converting CDs into MP3 format and burning them on a CD-ROM constitute examples of multimedia. As times change, so does the relevance of multimedia. What will we think of as multimedia ten years from now?

Technically speaking, multimedia refers to the combination of sounds and images in digital format on a computer. In the past few years the definition of multimedia has grown to encompass QuickTime movies, Musical Instrument Digital Interface (MIDI), virtual reality, 3D rendering, and Moving Picture Experts Group Layer-3 (MPEG-3 or MP3). Mac OS X supports most of the multimedia capabilities of Mac OS 9.1; any shortcomings, such as the ability to play or create DVD movies, will be resolved by the time you read this book. For now, I'll demonstrate how you can use Mac OS X to implement the following multimedia applications:

- QuickTime, for playing QuickTime, QuickTime VR, and QuickTime TV movies

- Text-to-speech and speech-to-text

- iTunes, for listening to MP3s and burning custom CDs

- iMovie, for creating professional-looking movies

Together, these components give you a high-performance multimedia computer that can play movies, sounds, and MIDI files, and even speak back to you using a variety of voices. Captain Janeway would be proud of our progress, don't you think?

QuickTime

For years, Macintosh has led the way for personal computers in typography, graphics, sound, and high-resolution color. Version 5 of QuickTime, which ships with Mac OS X, continues this tradition by blazing the trail in video and audio capabilities. The multimedia framework of QuickTime makes moving images and sounds basic types of Macintosh data. All kinds of applications—word processors, databases, presentation graphics packages, page-layout programs—can incorporate these moving images as easily as standard graphics.

QuickTime is now an essential component of the Mac OS, and is also an option for users of Windows 95, 98, ME, NT, and 2000. QuickTime for Java enables any computer that can run Java to benefit from many QuickTime features that are found on the Mac and Windows platforms. The consumer version of QuickTime is available at no charge and is distributed in a number of different formats and channels:

- QuickTime 5 is included as part of Mac OS X.

- QuickTime can be downloaded from Apple's QuickTime Web site (**www.apple.com/ quicktime/**). It can also be downloaded from online services or obtained from most Macintosh user groups.

- Many QuickTime-dependent applications include QuickTime on their distribution disks.

Actually, QuickTime comes in two versions: QuickTime and QuickTime Pro. QuickTime is free and comes with Mac OS X; QuickTime Pro, on the other hand, costs around $30 and enables you to perform significantly more tasks. The Pro version provides many additional features, including:

- Creating new QuickTime movies from existing movies

- Editing QuickTime movies, including individual tracks within a movie

- Playing or exporting more than 50 types of multimedia file formats

- Viewing almost all the multimedia types on the Web with the QuickTime plug-in

- Creating slide shows

Although the standard version is fine if all you need to do is view movies over the Web, the Pro version opens up several new doors to the world of multimedia.

What's New with QuickTime 5

Many of QuickTime 5's new features are performance related or enable additional file formats to be opened or saved. Depending on your computer, movies can now vary from 240×180 pixels at 1fps (frames per second) to a full screen at 30fps. The QuickTime Player application replaces SimplePlayer, the application that shipped with earlier versions of QuickTime. In addition, the following features of QuickTime have undergone improvement:

- *QuickTime DataPipe*—The DataPipe, which improves performance on all types of CD-ROM drives, allows tracks to be preloaded into memory prior to playback.

- *Music*—Movies can now contain music tracks. Data is stored as a series of note commands in the same way that music is stored in MIDI files.

- *MPEG-1*—MPEG-1 is an international standard for digital video.

- *Timecode*—QuickTime can store a timecode in a movie.

- *Burnt text*—QuickTime 1.6 introduced anti-aliasing text; version 2 added the capability to store prerendered text in a compressed image for faster redraw.

- *Drag and drop*—Drag and drop selections of a movie or sound into other QuickTime documents. When you're in QuickTime Player, you can also drag a movie from the Finder into a sequence.

- *Copyright dialog*—You can now add copyright information directly to a movie. Use the Set Movie Information command in the QuickTime Player application to add the information in the authoring mode. You can then view the information with the Show Copyright command.

- *Sprites*—A sprite is a graphic that can be animated by commands that determine the sprite's movements (as opposed to storing a full frame for each step of the animation).

- *Improved Web support*—When you download a QuickTime movie from the Web, the movie will begin to play as soon as enough data has arrived; this is known as the fast-start feature.

- *Streaming*—QuickTime 4 and higher allow live Webcasts to be streamed over the Internet so you can watch or hear a live broadcast.

- *Performance*—The performance of just about every aspect of QuickTime, including audio and video compression, QuickTime VR (virtual reality), import and export features, and special effects, has been improved.

10

- *AppleScript*—QuickTime is scriptable in Mac OS 9.1 and Mac OS X; AppleScript supports the automation of tasks.

- *MP3*—The QuickTime Player is now capable of playing MP3 audio files.

- *Miscellaneous*—A number of other small changes have been added, including the ability to play Audio Interchange File Format (AIFF) and WAV sound files directly.

These are only a small fraction of the total improvements and capabilities of QuickTime—I could easily write an entire book on the details of QuickTime's capabilities and features. Instead, let me describe some of the basic features of QuickTime that you're most likely to utilize.

Preview Instead of PictureViewer

QuickTime allows Mac OS X to play many types of movie and sound formats. Image formats such as GIF and JPEG cannot be played, however, because the PictureViewer application is not included in QuickTime for Mac OS X (whereas it is included in QuickTime for Mac OS 9.1). Instead, Mac OS X uses the Preview application to open and save images in the following formats:

- BMP (the native, bitmap image format for Microsoft Windows)

- Joint Photographic Experts Group (JPEG)

- MacPaint

- PICT (the native image format for Mac OS 9.1 and earlier)

- Photoshop

- Portable Network Graphics (PNG)

- QuickTime Image

- Silicon Graphics

- Tagged Information File Format (TIFF)

- Truvision Advanced Raster Graphics Array (TARGA)

In addition to opening and saving images in these file formats, which mirror the file formats that PictureViewer can open and save, Preview can open documents in PDF format as well. Also, note that if you have QuickTime for Mac OS 9.1 in-stalled on your computer and you double-click on a file with the creator code for the PictureViewer application, Mac OS X will attempt to open the image using PictureViewer in the Classic environment. To open an image with Preview instead, launch Preview, choose File|Open (or Command+O), and select the image file.

QuickTime Basics

QuickTime has hundreds of features and numerous capabilities, but at its most basic level QuickTime enables you to perform the following three types of tasks:

- Play movies

- Navigate QuickTime VR panoramas

- Play audio

The basic QuickTime movie file format is called Movie; the file extension is .mov and the file type is MooV. Like other file formats, such as PICT, EPS, or TIFF, the Movie file format saves a certain kind of data—in this case, moving video, animation, or sound (or all of these)—in a way that can be viewed at a specified rate and quality. By defining this file format at the system level, Apple makes it easy for application developers to support this kind of data—which encourages them to develop sophisticated ways to work with data that changes or reacts to user input to create special effects or clickable hotspots to other movies or even Web pages. The major file import and export formats supported by QuickTime 5 are shown in Table 10.1.

Table 10.1   QuickTime for Mac OS X import/export file formats.

File Format	Import?	Export?	Application
3DMF	Yes	No	QuickTime
AIFF	Yes	Yes	QuickTime
AU	Yes	Yes	QuickTime
Audio CD Data (Mac OS)	Yes	No	QuickTime
AVI	Yes	Yes	QuickTime
BMP	Yes	Yes	Preview
Cubic VR	Yes	Yes	QuickTime
DLS	Yes	No	QuickTime
DV	Yes	Yes	QuickTime
FlashPix	Yes	No	QuickTime
FLC	Yes	Yes	QuickTime
GIF	Yes	No	QuickTime
JPEG/JFIF	Yes	Yes	Preview
Karaoke	Yes	No	QuickTime
M3U	Yes	No	QuickTime
MacPaint	Yes	Yes	Preview

(continued)

10

Table 10.1   QuickTime for Mac OS X import/export file formats *(continued).*

File Format	Import?	Export?	Application
Macromedia Flash 4	Yes	No	QuickTime
MIDI	Yes	Yes	QuickTime
MP3	Yes	No	QuickTime
MPEG-1	Yes	No	QuickTime
Photoshop	Yes	Yes	Preview
PICS	Yes	No	QuickTime
PICT	Yes	Yes	Preview
PLS	Yes	No	QuickTime
PNG	Yes	Yes	Preview
QuickTime Image File	Yes	Yes	Preview
QuickTime Movie	Yes	Yes	QuickTime
SF2	Yes	No	QuickTime
SGI	Yes	Yes	Preview
System 7 Sound	Yes	Yes	QuickTime
TARGA	Yes	Yes	Preview
Text	Yes	Yes	QuickTime
TIFF	Yes	Yes	Preview
Virtual Reality	Yes	No	QuickTime
WAV	Yes	Yes	QuickTime

A QuickTime movie acts much as any other text or graphic element—you can select, cut, copy, or paste it either within or between QuickTime-savvy applications. When you select a movie, the QuickTime Player displays a set of controls that enables you to adjust the volume (if it has sound) and play the movie, as well as fast forward, reverse, or jump anywhere in between the beginning or end. For example, Figure 10.1 shows a QuickTime movie embedded in a Web page.

The image you see in the QuickTime Player window when the movie itself isn't playing is called its *poster*. The poster is a selected image from the movie. Because it's often not the first frame of the movie, you'll see the image of the poster jump to another image when the movie begins.

A *preview* is a moving representation of the movie. Although not all movies have previews, most longer ones do. A preview gives you a quick look at the movie highlights. A series of standard file dialog boxes lets you choose whether to see the poster or a preview before you open a movie.

As in previous versions of the Mac OS, all these features are available whether you are viewing QuickTime files in a Web browser using the QuickTime plug-in (Figure 10.1) or through the QuickTime Player application, shown in Figure 10.2.

Figure 10.1
A QuickTime movie with its controls.

10

Figure 10.2
Use the QuickTime Player application to view QuickTime movies.

Configuring QuickTime

QuickTime's main configuration is accomplished through the QuickTime System Preferences, shown in Figure 10.3. However, because QuickTime is also an application and a Web browser plug-in, there are also shortcuts in each to configure the other. The Preferences screen contains the following options:

- *Plug-In tab*—Configure the QuickTime Web browser plug-in to play movies automatically when loaded, save the movie and sound files in the browser's cache file on the hard drive, and enable a kiosk mode, which is designed to prevent users from saving movies to disk. The MIME Settings button is used to set which types of data the QuickTime plug-in is allowed to handle from within the Web browser.

- *Connection tab*—Allows you to tell QuickTime the speed of your network connection. QuickTime uses this information to help download the best file size for movies that have been optimized for various connection speeds. As a general rule, faster connections can handle larger files, and larger files are capable of better image and sound quality. You can also configure streaming transport options, which the QuickTime Player application uses to receive streamed data by way of one of several Internet protocols.

- *Music tab*—Configures QuickTime to use a particular synthesizer to play MIDI and music data.

- *Media Keys tab*—Provided by content creators to allow you to access private files.

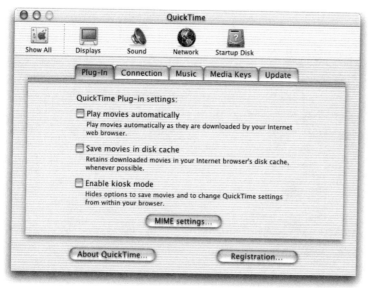

Figure 10.3
QuickTime System Preferences.

- *Update tab*—Allows you to update or install QuickTime and third-party software, as well as check for updates automatically. This feature works independently of the Software Update System Preferences feature.

- *Registration button*—The Registration section is where you go to register the Pro version of QuickTime.

In addition to these configuration options, you can also configure Web browsers to use the QuickTime plug-in for various types of multimedia. To configure the QuickTime plug-in, follow these steps:

1. Make sure the QuickTime plug-in is in your Internet Plug-ins folder, located in *<hard drive>*/Library/.

> Both Netscape Navigator and Microsoft Internet Explorer use Netscape-style plug-ins, so don't be alarmed if the plug-ins in your Internet Explorer folder have Navigator icons.

2. Review your browser's file helper configuration options to make sure QuickTime is properly defined as a file type. If not, open Explorer|Preferences|File Helpers and configure your settings like those shown in Figure 10.4.

3. Next, visit the QuickTime home page at **www.apple.com/quicktime/** and load one of the movies listed in the QuickTime Showcase section. If it won't load, check your browser's preferences and make sure it's configured to view QuickTime files via the QuickTime plug-in.

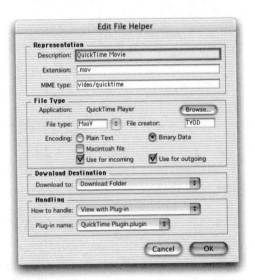

Figure 10.4
Your browser may need a bit of assistance in recognizing QuickTime files, although the presence of the QuickTime plug-in should be sufficient for most Web browsers.

4. If the QuickTime plug-in is properly recognized by the browser, the movie will begin streaming.

5. To configure the QuickTime plug-in, click on the triangle in the lower-right corner of the controls to reveal a shortcut to several of the QuickTime System Preferences.

6. When you're ready to save a movie or sound file (if you have the Pro version), just click on the triangle again and choose Save As QuickTime Movie, as in Figure 10.5, or Save As Source (to preserve the original file format).

Figure 10.5
Saving a QuickTime movie from within a Web browser.

QuickTime and Data Compression

One of QuickTime's most important technological breakthroughs is the real-time compression and decompression it provides to video, animation, and other graphics. QuickTime supports several built-in compression schemes and can easily support others as necessary. The built-in compression is a software-only solution, capable of achieving ratios as great as 25:1 without any visible loss in image quality. With specialized hardware, compression ratios as high as 160:1 are possible.

Compression is particularly important because of all the data needed to generate moving images and accompanying sounds. A good rule of thumb for estimating movie size is that every minute of motion consumes 10MB of disk space. As another example, a seven-minute, full-size, full-resolution movie could consume 200MB in its uncompressed form. Compressed, that same movie might need only 45MB. Of course, most movies are significantly shorter (lasting between 5 and 30 seconds), so files in the 200KB to 1MB range are common.

The actual size of a QuickTime movie depends on many things, including:

- *Frames per second*—Most QuickTime movies are recorded using 10, 12, 15, or 30 frames per second (fps). Without additional hardware for video acceleration, 15fps is the QuickTime standard; 30fps, which is the standard for commercial-quality video, is supported by QuickTime 5, although it will also support 29.97fps (which matches the frame rate of professional video equipment). The higher the frame rate, the larger the resulting movie file.

- *Image size*—Measured in horizontal and vertical pixels, the image size determines how large the movie will appear onscreen. The larger the image, the larger the movie file.

- *Resolution*—QuickTime supports all of the Mac's color bit depth—from 1 to 32 bit. The higher the resolution, the larger the movie file.

- *Audio sampling rate*—This rate can be thought of as the "resolution" of the sound. The Macintosh supports 8, 11, 22, or 44kHz audio sampling, although anything higher than 22kHz requires additional hardware. The higher the sampling rate, the larger the sound portion of a movie file.

- *Compression*—As mentioned earlier, QuickTime supports a number of compression schemes. You can select the degree of compression for each scheme. Increasing compression reduces movie size, but sometimes compromises playback quality. New compression schemes in QuickTime 5 should reduce or eliminate these kinds of problems.

- *Content*—Beyond the previously mentioned technical factors, the actual set of sounds and images contained in a movie is what will ultimately determine its size. This factor makes it difficult to estimate the size of a QuickTime movie based solely on its length or technical characteristics.

10

You can use QuickTime to watch movies (which may be included on CD-ROM disks, obtained from user groups or online services, or come embedded in documents you get from other Mac users), or you can create your own QuickTime movies. It's easy for almost anyone with a Mac to view a QuickTime movie, and with a digital camcorder and iMovie (discussed later in this chapter) just about anyone can create a movie and save it in QuickTime format.

Most QuickTime movies that are available now are part of CD-ROM–based information discs that provide education or information on music, history, sports, news, entertainment, or computer-related topics. CD-ROM is the perfect medium for QuickTime because it has huge storage capabilities (650MB), can be inexpensively reproduced, and has access times sufficient to deliver good-quality playback. CD-ROM support for QuickTime has recently been enhanced by faster CD drives and performance improvements included in QuickTime 5.

Using the QuickTime Player

The QuickTime Player has been slightly revised in QuickTime 5 to incorporate more intuitive (i.e., fewer) user controls. It also features QuickTime TV and an area in which you can store your favorite movies. And in addition to the QuickTime System Preferences, a few additional preferences that affect the behavior of the QuickTime Player are accessed via the QuickTime Player|Preferences|Player Preferences menu, including:

- *Open Movies In New Players*—Opens each movie in a new window.

- *Automatically Play Movies When Opened*—Begin playing a movie when opened in the QuickTime Player application.

- *Play Sound In Frontmost Player Only*—Mutes the sound of all movies and sound files except the one in the frontmost window.

- *Play Sound When Application Is In Background*—Continues to play the sound of a movie or sound file when QuickTime Player is in the background.

- *Ask Before Replacing Favorite Items*—Gives an alert when replacing one favorite with a new favorite.

To play a movie, double-click on any movie or sound file that has a QuickTime icon, or launch the QuickTime Player application from the Dock. When playing a movie, you'll notice that the QuickTime Player controls look different in comparison to those in previous versions of the application. Users complained that there were too many controls, and that they were not intuitive. Figure 10.6 illustrates the new controls.

Right off the bat, experienced users will notice the new Aquafied interface and the new TV button. Otherwise, the controls are self-explanatory and include volume, start/stop, and directional buttons. The TV button reveals a collection of QuickTime TV channels, shown in Figure 10.7, which are links to a combination of QuickTime-enabled Web sites with streaming and downloadable (non-streaming) content. For more QuickTime TV channels, see **www.apple.com/quicktime/qttv/**.

Clicking on the tab with the heart-shaped icon (next to the QuickTime TV tab shown in Figure 10.7) reveals a palette similar to that of the QuickTime TV channel palette. This palette, however, is blank—use this area to store shortcuts to your favorite QuickTime files. To add a favorite, just drag and drop its Finder icon to an empty channel slot. To view the QuickTime TV or Favorites channel palettes, you can also select them from the QTV menu in the QuickTime Player application.

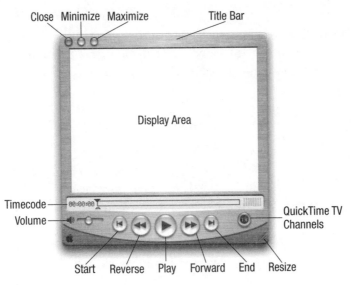

Figure 10.6
The QuickTime Player application sports a new set of controls.

Figure 10.7
Check out the QuickTime TV channels by clicking the round TV button in the QuickTime Player application.

10

Finally, the Pro version allows you to selectively play the audio or video track of a movie, as well as export it as a streaming QuickTime movie, among other formats. Of course, you can also create new movie and sound tracks if you have a digital input device for movies, such as a digital camera, or for sounds, such as a microphone or a CD-ROM.

QuickTime VR

QuickTime VR (QTVR) is a type of QuickTime movie that allows you to actually walk through a movie, spin around, look up and down, and manipulate objects from within the movie. QTVR takes digital images, stitches them together, and makes them look as if they were taken with a movie camera in three dimensions—pretty neat stuff. You can view QTVR movies from within a Web browser, thanks to the QuickTime plug-in, or using the QuickTime Player application. For more information on this, see the QTVR home page at **www.apple.com/quicktime/qtvr/**.

QTVR movies come in two basic types: one in which you move around within the movie, and another in which an object, such as a book, car, or planet, is manipulated. The difference is whether it's you or the object that is moving. A really complex QTVR movie can contain both. Figure 10.8 shows a sample QTVR movie of Grand Central Station in New York City. Notice the controls are a little different when viewing a QTVR movie. Typically, you can zoom in, out, or restart a QTVR movie.

Figure 10.8
Take a virtual tour using QuickTime VR.

Speech

Computer-generated speech has had an interesting history on the Macintosh. The very first program anyone saw running on a Mac in public was Macintalk, a text-to-speech generator that could create fairly realistic-sounding speech. At the introduction of the Macintosh, Steve Jobs pulled a Mac out of a carrying case and the Mac joked, "Thanks, it was hot in there." Ah, progress.

Apple eventually released Macintalk for developers to incorporate into their own programs; few took the opportunity, however, because Macintalk wasn't part of the standard system installation. Eventually, two forms of speech compatibility were incorporated into the Mac OS:

- *Speech recognition*—The ability of the Mac OS to recognize commands spoken through a microphone and perform tasks

- *Text-to-speech*—The conversion of written text into speech, output through the computer's internal or external speakers

Mac OS X incorporates all of the speech features found in earlier versions of the Mac OS, with a few cosmetic differences and a new set of built-in commands. The following sections describe the basics of these speech capabilities.

Speech Recognition

Mac OS X installs all the software necessary for your computer to listen for and execute a predefined set of commands. All you need is a microphone, which is built into most PowerBooks and iBooks. Speech recognition is not enabled by default, however; to get started, open the System Preferences and follow these steps:

10

1. Switch to the Speech pane, shown in Figure 10.9. Although Apple Speakable Items is the only system available at this time to implement speech recognition in Mac OS X, other systems may be developed or ported to Mac OS X in the future.

2. Enable Apple Speakable Items by selecting the On button in the On/Off section of the window.

3. Click the Helpful Tips button for a few pointers on topics such as how to best position the microphone.

4. Click the Open Speakable Items Folder button to get a better idea of what commands are available for execution using speech recognition.

Figure 10.9
Use the Speech Recognition section of the Speech System Preferences pane to configure your computer to execute voice commands.

5. Choose a feedback sound to play when a command has been recognized by Speech Recognition; this is helpful because it lets you know that your command has been accepted properly.

6. Click the Speak Text Feedback checkbox to have the Mac OS read alerts and dialog boxes to you.

Next, click on the Listening tab of the Speech Recognition section of the Speech System Preferences pane and configure how Mac OS X should listen for your commands. You have two basic options on how to issue commands, which are shown in Figure 10.10:

■ *Listen Only While Key Is Pressed*—Choose this option to press a key for one second prior to issuing a command. If you choose this option, select the Change Key button to identify a key on the keyboard, such as the Escape or F12 key, to hold down before the command.

■ *Key Toggles Listening On And Off*—Choose this option to use the selected key to turn listening on and off, and to not require the key to be depressed before each command. Instead, toggle speech recognition on and issue a command using a name for the computer in the Name field, and configure how the name is to be used in the Name Is field. The name can be anything you like, but I suggest that you don't

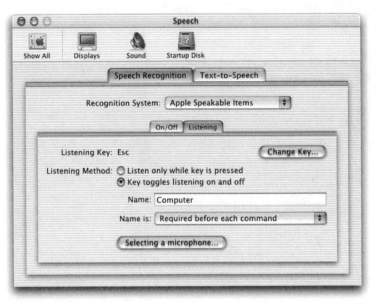

Figure 10.10
Configure how your computer should listen for commands.

use a monosyllabic name such as *Fred* or *Jane* for the computer. Another option is for the name to be completely optional, in which case the computer is constantly listening for commands, which might degrade system performance.

Finally, click the Selecting A Microphone button for a few tips on how Speech Recognition uses microphones to listen for commands, then quit the System Preferences.

Speech recognition works by matching commands you speak with those contained in the folder <*hard drive*>/<*user name*>/Library/Speech/Speakable Items. This folder contains about 62 items for you to try out, such as *Close this window*, *Open Sherlock*, and *Reply to sender*. When you issue a command, Mac OS X displays the command in a small floating window as a means of visual confirmation of the command. Another command, *Show me what to say*, opens a floating palette that lists all the commands found in the Speakable Items folder, which is very handy as you learn how to use speech recognition. This window, and an example of the confirmation window, are both shown in Figure 10.11.

Finally, you'll probably want to create new commands to suit your own needs rather than be limited by the canned commands that are installed by the Speech System Preferences. You have two options for creating new commands:

■ Create an alias to an existing Finder item, such as an application or document, and place the alias in the Speakable Items folder.

Figure 10.11
The *Show me what to say* command displays a list of all the commands that you can use.

■ Write an AppleScript to execute a command or series of commands, and place the script in the Speakable Items folder.

I'll cover AppleScript in the next chapter—in the interim, let me give you a quick example of how to make a useful command using an alias. iTunes has quickly become one of the most popular applications for the Mac OS, and the following steps will show you how to open iTunes using speech recognition:

1. Locate the iTunes application in the Finder.

2. Create an alias of iTunes and rename it *Play music*.

3. Open the Speakable Items folder in a new Finder window.

4. Drag the alias entitled *Play music* into the Speakable Items folder.

To try out your new shortcut, just speak the command *Play music*.

Next, let's look at how to convert text on your computer into spoken words.

Text-to-Speech

The Text-to-Speech section of the Speech System Preferences pane allows you to configure the Mac OS to speak alerts and the contents of certain dialog boxes, as well as speech-aware applications to speak the contents of documents. At this time, however, there are no speech-aware applications for Mac OS X to demonstrate, including Apple's TextEdit word processor.

However, the Mac OS and AppleScript can use text-to-speech. To configure the speech capabilities of Mac OS X, open the Speech pane of the System Preferences, and switch to the Text-To-Speech tab (shown in Figure 10.12) to configure the following two options:

■ *Voice*—The computer-generated voice, such as Fred or Kathy, used by Mac OS X to speak.

■ *Rate*—The rate at which the voice speaks. Some of the voices are slow and could use a little speeding up, so play around to configure a voice to which you'll be comfortable listening to on a regular basis.

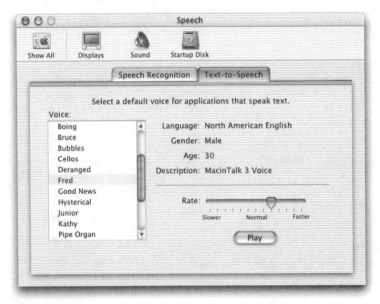

Figure 10.12

The Text-to-Speech section of the Speech System Preferences pane lets you select your computer's voice.

A number of different voices are available. They run the gamut from pleasant and understandable to difficult and unintelligible. Some are quite amusing—the Deranged voice speaks through a lunatic laugh, and the Good News voice sings your text to the tune of "Pomp and Circumstance."

iTunes

The latest craze in the multimedia world is MPEG Audio Layer-3 (abbreviated MP3), an ultra-efficient audio file format that is about 10 times more efficient than the standard CD-ROM audio format. The greatest thing about MP3 is that you can shrink an entire audio CD track, which is usually about 30MB, into a file that's 2 to

3MB in size. This is a very manageable file size for use on the Web, and it opens up new possibilities for artists who want to break into new markets without the overhead of mastering and distributing CDs. In fact, many people believe that the future of music distribution will be in a format similar to MP3, which can be downloaded over the Web instead of purchased in a music store.

iTunes, an MP3 player that runs natively on Mac OS X, allows you to convert audio CDs into MP3 format and store them on your hard drive, in addition to playing MP3 tunes. If you have a CD-R (CD-Record) or CD-RW (CD-Rewrite) drive, iTunes will also allow you to create (or "burn") CDs using the MP3 files on your computer. If you have an Internet connection, you can listen to streaming MP3 radio stations with iTunes. Download the latest version of iTunes from **www.apple.com/itunes/** and launch the iTunes application, an example of which is shown in Figure 10.13.

Figure 10.13
Playing an audio CD using iTunes.

iTunes performs most of the tasks you'll need from a multipurpose MP3 player. However, more and more players that incorporate different features are being created. Version 1.1.1 of iTunes is capable of performing the following functions:

■ *Play audio CDs*—To play a CD, just insert the CD and click on the small icon of the CD in the Source section on the left side of the iTunes window.

■ *Encode audio CDs*—Insert a CD, highlight the tracks you want to encode, and click the Import button in the upper-right corner of the application window. Alternatively, choose Advanced|Convert To MP3 and select a CD or other sound file when prompted. The files will be stored in the location specified in iTunes's preferences (iTunes|Preferences or Command+Y).

- *Burn audio CDs*—To create audio CDs from MP3 files, select the files and click the Burn CD button in the upper-right corner of the application window. iTunes will calculate the number of tracks, the total time for the tracks, and their physical size and display this information in the bottom center of the main window. Knowing the total time will help you decide how many tracks will fit on a CD; a standard audio CD can hold 74 minutes of music, although newer CD players accept 80-minute CDs. Stick to the 74-minute limit to ensure compatibility with the majority of CD players.

- *Categorize music*—You can create as many playlists (i.e., collections of songs) as you like by choosing File|New Playlist and dragging and dropping MP3 files to the new playlist.

- *Search for tracks*—To search for a particular track in your MP3 library, enter a search phrase in the Search field and iTunes will begin filtering through the information entered for all files. For example, Figure 10.14 shows the result of typing *fa* in the search field. Note that iTunes searched 89 files and found 3 matches.

- *Listen to streaming MP3s*—You can listen to a specific MP3 stream if you know the URL, or you can browse the Radio Tuner section and select from many categories. For example, Figure 10.15 shows two views of iTunes playing streaming MP3. The top view shows WUNC radio's streaming content (**http://152.2.63.108:8000**) in a compacted window, and the bottom shows one of nine stations in the Blues

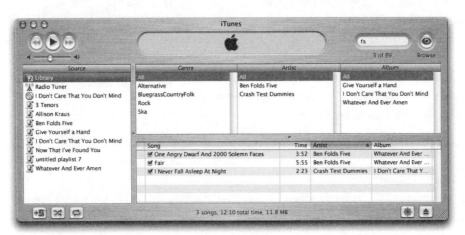

Figure 10.14
Use the search feature in iTunes to find an entry in your music library.

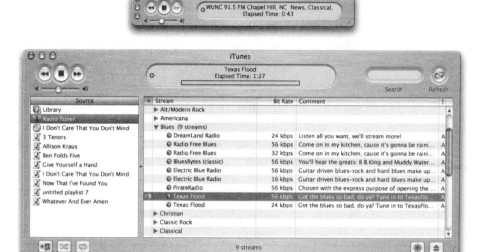

Figure 10.15
Two view of iTunes connected to streaming MP3 sites.

category. The quality of the stream depends on the speed of your Internet connection and the size of the streaming buffer as configured in the Advanced section of iTunes's preferences. With a fast connection and a large buffer setting, the quality of sound is very comparable to broadcast FM radio, but not quite CD quality.

QuickTime Player is also capable of playing MP3s. If you'd prefer a commercial MP3 player with more features than QuickTime Player or iTunes, check out SoundJam MP from Casady & Greene (**www.soundjam.com**). SoundJam MP uses a sleek, customizable interface and is very easy to use. Shown in Figure 10.16, SoundJam MP consists of a player (top left), an equalizer (top right), and a playlist window (bottom). You can also use SoundJam MP to encode sound files into MP3 format, as well as broadcast streaming MP3s over the Internet. For about $40, SoundJam MP is the best MP3 application for Mac OS X.

Finally, for the latest information about MP3 and links to FAQs and MP3 files, see the MP3.com Web site (**www.mp3.com**); for information about the most popular CD cataloging resource, see Gracenote (**www.gracenote.com**), formerly known as CDDB. The Gracenote (CDDB) database is a massive database of audio CDs that is used by iTunes and SoundJam MP to recognize CDs when they are inserted in your computer to display information about the CD's artist, tracks, genre, and so on.

Figure 10.16
SoundJam MP's player, equalizer, and playlist.

iMovie

iMovie, the latest addition to the Apple multimedia family, allows you to create professional-looking movies. iMovie is capable of incorporating QuickTime movies, images, sounds, MP3s, title tracks, and transitional and special effects into a multilayered movie that you can save to disk or, if you have a VHS camcorder, save to VHS. Figure 10.17 shows a tiny fraction of iMovie's capabilities.

iMovie works with many FireWire-enabled camcorders to acquire video, or you can use existing QuickTime movie and sound tracks as the basis for your new movie. Because the movie files you create can be huge, be wary about saving them to file. Instead of saving them to file, you can upload them to VHS through your VHS-based camcorder, burn them to CD or DVD, or upload them (small ones, anyway!) to your iTools account. For more information about iMovie, and to download the latest version, see **www.apple.com/imovie/**.

10

Figure 10.17
Use iMovie to create sophisticated movies.

Wrapping Up

Mac OS X has many powerful multimedia features that allow you to view, manipulate, or play audio, video, and 3D objects, although not all Macs have the same multimedia storage abilities of CD-R and DVD-R. The Mac OS is the leader in integrating multimedia into the home computer, and whenever a new technology comes to market before Apple can integrate it into the operating system, you can be sure that plenty of software developers will write an application to fill the void. In this chapter, you've learned about:

■ Playing video with QuickTime Player and Web browsers (using the QuickTime plug-in)

■ Viewing images with Preview

■ Using QuickTime VR to walk through virtual worlds and manipulate objects

■ Using speech recognition and text-to-speech

■ Listening to MP3s using iTunes and SoundJam MP

■ Creating movies with iMovie

In the next chapter, we'll look at how AppleScript can help automate tasks and provide shortcuts.

10

Scripting Mac OS X

Shortcuts are a way of life for many computer users. They help us save time and effort and are occasionally entertaining, but most importantly, they make us more productive. The Mac OS has a long history of providing shortcuts to applications and the Mac OS itself through key combinations and menus. In fact, it's safe to say that the graphical user interface's raison d'être is to enable the user to execute complex commands with a click of the mouse—perhaps the ultimate shortcut. Macintosh users can create their own shortcuts with AppleScript, a programming language that is unique to the Mac OS. Many elements of the Mac OS are scriptable (meaning that they "understand" AppleScript as a programming language), as are numerous applications that run under Mac OS X as well as Mac OS 9.1 and earlier.

The ability to control applications, repeat actions, and automate system tasks must originate in the operating system if it is to be successful. AppleScript was designed to provide these essential capabilities as part of an overall strategy to supply automation tools for Macintosh applications. A fully integrated part of the operating system, AppleScript is automatically installed as part of Mac OS X.

AppleScript can be utilized in an impressive variety of ways:

■ AppleScript lets you tailor applications to meet your needs.

■ AppleScript simplifies the work of developers, systems integrators, and value added resellers (VARs) by providing custom solutions based on standard Macintosh applications.

■ AppleScript allows you to write an applet, an intelligent agent, or a smart document that seamlessly integrates small components into larger solutions.

■ Software developers can create entirely new products with AppleScript.

This chapter looks at how AppleScript version 1.6 is implemented in Mac OS X. I'll also show you how to get your programming feet wet with AppleScript and then use your script-writing skills to become more productive.

What Is AppleScript?

Technically speaking, AppleScript is a high-level, object-oriented programming language. As far as programming languages go, AppleScript is the real thing: It can store variables and lists (records or arrays); repeat through looping; make decisions based on cases; do If-Then branching; compare; practice Boolean logic; and manipulate text, numbers, dates, times, and other values. AppleScript can also declare variables, create user-defined commands or subroutines, and store and manipulate data to return values. Of course, this is all meaningless if you're not a real computer geek, which goes to show that underneath the pretty interface, Mac OS X is a complex operating system.

AppleScript is termed an object-oriented programming language because it imposes actions on objects that are defined as part of its programming model. Objects can be applications (the Finder, TextEdit, BBEdit, and so on), files, resources, interface elements (buttons, windows, and so on), or data. In the Finder, objects can be a variety of computers, printers, and even AppleTalk zones on a network. Even the objects you see on your Desktop can be manipulated with AppleScript. Mac OS X also enables scriptable voice recognition and Sherlock scriptability; future versions might also reenable the ability to control other Macs over the Internet via AppleScript, which is available in Mac OS 9.1 but not in Mac OS X.

In AppleScript, objects have two additional characteristics that are part of the programming language: *inheritance* and *encapsulation*. Objects, like applications, can contain other objects (encapsulation); objects derived from other objects share common characteristics (inheritance). AppleScript is an object-oriented programming language, and scriptable applications serve as the objects upon which scripts act. The rules of scriptability from Apple impose regularity on objects by making them behave in ways you expect and come to learn intuitively, like rules of grammar.

AppleScript is different from most other programming languages because it uses *words* and *statements* instead of arcane programming characters and symbols to form a coherent group of commands into a script. Like the English language, AppleScript uses words as nouns (objects), verbs, and modifiers. In AppleScript, verbs are common action commands (such as open, close, print, or delete) that are often derived from standard menu commands. Statements are commands that can be conveyed in the form of messages to objects in other applications. Applications themselves are objects because they can be commanded to do actions. For example, consider the following:

```
tell application "Clock"
    activate
end tell
```

This three-line statement is a complete script that instructs the Finder to launch the Clock application. When viewed in the Script Editor program, a scripting tool installed by Mac OS X, you can see that this type of script uses bolded verbs, plain nouns, and italicized variables to make working with scripts easier than if all the text in the script were plain ASCII text. Often you'll see AppleScripts written in clegic logic (or hierarchical display) format, with indentations for each command structure. You can see an example of this formatting in the Current Date & Time.scpt script, which is located in the Example Scripts folder (discussed later in this chapter) provided by Apple as part of Mac OS X. Figure 11.1 shows what this script looks like in the Script Editor application, as well as the result of the script when the Run button is clicked.

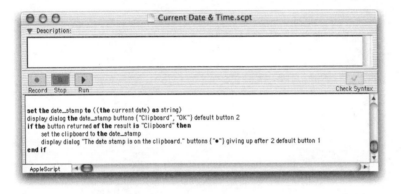

Figure 11.1
Current Date & Time.scpt, shown in the Script Editor (top) and the result of the script when it is run (bottom).

11

As much as possible, AppleScript is written in a manner similar to the way you normally write and speak—although the syntax is certainly much more precise and demanding. The intent is to lower the learning curve for AppleScript by employing words, expressions, and modifiers that you use in your everyday life.

Programs written in AppleScript, called *scripts*, are like those written for all other high-level programming languages. Scripts must be *interpreted* or *compiled* to run on your Macintosh. You can store your script for interpretation at run time or transform it into an interpreted read-only program, which you can then distribute freely to other users. When you compile a script, it is transformed into a dialect-independent format called *Universal AppleScript*. Upon opening a script, you'll see it displayed in the default language of the Macintosh you're working on—not necessarily the language in which the script was originally written. This means that the script has been translated from Universal AppleScript.

AppleScript isn't just a fixed set of commands. Instead, AppleScript is extensible by the scripting commands contained in each scriptable application, which are grouped into a scripting dictionary. Each scripting dictionary is composed of commands (verbs), objects (nouns), and modifiers that are accessible via AppleScript for that specific application, such as Mail or even the Finder. You can view the scripting dictionaries of all the scriptable applications on your computer by selecting the File|Open Dictionary command of the Script Editor, which presents the window shown in Figure 11.2.

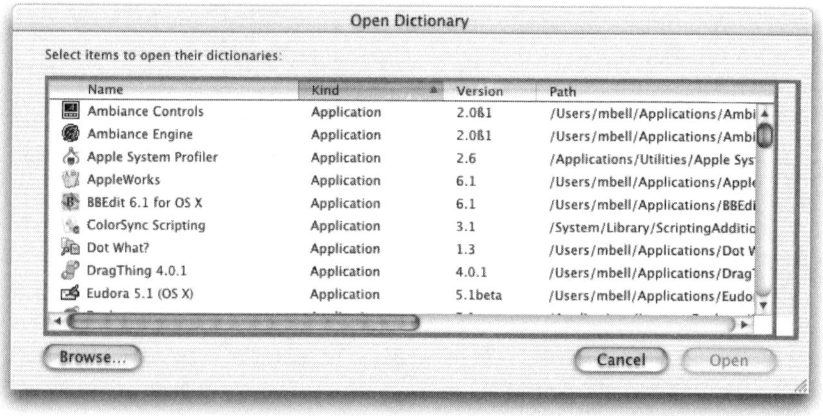

Figure 11.2
The new Open Dictionary command for AppleScript 1.6.

The ability to see all the scripting dictionaries at once is a new feature in AppleScript 1.6 for Mac OS X. However, you can still browse your computer for the scripting dictionary of a specific application by clicking the Browse button in the Open Dictionary window shown in Figure 11.2. You'll be asked to locate the application whose scripting dictionary you're looking for. Figure 11.3 shows an example of one item in the scripting dictionary for Internet Explorer. Although scripting dictionaries share many of the same elements, the dictionary of each scriptable application has at least a few elements all its own.

You can use applications other than Script Editor (such as BBEdit) to write AppleScripts, but at this time no applications other than Script Editor allow you to check syntax or open scripting dictionaries. Two popular applications for working with AppleScript—Scripter from Main Event (**www.mainevent.com**) and Script Debugger

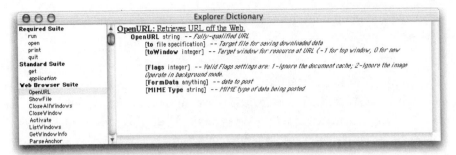

Figure 11.3
The scripting dictionary for Internet Explorer.

from Late Night Software (**www.latenightsw.com**)—are in the process of becoming Mac OS X compliant. Nevertheless, you can still use their applications in Classic mode or when booting into Mac OS 9.1 to write and edit scripts.

The AppleScript Architecture

Most programming languages require that you learn a new language. To minimize this inconvenience, Apple introduced the Open Scripting Architecture (OSA) as a language framework that other software venders could adopt, so that their applications could communicate with each other. A software vendor merely has to follow the OSA specifications to make an application scriptable.

The standards definition phase of OSA began in 1989 and is ongoing. OSA and the Apple Event Registry were released concurrently with System 7 in 1991. This marked the beginning of Interapplication Communication, which is the foundation of the AppleScript architecture. Some key applications that supported AppleScript with the original architecture (such as Excel 4.0, FileMaker Pro 2.0, PageMaker 4.2, and others) were released in 1992. Bundled with System 7 Pro, AppleScript 1.0 premiered as a separate product in 1993; version 1.1 and the Scriptable Finder appeared in System 7.5. The Scriptable Finder, a very important addition to the AppleScript architecture, removed the final advantage of text-based operating systems such as MS-DOS by allowing users to script the operating system. Mac OS X includes the latest version, AppleScript 1.6, and of course it is also highly scriptable using command-line scripts through the Terminal application. See Appendix C for information on learning basic Unix shell commands.

AppleScript is just one expression of OSA. OSA includes AppleEvents, the object model, and a reference library of objects and events that are codified by third parties through Apple. These components form the basis for an open standard that Apple

11

hopes others will build upon in the years to come. AppleScript uses AppleEvents as the messaging medium through which script commands are passed and results returned.

To prevent AppleScript from growing in nonstandard ways, Apple imposes a standard language. Objects in AppleScript are identified by compound names, called *references*. The overall naming scheme is called the *object model*. With this lexicon of references, the language allows you to refer to individual objects in several ways without worrying about how each application prefers to describe an object. Some commands have alternate expressions, as do some objects—fortunately, AppleScript validates both kinds in any application.

A standard syntax is imposed on developers only for common language tasks. Apple has organized events and objects into *event suites*, which are common ways to do tasks based on application categories: text processing, databases and spreadsheets, communications, page layout, and so on. Event suites extend across the programming language the concept of common menu-command language elements such as *copy* and *paste* to scripting commands such as **delete**, **contain**, **get**, and **set**.

Event suites are evolving as developers register their commands, objects, and suites in the AppleEvent Registry (available from the Apple Developer Connection, or ADC). The event suites in this registry are the approved language for interapplication communication; the registry serves as a standard reference for developers who want to implement AppleScript support within their own applications.

The commands that compose the language of AppleScript are contained in files called OSAX, which stands for Open Scripting Architecture Extension. These files are also called Scripting Additions. In previous versions of the operating system, Scripting Additions were contained in a single file called Standard Additions. This file, and other OSAX files, are now located in *<hard drive>*/System/Library/Scripting Additions/. In addition to this unification, a few of the features that extend a developer's abilities include:

- *User interaction*—Users can interact with scripts through script-generated dialog boxes, sounds, and text-to-speech.

- *File commands*—Scripts can request and present files and information about files, disks, folders, and volumes.

- *String commands*—Scripts can manipulate ASCII text, as well as summarize paragraphs or pages of text.

- *Clipboard*—Scripts can now access the data that is contained in the clipboard, set new data, or get information on the data.

- *Delay*—Scripts can incorporate a delay of a certain amount of time, specified in seconds. Scriptwriters use this to give scripts a more natural feel.

- *Choice menus*—A list of items can be presented to users, allowing them to make selections.

- *Timed dialog boxes*—A dialog box can assume a default value if a user does not respond to it within a certain amount of time.

Scripting Basics

AppleScript has been implemented using different components over the years. In earlier versions, AppleScript wasn't a mandatory part of the Mac OS, but eventually it became an integral part of the operating system. Mac OS X installs all the necessary components of AppleScript, including:

- *AppleScript framework*—Contains the AppleScript libraries necessary to interpret scripts for the Mac OS; also passes script commands and data between applications.

- *Scripting Additions folder*—Houses scripting additions that have been written in another programming language and added to scripts to provide additional functionality.

- *Scripts folder*—Stores scripts. Although AppleScripts can be placed just about anywhere on your computer, it makes sense to keep them in one place. Mac OS X provides such a place—a folder aptly named Scripts—in each user's home folder. Keep the originals in the Scripts folder and place aliases to your scripts in convenient locations elsewhere on your computer.

The AppleScript folder, located in the Applications folder, is the home folder for the three items you'll use most when working with AppleScript. The AppleScript folder includes:

- *Script Editor*—The primary application that enables you to write, record, edit, check the syntax of, compile, and run scripts. Shown earlier in Figure 11.1, the Script Editor is a basic but effective means of manipulating AppleScripts. The Script Editor Help covers the basics of writing AppleScripts and using the Script Editor. Choose Help|Script Editor Help to activate the Help Viewer application, shown in Figure 11.4.

- *Script Runner*—A new application that provides easy access to the contents of your Scripts folder, which are described in detail a little later in this chapter.

- *Example scripts*—A folder of example scripts that you can execute or explore with the Script Editor to help teach yourself about AppleScript.

11

Figure 11.4
Script Editor Help provides information about using AppleScript and Script Editor.

Because AppleScript support is added to an application by its developer, not all applications are scriptable in Mac OS X. Moreover, an application may or may not support each of the three levels of scriptability, which are referred to as:

■ *Scriptable*—A scriptable application represents the highest level of AppleScript support. These applications can understand and respond to AppleEvents generated by scripts, and can be controlled by an AppleScript.

■ *Recordable*—A recordable application is capable of sending itself AppleEvents (the messaging medium through which script commands are passed and results returned) and reporting user actions to the Apple Event Manager so that a script summarizing these actions can be recorded. When you use the Record button of the Script Editor, recordable applications allow you to create and compile scripts as applications. This is probably the easiest way to create a script, as it requires no knowledge of scripting. For many users, pressing the Record button and then opening an application is easier than typing the corresponding commands into the Script Editor.

■ *Attachable*—This type of application can trigger a script as a response to a user action (such as clicking a button or entering a text string). Apple describes an attachable application as "tinkerable." Attachable applications are useful as menus to other applications.

Any combination of these three levels of scriptability is possible—you can have an application that is scriptable and recordable, recordable and attachable, scriptable and attachable, or all three. Apple publishes a Web page entitled Scriptable Applications with a listing of each application's capabilities. To view the list or to add an application to the list, you can visit the Apple Web site at **www.apple.com/applescript/enabled. 00.html**.

The Script Editor

The Script Editor, which Apple provides with AppleScript, is the application that allows you to open, run, record, edit, and save scripts in various forms. The following sections illustrate many of the basic principles used in creating and working with AppleScripts.

Recording a Script

The Script Editor comes with a recorder feature that enables you to create scripts based on your actions. Other scripting programs call this a "watch me" kind of programming. As described previously, applications can be scripted in this way only if they are recordable, and the easiest way to determine recordability is to try it out. To record a script, follow these steps:

1. Launch the Script Editor.

2. Click the Record button to turn on the recording feature, or press Command+D.

3. Switch to the application of your choice, including the Finder.

4. Perform the actions in the sequence in which you want them to be recorded.

5. Switch back to the Script Editor window and click the Stop button, or press Command+. (Command+period).

What if you follow these steps and only some of what you did shows up in the Script Editor window? This means that the actions you attempted to record are not in the scripting dictionary of the application(s) involved in creating your recorded script. For example, Figure 11.5 shows the results of recording a script designed to switch to the application BBEdit, create a new document, and type "Hello world" in the new document.

You will notice that the Script Editor has recorded all the commands that correspond to my actions in this example except for the typing of "Hello world" within the BBEdit document. As with other keystroke macro recorders, only certain actions can be captured by the Script Editor: using menu commands, pressing keys, saving files,

11

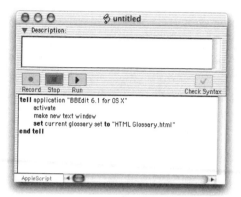

Figure 11.5
The Script Editor window with a sample recorded script.

opening and closing windows and files, and clicking the mouse. Drags and clicks are not captured because they usually don't result in any actions or changes. However, when a click or drag does result in an action, such as activating a button or moving a file to a new folder, that action is recorded. In this example, typing in a BBEdit document is not a recordable action.

 You can also use the commands in the Control menu of the Script Editor in place of the buttons you see in the Script Editor window.

Finally, because the actions were recorded as a script, the syntax does not require checking—therefore, the Check Syntax option (described later) is not available in the Script Editor window.

Saving a Script

When you stop the recording of a script in the Script Editor, or when you've made changes to an existing script, you can save the script from within the Script Editor via the Save As command, as shown in Figure 11.6. Using Script Editor, you can save your script in any of the following five formats:

■ *AppleScript Text*—When saving a script that was created using another text editor, such as BBEdit, the first option listed in the Format section of the Save As window is AppleScript Text. This converts the file creator code from BBEdit (or whatever was used to create the file) to Script Editor, but otherwise doesn't alter the script.

■ *Text*—It's best to save a script as a plain ASCII text file if you intend to use it in programs such as BBEdit, a program that's very popular with application and script authors. Figure 11.7 shows what the example recorded script in Figure 11.5 looks like when viewed in BBEdit as a text file.

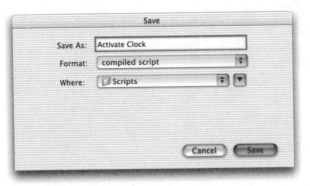

Figure 11.6
The Script Editor Save dialog box.

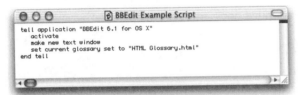

Figure 11.7
An AppleScript saved as a text file, viewed in BBEdit.

- *Compiled Script*—Scripts saved as compiled scripts are designed to be used from within applications or by other scripts, rather than by you, the user.

- *Classic Applet*—Scripts can be saved as applets (small applications) for use in the Classic environment or for Mac OS X. When you double-click on an AppleScript that was saved as a Classic applet, the applet runs by itself without the assistance of the Mac OS 9.1 Script Editor. When you save a script as an application, use the checkboxes in the lower-left corner of the Save dialog box to specify that applications be kept open after the script is run (Stay Open) or that the Script Editor be closed (Never Show Startup Screen) when the script starts up (see Figure 11.8).

  Earlier versions of AppleScript supported various languages, and compiling translated a script from its language of origin into Universal AppleScript, a pseudocode that your Macintosh can read. Since Mac OS 8.6, however, AppleScript has supported English only.

- *Mac OS X Applet*—A script saved as a Mac OS X applet is capable of running on any computer with Mac OS X or an earlier version of the OS that contains and supports the CarbonLib extension, a component that helps support Mac OS X.

Finally, you can save an applet or compiled script as a *runtime*—or as AppleScript calls it, *run-only*—version of your script; you cannot, however, save text files as run-only. A

11

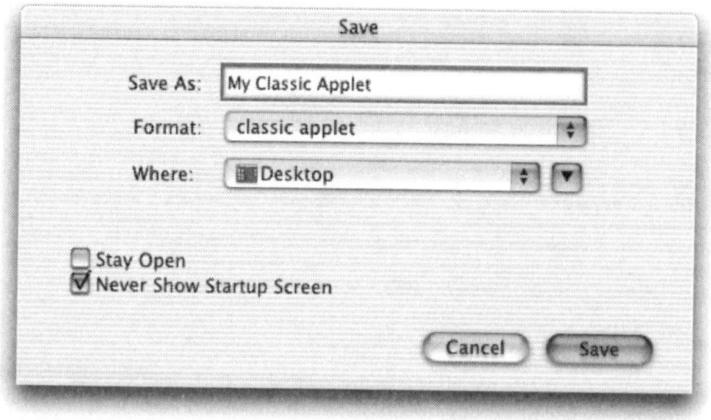

Save
Save As: My Classic Applet
Format: classic applet
Where: Desktop

☐ Stay Open
☑ Never Show Startup Screen

Cancel   Save

Figure 11.8
Saving an AppleScript as a Classic applet.

run-only script is kind of like a compiled application in this respect because you cannot "reverse-engineer" this type of script to see what it looks like in the Script Editor. To save a run-only version of a script, choose the Save As Run-Only command from the File menu. The resulting dialog box will ask you to specify the script's location, name, and format.

 To save a script in a non-editable format, choose Save As | Run-Only from the File menu.

Running a Script

Once you have recorded, written, edited, and saved a script, you can run it in several ways, depending on how the script was saved. You can run the script, or you can run an alias to the script as if it were the script itself. Aliasing scripts allows you to access scripts through various locations as well. For example, if you store all your scripts in your Scripts folder, you can still alias certain scripts in other locations as well, such as from within an application's own Scripts folder. The main ways to run a script include:

■ Select a script from within applications such as BBEdit and GraphicConverter, each of which has its own script folder for AppleScripts. Figure 11.9 shows the Script menus for BBEdit (left) and GraphicConverter (right).

■ Double-click a script saved as an applet from within the Finder.

■ Open a script in the Script Editor and click the Run button.

■ Run a script from within another script or applet.

■ Add a script to the Login Items pane of the Login System Preferences.

■ Use the Script Runner application, described in the following section.

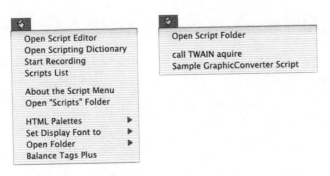

Figure 11.9
Many applications have robust support for AppleScript and even have a Script menu for easy access to scripts from within the application, such as BBEdit (left) and GraphicConverter (right).

When you launch an AppleScript application, a startup screen like the one shown in Figure 11.10 may appear if you didn't choose the Never Show Startup Screen option (refer to Figure 11.8) in the Save dialog box. Click the Run button or press the Return key to run the script; click the Quit button or press Command+Q to abort the script.

Figure 11.10
An AppleScript application startup dialog box.

Running a script results in a visible or invisible action. Some scripts return a value or expression based on the results of their actions. If you expect an outcome and want to see it displayed in a window, choose the Show Result command from the Script Editor Control menu. If there is an error in your script, you may see an error message in the Result window.

Scripts also can be saved in the form of a *droplet* (a drag-and-drop–enabled application). Droplets contain a handler that uses the **On Open** command and can be identified by the down-pointing arrow on their icons. To launch an AppleScript droplet, first decide what object will be on the receiving end of the droplet's action. Then simply drag that object's icon over the droplet's icon or alias. (This process is similar to opening a document with a particular application by dragging the document's icon onto the application's icon.) If the droplet supports the object, the action will take place immediately; otherwise, an error message will appear.

11

Scripts can, of course, be embedded inside other applications or files. Scripts in this form can be called up in many ways. Some embedded (or attached) scripts will be under your control; others will not. You'll often see scripts attached to buttons—when you click the button, the script runs. Other scripts will look for a text string in a field, check a condition, or enact other tasks that may not be obvious to you. These scripts can often run in the background and escape your detection.

Using Script Runner

The Script Runner application, a new addition to AppleScript in Mac OS X, is located in the main AppleScript folder alongside the Script Editor application. The Script Runner provides a floating palette in which you can access all of the scripts located in your personal Scripts folder. Figure 11.11 contains an example of Script Runner, which floats above all other windows on your screen.

Figure 11.11
The new Script Runner application provides a shortcut to the scripts stored in your Scripts folder.

Script Runner recognizes individual scripts in the Scripts folder, as well as subfolders of scripts that you can customize. Try out Script Runner's features by following these steps to move the example scripts that come with Mac OS X into your Scripts folder:

1. Open the Scripts folder located in the Library folder of your home folder.

2. Using a new Finder window, open the Example Scripts folder in the main AppleScript folder, located in the Applications folder.

3. Move the contents of the Example Scripts folder into the Scripts folder.

4. Launch Script Runner from the AppleScript folder.

5. Click on the Script Runner window to reveal the contents of the Scripts folder, an example of which is shown in Figure 11.12.

Script Runner will display all types of scripts and applets. It will not, however, display scripts saved as text because technically, these are document instead of scripts and cannot be run or launched to perform an action, as can scripts and applets. Use the Open Scripts Folder option in Script Runner to open the Scripts folder in the Finder, or select the Script Runner Help option to access more information via the Help Viewer. Finally, Script Runner won't recognize any new scripts or applications in your Scripts folder until you quit and relaunch Script Runner. To do this, click the Close

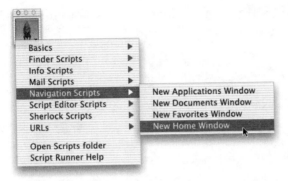

Figure 11.12
Using the Script Runner to access the contents of the Scripts folder.

button on Script Runner's floating palette—Script Runner doesn't have a Dock icon or even a menu from which you can choose Quit. You can relaunch Script Runner from the AppleScript folder.

Modifying a Script

Scripts recorded in the Script Editor are fully editable in the script window, as is any text document. To begin modifying a script, launch the Script Editor and use the Open Script command from the File menu to open the script by name. Most of the text editing actions in the Script Editor should be familiar to you from your word processor. Just type in your changes and save the results. In addition to simple clicks and drags, you can use the following shortcuts in the Script Editor window:

- Double-click to select a word; triple-click to select a line.

- Use the arrow keys to move the insertion point.

- Use the Command+left arrow or Command+right arrow keystrokes to move to the beginning or end of a line, respectively.

- Use the Command+up arrow or Command+down arrow keystroke to move to the beginning or end of the script, respectively.

- Use the Tab key at the beginning of a line to indent it. Tabs typed in the middle of a line are converted to space characters when you apply syntax formatting.

- Use the Return key at the end of an indented line to apply indenting automatically to the next line.

- Use the Option+Return keystroke to insert a continuation character (¬) and move to the beginning of the next line. This shortcut lets you work with a line that is too long to fit in the view of the active window. AppleScript ignores the continuation character and treats the lines on either side of it as one line.

■ Use the Shift+Return keystroke to move the insertion point from the end of an indented line to the beginning of a new, unindented line.

The Script Editor has a Check Syntax button for written or modified scripts. This feature will run through a script to check that the syntax of programming steps is correct. Syntax is the collection of grammar rules for a programming language. For example, if you have a command that requires a companion command, and if you forgot to put it in, you'll get an error when you click on the Check Syntax button. The Check Syntax button will check for errors in construction only, not errors in programming logic.

When applied, the Check Syntax feature returns the first error as selected text. If there is an error in the text, no formatting is applied to the text in the Script Editor window. When the error is corrected, the Script Editor compiles the script, showing it with clegic (indented) formatting and other formatting options.

Some Script Editor features let you set the formatting of the script to make it easier to read. Some programs call this *beautifying* the script. You can change fonts, styles, sizes, and colors that are used in your scripts. Whereas these formatting styles make it easier to read the script and understand it, they have no effect on the operation of the script. To set formatting options, choose the AppleScript Formatting command from the Edit menu; an example of the AppleScript Formatting window is shown in Figure 11.13. Changes you make in this window will affect any script you open from the Script Editor.

Figure 11.13
The AppleScript Formatting preferences window.

The elements of formatting that you can apply, based on the AppleScript formatting window, are as follows:

- *New Text*—Any modifications you make to a script before you check its syntax, run it, or save the results. Formatting these modifications allows you to easily discern your changes from a "wall of text."

- *Operators*—Actions (verbs) applied to objects in AppleScript.

- *Language Keywords*—Commands available as part of the AppleScript language. They are often also actions and verbs.

- *Application Keywords*—Language extensions added to AppleScript by an application referenced from within a script.

- *Comments*—Explanatory text that you add to a script to make its purpose understandable. Some people add comments to the beginning of a script as a header, to the beginning of a procedure, or even after important lines in a script. Comments in AppleScript are preceded by a double hyphen. Anything on a line to the right of the double hyphen is formatted in italics when compiled and then ignored at execution time or during a syntax check. For a multiline comment, use an asterisk to mark the beginning and end of the comment. Supplying brief yet cogent commenting is an art and the sure sign of a good programmer. For beginners, it's better to over-comment script than under-comment it.

- *Values*—Data or information, such as names, words, and numbers, used by AppleScript.

- *Variables*—A phrase you identify that can contain multiple values. Values can change according to conditions.

- *References*—A pointer to an object. When you describe "window 1 of application BBEdit," AppleScript knows you're referring to the first opened BBEdit window. Reference formatting appears in the Result window, not in the script window.

To change the style of text for a category, select the category by clicking on it once, then select a font from the Font menu, and then a style from the Style menu. To erase your changes and revert to the default styles for all the categories, select the Use Defaults button.

Scriptable Applications

Every application has its own set of terms to add to the AppleScript vocabulary. Those terms are described in the application's scripting dictionary, as mentioned earlier in this chapter. Items, commands, and other verbs that are scriptable by the application

11

are organized into categories called event suites. Because Mac OS X recognizes both Classic and Mac OS X scriptable applications, you need to be careful about selecting the correct scripting dictionary. In addition to the Finder, several of Mac OS X's applications are scriptable, including:

- Apple System Profiler
- ColorSync Scripting
- Image Capture Extension
- Internet Explorer
- Mail
- QuickTime Player
- Sherlock
- StuffIt Expander
- TextEdit
- URL Access Scripting

When you click on a dictionary item, the definition of the command appears in the right panel of the window; click on a category and all the commands for that category are displayed, as illustrated in Figure 11.14. You'll also see information about the item, such as the kinds of objects that it acts on, the information or values that it requires, and the results that are returned. Nearly every AppleScript-aware application supports the required and standard suites of commands.

For applications that support AppleScript, you may find that you can copy an object in the application and paste that object's reference into an AppleScript that you're building in the Script Editor. This trick isn't supported by all applications, so you'll have to try out objects based on what you see in an application's dictionary to see what works. An object can be scriptable and recordable without allowing the pasting of object references.

When you can paste an object, the procedure is simple. Select the object in your application, and copy it using the Copy command from the Edit menu. Then switch to the Script Editor and place the insertion point in the desired location. Issue the Paste Reference command from the Edit menu. The reference then appears at the insertion point. For example:

```
"word 2 of document 'Untitled'"
```

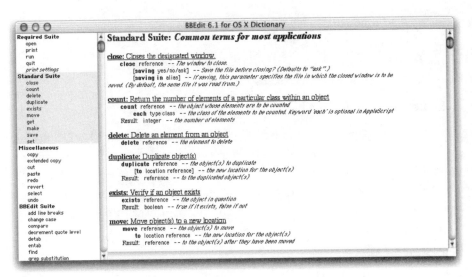

Figure 11.14
The Standard Suite of BBEdit's scripting dictionary.

With former incarnations of AppleScript, scriptwriters have complained that the dictionaries of various applications are very hard to understand. The greatest difficulty has been the tendency of the commands that are specific to an application to be presented in a single, unorganized list. While this presentation format is concise, it's difficult for a scriptwriter to find the name of a script command without having some idea of where the command is located alphabetically. In the current version of AppleScript, dictionaries are more typically subdivided into sections that represent different types of functionality. This allows a scriptwriter to narrow a search without previous knowledge of the component, but again, it is up to the application developer to organize the scripting dictionary according to Apple's recommended guidelines.

What's Different in AppleScript 1.6

AppleScript 1.6 is supported simultaneously in Mac OS X and Mac OS 9.1, but not without a few limitations due to the differences between the two operating systems. For the most part, scripts will work in both modes with little or no modification; keep in mind, however, the following points when creating scripts for use on one or both platforms:

- Scripts created in Mac OS 9.1 will work in Mac OS X, and vice versa as long as the CarbonLib Extension is installed in Mac OS 9.1.

- Scripts now support Unicode text in both operating systems.

- Preferences cannot be scripted in Mac OS X.

11

- Scripting over a network isn't supported in Mac OS X.

- Folder actions are not supported in Mac OS X.

- Printers cannot be scripted in Mac OS X.

- Program linking is not possible in Mac OS X.

The quickest way to check the compatibility of a script created in Mac OS 9.1 is to open the Script Editor in Mac OS X and select the Check Syntax button before running the application. For more assistance with compatibility issues, refer to the AppleScript home page (**www.apple.com/applescript/**) and the Knowledge Base section of the Support area of Apple's Web site (**http://kbase.info.apple.com**).

Example Scripts

The default installation of Mac OS X includes numerous example scripts, which were mentioned earlier in the section entitled "Using Script Runner." The three dozen or so example scripts are divided into the following categories:

- *Basics*—Scripts for working with the Script Editor and getting help

- *Finder Scripts*—Scripts for working in the Finder in Mac OS X

- *Info Scripts*—One script for getting the current date and time (see Figure 11.1)

- *Mail Scripts*—An example script for the Mail application

- *Navigation Scripts*—Scripts for manipulating Finder windows

- *Script Editor Scripts*—Advanced scripts for manipulating the Script Editor

- *Sherlock Scripts*—Scripts for searching with Sherlock

- *URLs*—Example scripts for opening URLs in a Web browser

In addition to these scripts, you may also download numerous samples from **www. apple.com/applescript/scripts/scripts.00.html**. Many of the scripts found at this site may not be compatible for Mac OS X; nevertheless, many of them contain useful examples and information that can help you understand the fundamentals of scripting. In addition to these sample scripts, the main AppleScript site has links to several valuable resources for learning more about AppleScript, including these online resources:

- AppleScript Guidebook

- AppleScript Beginner's Tutorial

- AppleScript primers

- Numerous scripting Web sites and resources

The AppleScript site also links to several companion software developers who make products that complement AppleScript, including:

- FaceSpan

- PreFab Player

- Real Basic

- Script Debugger

- Scripter

- Smile

Finally, check out your favorite online bookstores for the latest books about AppleScript.

Wrapping Up

AppleScript fulfills a long-standing promise to provide automation capabilities within the Macintosh operating system. Although the Mac OS X version is still playing catch-up, AppleScript is thorough and rigorous in its implementation, laying the groundwork for more important and convenient expressions to come.

In this chapter, you've learned how to use AppleScript to:

- Record actions with the Script Editor

- Save scripts that you can run as applications, or as compiled scripts that you can call from within other scripts

- Work with applications that are AppleScript aware (recordable, scriptable, and attachable)

The next chapter will explore an important, but often overlooked, feature of Mac OS X: Java.

11

Using Java

12

It seems that anyone who knows anything about computers these days has heard about Java. Hailed as the greatest advance in computer programming since the one and the zero, to some extent Java has yet to live up to the hype.

Java was developed by Sun Microsystems as a platform-independent language for the Internet. It was originally designed as a language for embedded systems (the tiny computers in your car or VCR, for example), but Sun quickly realized that Java could be used to create software that would perfectly suit the needs of the Internet. Because the majority of users access the Internet over modems and phone lines instead of broadband or Ethernet networks, Internet-based software must be relatively small so that it can be downloaded quickly. It's also essential for Internet-based software to understand TCP/IP as well as the higher-level applications that use it, such as Web servers and FTP servers. With its small executable files and vast networking capabilities, Java meets these needs.

Many of the programming concepts used in Java come from other languages; its syntax is very close to C++, and its object orientation is very much like Smalltalk. Many Web sites use Java applets (small applications) to make a page dynamic—so it's more than likely that you've already used Java.

Apple has embraced Java in a big way. Mac OS X is the first major desktop operating system to ship with Java 2 Standard Edition (J2SE), the latest version of Java from Sun. In fact, Apple expects programmers to move to Java, and is ensuring that the new system software can be accessed by Java programs by including more complete support for both Java and QuickTime within Java applications. Mac OS X also boasts several Java-specific performance enhancements, including multiprocessor support. So you can see why you, as an Apple user, should spend some time getting to know Java. This chapter will tell you what Java is and how you can run it on your Macintosh.

Java on the Macintosh

Apple began supporting Java with Macintosh Runtime for Java in late 1996. Now, J2SE is bundled with Mac OS X so that all Macs can run Java programs without needing any additional software—or even a Java-enabled Web browser. Java programs are usually referred to as applets because most Java applications are tiny in size and focused on providing a small set of features. However, there's no reason why a full-featured application can't be written in Java—in fact, most software vendors would love to have their applications written in Java. Why? Because a program created in Java could be written and debugged once, and then work on everybody's computer without the necessity of porting between all the different platforms. Software developers could make more money with less effort, and updates for all platforms would be released more quickly. Eventually more developers may use Java to create the programs we use every day because of the many unique features that Java offers, including:

- *Cross-platform compatibility*—Java applets use what's called byte code, which any computer can read using a Java Virtual Machine (commonly abbreviated VM). A VM is all any operating system needs to run Java applets; in the case of Mac OS X, HotSpot is the VM. Thanks to the VM, a single Java applet can be run on a Mac, a Windows computer, or a Sun workstation.

- *Apple support*—Apple has, in its infinite wisdom, included Mac Runtime for Java (MRJ) in all versions of the operating system since Mac OS 8.

- *Small*—Because Java is an object-oriented language, applets "inherit" features of the language that reside on the user's computer; therefore, these features don't need to be downloaded. Java also features built-in compression features so that bitmaps and sounds, for example, can be as small as possible.

- *Security*—Java applets are restricted in many ways so that your computer can't be harmed by applets written by malicious (or inept) programmers.

- *Network-readiness*—Java includes a rich feature set for connection over the Internet. Java applets can connect to Web servers, FTP servers, chat servers, or just about anything else that uses TCP/IP.

- *Performance*—Although the execution speed of many Java programs is slower than programs written for a specific operating system, special technologies such as Just in Time (JIT) and HotSpot compilers are closing this gap. Java also offers other performance benefits, particularly in networked applications. The Java Virtual Machine monitors the memory use of Java programs with a technique called *garbage collection*, which ensures that the programs don't suffer from memory leaks, one of the most common causes of software crashes.

These features make Java a great language for any computer, and especially for the Mac. Over the years, Mac users were often left out in the cold waiting for developers to make Mac versions of new software developed for Windows-running PCs. Java eliminates this discrepancy because any Java applet that runs under Windows will run under the Mac OS. As more and more software is created for Java, the Mac will benefit greatly.

Many of the applications written for Java run on the "back end" of large, expensive corporate servers to provide networking and intraoperating system integration because of Java's crossplatform capabilities. Java enables mainframe computers to talk with mini computers, workgroup servers, workstations, and even hand-held devices because they all can speak the same language—Java. However, Java applications are appearing more and more in the form of personal productivity applications and games. For example, Moneydance is a personal accounting application written entirely in Java not only for Mac OS X, but for Mac OS 8 through 9.1, FreeBSD, OS/2, Linux, Solaris, and multiple versions of Microsoft Windows as well. Shown in Figure 12.1, Moneydance has the look, feel, and speed of any Carbon or Cocoa application for Mac OS X, and includes the features you'd expect to find in most popular financial management applications, including online banking, stock management, check printing, and account reconciliation.

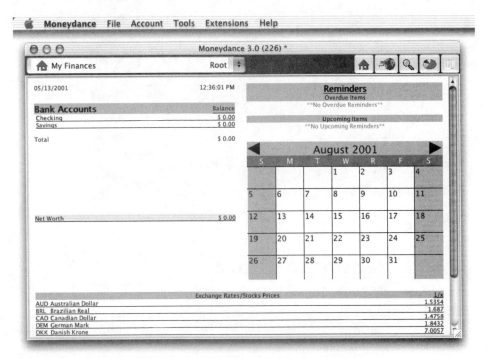

Figure 12.1
Moneydance is a sophisticated application written entirely in Java.

Java applets are also appropriate for fun and games, and can be used as part of a Web page instead of just as a standalone application. Art Safari, shown in Figure 12.2, is a Java applet that is served from the Web site of the Museum of Modern Art (MoMA). This Java program, which works on most Java-enabled browsers, offers a palette for young artists to experiment with. Take a look at the article about Art Safari at **http://java.sun.com/features/1999/02/moma.html**. Like all Java programs, Art Safari became available to Mac users as soon as it was available to Windows users.

Figure 12.2
The Art Safari applet.

Macintosh Runtime for Java

When you install Mac OS X, Java 2 Standard Edition is installed along with the HotSpot VM and the Java Development Kit. Apple refers to its Java implementation as version 3 of Macintosh Runtime for Java (MRJ 3). MRJ 3 installs three types of frameworks to integrate Java into Mac OS X:

- *Application framework*—A code base necessary to build Java applets

- *Development environment*—Tools to create Java applets

- *Runtime environment*—Resources to execute Java applets

MRJ 3 provides a number of new features and improvements over previous versions of MRJ, including:

- Processes graphics with the Quartz imaging model, including antialiasing of text and the ability to use Mac OS X's implementation of OpenGL to render 3D objects

- Includes HotSpot 1.3 VM for acceleration of Java code execution

- Includes support for the crossplatform Swing implementation

- Supports preemptive multitasking of application threads

- Supports Macs with multiple processors

- Includes the full Java Development Kit (JDK)

- Includes QuickTime for Java

- Supports Unicode language and font support

- Supports Apple's WebObjects

- Has the ability to embed Java applets within Web pages

Java is built into the layered framework of Mac OS X (described in Chapter 1), whereas it was an optional installation in earlier versions of the Mac OS. When using Java in Mac OS X, the resources required by your Web browsers and Java-enabled applications are automatically available; very few configurations are required on your part. The next section explains how to use a few example applets included as part of MRJ 3.

Other Java VMs

Apple isn't the only maker of a Java Virtual Machine for Mac OS X. Because Java is an open standard, any company is welcome—in fact, encouraged—to try its hand at producing Java software. At least one other company makes a Java Virtual Machine and development environment for Mac OS X. Metrowerks (**www.metrowerks.com**) makes CodeWarrior, the premiere programming environment for the Mac, and has created a fast VM that Microsoft included with previous versions of Internet Explorer (i.e., Mac OS 9.1 and earlier).

12

Unlike HotSpot, third-party Java VMs aren't integrated into Mac OS X and must be installed independently. Earlier versions of the Mac OS often included two different VMs, and not all Java applets worked properly with both VMs. A user would sometimes have to reconfigure the Web browser to select the VM that worked best with a particular applet. This situation may recur with OS X. For now, the HotSpot VM is the only VM demonstrated in this chapter.

Running Java Applets

From a user's perspective, the runtime environment is the most important of the three frameworks that constitute MRJ. Java applets can be executed in a number of ways in Mac OS X, including:

■ As part of a Carbon or Cocoa application

■ From a command line using the Terminal application

■ As a double-clickable application

■ By using the Applet Launcher

■ From within a Web browser

Moneydance is an example of a double-clickable application, and Art Safari is a creative example of a Java applet embedded within a Web page. Let's look more closely at the two most popular ways to run Java applets: the Applet Launcher and a Web browser.

Applet Launcher

The Applet Launcher, a standalone application located in the Utilities folder, can be used to explore the several example applets that are installed as part of Mac OS X, or any applets that you download from the Web. To run a Java applet:

1. Open the Utilities folder and double-click the Applet Launcher.

2. Click the Open button, shown in Figure 12.3, or press Command+O.

3. Navigate your hard drive using the dialog box shown in Figure 12.4 and select an applet.

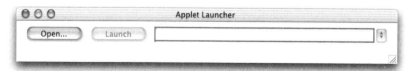

Figure 12.3
The Applet Launcher.

Figure 12.4
Selecting an HTML document containing a Java applet.

If you're a Unix geek and you want to type in the path of an applet, just enter it in the path area of the Applet Launcher and then either click the Launch button or press the Return key. The path should be in the form of a file accessed using a URL, like the one shown in Figure 12.5. Files are accessed using three forward slashes, unlike HTML documents, which require only two slashes.

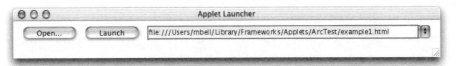

Figure 12.5
Type the path to a Java applet using the Applet Launcher.

The Applet Launcher has no preferences or configuration options to speak of, and few interface features with which you'll need to become familiar other than the Open button (Command+O) and the Launch button.

Unlike earlier versions of the Mac OS (in which the Applet Launcher is called the Applet Runner), you can't drag an HTML file containing a Java applet onto the Applet Launcher. However, you can use Applet Launcher to review and configure some aspects of an applet's preferences once the applet is running. When an applet is running, you'll see the following options in the Applet menu:

■ *Restart*—Forces the applet to start again from the beginning.

■ *Reload*—Dumps the applet from RAM and loads it freshly from the disk.

■ *Stop*—Pauses the applet.

12

- *Save*—Saves the applet to disk.

- *Start*—Continues a paused applet.

- *Clone*—Re-creates the applet in a second window.

- *Tag*—Reveals the HTML code used to embed the applet in an HTML document, which is useful if you want to see how the code is used.

- *Info*—Displays information and parameters provided by the applet's developer.

- *Edit*—Allows you to edit the applet (if enabled).

- *Character Encoding*—Reveals information about language options used to display the applet.

- *Print*—Prints the window containing the applet.

- *Properties*—Opens the window (shown in Figure 12.6) in which you can configure how the Applet Launcher accesses a network and determine whether the applet's code is a security risk. The Properties window also allows you to configure the following features:

  - *HTTP Proxy Server*—The Internet address of the proxy server used to access the applet.

  - *HTTP Proxy Port*—The TCP/IP port of the HTTP proxy server; the default port for all Web servers is 80.

  - *Class Access*—Choose between Restricted and Unrestricted to determine whether applets are allowed to write files to the local file system.

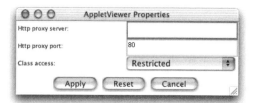

Figure 12.6
Use the Properties option to configure additional preferences.

Each the above options, except for the Properties option, relates to the frontmost applet. To affect another applet, launch that applet and review the settings in the Applet menu.

For security purposes, applets are usually restricted in what they can do. For instance, applets usually can't write files to the user's hard disk; this restriction prevents an applet from overwriting important files.

Unless you make changes, the default settings ensure that a Java applet cannot cause harm to your system. No other safety measures are necessary.

Java Applets with Web Browsers

At this time, Internet Explorer 5.1 and OmniWeb 4 are the two Web browsers that support Java under Mac OS X; more browsers will undoubtedly support Java in the future. Internet Explorer is installed automatically by the Mac OS X installer; OmniWeb is a commercial product (it costs about $30) and can be downloaded from Omni Development Group (**www.omnigroup.com**). Both are easily configured to support Java applets. To configure Internet Explorer:

1. Launch Internet Explorer from the Dock or the Applications folder.

2. Choose Explorer|Preferences and select the Java section, as shown in Figure 12.7.

Figure 12.7
Internet Explorer's Java configuration options.

12

3. Check the Enable Java option in the Java Options section; the other options in this section are not necessary to enable Java. They merely enable alerts to errors and logging options, such as the Log Java Exceptions option I have checked in this example.

4. The Security section provides a way for you to protect the Java code that is executed on your computer. The Byte-Code Verification option tells Internet Explorer to check the code of local applets only, all Java code accessed over a network, or not to check code at all. The Network Access options control how an applet in a Web page connects to the Internet, with three options to choose from:

- *No Network Access*—The applet can't use the network at all.

- *Applet Host Access*—The applet can use the restricted network access provided for applets.

- *Unrestricted*—The applet can use the network in any way it wishes.

5. Check the option entitled Restrict Access To Non-Java Class Files to prevent applets from accessing files that are not part of Java, such as operating system files, documents, or other applications.

6. Click the OK button.

Now you're ready to visit a Web site that uses Java, such as the Art Safari Web site mentioned earlier, or one of the example applets installed by Mac OS X (discussed in the following section).

OmniWeb is a bit easier to configure. After you have downloaded the latest version from the Omni Development Group's Web site, Choose OmniWeb|Preferences, select the Java section (shown in Figure 12.8) and choose from the following three options:

- *Run Automatically (When Loading Page)*—Allows a Java applet to load in a Web page automatically as soon as all the Java code has been read by the Web browser.

- *Run Manually (When Clicked)*—Presents an icon of a cup of coffee to indicate where an applet will be loaded in a Web page when clicked. This option gives you the ability to approve an applet before it loads, although you may have no idea what the applet will do when it is loaded.

- *Don't Allow Applets*—Prevents applets from being loaded by OmniWeb automatically or manually.

Let's explore a few sample applets using the Applet Launcher, Internet Explorer, and OmniWeb.

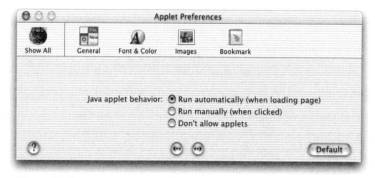

Figure 12.8
OmniWeb's Java configuration options.

Example Applets

Mac OS X installs a number of example Java applets in <*hard drive*>/Users/<*user name*>/Library/Frameworks/Applets/. Applets often are embedded in HTML documents; and although the example applets included here end with the file extension .html, they can also end in other extensions—including .htm. For example, Figure 12.9 shows a Java applet called ArcTest. Although this applet isn't particularly helpful in real-life situations outside of a trigonometry class, it could be a useful example of how to draw angles if you're trying to learn how to program with Java. Here you see the applet in both Internet Explorer (left) and Applet Launcher (right). Notice how the applet is accompanied by additional HTML code at the top (the name of the applet) and bottom (hyperlink to view the source code) of the Web browser window.

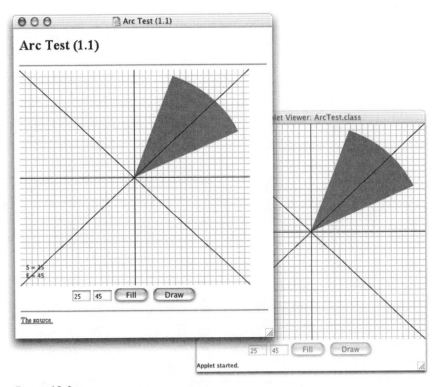

Figure 12.9
The ArcTest applet in Internet Explorer (left) and in Applet Launcher (right).

Some of the example applets, such as the Bar Chart applet, are actually useful. This applet takes configuration data from an HTML file and makes a bar chart. Figure 12.10 shows the Bar Chart applet using Applet Launcher.

One of the advantages of using Java applets, rather than plain HTML, in Web pages is that Java is so dynamic. HTML is limited to loaded images and

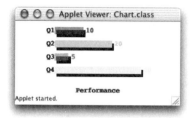

Figure 12.10
The Bar Chart applet.

components such as buttons, whereas Java allows interactive pictures to be drawn. The Draw Test applet, illustrated in Figure 12.11, presents a canvas on which you can draw by dragging the mouse across the canvas or by selecting straight lines from the pull-down menu.

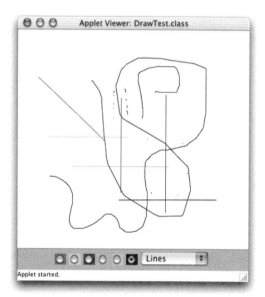

Figure 12.11
The Draw Test applet.

Applets have varying degrees of utility on Web pages. They can be used for navigation, interaction with the user, or for display purposes. The Gauge Lightweight Component demo in Figure 12.12 is an example of how Java can show dynamic results (horizontal bars) superimposed over a JPEG image displayed by Internet Explorer.

The SunSphere applet, shown in Figure 12.13 using Internet Explorer, is an example of a more sophisticated Java applet that is informational and interactive. You can view the position of the sun's light on earth relative to your time zone (which the applet reads from the Date & Time System Preferences settings).

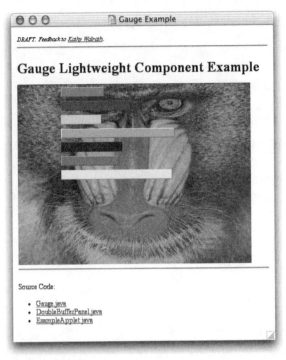

Figure 12.12
The Gauge Lightweight applet.

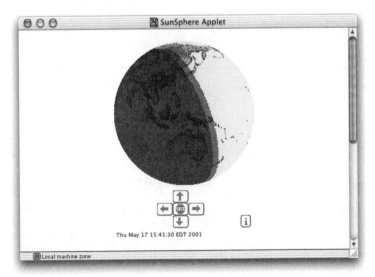

Figure 12.13
The SunSphere applet.

12

The Look of Cross-Platform Programs

From the beginning, Java programs were designed to blend in with other programs on each operating system. When a Java program contains a button and the program is run on a Macintosh, the button appears to be a Mac button. When the same Java program is run on a Windows computer, the button looks like a Windows button. The person who writes the program has no control over this—it's an element of Java itself. Swing is a special type of Java code that allows an applet to take on the appearance of the host operating system. For example, Figure 12.14 shows two examples of an applet that implements the Swing class to give the contents of the applet the appropriate look and feel for Mac OS X (top) and Windows 98 (bottom).

Although in some ways it's desirable to have your applets automatically assume the look of an operating system, some definite disadvantages exist:

- *Excessive need for testing*—A program that will use different components on different platforms must be tested on each platform to make sure that it looks correct in the different platforms.

- *Limited number of components*—This mechanism imposes a limit on the number of components that could exist in Java. The only components that can be used are components that are available on all platforms.

- *Loss of control*—In the software business, it's never good to completely remove options. A developer should have ultimate control over how a component will look.

When Sun and other companies realized these limitations, writing the components completely in the Java language became the solution. In Java Foundation Classes (JFCs), developers were taught to use the Java language to overcome the problems described above.

Note: Swing was the original code name for the Java Foundation Classes. One of the Sun creators of JFC was a big fan of Duke Ellington, who popularized a song containing the lyric "It don't mean a thing if it ain't got that swing." He assigned the Ellington reference as a temporary name for the evolving JFCs, which were so eagerly anticipated even before their release that the code name became a common term.

To sum things up, Swing and the Java Foundation Classes not only give developers the option to use more components, but also the ability to determine exactly how each component will look.

Mac OS X

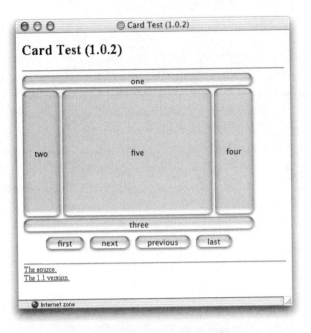

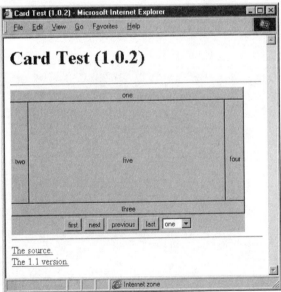

Figure 12.14
Swing allows Java developers to deliver the look and feel of the host operating system, such as Mac OS X (top) and Windows 98 (bottom).

12

Wrapping Up

Mac OS X includes robust support for J2SE, the latest version of Java. The most significant characteristic of Java is that it allows computer programmers to write one version of a program, such as a money management application, which can then be run on many different types of computers without modification. Programmers refer to this as the "write once, run anywhere" capability. Developers no longer have to choose a target platform when writing software. The popularity of Java means that software debuts for the Mac at the same time that it comes out for Windows. With Java-written software available for every platform at once, users will be free to choose the operating system that is most comfortable, and businesses will choose the OS that is easiest to support.

This chapter has demonstrated several aspects of J2SE on Mac OS X, including:

■ Macintosh Runtime for Java (MRJ)

■ How to run Java applets using the Apple Applet Launcher and a Web browser

■ Additional Java virtual machines

■ How Java can emulate the look and feel of just about any operating system

The next chapter will wrap up this section of the book by looking at ways to prevent problems with your Mac and how to troubleshoot problems when they arise.

Troubleshooting Mac OS X

Every type of computer and operating system has its own quirks and challenges, and Mac OS X is no exception. In fact, Mac OS X introduces a number of new support issues because it is essentially a new operating system. Many of the issues that faced users of Mac OS 9.1 and previous versions of the operating system simply do not exist in Mac OS X, although they do indeed relate to troubleshooting in the Classic environment. In earlier versions of the Mac OS, you could troubleshoot the operating system itself by disabling certain Extensions and Control Panels. Troubleshooting Mac OS X, on the other hand, is more about tweaking applications and user configuration features because the components of Mac OS X cannot be modified easily by the typical user. Solutions to the kinds of problems Mac users were once able to fix on their own are more likely to be found in updates of the operating system from Apple.

Using a handful of tools for Mac OS X and Mac OS 9.1, however, you can help prevent—and even troubleshoot—some of the most common problems in Mac OS X. In this chapter, I'll discuss prevention and treatment, as well as list a select number of online resources you can use to research technical problems and locate solutions from third-party developers.

Preventing Problems

Problems are a fact of computing life, but you can take several steps to prevent trouble down the road. These steps are no guarantee that you'll never have problems—instead, think of them as vaccinations that help ward off problems. Take these measures as a first line of defense against problems on your Mac:

- *Back up your data*—It's a good idea to perform full backups on a regular basis, and incremental backups in between. At a minimum, back up your documents and keep the installation disks and CDs handy in the event that you have to reinstall the Mac OS and/or your applications. Check out the following backup solutions to protect your data:

- FolderSynchronizerX (softoBe)—**www.softobe.com**

- Personal Backup (Intego)—**www.intego.com**

- Retrospect Client (Dantz)—**www.dantz.com**

- SwitchBack (Glendower)—**www.webnz.com/glendower**

- Synchronize! (Qdea)—**www.qdea.com**

- Synk X (Randall Voth)—**http://mypage.uniserve.ca/~rvoth/synkx.html**

- *Remove unneeded documents*—The fewer large documents on your drives, the easier (and faster) it will be for the Mac OS to manage your file systems. If you really need to keep large documents around for a while, consider purchasing a CD recorder to create archival copies of important collections of folders and documents. Use Sherlock to search for large documents that may be candidates for archiving, or for documents whose modification dates may indicate that they are no longer accessed.

- *Keep a record of important settings*—If your disk crashes and you must reinstall all your software, how will you be able to reconfigure your Internet settings? Periodically write down or print out any information that is critical to getting you up and running after a catastrophic failure such as a drive failure, lightning strike, or theft.

- *Retain all software installers*—Keep all your software installation CDs handy in case you have to reinstall Mac OS X or your third-party applications and utilities.

- *Read installation notes*—Because Mac OS X is a new operating system, I encourage you to read all the installation notes for Mac OS X and your applications before loading or updating software. Mac OS X is very particular about how and where many applications are installed!

Common Problems and Their Solutions

The vast majority of problems you're likely to encounter with Mac OS X revolve around a handful of common scenarios that are easily resolved. You might encounter some of the following problems on more than one occasion, and never see others. Take a look at each of the following scenarios so that you'll at least be familiar with each problem, its possible cause, and solutions. For more information, see the following section of this chapter ("Useful Tools"), as well as Appendix A to learn where to go for help.

Computer Won't Start Up

On startup or restart, the computer won't start at all. The screen displays no activity, and/or you don't hear anything coming from the central processing unit (CPU).

Cause

Power is not flowing to the computer and/or the monitor, or the power isn't reaching the CPU or monitor. The first is easier to detect than the second.

Solution

Be sure that the computer is plugged into a surge-protected outlet that is itself receiving power. If your monitor is plugged in through the courtesy outlet on the back of the CPU, make sure that the connection is secure. If it isn't, the CPU may be receiving power but isn't passing it on to the monitor, even though the monitor is turned on. To test the outlet for power, plug in a lamp or other device and turn it on; if it works, the outlet is receiving power.

If your computer is plugged into a surge protector (and it should be!), check to see if the surge protector is turned on. Most surge protectors have an On/Off switch. If the surge protector has a Reset button, try it; a power surge may have tripped it. Finally, if your surge protector has a fuse, shut down everything that's plugged into it, unplug the surge protector from the outlet, and check the fuse.

If your computer is receiving power but still doesn't start up, two possible explanations remain—but both require the services of an Apple-authorized repair center. First, the power supply in your CPU may be damaged. The power supply converts the current received from an outlet into a form that the computer can use. It's not uncommon for a power supply to go bad, especially if the computer is left on for extended periods of time. The minimal life span for a power supply that's left on 24 hours per day should be several years—I own a Mac Classic whose power supply is still going after nine years! The worst-case scenario requires replacing the logic board because it can no longer transfer the power received from the outlet by way of the power supply to the necessary components of the computer. PowerBooks are especially susceptible to simultaneous power supply and logic board failure because of the way the power cord plugs into the back of many older models.

Blinking Question Mark on Startup

On startup, the CPU and monitor receive power, but a blinking question mark appears on screen and no further startup activity occurs.

13

Cause

The computer cannot detect a startup disk containing the Mac OS. Either the drive is bad or one or more of the essential components is missing.

Solution

Approximately half of the infamous blinking question mark's appearances are due to the computer's inability to locate the designated startup disk. Most Macs only have one hard drive, and many computers have a booting utility built into the Read-Only Memory (ROM) chip on the motherboard that allows you to see what drives are available for booting before the booting routine actually begins. If the designated disk can't be found, the computer looks for additional disks containing the Mac OS. To use the boot utility to select a disk containing Mac OS X:

1. Restart the computer.

2. Hold down the Option key until the boot menu presents itself.

3. Select the drive containing Mac OS X and click the Continue button.

If the boot utility doesn't appear, then your computer doesn't support this feature.

The next line of defense is to reset, or *zap*, the computer's parameter RAM (PRAM), which is kind of like giving the computer a loud wakeup call to restart and behave! To zap the PRAM:

1. Restart the computer by pressing Control+Command+Power key (also known as a hard restart, a hard boot, or a three-finger salute). If your keyboard doesn't have a power key, or if your computer doesn't have an easily accessible Restart button (like the Cube), press the round On button for about six seconds to force the computer to switch itself off. Wait 20 seconds and press the On button again to start the computer.

2. Hold down the Option+Command+P+R keys while the Caps Lock key is *not* depressed.

3. Keep holding down these keys until you hear the startup chime a second time, then release.

If you also have Mac OS 9.1 installed on your computer and it starts Mac OS 9.1 instead of Mac OS X, the computer probably cannot find all the Mac OS X components, such as the mach.sym or mach_kernel files, that are necessary to boot properly. In this case, allow the computer to boot into Mac OS 9.1 and follow these steps:

1. Download and install the latest version of the Startup Disk Control Panel using the Software Update Control Panel, or by visiting the Apple Support Web site (**www.apple.com/support/**). At this time, version 9.2.1 is required to properly boot into Mac OS X.

2. Restart into Mac OS 9.1 and open the Startup Disk Control Panel.

3. Select the volume containing Mac OS X and click the Restart button.

If you cannot boot into Mac OS X or Mac OS 9.1 on your hard drive, you'll have to boot from an alternative source of Mac OS 9.1 or Mac OS X, such as an installation CD-ROM. When a Mac boots up, it looks for a valid operating system in the following order:

1. Floppy drive (if installed)

2. Hard drive designated in the Startup Disk System Preferences (Mac OS X) or the Startup Disk Control Panel (Mac OS 9.1)

3. Additional hard drives

4. CD-ROM drive

The most common method is to start up from a bootable CD-ROM, which you can do in two easy steps:

1. Insert the CD-ROM.

2. Restart while holding down the C key until the computer boots from the CD-ROM.

Once the computer has restarted from CD-ROM, the Installer program will automatically run. However, instead of reinstalling Mac OS X at this point, follow these steps to run the Disk Utility application from the Mac OS X installation CD-ROM to verify and/or repair the startup disk:

1. Choose Open Disk Utility from the Installer menu.

2. Select the First Aid button and then select the disk containing Mac OS X. Click the Verify button to verify the integrity of the drive or the Repair button to scan for problems and repair them automatically, if any problems are encountered. Figure 13.1 shows the Disk Utility in the process of verifying a drive containing Mac OS X.

3. Follow any on-screen instructions and choose Quit Disk Utility (Command+Q) from the Disk Utility menu to return to the Installer.

4. If you believe that a repair that is likely to have a positive impact on your drive was made, choose Quit Installer from the Installer menu and then click the Restart button in the Installer window. If you doubt that the Disk Utility was successful in repairing your drive, reinstall Mac OS X by choosing the Continue button—and be prepared to reinstall the entire operating system.

13

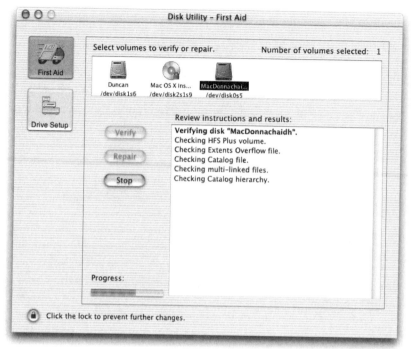

Figure 13.1
Checking a drive for errors using Disk Utility while booting from the Mac OS X installation CD.

Reinstalling Mac OS X is a last-ditch effort, so be sure that all the necessary installation CDs for the operating system and your applications are handy. Of course, if you've backed up all the important files on your computer regularly, reinstalling won't be too much of an inconvenience.

Application Stalls During Use

An application stalls during use and displays an error message or will not return control to the user.

Cause

The application performs an illegal operation or contains a programming error.

Solution

Application programming is an extremely sophisticated business, and sometimes programmers make mistakes that lead to an application's failure during use. Because Mac OS X introduces protected memory, described in Chapter 1, the offending application should not affect other applications or the Mac OS itself. If the application doesn't automatically terminate itself and just hangs there without allowing you to quit the application, follow these steps to *force quit* the application:

1. Press Option+Command+Escape simultaneously.

2. Select the application from the window shown in Figure 13.2.

3. Click the Force Quit button.

4. Dismiss the Force Quit window by clicking the close button.

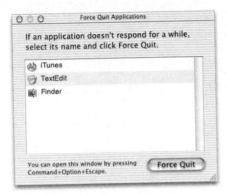

Figure 13.2
Choose Option+Command+Escape to force quit an application that is misbehaving.

Forcing an application to quit no longer necessitates restarting the entire computer to prevent a cascading effect with other applications or the Mac OS itself. If the misbehaving application is the Finder, however, I recommend that you quit all other applications and restart your computer.

Won't Shut Down

The Mac OS won't respond to the Shut Down command.

Cause
The Mac OS or an application is preventing the partial or full execution of the Shut Down command.

Solution
When you select Shut Down, the Mac OS issues an AppleEvent instructing all open applications to quit. If an application doesn't receive the AppleEvent or cannot interpret it properly, then the Mac OS will not comply with the final steps of the shutting down process. The best solution is to retry the Shut Down command. If that fails, then manually quit any applications that have not successfully quit in response to the AppleEvent. If all the applications do indeed quit, leaving only the Finder open, initiate a force quit of the Finder or restart the computer according to the steps outlined in the previous section. If all else fails, try Command+Control+Power key to

13

reboot the computer, or hold the power button for ten seconds. If that doesn't work, unplug the computer. If you have a PowerBook or iBook, you may need to eject the battery as well (after disconnecting the power cord) to deprive the computer of all sources of power.

Drive Not Recognized

One or more hard drives are not recognized during startup (they don't appear on the Desktop or you are asked to initialize the internal hard drive).

Cause

The Mac OS cannot find a boot partition or driver for a drive.

Solution

If the Mac OS cannot find a hard drive, follow the steps outlined earlier in the section entitled "Blinking Question Mark on Startup" and boot from the Mac OS X installation CD. After the Installer has launched, follow these steps:

1. Choose Open Disk Utility from the Installer menu.

2. Select the Drive Setup button and the disk containing Mac OS X, as shown in Figure 13.3.

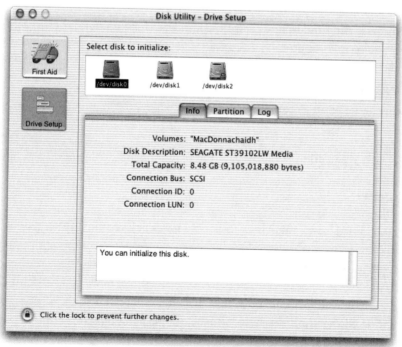

Figure 13.3
Selecting a drive using the Disk Utility application.

3. Review the Info tab and make sure the drive name is recognized. If the drive is significantly corrupted, the drive name and information in the Disk Description section may not be available. In this case, you may need to repartition the drive and install Mac OS X from scratch. Don't attempt to repartition the drive from within the Drive Setup section of the Disk Utility; instead, refer to Appendix E for instructions on installing Mac OS X and let the Installer repartition the drive for you.

Every hard drive contains a special partition, or section of the drive, called the *boot partition*. In order to load the drivers and information required for mounting the disk on startup, the OS must be able to access the boot partition. If the boot partition is corrupted or the driver information is unreadable, the drive will not be mounted until it has been repaired.

In the case of Apple hard drives, the Drive Setup section of the Disk Utility application is the best solution to try first. If this doesn't work, and if you can afford it, however, you can't go wrong with purchasing a commercial utility that specializes in disk storage. In the worst-case scenario—in which you cannot reinstall the proper driver for a drive or repair it—you may have to reformat the drive, which will cause all of your data to be lost anyway.

If the drive that is not recognized is a secondary drive (i.e., not the original, internal hard drive that came with your computer), the problem could be a Small Computer Serial Interface (SCSI) ID conflict or an Integrated Drive Electronics (IDE) master/slave configuration error. Each SCSI disk must have a unique ID; if it shares the ID of an existing drive, it will not boot. IDE drives have a similar problem, but they allow for only two drives on each Advanced Technology Attachment (ATA) bus—a master and a slave—whereas SCSI buses allow for seven IDs. Macs can have multiple SCSI and ATA buses, which can cause confusion when you're trying to assign IDs and configure multiple drives. Use the Apple System Profiler's Devices and Volumes tab for a detailed listing of all the SCSI, ATA, and USB devices connected to your computer (discussed later in this chapter).

Can't Connect to a Network/Internet

Computer cannot see AppleTalk devices over the network or access the Internet.

Cause

Your computer has been physically disconnected from the network or a software error has occurred. Also, the network may be down, in which case your Mac is not the problem.

13

Solution

The first possible solution is to make sure your Ethernet cable or modem is properly connected. Network cables and hardware devices such as Ethernet cards and modems rarely go bad, however. The most likely solution to this type of problem can be found by checking your Network System Preferences according to the following steps:

1. Choose System Preferences from the Apple menu.

2. Select the Network pane.

3. Make sure that the proper Location, such as Home or Work, is selected.

4. Determine whether the proper type of interface, such as Built-in Ethernet or Modem Port, is selected in the Connection section.

5. If you are on a local area network, review the TCP/IP settings for accuracy.

6. If you are dialing into an Internet service provider (ISP) using a modem, check the Point-to-Point Protocol (PPP) settings.

7. If you are using any proxy servers to connect to the Web or other Internet resources, check the Proxy section.

8. If you are dialing into an ISP using a modem, check the Modem section to make sure that the proper modem is selected.

Modems present errors that are usually related to configuration errors in the PPP and Modem sections of the Network System Preferences. Dial-up connections are often very difficult to troubleshoot because of the hardware and software differences between the types of modems used by ISPs and those found in Apple computers. Make sure that your ISP supports the type and speed of your Mac's modem; for example, some ISPs do not support the 56Kbps V.90 modem, which is found in most Apple computers.

Mouse and Keyboard Won't Work

The mouse and/or keyboard won't work.

Cause

The Apple Desktop Bus (ADB) or Universal Serial Bus (USB) cables connecting the mouse and keyboard to the CPU have become disconnected, or the mouse or keyboard is broken.

Solution

In about 70 percent of cases, the answer to this problem is simply that the cables connecting the mouse or keyboard have become disconnected. All pre-iMac and G4 computers use the ADB-style cable to connect the mouse to the keyboard and the keyboard to the CPU. In some of these computers, the ADB cable passes through the monitor, connecting the mouse and keyboard independently to the monitor, which is then connected to the CPU. First check to see if any of these cables is loose, especially if your keyboard is one of the models that has ADB connectors on either side (these are notorious for becoming bent and broken). If all cables are connected properly and the problem persists, you could have a bad mouse or keyboard. Try borrowing a similar mouse or keyboard from a coworker or friend before buying a new one—you can quickly determine if the mouse or keyboard is suspect.

For iMacs, Cubes, and G4s, the USB cable may have become disconnected. Although the connectors on USB cables are a great improvement over ADB connectors and are much less prone to failure, you should be aware of one issue when using USB hubs to connect USB mice, keyboards, and peripherals: USB hubs are either unpowered or are powered by an external power supply, and some USB devices draw more power than can be provided by an unpowered USB hub. So, if you intend to connect multiple USB devices and are in need of a hub, consider purchasing a hub with its own external power supply to ensure that your peripherals get enough juice.

 Whenever possible, shut down the computer before connecting and disconnecting ADB cables. USB cables may be freely connected and disconnected at any time, however.

Application Crashes

An application crashes periodically or consistently.

Cause

The application may have a bug or may conflict with the Mac OS or another application.

Solution

Applications crash for mysterious reasons; fortunately, Mac OS X prevents wayward applications from taking down other applications or the operating system itself. If you can re-create the same error a second or third time, the problem is most likely related to the application rather than the Mac OS. To remedy a problem with an application, follow these steps:

1. Check the documentation on the offending application for any mention of known problems with the application itself or when it interacts with other applications.

2. Check the software creator's Web site to see if any new information or updates to the application have been posted.

13

3. Delete the application's preference file, located in *<hard drive>*/Users/*<user name>*/ Library/Preferences. Apple encourages software developers to give their program's preference file a name that incorporates their company domain name. This practice ensures that all preference files for that company's products are grouped together. For example, Figure 13.4 shows the preference file for Sherlock grouped with all the other application preference files for Apple products.

4. Reinstall the application as a last resort.

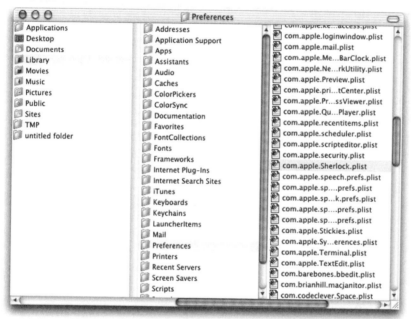

Figure 13.4
Try deleting the preference file of a troublesome application to solve a problem.

Of course, if you delete a preference file or reinstall an application, you risk losing application settings, custom dictionaries, and other files that store your preferences—so be prepared to reenter them.

Colors Won't Display Properly

Colors displayed on screen look odd, especially when browsing the Web.

Cause

A loose connection, corrupted preference file, or erroneous Monitors settings.

Solution

Color problems are typically due to one of two causes. First, your monitor cable may be loose, preventing one or more of the pins in the cable from making a good connection. This results in a display with an unusual color balance, such as a green or amber wash over the entire screen. Securing the cable will usually take care of this problem, but if it persists, it could indicate a bad monitor or a malfunctioning video card.

Second, open the Displays System Preferences and check the color depth and resolution settings. As a rule of thumb, configure your computer's display as follows:

■ As many colors as possible

■ The highest resolution you're comfortable with

■ A refresh rate of 75Hz or higher

The color depth setting is especially important because it controls the quality with which Web images are displayed.

If looking at your monitor makes you queasy, check the refresh rate to make sure that it's set to 75Hz or higher (I prefer 85Hz). Accountants, graphic designers, and others who sit at their computers all day have been known to become squeamish if the refresh rate is too low.

Computer Won't Print

Computer won't print to the connected printer.

Cause

Printer is physically disconnected, Network System Preferences are misconfigured, or print driver is improperly selected via the Print Center.

Solution

Check your USB cable to ensure connectivity, if you're connected locally to the printer. Both ends of the cable should be tightly connected and the cable should not be crimped. If you're using a networked printer, check the network connectivity for your computer and the printer. Physical connectivity is usually pretty easy to troubleshoot:

1. Shut down the Mac and the printer.

2. Start the printer; once the printer is online, start the Mac.

If you're certain that the printer is connected properly, open the Print Center and look for the printer—it should be listed under its proper connection method, such

13

as USB or AppleTalk. If necessary, you may have to resort to connecting to the printer from scratch. Refer to Chapter 9 for instructions on selecting a printer using the Print Center.

Documents Won't Open

A document won't open even though you think you have the application that created it.

Cause

An incomplete application database.

Solution

Mac OS X uses a database to keep track of information about documents and the applications used to create them. Sometimes the OS doesn't have a complete picture of all the files and their associated applications. In earlier versions of the operating system, this information is stored in a database (referred to as the Desktop database) on a volume-by-volume basis. Because Mac OS X is a true multiuser operating system, it stores information about the applications favored by each user on a person-by-person basis. When a user initially launches an application, information about that application is added to the user's application database, which is loaded on startup each time the user logs in to the computer.

It's not unusual for a computer to contain tens of thousands of files—no wonder the Mac OS gets a bit confused about which documents were created with what application. If you're using a previous version of the Mac OS, the solution to this problem is to "rebuild the Desktop." This process involves holding down the Command+Option keys at startup; a dialog box appears and asks if you want to rebuild the Desktop database in order to reassociate all applications with the appropriate documents. Although you cannot manually rebuild the application database in Mac OS X, you can follow these steps to refresh the information available to the operating system:

1. Restart the computer and log in to your account.

2. Open a Finder window in column view and navigate to the folders containing your applications.

3. Try opening the document again.

Mac OS X refreshes the application database for each user at startup and whenever a folder is opened in a Finder window. It does not search for every application on the entire hard drive, as in previous versions of the Mac OS. Instead, Mac OS X looks in the Applications and Utilities folders and records the information about each application's type and creator codes, if this information exists (not all Cocoa applications have creator types and codes). This information determines what types of documents an application can open. When a document is double-clicked, Mac OS X attempts to match the Finder attributes of that document with all applications associated with that user. If a matching application is found, the OS opens the document with the appropriate application. If a match cannot be made, the Finder responds with a dialog box to inform you that the correct application is not available, as illustrated in Figure 13.5 (top).

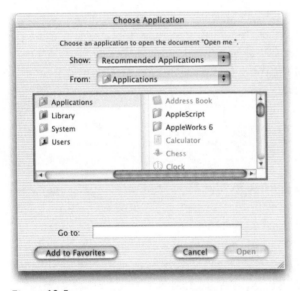

Figure 13.5
Searching for an application.

To search for an application to open the document:

1. Click the Choose Application button shown in Figure 13.5 (top).

2. Choose Show Recommended Applications (shown in the bottom window of Figure 13.5), which allows the Finder to weed out applications with little or no chance of opening the document. Recommended applications are chosen on the basis of the Finder type and creator codes stored in your application database.

3. Choose Show All Applications to attempt opening the document with a non-recommended application.

4. Choose the location for the recommended application, such as the Applications folder, or browse your hard drive for additional applications.

If the document still won't open, try launching an application that is likely to open the document and then open the document from within the application (instead of double-clicking the document from within a Finder window or the Desktop). If that fails, too, you can assume that either the document is corrupted or you truly don't have the appropriate application for the job.

In the next section I'll look at the best tools for diagnosing and repairing the most common hardware and software problems.

Useful Tools for Mac OS X

Mac OS X includes several helpful tools for gathering information and repairing and monitoring your computer's resources. In addition to these tools, several third-party applications and utilities are available to help you troubleshoot Mac OS X. The following list describes some of the more frequently used tools that you should consider adding to your troubleshooting tool kit, and tells you where you can get the latest versions. For those of you who rely on Classic mode, a handful of the most essential Mac OS 9.1 utilities are listed as well.

Software Update

Apple is constantly working on updates to Mac OS X to provide performance enhancements and resolutions to known problems and to incorporate new features. You can use the System Preferences' Software Update feature to check for updates to Mac OS X manually, or on a daily, weekly, or monthly schedule. Appendix E contains detailed information on how to update Mac OS X using the Software Update feature, as well as how to download the updates from the Apple Web site.

Get Mac OS X Software

Instead of banging your head upside a virtual wall over a misbehaving application, look for an updated version of the application after reading the release notes that come with the application currently on your hard drive. New and updated applications for Mac OS X are being released every day, and Apple has made it as easy as possible for you to stay abreast of all the news about the latest software for Mac OS X. To connect to Mac OS X Downloads, Apple's news and software download site, choose

Get Mac OS X Software from the Apple menu, which opens the Web site shown in Figure 13.6. The applications are categorized, so it's easy to find the type of software you're looking for, and the most popular downloads are featured on the first page of the site. Developers can easily update or add new descriptions of their software on the Mac OS X Downloads site.

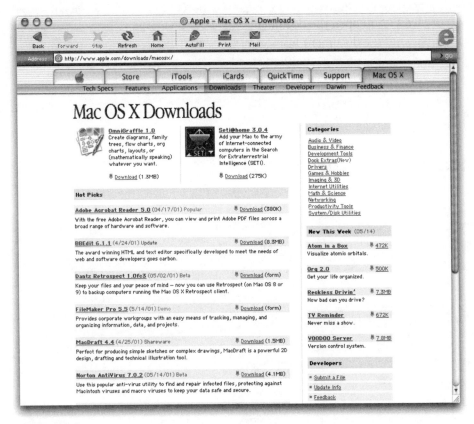

Figure 13.6
The Get Mac OS X Software command from the Apple menu gives you easy access to the latest applications for Mac OS X.

Mac Help

Mac Help is an essential resource when troubleshooting Mac OS X or an application. However, the help documentation for some applications or Mac OS X components was not written for the Help Viewer application, so don't be surprised if the menu is disabled when you need it most. For additional information on getting help from the Mac OS and its applications, see Appendix A.

13

Apple System Profiler

The Apple System Profiler utility is a great tool for learning about what resources and devices are connected to your computer and recognized by Mac OS X. The Apple System Profiler, located in the Utilities folder, catalogs your computer's hardware and software attributes for reference and for use by trained support professionals. It records just about every conceivable aspect of your Mac, including hardware specifications, Mac OS version, and what frameworks, Extensions, and applications are installed on your computer. For example, Figure 13.7 shows the general profile information about a dual-processor G4.

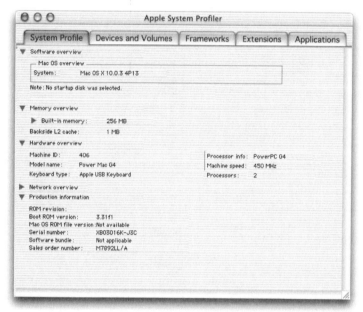

Figure 13.7
A small portion of the information gathered by the Apple System Profiler.

Console

The Console, a somewhat geeky utility, displays a variety of error messages from the operating system that may prove useful to some users. Shown in Figure 13.8, the Console logs all types of anomalies about Finder operations, networking errors, printer communication problems, and errors about communications with other peripheral devices such as the mouse and keyboard.

CPU Monitor

Sometimes your computer might seem a little sluggish, especially when you're running several applications at the same time. You can use the CPU Monitor utility to track

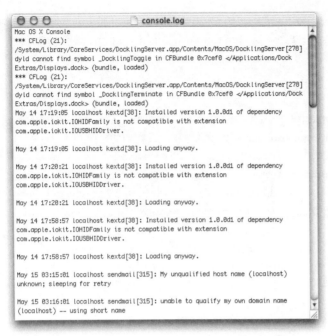

Figure 13.8
Use the Console utility to view error messages logged by the operating system.

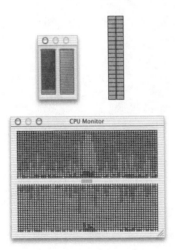

Figure 13.9
Three views of the CPU Monitor.

processor resources and potentially eliminate the processor as the reason for unresponsiveness, and you can display the activity levels of your processors in a variety of ways. For example, Figure 13.9 shows the CPU Monitor in Standard (top left), Floating (top right), and Expanded (bottom) views. Select CPU Monitor|Preferences to

13

configure the monitor's on-screen display, including colors and level of transparency. My preference is to display the Floating version with slight transparency to minimize the distraction caused by the CPU Monitor.

ProcessViewer

The ProcessViewer, a companion utility for the CPU Monitor, provides detailed information about the processes and applications running on your computer. Most Unix operating systems provide this ability as a way for system administrators to closely monitor the performance of mission-critical computers and keep track of processor resources. You can view all processes in a window like the one shown in Figure 13.10, or only those processes belonging to the current user, administrative processes (used by the operating system), or processes belonging to the NetBoot feature. Even if you are not using a NetBoot server to boot your computer over a network, a few NetBoot processes will be running, so don't be alarmed.

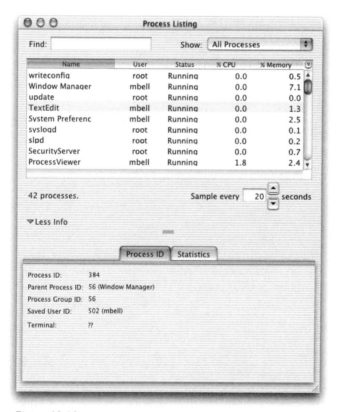

Figure 13.10
The ProcessViewer.

To get information about a particular process, select it from the list of processes in the upper half of the window. The Process ID and Statistics tabs in the lower half of the window provide some rather technical information about the process you've selected, which you can also terminate from within the ProcessViewer by selecting Process|Quit Process (or Command+Shift+Q). If you ever doubted that Mac OS X is really a Unix operating system with a very friendly user interface, doubt no more!

Disk Utility

The Disk Utility was described earlier in this chapter in the context of booting from the Mac OS X installation CD-ROM to troubleshoot and partition hard drives. However, you may also launch Disk Utility from the Utilities folder when the computer has finished booting from the hard drive containing the Disk Utility instead of an external boot source such as a CD-ROM or Mac OS 9.1 disk. However, you cannot repair a disk that has been used as the startup disk, a locked disk (such as a CD-ROM), or a disk containing open files. You can verify these disks, but not repair them.

Useful Tools for Mac OS 9.1

Because Mac OS 9.1 will continue to be a part of the Mac experience for the foreseeable future, consider the following utilities for use with your computer when booting directly into Mac OS 9.1. Some of these utilities may work from within Classic mode, but I strongly recommend that you boot into Mac OS 9.1 if you're attempting to repair a drive or resolve especially difficult startup problems. Many of the utilities mentioned here are in the process of being Carbonized for use in Mac OS X, so keep checking for new versions.

Disk First Aid

The Disk First Aid utility comes with the Mac OS and is an essential tool for diagnosing and repairing Apple hard drives, much like the Disk Utility for Mac OS X. It can verify the physical integrity of a disk, as well as make some repairs.

Drive Setup

The Drive Setup utility, the companion tool to Disk First Aid, is used to format and initialize drives, including partitioning, low-level formatting, and updating disk drivers. The Disk First Aid and Drive Setup utilities are included on the Mac OS 9.1 CD-ROM.

13

Extension Manager

As you've seen in Chapters 2 and 3, Mac OS 9.1 relies on Extensions to provide essential functionality for your computer. The Extensions Manager is the best way to manage these Extensions, as well as Control Panels and Startup Items.

MacsBug

http://asu.info.apple.com

MacsBug is an advanced programming utility that loads before Mac OS 9.1 at startup and is particularly useful in identifying what causes an application to crash. When an error occurs and is trapped by MacsBug, detailed information about what crashed and why appears in a bizarre on-screen display. The benefit for the beginner user is that at least you'll know what crashed and be able to recover control of the computer by typing one of several commands, such as **es** to exit the offending application, **ea** to restart the offending application, or **rb** to reboot the computer.

FWB Hard Disk Toolkit

www.fwb.com

FWB Hard Disk Toolkit is a powerful application that specializes in the formatting, performance optimization, and repair of hard drives. In addition to individual drives, it supports RAID (redundant array of inexpensive disks) drives as well. If you aspire to be a power user, then you should have this utility.

Norton SystemWorks and Norton AntiVirus

www.norton.com

Norton SystemWorks is a suite of utilities that provides serious repair capabilities in addition to disk optimization, added protection against crashes, and file and disk recovery. Norton, as it is known in tech support circles, is probably the best-known repair utility for the Mac OS, and for good reason. Be sure to add it to your tool kit.

Norton AntiVirus is a powerful commercial application that detects and automatically repairs viruses, including Microsoft Word macro viruses, and updates its virus library over the Internet. It also includes a bootable CD-ROM.

TechTool Pro

www.micromat.com

Another tool that has become essential to the Mac OS troubleshooting tool kit is
TechTool Pro from MicroMat. TechTool Pro is a real geek's tool, but it provides a
clever front end that allows you to select a Simple or Standard interface—in case
you're intimidated by the Expert interface.

File Buddy

www.skytag.com

File Buddy is a wonderful (and cheap!) utility that provides a number of functions
such as finding duplicate or hidden files, checking the integrity of aliases, cleaning out
unnecessary files, inventorying drives, and rebuilding the Desktop. One of the most
popular features of File Buddy, however, is its powerful Get Info command, which
allows you to contextual-click on an item in the Finder and view detailed information
about that item.

Extension Overload

www.extensionoverload.com

Extension Overload from Teng Chou Ming and Peter Hardman is an award-winning
utility that helps users manage the dozens of Extensions in the System Folder. In fact,
this utility contains information on over 1,200 items! Extension Overload provides
detailed information about each item and offers a searchable interface to help you
locate a specific Extension or Control Panel.

Conflict Catcher

www.casadyg.com

Conflict Catcher helps resolve Extension conflicts and startup problems by identifying
offending items. It works by cataloging your System Folder and performing a series of
restarts, identifying problems along the way.

SysErrors

http://cptech.free.fr

SysErrors by Caerwyn Pearce is a database of error codes with a handy interface that
allows you to search for a particular error or browse categories of error codes for

13

specific elements of the Mac OS, such as the Memory Manager. Remember that Mac OS error codes come in two formats, positive errors and negative errors, so be sure to look up the error using a minus sign for negative errors.

Virex

www.mcafee.com

Virex is another commercial application that provides substantial protection against viruses, as well as automatic updates and scheduled scans of your drives and network volumes. A version of Virex for Mac OS X is currently under development.

Useful Resources

Many new Web sites are devoted to helping you troubleshoot problems and providing software solutions for Mac OS X. Several of these sites will be familiar to the experienced Mac user because they've been around for years and should be regarded as reliable. For additional information about where to go for help with Mac OS X, refer to Appendix A.

AppleCare Service and Support

www.apple.com/support/

The Apple support Web site continues to evolve to provide more information about Mac OS X. The site has several subsections, including the new Knowledge Base search engine (**http://kbase.info.apple.com**), an example of which is shown in Figure 13.11. The Knowledge Base search allows you to select a broad topic, such as Mac OS X, and then narrow the search to a subcategory such as configuration, and then type in the search term for that subcategory. You can further narrow the search to a specific type of computer, such as iMac, iBook, PowerBook, or Desktop, or all of these Macs.

You can also perform an advanced search using natural language and Boolean logic, such as "Mac and OS and X and installation", as well as search the Tech Info Library or browse the AppleSpec database for technical information about your particular model of Mac.

MacNN: OS X News

www.osx.macnn.com

The Mac OS X section of the MacNN Web site is my site of choice for news about Mac OS X, applications, and discussion forums. Their slogan is ReadMe First for a good reason!

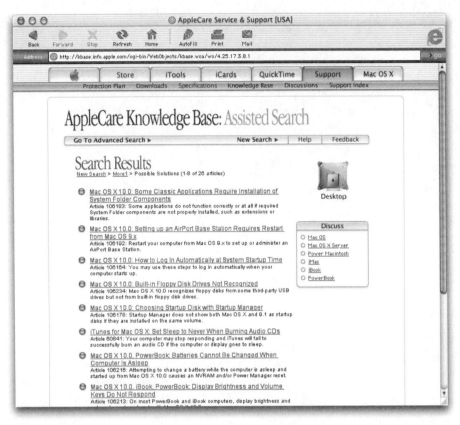

Figure 13.11
Use the Knowledge Base search to help troubleshoot a problem with Mac OS X.

Macintouch: Mac OS X Reader Reports

www.macintouch.com/mosxreaderreports.html

The Mac OS X section of Macintouch is less organized than that of MacNN, but it is nevertheless a great resource because of the sophisticated level of contribution by loyal Macintouch readers.

MacFixIt: Troubleshooting for Mac OS X

www.macfixit.com/macosx.shtml

MacFixIt is the most thorough site for troubleshooting Mac OS software and hardware. It has a great forum for discussing technical issues and troubleshooting tips, as well as a good search engine to look for tips in their archive of information.

Mac OS X Apps

www.macosxapps.com

Mac OS X Apps is the newest Web site that I follow every day. This site tracks new and updated Mac OS X applications, which are organized in numerous subcategories such as Docklets, Games, Productivity, Security, and Utilities. It also has a good search engine and links to news stories.

Version Tracker: Mac OS X

www.versiontracker.com/vt_mac_osx.shtml

Version Tracker, which is similar to Mac OS Apps, has a membership section that allows you (for a fee) to be notified of changes to the applications and utilities you want to track. Between Mac OS X Apps and Version Tracker, you won't need any other resources for keeping up to date with software for Mac OS X.

Mac OS X Hints

www.macosxhints.com

Mac OS X Hints is a really cool site that organizes readers' hints, tips, and tricks about Mac OS X into Applications, Classic Environment, Desktop, Help Requests, Install, Internet, Networking, Site News, System, and Unix. The search engine allows you to search for hints by keyword, such as Dock, and returns entries in all the above categories.

Wrapping Up

Troubleshooting the Mac OS is fairly easy when compared to other operating systems—but a lot of good this observation will do if you're the one trying to resolve a problem! Don't underestimate the effectiveness of preventative maintenance, however, and above all else, *back up your data on a regular basis*. Your number *will* come up one of these days! If you do have a problem, keep in mind the most common problems and their solutions discussed in this chapter, including:

■ Startup and shutdown problems

■ Freezing up during use

■ Hard-drive problems

■ Networking difficulties

■ Mouse, keyboard, and USB issues

■ Problems with monitors, applications, and documents

■ Printing problems

■ Mac OS X diagnostic and repair tools

■ Mac OS 9.1 diagnostic and repair tools

■ Web sites for Mac OS X troubleshooting and applications

In the next section, I'll look at how to use your Mac on a variety of networks, starting with the Mac OS's built-in File Sharing and Web Sharing features.

13

Part 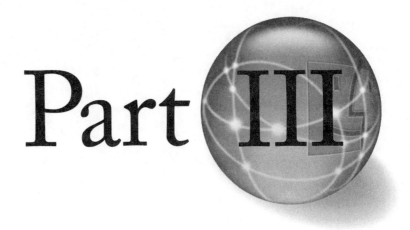 III

Networking

File and Web Sharing

File Sharing is one of the many areas in which the Macintosh was ahead of its time when it debuted in 1984. The first Macintosh supported the AppleTalk networking protocol, allowing any number of Macintosh computers to be strung together with inexpensive telephone cable to form what is known as a *peer-to-peer network*. Back then, however, sharing word processing documents was probably the most compelling reason to create a Macintosh network.

With Web Sharing, you can publish HTML documents on the World Wide Web just as easily as you can share files—word processing or otherwise. Web Sharing is designed for individuals who want to share information over the Web without having to install, configure, and manage a commercial Web server. Mac OS X includes a complete version of Apache, the most popular Web server in the world; you can use it to share just about anything on your Mac, including HTML documents, images, word processing documents, spreadsheets, and much more.

Mac OS X makes significant changes to the way you can share files and HTML documents on a local area network (LAN), an intranet, the Internet, and the Web. This chapter explains everything you need to know in order to share documents safely in the multiuser environment of Mac OS X.

What Is File Sharing?

File Sharing is a quick and easy way to share any file or folder with users on just about any type of network—whether it's a small peer-to-peer network of just two computers, or the mother of all networks, the Internet. But why, exactly, would you want to share files? You may be motivated to put your Macintosh on a network and share files for two main reasons:

- *Computer-to-computer communications*—Networked Macs can transfer files directly from one computer to another, eliminating the need to transfer files via *sneakernet* (which employs the Nike or Converse protocol) or FedEx.

- *Centralized or distributed file servers*—Storing large amounts of data on file servers provides an easy way to share information, allows a number of people to participate in group projects, and reduces the data storage requirements of individual users. But because File Sharing has its limitations, Apple also produces an industrial-strength version of File Sharing in the form of Mac OS X Server, which is capable of supporting thousands of users. Of course, the ultimate form of File Sharing is Apple's iDisk, which supports millions of users.

Mac OS X File Sharing allows you to share the contents of one main folder, called Public, that is located in your home folder. This differs from earlier versions of the Mac OS, in which you can designate up to 10 folders for sharing, regardless of their location on your computer. Because Mac OS X is a multiuser operating system, the number and location of folders has been limited to prevent unauthorized access to files. However, for each shared folder within the Public folder, you can restrict access to users who have accounts on your server.

In addition to sharing files that reside on your computer with others, a second File Sharing strategy allows you to access folders and volumes located on other Macs—provided you've been granted access privileges. After you've accessed them initially, folders and volumes from other Macs appear on your Desktop and can be viewed in a Finder window. For example, Figure 14.1 shows an example of the Desktop icon for a shared volume (top) and the contents of the volume (bottom). Now you can use the contents of the mounted folder or volume as if they were your own.

In networking parlance, when your computer is sharing files, it's acting as a server; when it's accessing files from another computer, it's acting as a client. File Sharing allows every user on a Macintosh network to be a server, a client, or both. Sharing

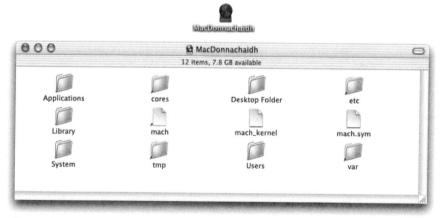

Figure 14.1
A volume shared over the Internet using File Sharing.

data from your Macintosh and accessing data shared by others on your network can increase your capabilities and productivity in many ways. Here are some examples of resources that can be shared:

- *Central libraries*—Reference files such as clip art, templates (or stationery), and historical records can be kept in one location and shared with the entire network.

- *Drop-box folders that send and receive files*—Each network user can define an electronic Out box and In box. By assigning access privileges, you can use an In box to let everyone add files (but not look at the folder's contents), and an Out box to let users pick up the files they need (but not add any files).

- *Temporary access*—File Sharing is the perfect delivery system for members of the desktop publishing and printing industries who often transmit large files to and from customers. The alternatives are copying the files to a removable medium such as a Zip or Jaz cartridge or burning a CD and then mailing it; compared to File Sharing, both approaches waste time and resources.

Mac OS X's File Sharing isn't the answer to all your needs, however.

The Limits of File Sharing

Although the capabilities of File Sharing are impressive, it's important to understand that File Sharing is only a "personal" method of sharing files over a network. Mac OS X Server, Apple's dedicated file server software, accommodates thousands of shared items and allows Windows-based computers to connect to the Mac server as well. For a small number of Macs, File Sharing is sufficient, whereas larger or more heavily used networks should utilize a combination of Mac OS X Server and File Sharing. In most of these situations, File Sharing will supplement Mac OS X Server, not replace it.

Here are a few observations about using File Sharing that you might want to consider:

- *Administration requirements*—As you'll see later, the administrative requirements of File Sharing are not incidental. When many users need frequent access to numerous files and folders, centralized File Sharing administration (provided by central file servers such as Mac OS X Server) is usually more efficient than distributed administration.

- *Security risks*—To lighten the burden of administrative requirements, users often neglect security issues and leave confidential or sensitive data unprotected. This is less likely to occur on centralized, professionally managed file servers.

14

■ *Performance degradation*—Even with a very fast processor and a very fast hard drive, File Sharing takes a noticeable toll on computer performance. Macintoshes or peripherals that aren't particularly speedy to begin with make the problem even worse. The benefits outweigh the inconveniences for casual or infrequent users. For frequent uses, however, regularly encountering long delays can be annoying and counterproductive. A centralized server with resources dedicated to the burdens of serving network users is the practical alternative in these circumstances.

■ *Access limitations*—Unlike previous versions of the operating system, Mac OS X File Sharing cannot strictly limit access to files and subfolders. Anyone who has been granted administrative access through the Users section of the System Preferences has total access to the entire computer. In many cases, these privileges are too promiscuous and could lead to trouble. Furthermore, the sharing Macintoshes must be left on all the time to ensure that files are always available on the network.

A File Sharing Quick Tour

File Sharing's capabilities are powerful and therefore require more preparation and attention than most other Mac OS X features. Here is a quick tour of the steps I feel are essential for File Sharing:

1. *Prepare your Macintosh*—This includes physically connecting to a network, placing the files to be shared in the proper locations, and activating AppleTalk if you want users to see your computer over legacy AppleTalk networks.

2. *Start File Sharing*—The Sharing System Preferences provides configuration information and the master switch to turn File Sharing on and off.

3. *Configure users*—Users must be defined in the Users portion of the Sharing System Preferences.

4. *Specify folders to share*—To share most folders with guests over a network, you must place the folders in a special location; users with administrative access will have rights to see any folders on the computer.

5. *Connect with others using File Sharing*—In order to access folders and volumes that are shared by others, use the Connect To Server command to log on to other computers. Mac OS 9.1 users can use the Chooser or Network Browser.

The remainder of this chapter considers these steps in detail. Chapter 15 covers even more information about File Sharing and networking.

Preparing for File Sharing

File Sharing success depends on physically connecting your computer to a network and properly configuring network settings. The simplest and most common Macintosh networking scheme uses standard Ethernet and a hub to connect multiple computers to each other. Sophisticated networks, which run at increased speed and use switches rather than hubs, require Fast Ethernet or Gigabit Ethernet adapters because they can route packets of data more efficiently than hubs. All PowerMacs capable of running Mac OS X are equipped with built-in Ethernet, and additional Ethernet cards may be added via PCI slots (or in the case PowerBooks, a PCMCIA slot). It's also possible to implement File Sharing over a wireless network using Apple's Airport networking technology.

 You will need administrative privileges in order to change your network settings.

Once the physical elements of the network are properly configured, you need to configure your network interface using the TCP/IP and AppleTalk sections of the Network System Preferences. File Sharing works without AppleTalk being active, but users on your network need to know the IP address of your computer in order to connect to it; your computer will not show up in the Chooser or Network Browser of computers running earlier versions of the OS, or in the selection tool of Windows-based computers running utilities such as PCMACLAN that allow them to connect to Apple-based networks. To configure your computer for network access, obtain the proper settings from your Internet service provider or LAN administrator. Once you have the proper network settings, launch the System Preferences, choose the Network pane, and follow these steps:

1. Choose the proper network interface, such as Built-In Ethernet (shown in Figure 14.2), and click the TCP/IP tab.

2. In the Configure section, choose the method for obtaining your Mac's IP address, such as manually or using a Dynamic Host Configuration Protocol (DHCP) server.

3. Complete the remaining IP-related settings, such as the IP Address, Subnet Mask, Router, Domain Name Servers, and Search Domains. These options will vary depending on how your Mac obtains an IP address. For example, if you choose DHCP, you'll see a much different group of settings.

14

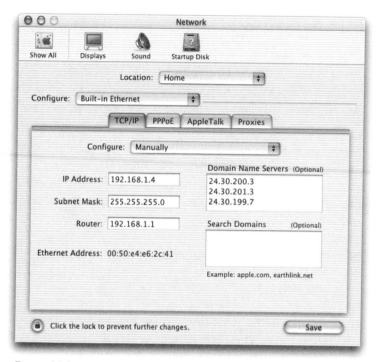

Figure 14.2
You'll need to configure your computer's TCP/IP settings before starting up File Sharing.

4. Click on the AppleTalk tab and choose Make AppleTalk Active if you want your computer listed in the Chooser and Network Browser of Macs running earlier versions of the Mac OS. Figure 14.3 shows the AppleTalk tab of the Network System Preferences.

5. Configure any remaining AppleTalk-related options and click the Save button.

The next step in preparing your Mac for File Sharing is confirming connectivity to a network. For this task, use a network monitoring tool such as Apple's Network Utility, located in your Utilities folder. Choose the Info tab in the Network Utility window (as shown in Figure 14.4) and then select the network interface that you configured in the TCP/IP section of the Network System Preferences and confirm the following settings:

- *Hardware Address*—Ensures that the computer properly recognizes the Ethernet adapter, which has an (allegedly) unique hardware address.

- *IP Address*—Shares your IP address with the network by way of the Network System Preferences.

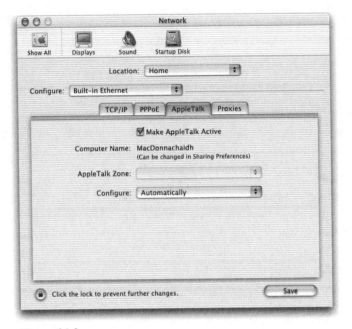

Figure 14.3
Although AppleTalk isn't required for File Sharing, enabling it will display your computer in the Chooser and Network Browser of Macs running earlier versions of the Mac OS.

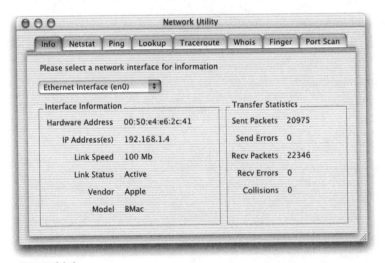

Figure 14.4
Use the Network Utility to verify your network connectivity.

14

- *Link Speed*—Determines whether your Ethernet adapter is communicating at the optimal speed with the hub or switch through which it is connected to the rest of your network.

- *Link Status*—Indicates whether you are on (Active) or off (Inactive) the network.

If you're really curious about the performance of your network connection, check out the Transfer Statistics section of the Info tab. It contains some geeky stuff, but it can also alert you to network traffic errors.

After verifying that you are properly connected to a network, the final step in preparing to start File Sharing is to give your computer a name, or identity, for use in File Sharing and AppleTalk networks. To assign a name to your computer, open the Sharing section of the Network System Preferences and enter a name in the Computer Name field of the Network Identity section. For example, Figure 14.5 shows that I've entered MacDonnachaidh as the name for my computer (that's Gaelic for "son of Duncan," in case you're wondering).

Once you've completed all these steps, you're ready to start sharing!

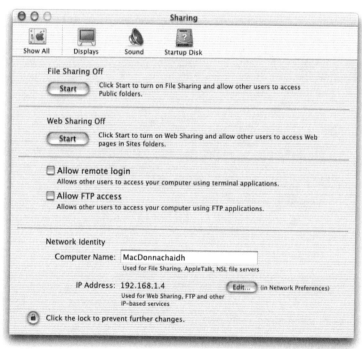

Figure 14.5
Give your computer a name in the Sharing section of the System Preferences.

Starting File Sharing

Once your physical (or wireless) network is installed and your Network System Preferences are configured, you're ready to launch File Sharing. As a security precaution, File Sharing is not automatically enabled when you first install Mac OS X. By default, Web Sharing, remote access (Telnet), and File Transfer Protocol (FTP) are also not initially enabled. To start File Sharing, open the Sharing System Preferences (shown in Figure 14.5) and click the Start button in the File Sharing section. It will take several seconds to complete the startup task, and you can expect to hear your computer's hard drive reading and writing during the startup process. The startup process is considerably quicker in Mac OS X than in previous versions of the Mac OS; however, just *how* quick will depend on the speed of your processor and the quantity of files and folders that are being shared.

Once File Sharing is running, the Start button shown in Figure 14.5 becomes the Stop button. To halt File Sharing, just click the Stop button; a dialog box like the one in Figure 14.6 asks you how many minutes remain until file sharing is turned off. Enter a number between 0 (for immediate shutdown) and 999 (for delayed action). Finally, the optional warning message is sent to users as a courtesy.

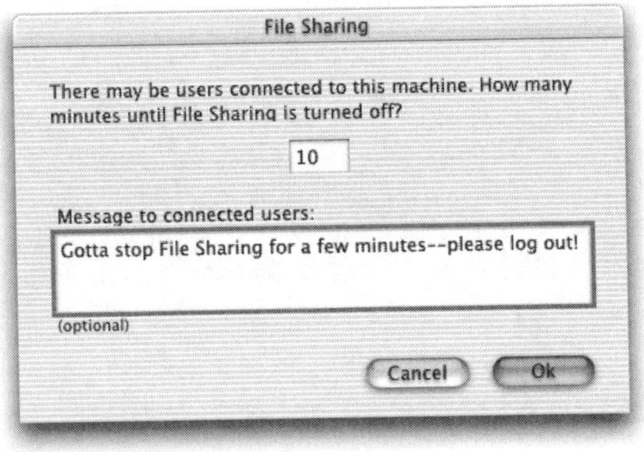

Figure 14.6
The File Sharing shutdown dialog box.

After you click OK in the shutdown dialog box, a status message informs all users who are logged into your Mac that File Sharing will be turned off in the amount of time that you specified; it also conveys the message entered in the dialog box shown in Figure 14.6. If you cancel the shutdown command before the time limit expires, users will receive a second message stating that the shutdown procedure has been canceled. If you choose the 0 minutes option, cutoff will occur without warning. Figure 14.7 contains examples of the various messages that your computer may issue during the File Sharing shutdown process.

14

Figure 14.7
Users logged into your computer may be notified of an impending disconnection or a cancellation of the shutdown command.

In earlier versions of the Mac OS, File Sharing is also scriptable via AppleScript; however, this is not the case in Mac OS X. Perhaps a future release will include this handy feature.

Configuring User Access

Mac OS X's method of assigning access to users differs significantly from Mac OS 9.1. In fact, File Sharing is a little less flexible in Mac OS X because of the operating system's multiuser capability. File Sharing access is limited to three types of users:

- Administrative users
- Users
- Guests

Users and administrative users have accounts on your computer that are created in the Users section of the System Preferences; guests can access your computer through

File Sharing without your creating guest accounts. Refer back to the section entitled "Working with Multiple Users" in Chapter 5 for detailed information on creating and managing user accounts. Although Mac OS X doesn't allow you to easily create and manage groups of users, users with advanced Unix administration skills can use the Terminal application to manipulate the Group ID (GID) property. Let's take a look at the three different types of File Sharing users in Mac OS X.

Administrative Users

In Mac OS X File Sharing, an administrative user has more read and write privileges than a user. When an administrative user logs into your Mac via File Sharing, she has access to most files and folders from the root level on up, including those in the home folders of other users and all the files and folders. By contrast, non-administrative users are typically restricted to the contents of their own home folder and the Public folders of other users, a distinction I'll illustrate a little later in the chapter.

The second difference between administrators and users is rather curious: Administrators have more access to the contents of a hard drive when logging in remotely than when physically logging into a Mac OS X computer by sitting down at the keyboard. Specifically, logging in remotely allows administrators to see inside all the home folders of all the users on the computer; when physically logged in, administrators cannot see inside these folders.

Furthermore, Mac OS X doesn't clearly distinguish between administrators and the owner of the computer, often referred to as the *superuser* or *root user*. In other Unix-based operating systems, one username and password has absolute control over all file, folder, and application access. With root access, you can add and delete any data on the computer and bestow administrative privileges to others; administrators can manage limited amounts of data, as well as the accounts of others; users are often strictly limited to certain portions of the folder structure and may be limited to launching certain applications. In Mac OS X, administrative users have most of the capabilities of a Unix-style superuser, but not all of them.

To summarize, Mac OS X File Sharing is like a three-story office building: the farther you are from the ground, the more privileges you have. Administrators occupy the third floor and have the best view; the occupants of the second floor are the registered users; the ground floor is for guests. As far as File Sharing is concerned, however, the building has no owner—only multiple administrators. To assign administrator status to a user, read Step 3 in the following section carefully.

14

Users

File Sharing grants access to your computer to users who've been assigned a username and password through the Users System Preferences. In addition to being able to access your computer, they can also share their Public folders with other users and guests. To create a user account, follow these steps:

1. Launch the System Preferences from the Apple menu or the Dock and choose the Users pane.

2. Click the New User button and enter the necessary information, as shown in Figure 14.8.

3. Do not click the Allow User To Administer This Machine checkbox unless you wish to grant administrative access to the computer to the new user.

4. Click the Save button and quit the System Preferences.

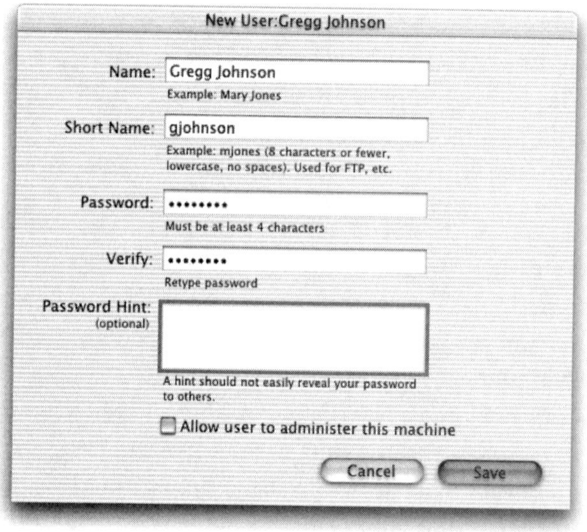

Figure 14.8
Create new user accounts for File Sharing access, as well as other types of access, in the Users System Preferences.

In addition to creating the standard set of folders, such as the Desktop and Documents folders, in the new user's home folder, Mac OS X also creates a folder called Public for use in File Sharing. I'll explain more about this folder in the section entitled "Sharing Folders and Volumes."

Guests

Occasionally you may want to share files with someone who is physically connected to your network but doesn't have a user account for File Sharing. Thanks to File Sharing's support of guests, this is possible. By default, guests are allowed in the Public folders of each user account on your computer. In Mac OS X, guest accounts cannot be globally enabled or disabled, whereas Mac OS 9.1 includes this option in the Users & Groups section of the File Sharing Control Panel. Guest access is turned on by default; however, File Sharing is not enabled by default when Mac OS X is installed so guests cannot connect to your computer by default.

It is possible to disable access to the Public folder, however; I'll describe this procedure later in the chapter. Moreover, you can selectively disable guest access to individual user accounts.

Sharing Folders and Volumes

The previous section describes in detail the three different types of File Sharing users; this section covers what you need to know about the various locations that can be accessed through File Sharing. As you know, users of your computer can share the contents of their Public folders. However, users can also share the entire contents of their home folders; users with administrative access can share the contents of the entire computer, in addition to their own Public folders. So, to summarize, Mac OS X File Sharing allows for essentially three types of users (administrator, user, guest) and three accessible areas of the computer (the entire computer, a user's home folder, and a user's Public folder). Table 14.1 illustrates the intersection of this set of threes.

Mac OS X preprograms, or *hard codes*, the Public folder in each user's home folder for File Sharing, just as it names the home folder with each user's Short Name as configured in the Users System Preferences. You can't change the name or location of either of these folders. However, a user can share other folders by moving them into the Public folder and modifying access privileges to change the rights that administrators, other users, and guests have to the Public and Sites folders.

Table 14.1   Mac OS X File Sharing access privileges.

Type of User	Computer	Home Folder	Public Folder
Administrator	Yes	Yes	Yes
User	No	Yes	Yes
Guest	No	No	Yes

14

Selecting a Folder to Share

Before you can share a folder with others on your network or over the Internet, you must initiate File Sharing and specify access privileges in the Privileges section of the Show Info command; otherwise you'll be stuck with the default set of privileges. To review or change the sharing privileges of a folder located in your Public folder, select the folder and follow these steps:

1. Choose File|Show Info or press Command+I.

2. Select Show Privileges.

For example, Figure 14.9 shows the Privileges section for a folder named Docs in my Public folder. This dialog box allows me to assign the access privileges for this item and transfer the same set of privileges to any folders contained in the Docs folder. Access privileges, as you learned earlier, determine who is allowed to see the folders and volumes as well as the files inside those folders and volumes, and who can make changes to existing files or store new files. (I'll talk more about access privileges in the upcoming "Understanding Access Privileges" section of this chapter.)

Figure 14.9
The Privileges section of a Show Info window.

The Privileges section of the Show Info window allows you to configure a number of important options, including:

■ *Name*—The name of the folder, which you can edit by typing into this field.

■ *Owner*—This option specifies the owner of the selected folder or volume and the owner's access privileges. Unlike previous versions of the operating system in which you can reassign ownership of the folder to another user, you are the sole owner of shared folders in your Public folder.

■ *Group*—Mac OS X assigns users of your computer automatically to a group called Staff, which you cannot change, as you can in Mac OS 9.1. This marks a significant change in File Sharing from previous versions of the Mac OS. Perhaps a future release of Mac OS X will restore some capability for creating and assigning groups.

■ *Everybody*—This section specifies access privileges granted to guest users on your Macintosh. As mentioned before, anyone on your network can log on to your Mac as a guest—as long as you've enabled File Sharing and have at least one user account with a Public folder whose privileges have not been further restricted.

■ *Copy These Privileges To All Enclosed Folders*—When you share a folder, all enclosed folders are also automatically accessible to users with access to your computer. You can change the access privileges of an enclosed folder so that they don't match those of the enclosing folder, and this option is used to reset the access privileges of the enclosed folders so they match those of the currently selected folder or volume. Think of this option as a kind of reset button.

After making any changes to these options, click the close button in the title bar to close the Show Info window and apply the selected options to the folder in question.

Unsharing a Folder

Sharing folders has been the central topic thus far, but what about unsharing a folder? Mac OS X provides several strategies that you can use to stop sharing a folder, including:

■ Turn File Sharing off completely

■ Stop sharing a selected user's Public folder

■ Stop sharing a selected folder within a user's Public folder

■ Remove or relocate a folder outside the Public folder

Of course, turning off your Mac or disconnecting its network cables will also do the trick!

To turn File Sharing off completely, open the Sharing System Preferences and click the Stop button, described earlier in this chapter. When File Sharing is turned off, the settings and access privileges that you set with the Sharing command are retained for all shared folders and volumes; they will be reactivated when File Sharing is turned on again. This option is easiest if you're the only user of the computer. If not, you'll automatically disable File Sharing for everyone else who uses your computer.

14

To turn off the Sharing of a particular folder only, the easiest approach is to remove it from your Public folder, instead of trying to manipulate the sharing privileges for that folder. I don't recommend that you stop File Sharing for the entire Public folder unless some users of your computer don't want to share their folders while others are still willing to share their Public folders. In this case, the only option is to disable access to a user's Public folder. The following section will help you understand how access privileges work so you can alter access to specific folders.

Understanding Access Privileges

Shared folders, volumes, and folders enclosed within shared folders and volumes are available to other network users according to the access privilege settings you apply in the Privileges section of the Show Info window. These privileges are the key to controlling File Sharing.

As shown in Figure 14.10, the three access privilege options are assigned to three different users or groups. Your choice of option settings and combinations determines how network users can access and modify your shared data and storage space.

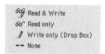

Figure 14.10
The access privilege options for Mac OS X File Sharing.

Let's look at these access privileges, the users and groups they can be assigned to, and the results of applying them in different combinations, starting with the fewest privileges offered to the most users:

■ *None*—With no privileges specified, a shared folder is inaccessible to users. If that folder is enclosed within another folder to which a user has at least read access, the folder that has no privileges will look like the Docs folder shown in Figure 14.11. If

Figure 14.11
Folders with no access privileges appear with a small stop sign to indicate that you cannot go any further.

the Public folder is assigned this option, it will not appear in the Select The Volumes You Wish To Mount section of the Connect To Server command. In other words, when someone attempts to log into your computer and your Public folder is not shared, they will not even know you have an account on the computer.

■ *Write Only (Drop Box)*—This privilege hides the contents of folders from a specified user or group—users don't even know what, if anything, is inside this type of folder (selecting Show Info will reveal 0KB of contents). Users can place files in the shared folder, but only the owner can see and manage its contents. When a folder is shared as a Drop Box, it will appear with a small downward arrow like the folder named Drop Box in Figure 14.11.

■ *Read Only*—This option limits a user to viewing (or reading—hence the name) the contents of the folder. No changes can be made within the shared item. When the Read Only option is selected, an icon appears in the upper-left corner of the title bar of windows accessed via File Sharing to let the user know that the folder or volume is write protected (see Figure 14.12). Users are prohibited from writing to this folder, as well as from editing or deleting files and folders.

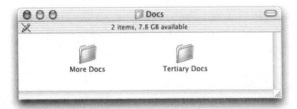

Figure 14.12
A shared folder with Read Only privileges displays a read-only icon in the status bar.

■ *Read & Write*—When the Read & Write privilege is set, the user can save new files, change existing files, and create new folders. He or she enjoys almost unlimited access to the folder and its contents and can delete the contents of these folders.

Privilege can be assigned to the following three types of users (although the Groups section below is a little fuzzy in Mac OS X because everyone is a member of the Staff group by default):

■ *Owner*—The owner of a folder or volume is the individual or group who can change the access privileges of that folder or volume while accessing it over the network. The person in whose home folder hierarchy a folder exists is automatically the owner of it. Therefore, by default, you're the owner of only the folders in your home folder; the other folders created by Mac OS X belong to another user ID called System.

14

- *Group*—The Group category assigns access privileges to a specific user or group. When sharing folders or volumes, you cannot change the Group assignment unless you are a proficient Unix system administrator. Please do not try this at home!

- *Everybody*—The Everybody category grants access privileges to all registered users, groups, and guests who connect to the Macintosh that contains the selected folder.

For example, refer to Figure 14.11 in which my Public folder contains two folders, Drop Box and Docs. The Drop Box folder is marked as follows:

- *Owner*—Read & Write

- *Group*—Write Only (Drop Box)

- *Everybody*—Write Only (Drop Box)

Although no user will be able to see the contents of this folder, they will be able to add items to it via File Sharing. The Docs folder in the same example is not readable by anyone other than the owner and other administrative users (who have access even though users and guests do not). The Docs folder has the following privileges:

- *Owner*—Read & Write

- *Group*—Read Only

- *Everybody*—Read Only

Finally, any folder you want to be open to anyone should have the following privileges selected in the Privileges section of the Show Info window:

- *Owner*—Read & Write

- *Group*—Read & Write

- *Everybody*—Read & Write

Now that you have a better understanding of the various types of users, locations for sharing folders, and levels of access, let's take a quick look at a few strategies for using File Sharing.

 The Mac OS uses different folder icons to indicate the level of access privileges assigned to a folder. This enables you to know at a glance whether you have read, write, or no access to a folder.

Access Privilege Strategies

Mac OS X provides various levels of privileges to control the way files can be accessed via File Sharing. Several common ways of using access privileges are as follows:

■ *Create an Inbox folder*—People can drop items into an Inbox folder but can't see what's already there or delete items from the folder. This is accomplished by granting Write Only (Drop Box) privileges to users in all categories (except the owner).

■ *Create an Outbox folder*—An Outbox folder allows users to see files and folders, but prohibits them from adding or deleting items. For example, an Outbox folder is an effective way to maintain an unsullied master copy of a document because it prevents other users or guests from tinkering with the document. This type of limited access is designated by granting Read Only access to everyone other than the owner, who has Read & Write privileges.

■ *Provide a workgroup area*—You can create a folder with several subfolders for access by groups who are working on related projects is a common way to utilize File Sharing. For example, you can create a folder to which everyone has Read & Write access—just be sure that the users are aware of their responsibility to refrain from deleting or modifying documents that don't belong to them. Think of this strategy as a form of cooperative multitasking among File Sharing users.

Logging In

You can log in to a Mac running File Sharing, Mac OS X Server, or AppleShare IP using the Connect To Server command in the Go menu of the Finder, or by pressing Command+K. The Connect To Server command, also known as simply the Connect command, combines the functionality of the Chooser and Network Browser of Mac OS 9.1 into a single application.

To connect to a server after issuing the Connect command, follow these steps:

1. Select a server from the drop-down list of recent or favorite servers, or enter the domain name or IP address of a server in the Address field, as shown in Figure 14.13.

2. Click the Connect button to connect to the server, Cancel to dismiss the Connect to Server window, or Add To Favorites.

3. When prompted for a username and password, as in Figure 14.14, click the Guest radio button to log in as a guest, or enter the username and password for an administrative or user account on the computer.

14

Figure 14.13
Selecting a File Sharing server.

Figure 14.14
Logging in to a Mac OS X computer running File Sharing.

4. Click the Connect button to display a list of volumes to which your user account has permission to access, as shown in Figure 14.15. Technically, some of the volumes are actually not volumes but the Public folders of users who have accounts on the computer. You may also hear these volumes referred to as *mount points* or *share points*. You can click one or more of the items shown in this window by Command+clicking the volumes.

5. Click the OK button to mount the volumes on your Desktop—if you have selected the Show Disks On The Desktop option in the Finder Preferences. If not, you can choose Go|Computer to open a new Finder window and see the

Figure 14.15
Select one or more volumes to connect to.

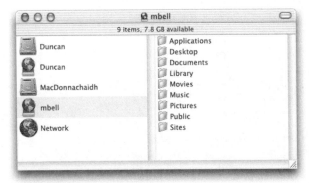

Figure 14.16
Using any type of Finder window, you can browse the contents of a mounted volume as if it were a local volume.

volume(s) mounted on your computer. For example, Figure 14.16 shows two volumes from the same server mounted at the same time: mbell and Duncan. The mbell volume is selected in a column view. Because you can see the contents of the home folder in this example, you know that I'm logged in either to my own home folder or someone else's home folder that I have administrative access to. Otherwise, I would only see the contents of the Public folder for this user.

If you're on a LAN and want to connect to a server running File Sharing, Mac OS X Server, or AppleShare IP, you can expand the Connect window and browse the contents of the network. This process is described in detail in the following chapter.

Now that you know the basics of configuring your computer for File Sharing, let's explore the second method of sharing files using your Mac, Web Sharing.

14

Web Sharing

The second way you can share files with other users over a LAN or the Internet is with Mac OS X's Web Sharing feature. Although Apple has included a personal Web server with the Mac OS in the past, Web Sharing is different. It's more than just a lightweight Web server—it's a fully functional installation of the Apache Web server. Apache, the most popular Web server on the Internet since 1996, now accounts for 60 percent of all Web servers in use today. Because Apache is an open source Web server, much like Darwin is an open source operating system, the two are a great match. For more information about the Apache Web server and other open source projects that support or compliment Apache, consult the Apache Software Foundation home page (**www.apache.org**).

If you can point and click a mouse, then you can be a Webmaster and run an Apache Web server on your computer, thanks to Mac OS X. This chapter explores a few tidbits about how the Web works; how to enable and configure Apple's Web Sharing feature; and how a special third-party application from Tenon Intersystem can unlock the power of Apache and turn your computer into a customized and highly configurable commercial Web server.

The Web and HTML

The Web is a collection of Web servers that are accessed by Web browsers such as Microsoft Internet Explorer, Netscape Navigator, iCab, OmniWeb, and many others. Web browsers are available for virtually every computer hardware and software platform; hand-held personal digital assistants (PDAs), such as the Palm Pilot; and mainframe computers. The Hypertext Markup Language (HTML) makes it possible for one document to be read by so many different types of computers. HTML is a low-level programming language called a markup, or page description, language; it's very unsophisticated and easily implemented into existing applications such as Microsoft Office and operating systems like Mac OS X. HTML uses simple formatting instructions like the following example to make portions of the document appear underlined, boldface, and centered, as well as insert images and citations:

```
<HTML>
<HEAD>
   <TITLE>HTML Basics</TITLE>
   <META NAME="generator" CONTENT="BBEdit 6.1.2">
</HEAD>
<BODY>
```

```
<P>
<CENTER><FONT FACE="Lucida Grande">
   This is an example of <U>underlined</U> and <B>bold</B>
   text centered on the page.
   <IMG SRC="1971.jpg" ALT="My First Bike" WIDTH="429" HEIGHT="429"><BR>
   <CITE>This is a citation.</CITE>
</FONT></CENTER>
</P>

</BODY>
</HTML>
```

HTML is really just a collection of commands written in easy-to-understand ASCII text that tells Web browsers how to display formatted text, insert images, and link to other pages on the Web. Figure 14.17 shows what this example looks like in Internet Explorer when served using Web Sharing.

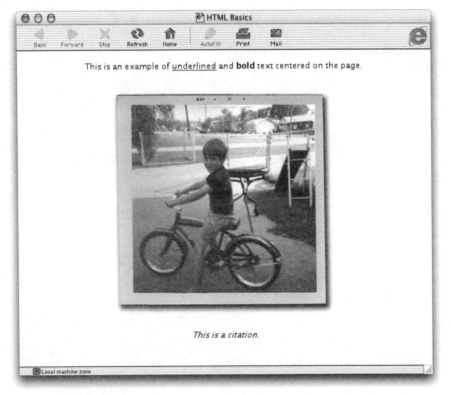

14

Figure 14.17
Web pages are composed of HTML code that tells Web browsers how to display text as well as images, movies, and sounds.

You'll need a good HTML editor if you plan to get serious about creating and modifying Web pages, and BBEdit for Mac OS X is a great place to start. To obtain a fully functional demo version of BBEdit, visit the Bare Bones home page (**www.barebones.com**). The full version costs about $120; you can upgrade to the Mac OS X version for as little as $39. It will be a worthwhile investment.

Web Server Configuration

Mac OS X implements the Apache Web server in an interesting way: It hides all the complex configuration options and expansion modules so that you can start serving Web pages for every user on your computer with a single mouse click. Apple doesn't disable Apache's advanced options—it just hides them by making the folders containing the configuring files invisible. This is not a problem for people who want to use more of Apache's features, however. Experienced Apache users can enable many of the hidden features using the Terminal application to issue command-line instructions. This requires a working knowledge of Unix file permissions as well as Apache administration experience. A second option is iTools from Tenon Intersystems (**www.tenon.com**), which I'll demonstrate a little later in the chapter. The rest of this section details how to start and stop Web Sharing, as well as a few points about file names and folder locations.

Starting Web Sharing

When Mac OS X is first installed, Web Sharing isn't active by default, but starting it up is easy. Once you've configured your Mac as part of a network (outlined earlier in this chapter), you're ready to start the Web server. Just follow these steps:

1. Open the Sharing System Preferences, shown earlier in Figure 14.5.

2. Click the Start button in the Web Sharing section, and the default access settings are applied.

3. The Web server will check to see if a valid network connection can be made and will then start up.

Because Mac OS X is a multiuser system, the amount of time it takes to complete the startup process depends on how many user accounts are configured on your computer and how many files and folders are located in the locations that have been designated for serving content. I'll explain this last point in just a moment. When the Web Sharing startup process is completed, the Start button will transform into a Stop button.

Stopping the Web Server

Once you've started the Web server, it will continue to provide access to your computer until you stop it. If you shut down your Mac without stopping the Web server, access will no longer be available. Once you restart your Mac, however, users will again have access. To stop the server, you can either shut down your Mac or open the Sharing System Preferences and click the Stop button in the Web Sharing section.

The server will not be accessible again until you manually restart it using the steps detailed in the previous section.

Locating Web Folders

When Mac OS X is installed, the Web server and its components are installed into a variety of locations on your Mac OS X hard drive. The Web server designates two folders from which files are actually served to Web browsers over the Web. The Apache Web server has a default folder in the following location: <*hard drive*>/Library/WebServer/. The Web server stores your HTML documents, images, and "other content" in this folder (which is known as the base directory, root folder, or docs folder in Webmaster-speak). Because of an Apple-imposed limitation in the Web server, the name and location of this folder cannot be changed. It contains two folders, one called Documents that contains documentation for the Apache Web server and also doubles as the default home page for your computer, and a folder called CGI-Executables for storing small applications called Common Gateway Interfaces (CGIs). CGIs provide Web site features such as shopping carts and forms that may be filled out and submitted, as well as site navigation or other interactive features.

The second default folder is called Sites and is located in the home folder of every user on your computer. Although each user has only one Sites folder, you can create subfolders in the Sites folder, as illustrated in this example:

■ <*hard drive*>/Users/<*username*>/Sites/

■ <*hard drive* >/Users/<*username*>/Sites/Docs/

■ <*hard drive*>/Users/<*username*>/Sites/Images/

■ <*hard drive*>/Users/<*username*>/Sites/Images/gifs/

The Sites folder is owned by a specific user and is accessible to anyone on the Web unless you manually disable access to the Sites folder. As is the case with File Sharing,

14

you may encounter some users who want to share their Sites folders and others who do not. In such a situation, your only options are to completely disable Web Sharing for the entire computer or disable access to the Sites folders by following these steps:

1. Have the user log in to your Mac with the appropriate username and password.

2. Open a Finder window and navigate to *<hard drive>*/Users/*<username>*/.

3. Select the Sites folder and choose the Show Info command from the File menu (or press Command+I).

4. Reduce the access privileges from Read Only to None in the Groups and Everybody sections. Figure 14.18 shows a before (left) and after (right) example of the Show Info window after revoking access to the Sites folder for the user mbell.

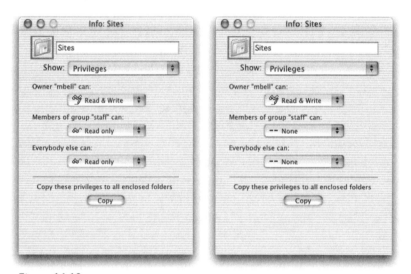

Figure 14.18
Reduce the access privileges of the Sites folder to disable Web Sharing for a particular user.

You can't reduce the access privileges to the WebServer folder, however, because the operating system—rather than you or any of the other administrators of your computer—owns it. To disable access to the WebServer folder, you must completely disable Web Sharing.

Selecting a Home Page

All Web servers have what is known as a *default* home page. This means that when you open a Uniform Resource Locator (URL) to that server without specifying a particular HTML document, the Web server gives you a document anyway. For example, when you go to **www.apple.com** (and you should!), the Web server gives you **www.apple.com/index.html** instead because index.html is specified as the default home page. Moreover, when you open a URL to a directory within a Web server without specifying a document, any document in that directory named index.html will be served by default. The names of the most common default pages include:

- index.html

- default.html

- home.html

Because Web servers on Windows-based PCs often use the extension .htm instead of .html, you may encounter home.htm or default.htm, for example.

Web Sharing uses a file named *index.html*, which is the default file name specified in the configuration files for the Apache Web server, as the default for serving HTML documents in each directory in the Web server. You can only override this file name using a Terminal command or an application like iTools.

iTools

Like Mac OS X's Web Sharing, iTools from Tenon Intersystems is a smart application that provides a graphical, Web-based interface to the complex tasks associated with managing an Apache Web server. iTools does much more than just add a pretty interface to Web Sharing—that's why it isn't cheap. Considering that iTools costs a few hundred dollars, it may be worthwhile if you want to provide sophisticated services such as:

- Web-based configuration of all services, including Apache

- Domain Name Services (DNSs)

- Search engine for all virtual Web sites

- Secure Socket Layer (SSL) 3.0

- Users and groups, independent of Mac OS X

- Virtual Web sites and FTP accounts

- Web site caching for increased performance

- Web-based email accounts

14

iTools is derived from a previous BSD-on-Macintosh product from Tenon called WebTen, so you can be confident that iTools is a well-tested product. For example, Figure 14.19 illustrates how iTools eases the complex configuration of the Apache Web server into a series of buttons instead of archaic commands typed into the Terminal application.

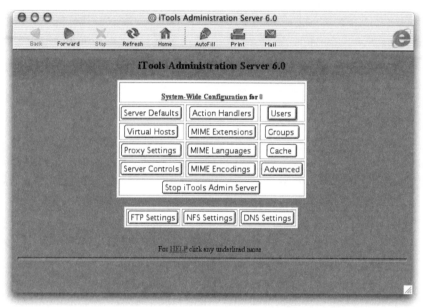

Figure 14.19
iTools uses a thoughtful, Web-based interface to configure the Apache Web server used by Web Sharing.

One of the best features of iTools is its support of usernames and passwords for specific areas of your Web site, a feature that Web Sharing doesn't implement. In fact, Web Sharing has no security features at all, nor does it have the ability to create groups of users for whom passwords may or may not be required. iTools allows you to create and maintain groups of users without requiring you to give them an account on your computer via the Users section of the System Preferences. Figure 14.20 shows an example of the Users configuration area of iTools, where you configure the Web, email, FTP, and group access privileges for each user.

iTools is overkill (and over budget) for users who want to serve simple Web sites using Web Sharing and Apache. However, if you want to enable all of Apache's advanced features with a super-simple interface, iTools is a great place to start.

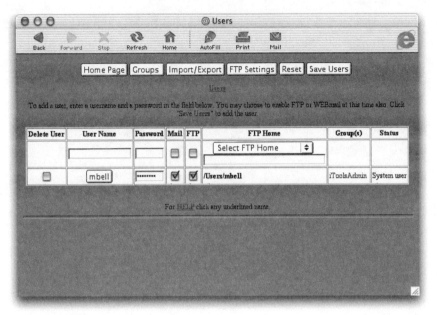

Figure 14.20
An example of the Users configuration capabilities of iTools.

Wrapping Up

The power and flexibility of File Sharing and Web Sharing can change the way you work on a local network or the Internet. File Sharing and Web Sharing remove almost all the barriers that prohibit flow of data between computers. With File Sharing and Web Sharing, you can:

■ Share the Public folder and subfolders for each user on your computer over a LAN or the Internet using TCP/IP

■ Share files with administrators, users, and guests

■ Selectively disable access to a particular user's Public folder

■ Create a Drop Box for each user that no one can view or modify

■ Serve HTML documents for the computer and for each user with an account on your Mac

■ Create subfolders for HTML documents

■ Explore alternative applications such as iTools to configure Web Sharing and provide additional Internet services such as Web-based email and DNS

14

The File Sharing and Web Sharing services provided with Mac OS X are designed for the basic user in mind, although the power of these services can be unlocked and enhanced with a little assistance. In the next chapter, I'll demonstrate several tips and strategies for collaborating on a network and the Internet.

Collaborating on a Network

Mac OS users have long known the benefits of computer networking—the very first Macs were designed to easily connect to a network, as are Macs running Mac OS X. Networked printers (see Chapter 9), File and Web Sharing (see Chapter 14), and access to network file servers are commonplace on almost every Mac network. In this chapter, I'll focus on using your Mac to collaborate via a local area network (LAN) for the purpose of accessing the services and resources associated with LANs rather than the peer-to-peer services associated with File and Web Sharing. Specifically, this chapter explores connecting to Mac OS X Server and AppleShare volumes; File Transfer Protocol (FTP) and Secure Shell (SSH) services; screen-sharing utilities such as Timbuktu and the Virtual Network Computing (VNC) protocol; and how to store passwords to these types of services in the Keychain. You'll also learn how to sign up for an iTools account and access your iDisk. What's not covered here will be discussed in Chapter 16 (including how to access the Internet using a dial-up ISP) and Chapter 17 (additional Internet-based applications and utilities included with Mac OS X). Let's start with connecting to file servers using Mac OS X.

Accessing Network Volumes

As described in Chapter 14, every Mac on your network—thanks to the wonders of File Sharing—is capable of sharing files, folders, or volumes with other users over your LAN or the Internet; Web Sharing enables you to share documents over the World Wide Web as well. In addition to these limited resources, dedicated file servers can make a virtually unlimited number of files, folders, and volumes available to all network users according to highly specific access privileges. Connecting to file servers running Mac OS X Server or AppleShare is easy, and this section describes both how to connect to and how to manage the data stored on these types of servers. (Other types of file servers, including Microsoft Windows, Novell NetWare and IntranetWare, and various Unix-based servers, do exist—they're just not discussed here.) The following section covers connecting to your iDisk, possibly the largest Mac-based file server in the world.

Before attempting to connect to a file server, make sure your computer is physically connected to a network and that the Network settings in the System Preferences are properly configured. For detailed information on connecting to the Internet using an Internet service provider (ISP), refer to Chapter 16. Once you're connected, proceed with the instructions that follow. If you don't understand the options as they're presented, talk to a network administrator or see Appendix A for more information on where to find help with connecting to a network and other Mac OS X–related questions.

Connecting to a Server

The first step in accessing network data is to issue the Connect To Server command, often referred to simply as Connect. As I've mentioned before, Connect replaces both the Chooser and the Network Browser (found in Mac OS 9.1) as the sole means of connecting to file servers. You can also access Network File Services (NFS) volumes with Connect, something the Chooser and Network Browser cannot do without the assistance of a third-party utility. To issue the Connect To Server command, switch to the Finder and choose Go|Connect To Server, or press Command+K. A window similar to the one shown in Figure 15.1, which is the contracted version of the Connect window, will be displayed. Clicking on the disclosure triangle in the upper-right of this window reveals additional options I'll discuss in a moment.

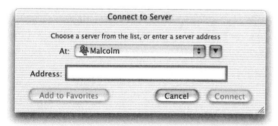

Figure 15.1
The Connect To Server window.

The Connect To Server command gives you two ways to access a file server. First, you can enter the IP address or domain name of the server in the Address field (much like a URL in a Web browser). File server URLs begin with afp:// (which stands for AppleTalk Filing Protocol), followed by the address of the server, like this example:

```
afp://myserver.macosbook.com
```

The second way to access a file server via the Connect To Server command is to browse a list of servers that advertise themselves as AFP servers on your LAN. This distinction is significant because not all AFP servers advertise on a LAN. AFP servers communicate using the AppleTalk protocol, the TCP/IP protocol, or both, depending on how the server administrator configures the server. Because AppleTalk is known as a "chatty" protocol that creates a lot of unwanted traffic on a network, some server administrators only permit connections via TCP/IP, which is not chatty and allows for much quicker file transfer speeds. Figure 15.2 shows two views of a Connect window that has been expanded to view the Local Network option, which is selected and displays several servers on a LAN.

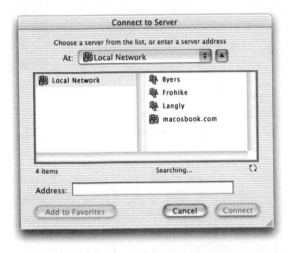

Figure 15.2
Browsing a list of servers on a LAN.

The list of file server names includes a dedicated Mac OS X Server and AppleShare file servers as well as the Macs on your network that use File Sharing. From the listing, it's not easy to tell which servers are which. In any case, as a client accessing a

15

server over the network, it makes no difference to you whether you're accessing data from a dedicated file server or from a Mac that's running File Sharing.

There are four servers in this example: Byers, Langly, Frohike (top), and another server called Roswell in the network segment called macosbook.com (bottom). Each of these servers is configured to use the AppleTalk protocol to advertise itself on the LAN; when connecting to a server, however, each server connects using TCP/IP instead. In fact, Mac OS X requires TCP/IP to connect to another server.

 Servers that do not advertise with AppleTalk can still be accessed by entering the IP address or domain name of the server in the Address field described above and in Chapter 14.

When you've located the file server you wish to access, double-click the name of the server or click the name once and then click the Connect button to open a connection to the server. The connection dialog box offers you the option of connecting to the selected file server as a guest or as a registered user:

- *Guest*—Although connecting as a guest is a simple matter, guests usually have very restricted access privileges. Of course, this is your only option if you're not a registered user. To connect as a guest, click the Guest button and then click the Connect button. If the selected file server does not allow guests to connect, the Guest button will be dimmed. If this is the case, the only way to connect is to contact the server administrator and ask to become a registered user.

- *Registered User*—To connect as a registered user, select the Registered User option in the connection dialog box. The information specified in the Name field of your User System Preferences will be entered for you in the Name field of the connection dialog box.

Refer back to Figure 14.15 for an example of the connection dialog box. If you're connecting as a guest, the Options button will be dimmed because, well, you just don't have many options as a guest! If you're a registered user, however, you can select from several preferences.

Choosing Connection Preferences

Once you've entered a valid username and password in the Connect dialog box, you can select the Options button to modify several preferences associated with logging into a particular file server. The Options button opens a preferences window, shown in Figure 15.3, that allows you to change the settings or perform the following actions:

- *Add Password To Keychain*—Creates a new Keychain entry that associates the username and password entered in the previous step with the file server in question.

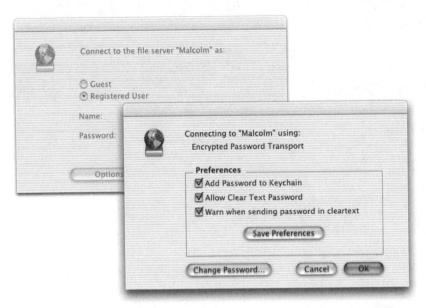

Figure 15.3
Configure connection preferences by clicking the Options button before logging into a file server.

See the section later in the chapter entitled "Storing Passwords in the Keychain" for detailed information.

■ *Allow Clear Text Password*—Permits the password to go across the network to the file server unencrypted (in clear text), which is a significant security risk. This option and the following option are enabled because not all file servers accept encrypted passwords.

■ *Warn When Sending Password In Cleartext*—Allows a clear text password to be sent, but issues a warning before it's actually transmitted across the network to the file server. By warning you about the risk, this option provides some level of security while still enabling you to connect to the maximum number of servers.

■ *Save Preferences*—Saves the previous three settings, which can then be used by the Connect To Server command for subsequent access to all file servers.

■ *Change Password*—Allows you to reset a password to the file server by clicking this option, entering your old password, and then entering a new password. You'll also be asked to reenter the new password for verification.

When you have reviewed the connection settings for a particular server, click the OK button to return to the main Connect dialog box. The next steps are authentication and to select the volumes that you wish to access, described next.

15

Authentication

After identifying yourself as either Registered User or Guest, click the Connect button to submit your request for access to the server. If you entered an incorrect name or password, an alert dialog box will inform you that your attempt to log in to the server failed because of one or more of the following reasons:

- Unknown user

- Incorrect password

- Log on disabled

As another security measure, the Connect To Server command doesn't reveal which error caused the failure. For example, if a hacker's attempt to log in to a server is unsuccessful and the server tells the hacker precisely why, then the hacker has just picked up a free clue about how to (or how not to) get into the server. An error message such as "The password you entered is incorrect" reveals that the username, but not the password, used by the hacker was correct. Therefore the error message is designed to be purposefully vague.

Selecting and Mounting Specific Volumes

After the file server has authenticated your username and password, the Mac OS opens a volume selection window in which you choose the volume you want to mount. (In case you're wondering, *mounting* is merely computer jargon for making a file system available to your computer over a network.) Whereas some file servers have only one volume to mount, others have multiple volumes—and quite often, these aren't volumes at all, but something Apple refers to as *mount points*, or folders that the server has designated for sharing. Servers can have anywhere from one to multiple volumes or mount points.

For example, Figure 15.4 shows two views of the same File Sharing server's mount points. The top view shows the mount points that are listed when you log in as a guest to a server that only permits access to the Public folders of its user accounts. The bottom view shows the mount points that are available when you log in to the same computer as a registered user. Note the differences in mount points depending on guest versus registered user access privileges.

 Because it's usually impossible to differentiate between shared folders and shared volumes, the term *volumes* is used generically to refer to mount points.

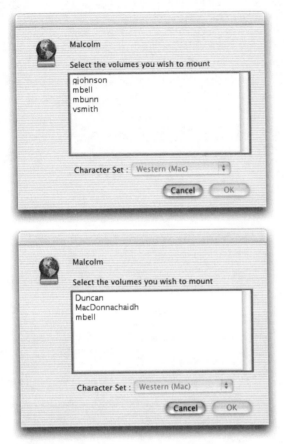

Figure 15.4
The list of mount points displayed by a file server differs according to your status as a guest (top) or a registered user (bottom).

To select one or more volumes to mount, click once on each of the volume names and then click the OK button. The volumes will be mounted on the Desktop, assuming you haven't disabled the Show Disks On The Desktop option in the Finder|Preferences menu, as described in Chapter 5. Regardless of whether you've chosen this option, you'll be able to access any mounted network volumes by switching to the Finder and selecting Go|Computer, or by pressing Command+Option+C. Now you can use the network volume.

To mount additional volumes from the selected file server, repeat the preceding steps. This time, however, you will not be prompted to enter a username or password because your access privileges have already been authenticated. Also, any volumes that you've already mounted will appear grayed out in the volume selection list.

15

Remote Volumes and Access Privileges

File server volumes are used in the same way as local volumes (those physically connected to your Mac), with one exception: Any restrictions imposed by the file server also apply to the volumes. This means that you can't save or copy a file to a volume unless you have Read & Write privileges. In Save dialog boxes, the Save button is dimmed when the selected volume is write-protected in this way, and in the Finder, any attempt to copy or create files brings up an alert telling you that the volume cannot be modified. Finder commands such as File|New Folder are disabled as well.

The Privileges section of the Show Info command (shown in Figure 15.5) contains the access privileges for any volume you're allowed to mount. To view this information, select the volume icon and choose Show Info from the File menu (or press Command+I). When you create a folder on a shared volume, you're automatically designated as the folder's owner, and as the owner, you can use the File menu's Show Info command to reset the access privileges.

Figure 15.5
Use the File|Show Info command to view the sharing privileges for a volume mounted on the Desktop.

Volume Access Shortcuts

Want to avoid going through this lengthy process every time you mount a networked volume? You can create an alias of a volume that appears on your Desktop and store the alias in a convenient spot on your hard drive, perhaps in your Documents or Favorites folders.

Double-clicking on the network volume alias icon mounts the volume as soon as you supply the necessary passwords. If the username and password are stored in the Keychain, however, the volume will be mounted automatically—no questions asked. How's that for quick and easy?

After you've mounted a network volume, that volume will appear in the Recent Servers list in the At section of the Connect To Server window (for example, the server named Malcolm, shown earlier in Figure 15.1). Because the Recent Servers section remembers only a few servers at a time, the volume you're interested in may not stay there for long—it depends on how many other servers you've accessed since the last time you accessed the server in question. By way of the Connect To Server window, you can add the server to your Favorites folder and then remove it, if you change your mind. Shortcuts like these are real timesavers when you're working with a frequently accessed network volume.

 Placing an alias or an original file server volume in the Dock isn't a good idea. For some mysterious reason, the Dock doesn't like items that have remote original locations.

Disconnecting from Remote Volumes

After you've logged in and mounted one or more remote volumes, you can disconnect a mounted network volume in any of the following four ways:

- *Trash the volume*—Simply drag the volume icon into the Trash in the same way that you would eject a removable disk.

- *Shut Down or Restart*—All mounted volumes are released when you execute the Shut Down or Restart command.

- *Eject*—The File menu's Eject command, or its keyboard equivalent, Command+E, dismounts any selected volumes.

- *Contextual menu*—Control+click on a volume from within a Finder window or on the Desktop and then choose Eject from the contextual menu.

None of the four commands is labeled well. It would be a little more intuitive if Apple changed the Eject command to Logoff, Logout, Dismount Volume, or something similar.

Accessing Your iDisk

With Mac OS X, you get free access to an iDisk, which is an account on Apple's Internet-based file server that is provided as part of the iTools package of services. In addition to the iDisk, iTools also includes several very cool services, such as:

- *iCards*—Customizable electronic greeting cards

- *Email*—Your very own Mac.com email account

- *HomePage*—A Web site creation and storage tool

- *KidSafe*—A resource for kid-friendly Web sites

The entire iTools suite of services is free; for a fee, you can increase the amount of storage space on your iDisk. The entry-level amount of storage space is 20MB with an unlimited daily transfer rate; additional storage space is about $1 per megabyte per year. Other restrictions for your iDisk include:

- *Access to your iDisk depends on the size and frequency with which you access your disk.* Your iDisk will time itself out, or automatically disconnect, when left inactive for a certain period of time. The more storage space you have or purchase, the longer the disk will stay mounted when left inactive.

- *The Public folder in your iDisk can be shared via Guest access.* You can share any file, folder, or data placed in the Public folder with anyone else who has an iTools account and knows your username.

- *You can use the Sites folder in your iDisk to share documents with anyone on the Web.* Use the Sites folder in your iDisk to allow guests to access your documents—just like the Web Sharing feature. The URL for the Sites folder on you disk is **http://homepage.mac.com/ <user name>/**.

- *Although Apple places the latest Mac OS X software on your iDisk, it doesn't count toward your storage limitation.* Apple includes its own software that has been designed for Mac OS X, as well as popular third-party software such as a BBEdit demo.

In addition to the special Public, Sites, and Software folders, the iDisk also includes folders called Documents, Music, Pictures, and Movies, much like the folder structure of your Mac OS X home folder. For example, Figure 15.6 shows an example of my iDisk.

To sign up for an iTools account:

1. Configure your computer to access the Internet.

2. Open the System Preferences from the Dock or the Apple menu.

3. Choose the Internet pane of the System Preferences, as shown in Figure 15.7.

4. Click the Free Sign Up button to open the registration page in your Web browser; then complete the registration process.

5. Return to the Internet section of the System Preferences and enter your username and password.

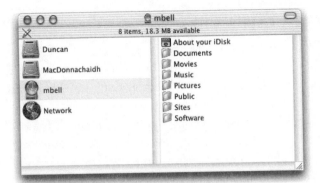

Figure 15.6
Sign up for a free iTools account to get a 20MB iDisk, which you can mount on your computer like any other server.

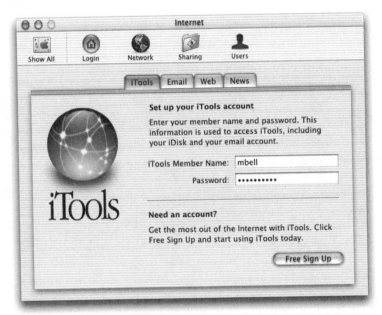

Figure 15.7
Configure your iDisk username and password via the Internet System Preferences.

 For more information about iDisk and iTools, visit **www.apple.com** and click on the iTools icon.

To mount your iDisk once your account has been set up, choose Go|iDisk from the Finder or choose Command+Option+I. Your iDisk will be mounted like other server volumes, but without the log-in procedures outlined above (provided that the correct username and password are entered in the Internet System Preferences). You can log out of your iDisk just as you would from any other file server volume.

15

Accessing and Sharing Files via FTP

The File Transfer Protocol (FTP) is another way to access, and even share, files with other users on your network. Mac OS X gives your Mac the ability to perform the role of an FTP server and provides you with Terminal and Internet Explorer—two ways of logging in to an FTP server. FTP is a simple protocol that basically enables you to *get* files from a server and *put* files on a server using an appropriate FTP client. Internet Explorer, for example, is good for getting files but has limited abilities for uploading, or putting, files on an FTP server. The Terminal application allows you to get and put files, but requires you to use a command-line interface.

Beyond Terminal and Internet Explorer, however, several full-featured FTP applications are available for a reasonable price. The FTP clients I recommend include:

■ Transmit, from Panic (**www.panic.com**)

■ Fetch, from Fetch Softworks (**http://fetchsoftworks.com**)

■ NetFinder, from Peter Li (**http://members.ozemail.com.au/~pli/**)

■ Interarchy, from Stairways Software (**www.interarchy.com**)

Each client takes a different approach to displaying files on an FTP server. I especially like the approach taken by Transmit, which is illustrated in Figure 15.8. The display of the categories of files called Your Stuff and Their Stuff is about as clear as it gets.

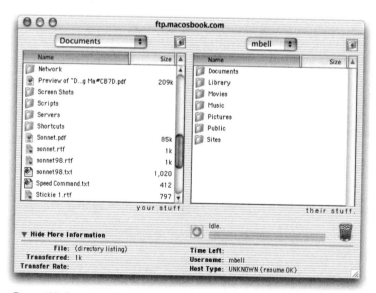

Figure 15.8

Use a graphical client such as Transmit for uploading and downloading files via FTP.

In addition to accessing FTP servers on your network for the purpose of uploading and downloading HTML documents and other data, you can enable your Mac to be an FTP server for yourself or any registered user—but not for guests. To enable the built-in FTP in Mac OS X, do the following:

1. Open the System Preferences and switch to the Sharing pane, shown in Figure 15.9.

2. Click the Allow FTP Access checkbox.

3. Quit the System Preferences.

Anyone with an account will be able to access your computer until you disable this selection.

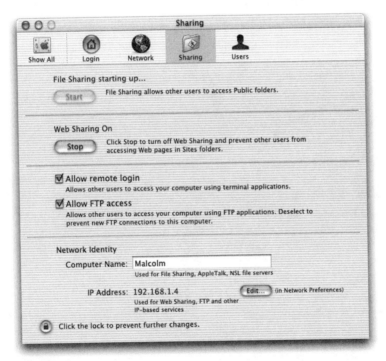

Figure 15.9
Use the Sharing pane of System Preferences to enable FTP.

Accessing and Sharing Files via SSH

Secure shell, or SSH, is a secure alternative to the remote login (rlogin) and remote shell (rsh) protocols used by various BSD-based operating systems, including Mac OS X. SSH, rlogin, rsh, and Telnet are all forms of *remote login* to a server on which a user has an account and may execute certain types of commands, several of which are explained in Appendix C. **ftp** is an example of a type of command that can

15

be executed from a remote login session; other examples include **ls** to list the contents of a folder and **man** to view the help manual for a particular application or command.

To log in to a remote server using the Terminal application and the SSH protocol:

1. Launch the Terminal application from the Utilities folder.

2. Choose Shell|New or press Command+N.

3. Type "ssh *<IP address of remote host>*" and press the Return key.

For example, Figure 15.10 shows a remote login session to 192.168.1.4. In this example you can see the login command on the first line, as well as authentication messages between the two computers on the following lines; eventually the remote computer asks for the password of the user account on the remote computer, after which the message *Welcome to Darwin!* is displayed. Next, I issued the **ls** command to list the contents of the current folder, which appears to be my home folder based on the names of the subfolders in this location. To be sure, I issued the **pwd** command to print the name of the current working directory on screen.

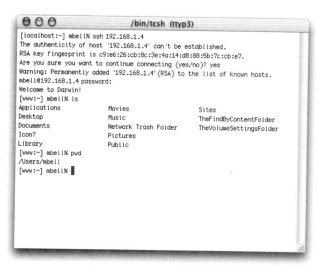

Figure 15.10
Use the Terminal application to open an SSH connection to a remote host.

Because the SSH protocol uses encryption fingerprint verification to authenticate remote hosts, it may take several seconds before anything happens once you've issued the **ssh** command.

You can enable SSH on your computer by following the same steps you used to enable FTP:

1. Open the System Preferences and switch to the Sharing pane, shown earlier in Figure 15.9.

2. Click the Allow Remote Login button.

3. Quit the System Preferences.

A user account is required to log in, and the user must be running an SSH-enabled client. Mac OS X doesn't permit Telnet connections even if the remote login option is enabled. Although SSH and Telnet are distantly related, Apple discourages users from enabling Telnet because of the significant security risk it presents.

Sharing Resources with Timbuktu and VNC

In my line of work, the most valuable network collaboration tool at my disposal is one that lets me see, control, and trade files with the Desktop of another computer. Timbuktu from Netopia (**www.netopia.com**) is the Ferrari of collaboration tools. It allows you to perform numerous collaboration tasks with computers running Mac OS 9.1, Mac OS X, and several versions of Microsoft Windows. Virtual Network Computing (VNC) is a freeware utility that performs most of the same screen sharing functions as Timbuktu. VNC is very limited in comparison to the overall capabilities of Timbuktu, but it's free, so what do you expect? When you compare the features of Timbuktu to the features of VNC, you'll see that Timbuktu is well worth the cost of about $100.

Timbuktu's main features include the ability to:

- Chat with a remote computer

- Control a remote computer

- Exchange files

- Exchange text messages

- Intercom with a remote computer

- Look at a remote computer without being able to control the computer

For example, I frequently exchange files between computers on which File Sharing is intentionally not enabled; because Timbuktu uses TCP/IP for all its communications, I can exchange files with any Mac or PC on the Internet on which Timbuktu is installed. For example, Figure 15.11 shows a Timbuktu connection between two computers over the Internet. The Exchange feature is very intuitive and easy to use.

The screen sharing feature, called Control, lets me control the mouse and keyboard of a remote computer, including the restart and shutdown commands. In short, you can

15

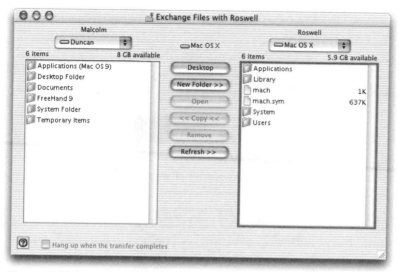

Figure 15.11
Exchanging files between two computers using Timbuktu.

perform almost any action on the remote computer that you can perform on your own Mac OS X computer, with the possible exception of issuing the Force Quit command. To speed up the transfer of screen information between computers, Timbuktu allows you to hide the Desktop on the remote computer. In Figure 15.12, however, I haven't enabled this feature because showing the Desktop better illustrates what a Control session looks like.

Unlike Timbuktu, VNC requires two different pieces of software: one to enable screen sharing on your computer (referred to as a VNC server) and one to browse remote computers (referred to as a VNC client). Several Mac OS X–supported VNC servers and clients exist, and most seem to work just fine. VNC is an open source application, which means that hundreds of capable programmers are developing VNC servers and clients for a variety of platforms, including Mac OS 9.1, Linux, Solaris, and Windows 95/98/2000/NT/CE, to name only a few.

In fact, the speed of screen sharing demonstrated in Figure 15.13 is a little snappier than in the version of Timbuktu shown in the preceding examples. Because VNC has fewer features than Timbuktu, it also has less application overhead to potentially bog it down.

The two VNC components I'm using in this example are:

- *VNC server*—OSXvnc (**www.osxvnc.com**)

- *VNC client*—VNCThing (**www.webthing.net**)

Figure 15.12
Controlling a remote computer (Malcolm) with Timbuktu.

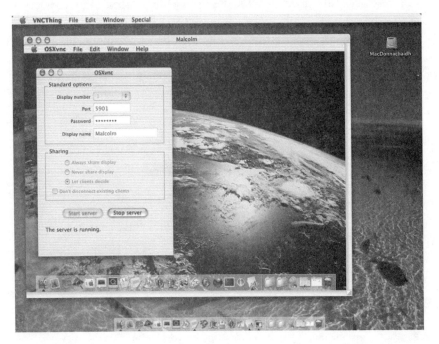

Figure 15.13
Controlling a remote VNC server with a VNC client.

15

The VNC server, seen in the inner window, shows the server configuration preferences, including the number of connections (1), port number (5901), password, and the computer's screen name (Malcolm).

For more information about VNC, including a list of over 36 different operating system platforms that support VNC servers or clients, visit the Virtual Network Computing home page of AT&T Labs at **www.uk.research.att.com/vnc/**.

Storing Passwords in the Keychain

After a long absence from the Mac OS, Apple reintroduced the Keychain in Mac OS 9. It's included in Mac OS X and is more useful than ever. The Keychain allows you to store login information (server, username, and password) and site certificates in a master file that is conceptually similar to the large, noisy collection of a couple of dozen keys that a building superintendent carries. In the Mac OS X Keychain, you can store login information for file sharing volumes as well as applications, including email clients such as Eudora and other network-related applications such as Timbuktu.

Using the Default Keychain

Mac OS X creates a default keychain (based on the Short Name and password) for each person who has an account on your computer. When the user logs in, the OS opens the default keychain, making the information stored in it available to pass on to servers or applications. Figure 15.14 shows the default keychain for the user account mbell.

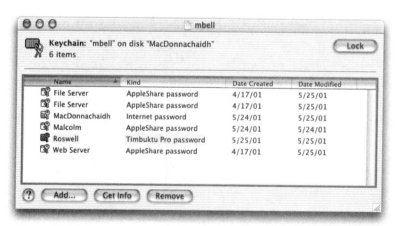

Figure 15.14
Mac OS X automatically creates a keychain for each user and unlocks it when that user logs in to the computer.

Adding Items to a Keychain

When logging into a remote computer or using any application that is Keychain-aware, look for an option called Add Password To Keychain (such as the one shown in Figure 15.3) that allows you to add an item to your default keychain. If the keychain is unlocked when you attempt to add an item to it, the Mac OS allows you to proceed—no questions asked. If the keychain is locked, on the other hand, you'll be prompted to unlock the keychain in which to store the information. Because only the default keychain is unlocked at startup, you may encounter a message like the one shown in Figure 15.15. Notice that the name and path to the keychain are identified (~/Library/Keychains/mbell) along with the name of the application requesting access (/System/Library/CoreServices/Finder.app).

Figure 15.15
Adding an item to a locked keychain requires that the keychain first be unlocked.

After a keychain has been selected and unlocked, information can be stored in it, as shown earlier in Figure 15.14. You can sort the items in a keychain by name, kind, date created, and date modified, as well as view the properties for a particular item by selecting it from the list of items in a keychain and choosing the Get Info button to reveal the General Information and Access Control options for that particular keychain item. You can even view the password for that item by selecting the View Password button. Figure 15.16 shows two views of an item in my keychain that stores information about a Timbuktu connection. The top portion of this figure shows the general information, whereas the bottom view shows the access information.

You can specify what applications have access to a keychain entry by opening the item from within the Keychain and viewing the Access Control settings, as shown in the lower half of Figure 15.16. Your access options include:

15

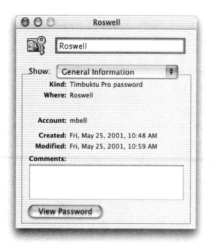

Figure 15.16
Viewing the properties of an item in a keychain.

- *Allow Access To This Item Without Warning*—You will not be prompted to verify access to an item in a keychain.

- *Allow Access By Any Application*—Any application on your computer may access this keychain entry.

- *Allow Access Only By These Applications*—Only the applications you specify may access the keychain entry.

When you select the third option, a keychain not only stores username and password information for a keychain resource, it also tracks applications that have permission to access an item in a keychain. The Finder provides a good example of this feature. As you know, the Finder is the application that allows you to access file servers using the

Connect To Server command, described in Chapter 14 and earlier in this chapter. When accessing a file server for which an entry has been made in a particular keychain, the Keychain application asks you about the level of access you want to allow. Figure 15.17 shows an example of this message, in which you can choose from the following possible answers:

■ *Deny*—Don't use the information in the keychain for this particular login attempt.

■ *Allow Once*—Use the username and password for the keychain entry in this particular instance, and prompt the user again the next time this server is accessed.

■ *Always Allow*—Use the username and password stored in the keychain for this particular server now and in the future.

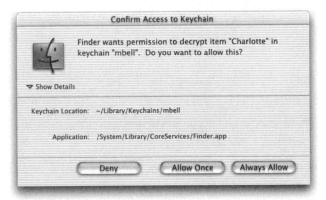

Figure 15.17
Choose what level of access to grant an application for an item in a keychain.

Adding and Deleting Keychains

You can add and delete keychains in addition to the default keychain. For example, you may want to create a keychain just for file or Web servers to help you track these specific resources. To create a new keychain, follow these steps:

1. Open the Keychain application from within the Utilities folder.

2. Choose File|New Keychain and give the keychain a name and passphrase (password). Be sure to enter the same password in the Verify field. If you enter two different passwords, the Keychain will prompt you to correct the password.

3. The keychain will be created, unlocked, and opened.

Each keychain has preference settings that you can modify to suit your security concerns. To configure a keychain, follow these steps:

15

1. While Keychain is open, choose the keychain you want to configure from the Keychains menu or the Keychains|Keychain List window.

2. From the Edit menu, choose "*<keychain name>*" Settings.

3. Review the settings shown in Figure 15.18 and make the necessary changes.

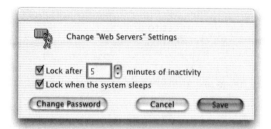

Figure 15.18
The settings for a newly created keychain called Web Servers.

The settings configuration window lets you change the master password for a keychain, as well as:

- Automatically lock the keychain after a specified period of inactivity (i.e., without touching the mouse or keyboard).

- Lock the keychain if the computer goes to sleep as configured in the Energy Saver System Preferences.

Finally, you can delete a keychain just as easily as you can create a new one by following these steps:

1. Choose Edit|Keychain List.

2. Choose a keychain to delete by clicking it once.

3. Select the Remove button in the Keychain List window.

4. Choose Delete File to delete the file containing the keychain's preferences. You cannot copy or move the keychain to another computer if you delete the file.

5. Choose Remove to remove, rather than delete, the keychain from your list of keychains. This option preserves the keychain file for later use on this or another computer.

 Your keychain files are stored in the /Library/Keychains/ folder of your Home folder. They can be moved or copied to other computers and used if the correct password is provided.

Keychains are very handy for storing all sorts of username and password information for Keychain-aware applications such as the Finder. Whenever an application asks for a password, look for an option that will allow you to store it in a keychain for future reference.

Wrapping Up

Most Macintosh users are initially motivated to connect to a network in order to share peripheral devices such as laser printers or network modems. But networks also make it possible for computers to communicate with each other and for data to be shared among computers or by accessing centralized file servers.

In this chapter you've seen how to make the most of these abilities:

- Using the Connect To Server command to select and mount file server volumes

- Accessing your iDisk

- Connecting to and sharing via FTP and SSH

- Sharing files and screens with Timbuktu and VNC

- Using the Keychain to store login information for remote servers and applications

Next, in Chapter 16, I'll show you how Mac OS X prepares you to connect to the biggest network in the world—the Internet.

15

Connecting to the Internet

If the big story of the eighties was the advent of affordable personal computers, then the big story of the nineties was the Internet and the World Wide Web. Now the story is about super-fast Internet access via cable modem and various versions of digital subscriber line (DSL). The Net is still a hot news topic, of course, and in just a few years the World Wide Web has grown from a handful of university pages to a massive conglomeration of commercial, personal, governmental, and educational sites. The Web provides an easy-to-use interface to the Internet's interconnectivity in much the same way that the Mac OS serves as an interface to powerful and complex computer hardware.

If you've ever used other computers to work on the Web, you know that a Mac is the best way to get online. The Mac OS—a superior multimedia platform—is the perfect complement to the Net's combination of text, sound, images, and movies. The people at Apple realized this, and have integrated Internet connectivity into the operating system itself. In addition, they included everything you need to connect to the Net as part of the basic installation of Mac OS X.

Each of the major applications and utilities you need to master the Internet and the Web is already installed on your machine; I'll discuss them in the next chapter. But first, let's talk about how Mac OS X can help you get online with a cable, DSL, or dial-up modem in just a few minutes.

Getting Connected: LAN vs. Modem

Connecting to the Internet requires, first and foremost, an Internet service provider (ISP). As far as most users are concerned, there are essentially two main types of ISPs: a private local area network (LAN) or a commercial provider. Most LAN users connect via a corporate or educational LAN using various forms of Ethernet network cabling, as well as other types of cabling and protocols, such as Token Ring, that are not supported by Mac OS X. Moreover, many large colleges and universities use their LANs to provide Internet access for their faculty, staff, and students while on campus, as well as dial-up access to their resources from off campus. Most people connecting to an ISP from home use one of several types of modems (dial-up, cable, or DSL) to establish a connection. Although the vast majority of home users still use a dial-up modem, the number of cable and DSL (both commonly referred to as *broadband*) subscribers is expected to increase along with the number of commercial ISPs that offer both dial-up and broadband access.

LAN Access

More businesses than ever have LANs that connect the various computers throughout an office or group of offices. LANs come in several varieties. For example, a group of LANs connected together makes up what is referred to as a *wide area network (WAN)*. An *intranet* is any private network that is accessible to the employees of an organization over a LAN or WAN. LANs, WANs, and intranets use communications software such as email clients, Web browsers, and collaboration software that utilize the same protocols as the Internet, so Mac OS X runs as smoothly on any type of LAN as it does on the Internet.

For novice users, connecting to the Internet through a LAN is generally less confusing than connecting through a modem. The steps that are necessary to connect to the Net by way of a LAN are extraordinarily easy, and most businesses with large networks have full-time computer and networking professionals on staff to take care of all the configuration details. The Mac OS X has streamlined the connectivity process to such a degree that most people will be able to set themselves up on a LAN with little effort.

Modem Access

Mac OS X users who access the Internet from home connect to their ISP with a modem and software installed by the operating system. No additional software is required, whereas in older versions of the Mac OS, third-party connectivity software was sometimes necessary. Although modems can still be tricky, all computers that support Mac OS X have the type of modem that is most compatible with the modems of the major ISPs. In fact, Apple has teamed up with Earthlink, naming it as the preferred Macintosh ISP, to ensure that the modems installed in Apple computers have the highest level of compatibility with Earthlink modems.

The greater availability of broadband cable and DSL modems presents new opportunities for Mac OS X users—and fortunately these types of connections are easy to establish and maintain, compared to dial-up modems. In fact, broadband connections more closely resemble LAN connections than dial-up connections in terms of configuration and troubleshooting. The following sections describe how to use the Network System Preferences to configure your Ethernet and modem ports to communicate over the Internet.

16

Ports and Protocols

Some people may be a little confused about various selection options for configuring Internet access. I believe the key to understanding how to configure the Network System Preferences and connect to any network is this: Most computers have multiple ports through which data flows, and each port may accept one or more protocols, or languages. The secret to configuring Mac OS X for Internet access is to select the right protocols for the right ports.

Modem connections make use of two sets of rules, called *protocols*: Transmission Control Protocol and Internet Protocol, commonly referred to as TCP/IP. The first determines how information is split into smaller parts and then reassembled at the destination, and the second determines the best path for the information to travel.

One of the great things about Mac OS X is the Location feature, which allows you to take the management of ports and protocols one step further and create sets of ports and protocols and easily switch among them from the Apple menu. Like Open Transport in Mac OS 9.1, the networking layer of Mac OS X allows you to switch between Locations without restarting the computer and use more than one type of network port or protocol at the same time. For example, Mac OS X enables you to use AppleTalk to communicate with a network printer while using TCP/IP to connect to the Internet.

Configuring Network System Preferences

As I've mentioned in several earlier chapters, the Network System Preferences pane (which replaces the old AppleTalk and TCP/IP Control Panels in Mac OS 9.1) is used to configure all the features that are essential to getting your computer on the Internet. In addition to the TCP/IP, AppleTalk, and modem settings, the Network System Preferences also supports several features of the old Location Manager. You can create multiple locations that allow you to easily switch between network configuration preferences—a feature that PowerBook and iBook users will find especially helpful when connecting on the road using a dial-up modem, and switching to Ethernet when in the office. Locations are helpful for other users as well, but the primary benefit is for mobile users. Let's start by looking at the Locations feature.

Managing Locations

The first option in the Network System Preferences is the Location field, which is shown in Figure 16.1. In the Location section, you can create, edit, and delete locations that identify what protocols are active on which ports on your computer. For example, you could have one location called "Earthlink" or "AOL" for your dial-up

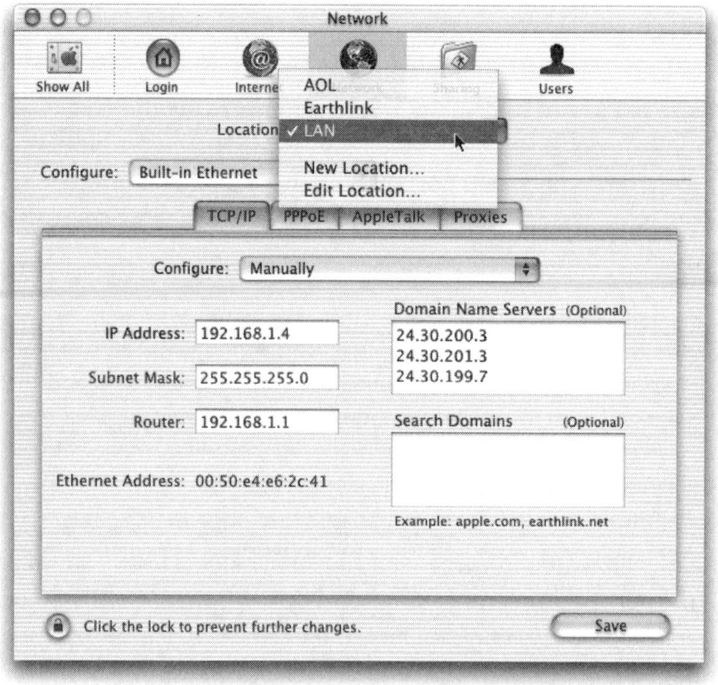

Figure 16.1
Use the Location feature to configure multiple collections of ports and protocols.

account on your PowerBook or iBook, and another called "LAN" for your Ethernet connection when in the office. Locations can be named whatever you wish. You can easily switch among locations from within the Network System Preferences or via the Apple menu.

To add a new location, open the Network System Preferences and then follow these steps:

1. Select the Location pop-up menu.

2. Choose New Location and give the location a name when prompted.

3. Select and configure the ports and protocols outlined in the next section.

You can add, delete, or rename a location at any time by following these steps:

1. Select Edit Location from the Location pop-up menu.

2. Select an existing location from the list of locations.

3. Click the Duplicate, Rename, or Delete button.

4. Choose Cancel to abort the process or Done when finished.

If you have only one port for accessing the Internet or a LAN, such as an Ethernet connection, multiple locations may be unnecessary. However, you can also use locations to easily change network settings for the same port. For example, you can create one location called "AT-On" that has the AppleTalk protocol enabled and another called "AT-Off" that disables AppleTalk to make changing between the two settings a simple matter. Once you've configured multiple locations, for whatever purpose, you can switch between them by following these steps:

1. While using any application, activate the Location section of the Apple menu, as shown in Figure 16.2.

2. Select a location from the alphabetized list.

Locations may also be selected from within the Network System Preferences by choosing Network Preferences from the Location pop-up menu.

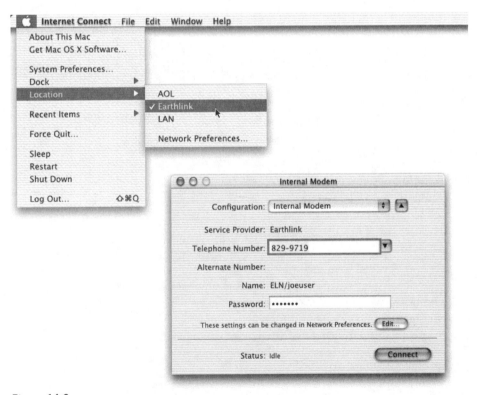

Figure 16.2
You can easily switch among locations for various dial-up accounts using the shortcuts provided in the Apple menu.

Configuring Ports

You configure the communications ports on your computer, as well as the protocols that flow through these ports, in the Configure section of the Network System Preferences. Most Macs have two ports, a built-in Ethernet port and an internal modem port, although it is possible to add more Ethernet ports and external modems. To make things a bit more interesting, Mac OS X also allows you to configure ports in two new ways:

- Selectively enable or disable each port to show or hide the port in a location.

- Prioritize each port within a particular location as a means of locating a port to connect to a network.

For example, let's create a configuration called LAN that uses the Built-in Ethernet port as the primary port through which the computer connects to the Internet. My computer has a PCI Ethernet card and two modems, in addition to the Built-in Ethernet port. In the Advanced section of the Configure menu, shown in Figure 16.3, I've selectively enabled the Ethernet ports, but disabled the modem ports because I don't want them to be involved in connecting to my LAN. The PCI Ethernet card is

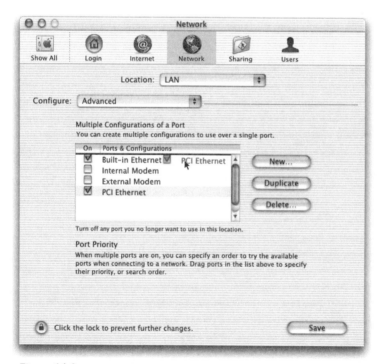

Figure 16.3
Mac OS X can prioritize selected ports for communicating over a network to increase reliability and to customize locations.

16

the fourth port found by the Mac OS, and I want to move it up to the first position so that it, instead of the Built-in Ethernet port, will be used as the primary port. The Built-in Ethernet port will serve as a secondary port in case the primary port becomes unavailable.

To select and prioritize ports, open the Network System Preferences and follow these steps:

1. Click the Configure pop-up menu and choose the Advanced option.

2. Place a check beside the ports you wish to enable. I recommend disabling unwanted ports—this decreases the amount of CPU time your computer spends managing ports and networking resources.

3. Drag the enabled ports to the desired location in the list to prioritize the ports, as in Figure 6.3.

4. Click the Save button.

You can rename the ports by double-clicking on the name of the port and typing a new name; the names of some ports are reserved, however, and cannot be changed.

Because different types of ports have different protocol configuration options, each port needs to be configured separately for the various protocols it supports. For example, Ethernet cards typically support the AppleTalk protocol for communicating over a LAN, but modems do not because they're not designed for LAN use. However, Ethernet and modem ports do share certain protocol configuration options, including some TCP/IP and proxy settings. The possible configuration options for the ports on a typical desktop Macintosh are described in the following sections.

Configuring Built-in Ethernet Protocols

Most G3 and G4 Macs have an Ethernet port built into the motherboard of the computer, and additional Ethernet and AirPort cards can be installed as well. The following protocols are typically found on any Mac with a built-in Ethernet port, an example configuration for which is shown in Figure 16.4.

TCP/IP

The Internet relies on the TCP/IP suite of protocols to connect the hundreds of millions of computers around the world. Fortunately, Mac OS X is based on the NeXTStep/OpenSTEP operating system, upon which the World Wide Web was invented. The TCP/IP section of the Network System Preferences has multiple configuration options that relate to how your Mac obtains an IP address—manually or

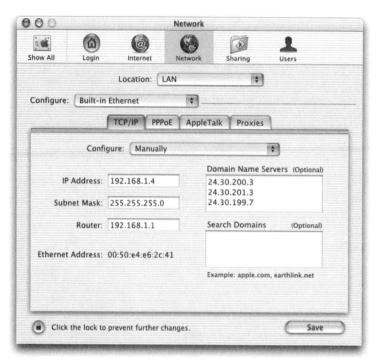

Figure 16.4
Most Macs have a built-in Ethernet port for connecting to an Ethernet network.

dynamically. Manually assigned IP addresses, which typically do not change over time, are coordinated by a system administrator who gives your computer an IP address. Dynamically assigned addresses, which are issued by a special type of server on a temporary basis, are commonplace in large network environments such as ISPs. IP addresses are in short supply around the world because only a limited number of addresses exist, whereas an unlimited number of computers are able to connect to the Internet. Dynamically assigned IP addressing enables unused IP addresses to be reclaimed and distributed to other computers, thereby decreasing the overall number of addresses in use at any one time.

The main ways in which Mac OS X obtains an IP address include:

- *Manually*—You or a system administrator manually enter the IP address. Additional configuration options, which are described below, must be completed as well.

- *Using DHCP*—The IP address is assigned by a Dynamic Host Configuration Protocol (DHCP) server. This method is typically used when connecting via cable or DSL modem. The IP address assigned using this method is "released" when the computer is shut down, and a new address is assigned when the computer is restarted.

- *Using DHCP With Fixed IP Address*—The IP address is assigned by a DHCP server, but the ISP gives you a static address, usually for an additional monthly fee. The DHCP server configures the remaining information, such as the router and Domain Name Server (DNS), required to connect to the provider.

- *Using BootP*—The IP address is assigned dynamically by a Bootstrap Protocol (BootP) server, which is becoming less common in favor of the DHCP server.

Whether your Mac obtains an IP address statically or dynamically, the networking layer of the operating system needs to know the IP addresses of several other types of servers in order to connect to a TCP/IP-based network such as the Internet. When selecting one of the four configuration options just described, the following information may be required:

- *IP Address*—Entered either manually by you or your system administrator, or dynamically by a server.

- *Subnet Mask*—Tells the Mac OS on what type of network it is connected to for IP addressing purposes.

- *Router Address*—The IP address of your LAN's router, which connects and routes IP traffic between subnets and to the Internet.

- *Domain Name Servers*—Enter one or more DNS server addresses here. However, the addresses may be assigned dynamically when choosing DHCP, in which case you may not be required to enter information in this section.

- *Search Domains*—Enter the names of other domains you would like to connect to without having to type the entire URL in the Address field of a Web browser such as Internet Explorer. For example, if you add apple.com as a search domain and type "www" in the Address field, the Network System Preferences tells the Web browser to append apple.com onto *www* to search for the address **www.apple.com**.

- *DHCP Client ID*—When connecting via DHCP, you may be required to enter a username assigned by your ISP.

Finally, your computer's Ethernet hardware address is also displayed in the TCP/IP section of the Network System Preferences. Each Ethernet adapter should have a unique address to assist in network management in the same way that each computer has a unique IP address.

PPPoE

The Point-to-Point Protocol Over Ethernet (PPPoE) protocol is a relatively new protocol used by wireless networks and broadband ISPs that combines the Point-to-Point Protocol (PPP) with standard Ethernet wiring. Apple's AirPort wireless base station, which is attached to a network via Ethernet or modem, and broadband connections, which rely on cable and DSL modems, sometimes use PPPoE as a means of dynamically assigning IP address information and performing user authentication. The main PPPoE configuration options, shown in Figure 16.5, include the following:

- *Connect Using PPPoE*—Click this option if your ISP requires a PPPoE connection in order to access their services. If checked, the following options become available:

  - *Service Provider (Optional)*—The name provided by your ISP.

  - *PPPoE Service Name (Optional)*—The name of the PPPoE service, also provided by your ISP.

  - *Account Name*—The username of your account.

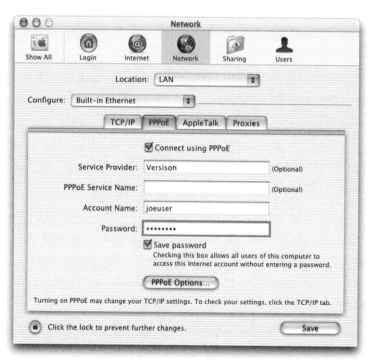

Figure 16.5
The PPPoE configuration section of a built-in Ethernet port.

- *Password*—The password for your dial-up or broadband account.

- *Save Password*—Check to save your password.

If you select PPPoE, several related protocol settings will be affected as well. For example, your TCP/IP settings will be modified to obtain an IP address via PPP (instead of Manually, Using DHCP, Using DHCP With Fixed IP Address, or Using BootP) because PPP and PPPoE obtain IP addresses dynamically using a PPP server. Also, the AppleTalk protocol, discussed in the next section, is automatically disabled when PPPoE is being used on the same port. However, it's possible to create a new port and run AppleTalk on that port (this option is also discussed in the following section). To complete the configuration of the PPPoE protocol, click the PPPoE Options button and review the following settings:

- *Connect Automatically When Starting TCP/IP Applications*—Initiates a connection to your ISP whenever an Internet application such as Mail or Internet Explorer is launched.

- *Prompt To Stay Connected If Idle For __ Minutes*—Issues a reminder to remain connected to the ISP after a certain amount of time, which is helpful if you're paying by the minute.

- *Disconnect If Idle For __ Minutes*—Releases the connection if you haven't touched the mouse or keyboard after a certain amount of time.

- *Send PPP Echo Packets*—Enhances the way Mac OS X communicates with your ISP's routers for the purpose of ensuring connectivity to the network.

- *Use Verbose Logging*—Increases the details entered into the Connection Log of the Internet Connect application when accessing an ISP by PPPoE, modem, or AirPort.

- *Cancel*—Cancels changes made to the PPPoE Options settings.

- *OK*—Approves changes made to the PPPoE Options settings.

AppleTalk

The AppleTalk section of the Built-in Ethernet port, shown in Figure 16.6, is where you can configure your computer to send and receive AppleTalk data over a LAN. Although it is not the preferred protocol in Mac OS X, AppleTalk is still useful for certain aspects of File Sharing and networked printing. Like the IP address of the TCP/IP protocol, the AppleTalk protocol identifies computers on a network by a unique number called a Node ID. Different segments of AppleTalk networks are identified by Zone names and the Network ID number. You can tell the computer to

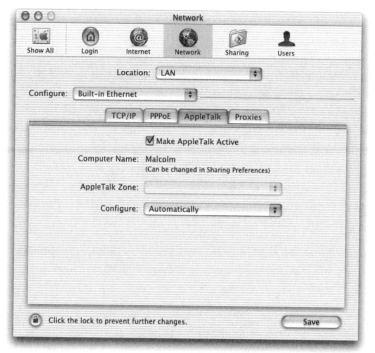

Figure 16.6
The AppleTalk section of the Network System Preferences.

assign these numbers automatically, or you can assign them yourself (although I don't recommend it). Depending on how you've chosen to obtain these numbers, your configuration choices may differ from those in Figure 16.6. If the Mac OS assigns the numbers automatically, your configuration choices will include:

■ *Make AppleTalk Active*—Enables AppleTalk.

■ *Computer Name*—Displays the name that your computer broadcasts over an AppleTalk network. To change the name, go to the Sharing pane of the System Preferences, as outlined in Chapter 14.

■ *AppleTalk Zone*—Choose the Zone to which your Mac should belong. If your network's routers are not configured to segment AppleTalk networks into Zones, your Mac will belong to the Default zone and you will be unable to make any changes for this setting.

■ *Configure*—Choose to configure the Node and Network IDs manually or automatically. You should attempt to manually configure these settings only if you are told to do so by a system administrator. If you do choose Manually, the following two options are displayed:

16

- *Node ID*—The numerical address of your computer, using a number between 1 and 253.

- *Network ID*—The numerical address of an AppleTalk network, using a number between 1 and 65534.

Proxies

The Proxies section allows you to identify the domain name or IP address and the port number of a proxy server for five of the most popular Internet protocols, as shown in Figure 16.7. When using a proxy server, your computer connects to a proxy server for a particular type of service, and the proxy server accesses that service on your behalf—hence the term *proxy*. This type of arrangement is widely used in corporate and university settings to keep unwanted users from accessing online resources, such as an online catalog or journal subscription. Proxy servers can also serve as part of a firewall through which a Web browser must pass to gain access to a network. Finally, proxy servers are also used to cache frequently accessed Web pages in order to increase the speed with which these pages are downloaded. For example, if 10 people on the same network access the CNN.com home page in a short span of time without the

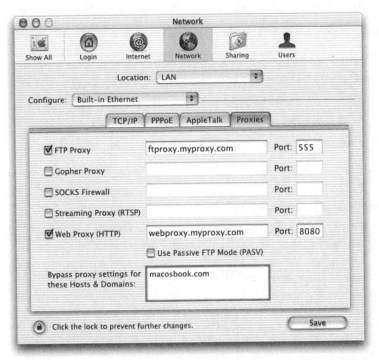

Figure 16.7
Proxy settings for the Built-in Ethernet port.

use of a proxy server, the CNN.com page is downloaded over the Internet 10 times. If everyone goes through a proxy server that is cached, however, the first user's request is fulfilled over the Internet and the remaining nine users obtain the CNN.com page from the proxy server.

Your network system administrator or ISP will tell you whether you need to use a proxy server to access an Internet protocol. The following five protocols are handled via the Proxy section of the Network System Preferences:

- *FTP Proxy*—For downloading files via FTP.

- *Gopher Proxy*—For access to Gopher servers, which are becoming increasingly rare.

- *SOCKS Firewall*—For access through a SOCKS firewall to access Internet services on the other side of the firewall.

- *Streaming Proxy (RTSP)*—For access to Real Time Streaming Protocol (RTSP) servers for QuickTime and other streaming multimedia.

- *Web Proxy (HTTP)*—For access to the World Wide Web.

For each of these protocols, you'll be required to enter the following information:

- *Domain Name or IP Address*—The IP address or domain name for the proxy server.

- *Port*—The TCP/IP port number over which a protocol flows. Typically, a proxy server will require that you use a non-standard port number, such as 8080 instead of 80 for Web proxy access.

And in addition to these settings, the Proxy section of the Built-in Ethernet port provides two other options:

- *Use Passive FTP Mode (PASV)*—Check this option to enable Passive FTP, a more secure mode of FTP. In passive FTP mode, the FTP client software makes all the requests to the server, unlike normal FTP, in which the FTP server sends data to the client via a prenegotiated communications channel. Although passive FTP can prevent certain types of attacks upon an FTP server, non-passive FTP is still the normal way for FTP clients and servers to communicate. Don't enable this option unless your network administrator tells you to.

- *Bypass Proxy Settings For These Hosts & Domains*—Enter the names of any domains that you would like to bypass when using a protocol for which a proxy has been configured. For example, you may need to use a proxy server for Web access, but there is one Web site whose firewall will not work properly through the proxy server. To bypass the proxy server for this domain, enter the root level of the domain, such as **macosbook.com** or **apple.com**, in this area, or the host name of the particular Web server, such as **www.macosbook.com** or **www.apple.com**.

These are pretty much all the settings you'll encounter for a typical Built-in Ethernet port. Let's take a look at the protocol settings for a typical modem port.

Configuring Modem Protocols

Although modems and Ethernet adapters utilize many of the same communications protocols, modems need additional protocols to communicate with the modem hardware. This is where things get a little tricky because of the vast array of modems available to the ISPs and consumers. Before you can configure a modem to work properly, you have to get Mac OS X to recognize and communicate with the modem—and then pray the modem works well with the ISP's modem on the other end of the telephone line. Fortunately, Mac OS X supports approximately 200 modems using *modem scripts*, or small files that tell the operating system how to communicate with each modem. Each modem script defines everything from getting the attention of the modem and dialing a telephone number to negotiating the speed of the modem port. One modem script for each supported modem is located in <*hard drive*>/Library/ Modem Scripts/. Each script contains several hundred lines of instructions that look something like this:

```
ifstr 5 1 "0"
serreset 115200, 0, 8, 1
jump 2
!
@LABEL 1
serreset 57600, 0, 8, 1
!
@LABEL 2
hsreset 0 0 0 0 0 0
settries 0
```

In most Mac OS X-capable computers, a modem has been installed on the motherboard, but modems can also be installed in a PCI slot or externally via a serial or USB port. If the modem is installed correctly and the proper modem script is available, you should be able to connect to the Internet as soon as you have an account with an ISP that offers a compatible modem. Check your modem's documentation and the support section of your ISP's Web site for information about modem incompatibilities. Some ISPs will give specific telephone numbers to dial for a specific type of modem.

Although the TCP/IP and Proxy settings are similar to those used when connecting to an Ethernet port and the PPP section is similar to the PPPoE section, the Modems section is unique. I'll point out the similarities and differences below. The following protocol settings should be reviewed and configured when using a modem to connect to an ISP:

- *TCP/IP*—Configure the computer to obtain an IP address manually, which is highly unlikely, or via PPP, which is very similar to DHCP in that the IP address and most other settings are entered automatically by the ISP's PPP server.

- *Proxies*—Exactly the same as described in the Built-in Ethernet section above.

PPP

PPP has made the old Serial Line Internet Protocol (SLIP) all but obsolete for dialing into an ISP. In the PPP section of the Network System Preferences (shown in Figure 16.8), you can configure how Mac OS X communicates with a PPP server using the following options:

- *Service Provider (Optional)*—The name provided by your ISP.

- *Telephone Number*—The primary telephone number dialed by your modem to connect to your ISP. Prefix this number with any additional numbers required to make a connection, such as 9 to access an outside line, or *70 to disable call waiting.

- *Alternate Number (Optional)*—A secondary telephone number to access your ISP.

- *Account Name*—The username of your account.

Figure 16.8
The PPP section of the Network System Preferences.

16

- *Password*—The password for your dial-up or broadband account.

- *Save Password*—Check to save your password.

Like the PPPoE Options button described earlier, clicking the PPP Options button reveals the following PPP-specific options:

- *Connect Automatically When Starting TCP/IP Applications*—Initiates a connection to your ISP whenever an Internet application such as Mail or Internet Explorer is launched.

- *Prompt To Stay Connected If Idle For __ Minutes*—Issues a reminder to remain connected to the ISP after a certain amount of time, which is helpful if you're paying by the minute.

- *Disconnect If Idle For __ Minutes*—Releases the connection if you haven't touched the mouse or keyboard after a certain amount of time.

- *Disconnect When User Logs Out*—Automatically disconnects the modem from the ISP when the user who initiated the connection logs out of Mac OS X using the Log Out command from the Apple menu. Of course, the connection will also be terminated if the user restarts the computer or chooses Shut Down instead of Log Out.

- *Redial If Busy*—Tells the Internet Connect application how many times to redial the main or alternative number to establish a connection, as well as how long to wait between tries. This feature is very handy if you frequently receive a busy signal when trying to dial in to your ISP.

- *Send PPP Echo Packets*—Enhances the way Mac OS X communicates with your ISP's routers for the purpose of ensuring connectivity to the network.

- *Use TCP Header Compression*—Speeds up the connection by telling the modem to compress the header information in TCP/IP packets as they are sent to the receiving modem. Not all modems support this feature, so try disabling this option if you have trouble connecting to an ISP.

- *Connect Using A Terminal Window (Command Line)*—Opens a Terminal window and requires that you manually type in commands to initiate the connection. Occasionally, your ISP may ask you to enable this feature to troubleshoot a connection problem. It enables the ISP rep to see the exact steps your computer is following and the response from the PPP server.

- *Use Verbose Logging*—Increases the details entered into the Connection Log of the Internet Connect application when accessing an ISP by PPPoE, PPP, or AirPort.

■ *Cancel*—Cancels changes made to the PPP Options settings.

■ *OK*—Approves changes made to the PPP Options settings.

Modem

The Modem protocol section, which is shown in Figure 16.9, is very easy to configure. Each modem script appears as an option in this section, so if you're not sure which modem is installed in your computer, check the documentation that came with your computer. If the documentation is not available, check the Support section of the Apple Web site at **www.apple.com/support/** for assistance. Otherwise, start with the Apple-brand modems.

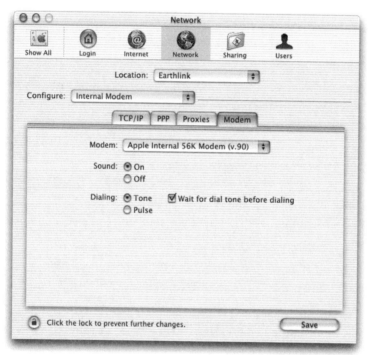

Figure 16.9
Configure your modem using the Modem section of the Network System Preferences.

Use the following settings to configure your modem:

■ *Modem*—Select one of over 200 modems from the Modem pop-up list.

■ *Sound*—Turn the modem's sound on or off.

■ *Dialing*—Choose between tone or pulse dialing; tone dialing is by far the most common of the two.

16

- *Wait For Dial Tone Before Dialing*—Tells the Internet Connect application to confirm a dial tone before initiating a connection. This helps to confirm whether any prefixes, such as *70 for call waiting, were entered correctly in the Telephone Number section of the PPP section and whether a dial tone is present.

When all the protocols have been reviewed and configured, you're ready to launch the Internet Connect application and connect to your dial-up ISP.

Connecting to an ISP with Internet Connect

Connecting to a network via Ethernet is typically a "configure-it-and-forget-it" operation. Unless your computer needs to change locations while on a network, you'll probably never have to revisit the configuration options. Dialing into an ISP via modem, on the other hand, requires that you use the Internet Connect application to initiate a session unless you selected the Connect Automatically When Starting TCP/IP Applications option described in the PPPoE and PPP sections earlier in the chapter.

After you've configured the ports and protocols outlined in the preceding sections, choose a location containing a modem, such as the Earthlink location shown in Figure 16.8, using the Location shortcut in the Apple menu. Then launch the Internet Connect application from the Applications folder. A window like the one shown in Figure 16.10 will appear.

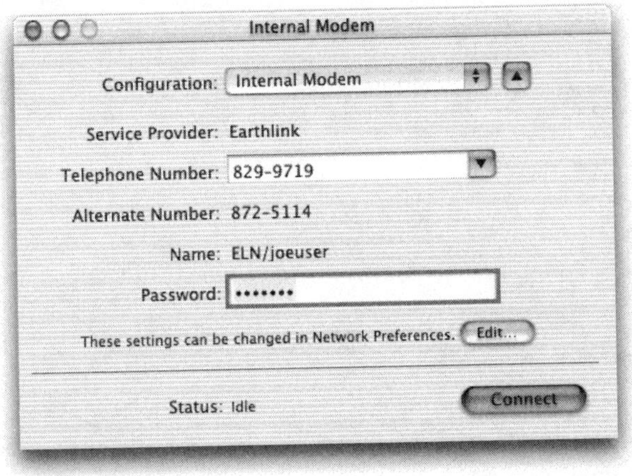

Figure 16.10
Use the Internet Connect application to initiate a dial-up connection to your ISP.

The name in the title bar of the Internet Connect window will reflect the name given in the Configuration field, not the location, which may be confusing to some users. Because the window is also collapsible, it may look smaller than the one shown in

Figure 16.10. To collapse or expand the window, click the disclosure triangle to the far right of the Configuration pop-up menu.

To connect to your ISP, click the Connect button and monitor the Status section of the window until you see information that confirms a connection has been made. Once the connection has been established, the Internal Modem window (shown in Figure 16.11) reveals the following details in its lower section:

- *Status: Connected To*—The IP address of the PPP server to which your computer is connected.

- *Send*—The level of information flowing from your computer.

- *Receive*—The level of information flowing to your computer.

- *Connect Time*—The amount of time your computer has been connected to the ISP.

- *IP Address*—The IP address assigned to your computer.

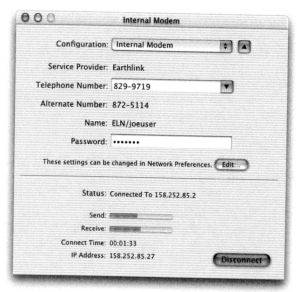

Figure 16.11
When connected, the lower section of the Internet Connect window displays technical information about the status of your dial-up Internet connection.

Once connected, you can minimize the connection window; or, if you want to monitor your connection while online, select the disclosure window to hide all but the most important information about your connection, as shown in Figure 16.12. To terminate the connection to your ISP, click the Disconnect button and quit the Internet Connect application.

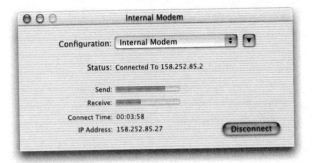

Figure 16.12
Retract the Internet Connect window to show only the necessary connection information to unclutter your display.

Wrapping Up

The Internet is an important part of modern life, and this chapter has shown you how Mac OS X has taken this fact into account:

- You've learned about the basic differences between connecting to a LAN and connecting to a modem.

- You've seen how to configure and prioritize the ports and protocols in the Network System Preferences to connect to a network.

- You've learned how to create locations to make switching between Internet access methods as easy as possible.

- You've seen how to use the Internet Connect application to dial into an ISP using a modem.

Once you've connected to the Internet, you'll want to explore all the Internet applications and utilities included with Mac OS X. I've discussed several of them along the way in the preceding chapters, and in the last chapter of this book I'll review these applications and discuss the others that have not been covered thus far.

Mastering Internet Applications and Utilities

Mac OS X lives up to the slogan "built for the Internet" by providing robust support for numerous Internet-related features, applications, and utilities. Even more impressive is Mac OS X's extensive backward compatibility with previous versions of the Mac OS and its enthusiastic appropriation of cutting-edge technologies such as Gigabit Ethernet and streaming multimedia. As I've shown in the preceding chapters in this section, Mac OS X makes it easy to set up File Sharing and Web Sharing, collaborate on a local area network (LAN), and connect to an Internet service provider (ISP). These developments uphold the Mac OS's reputation for being both the easiest and the most efficient operating system to use for networking.

Along with integrating Internet connectivity into the operating system itself, Apple has included as part of the basic installation of Mac OS X all of the major applications and utilities you'll need to master the Internet and the Web. In this chapter, I'll review the many components of the operating system that are Internet-related, including the applications and utilities that are essential to exploring and leveraging the vast resources of the Internet. Some of the third-party utilities are commercial products, but most are available as inexpensive shareware or even freeware.

Configuring Internet System Preferences

Numerous areas of the Mac OS X System Preferences either control Internet access or are themselves hooked into the Internet to provide a feature or perform a task. Most of these elements have been discussed earlier in the book, so I'll only review them here and refer you back to earlier chapters for more detailed information. Reviewing these features reminds us of how easy it is to take for granted the many ways in which Mac OS X relies on the Internet to provide features. A review of these preferences also serves to emphasize the fact that many of Mac OS X's features may not work properly without accurate configuration.

During the basic installation of Mac OS X, the installer leaves a few presents in the Applications and Utilities folders, including Microsoft Internet Explorer, Mail, QuickTime Player, and Network Utilities. And if that's not enough, you can download hundreds—perhaps thousands—of Internet applications and utilities for the Mac OS for free, as shareware, or as commercially packaged software. Let's take a look at the main configuration options that allow you to take full advantage of Mac OS X's Internet-related features.

Date & Time (Network Time)

Keeping track of the date and the time is one of the most basic tasks of any computer operating system. Of course it's important for you to know the correct date and time, but it's essential for Mac OS X to have the correct information in order to organize its files and services properly. To accurately track the date and time, Mac OS X accesses a Network Time Protocol (NTP) server through the Date & Time System Preferences, as shown in Figure 17.1.

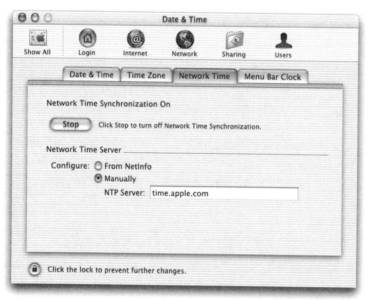

Figure 17.1
Connect to an Internet time server to keep your computer's clock as accurate as possible.

To configure your computer to connect to a time server, follow these steps:

1. Open the System Preferences and select the Date & Time pane.

2. Choose the Network Time tab.

3. Determine how the computer is to access a time server: by using the NetInfo Manager utility (which requires activation by a network system administrator) or Manually (from an NTP server over the Internet).

4. If you choose Manually, enter the domain name or IP address of a time server, such as **time.apple.com**.

5. Click the Start button to activate synchronization with the time server; click Stop to disable synchronization once synchronization has been initiated.

Mac OS X will periodically check the server for the correct time and update the computer's internal clock accordingly.

Internet

The Internet section of the System Preferences contains several Internet-related configuration options. Some of these options are populated after Mac OS X has been installed and the computer has been restarted for the first time. The Setup assistant asks several questions about your iDisk and email preferences and stores the answers in the Internet System Preferences. Specifically, the Internet System Preferences contains configuration information about four specific areas: iTools, email, Web, and Usenet News.

iTools

The iTools section of the Internet System Preferences contains information about your username (referred to as the iTools Member Name) and password, as well as a shortcut to the iTools Web site so you can create an account if you don't already have one. This information is requested during the initial setup stages of Mac OS X, but don't worry if you don't have an iTools account because it isn't required. Chapter 15 contains more information about iTools and the many features it provides, including an email account and your iDisk (free disk space on Apple's computer system).

Email

The Email configuration tab, which is shown in Figure 17.2, serves as a clearinghouse for the information your email application will likely require to connect to an email account. You can configure the following options to connect to an account that uses Post Office Protocol (POP) or Internet Mail Access Protocol (IMAP), both of which are Internet-standard email protocols. You can't configure these settings to work with proprietary email accounts that utilize transfer protocols other than POP or IMAP. To configure your computer to access an email account using an application such as Mail, open the Internet System Preferences, switch to the Email tab, and configure the following options:

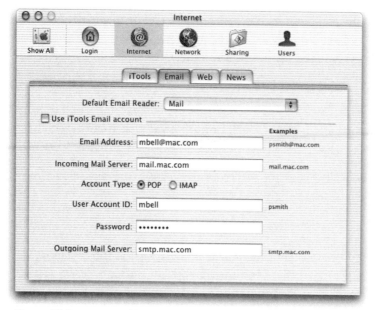

Figure 17.2
Configuring the Internet System Preferences to access an email account.

- *Default Email Reader*—Choose Mail or the Select option from the pop-up list and locate the proper application.

- *Use iTools Email Account*—Click this option if you wish to bypass the settings in this section and use the settings in the iTools tab to access your iTools email account. Internet System Preferences will plug in the username and password provided in the iTools tab, as well as all the remaining configuration options.

- *Email Address*—Enter the address to which people send you email.

- *Incoming Mail Server*—Enter the domain name of the server that hosts your POP or IMAP account.

- *Account Type*—Choose POP or IMAP.

- *User Account ID*—Enter the username for your email account.

- *Password*—Enter the password for your email account.

- *Outgoing Mail Server*—Enter the domain name of your Simple Mail Transfer Protocol (SMTP) server, which is used to send mail. It is often different from your incoming mail server, although they can be the same.

Web

The Web section of the Internet System Preferences contains several basic pieces of information that assist in the configuration and behavior of your Web browser. Like the Email section, the information entered here is shared with whatever Web browser you set as the default application for browsing the Web. However, because some applications may not be capable of importing these settings, you may have to configure your browser manually if you choose a Web browser other than Internet Explorer. To configure your computer's Internet System Preference, complete the following fields:

- *Default Web Browser*—Choose Internet Explorer or the Select option from the pop-up list and locate the proper application.

- *Home Page*—Designate the URL to use as the default, or home, page.

- *Search Page*—Specify the URL to use as the default Web page for performing Internet searches.

- *Download Files To*—Enter the path to the location on your computer's hard drive where you want downloaded files to be placed. The default location is the Desktop folder of your home folder (/Users/<*user name*>/Desktop), although you can click the Select button to identify another folder.

News

The News tab is used to configure the preferences for your preferred Usenet News client and server, although a client is not included in the initial release of Mac OS X. I'll make a few suggestions in the next section of the chapter, but for now you can fill in most of the following configuration options if the information is available from your ISP:

- *Default News Reader*—Choose the Select option from the pop-up list and locate the proper application.

- *News Server*—Specify the domain name of the Network News Transfer Protocol (NNTP) server.

- *Connect As*—Choose Registered User and complete the following fields, or choose Guest to connect without a username or password.

- *User Account ID*—Enter the username of your news account.

- *Password*—Enter the password of your news account.

Although Usenet News isn't as popular as the Web or email, it's been around for a long time and is a great way to share information. I'll talk more about Usenet News later in this chapter.

Network

As detailed in Chapters 14 and 16, the Network System Preferences is used to configure the TCP/IP settings to connect your computer to the Internet via Ethernet or a modem. You can choose from dozens of configuration options and configure *locations*, groups of settings that you can easily switch between when you want your computer to use different Internet settings.

QuickTime

Mac OS X installs the standard version of QuickTime 5, including the QuickTime Player application that enables you to view and listen to streaming multimedia over the Internet. The QuickTime format specifies different file sizes for different streaming rates so computers with fast Internet connections can view more complex files than computers with slower connections. This allows QuickTime developers to create content that is viewed in a way that is more meaningful to users. To configure QuickTime to accept data at the most appropriate rate for your computer:

1. Open the QuickTime pane of the System Preferences.

2. Click the Connection tab (shown in Figure 17.3).

3. Choose a Connection Speed between 28.8Kbps and 1.5Mbps.

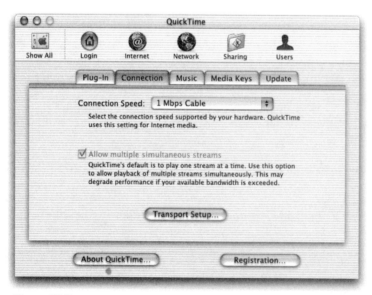

Figure 17.3
Configure QuickTime to accept streaming media at the appropriate speed over the Internet for optimal performance.

4. Click the Transport Setup button and either select the default protocol to receive QuickTime data or click on the Auto Configure button to let Mac OS X handle the configuration options for you.

For more information about QuickTime, refer to Chapter 10.

Sharing

Mac OS X includes a sophisticated infrastructure that enables each user with an account on your computer to share files over a LAN, the Internet, and the Web. (In the old days of the Mac OS, you could create File Sharing accounts for users and groups who didn't have Multiple Users accounts on your computer.) The Sharing pane of the System Preferences allows you to enable and disable File Sharing and Web Sharing, as well as remote access via Secure Shell (SSH) and FTP. In the Sharing pane, you can give your computer a name (such as Malcolm) and enter its IP address; the name you enter here is what will be available to select when browsing a LAN using the Connect To Server command. See Chapter 14 for more information on File Sharing and Web Sharing, and Chapter 15 for information on SSH and FTP.

Software Update

One of my favorite Internet-related features of Mac OS X is the ability to update the Mac OS over the Internet. I can still remember the old days of System 6 and 7, when updating the OS meant spending 10 or 15 minutes swapping system updates on floppy disks in and out of the computer. The Software Update section of the System Preferences allows you to check for updates to the OS manually or on an automated basis. When an update is found, Mac OS X asks you if you want to install the update, and handles the rest of it from there. For more information about updating Mac OS X over the Internet, see Appendix E.

Essential Applications

Mac OS X installs a number of applications that I consider essential to working efficiently on the Internet; however, depending on your needs, these applications may not paint a complete picture for you. I use the following applications almost every day and supplement them with several third-party applications (listed in the last section of this chapter) as well as a few Classic applications. Every day I find new Carbon and Cocoa applications that replace the functionality of the Classic applications, which I hope to retire as soon as possible. The applications in this section are installed by Mac OS X or can be downloaded from Apple at no cost.

Address Book

The Address Book is the first application from Apple (as far as I know!) that functions as an Internet-savvy contact manager. It's a powerful yet simple application to track information about people, including:

- Email addresses

- Web addresses

- Physical addresses

- Phone numbers

You can create custom categories, such as the Web and Mac.com fields shown in the bottom-left of Figure 17.4, as well as assign contacts to easy-to-manage categories such as Work, Family, and Friends.

The Address Book also has a Directory feature to search Lightweight Directory Access Protocol (LDAP) servers such as Bigfoot.com. The Directory feature is similar to the People search in Sherlock, which is discussed later in this section.

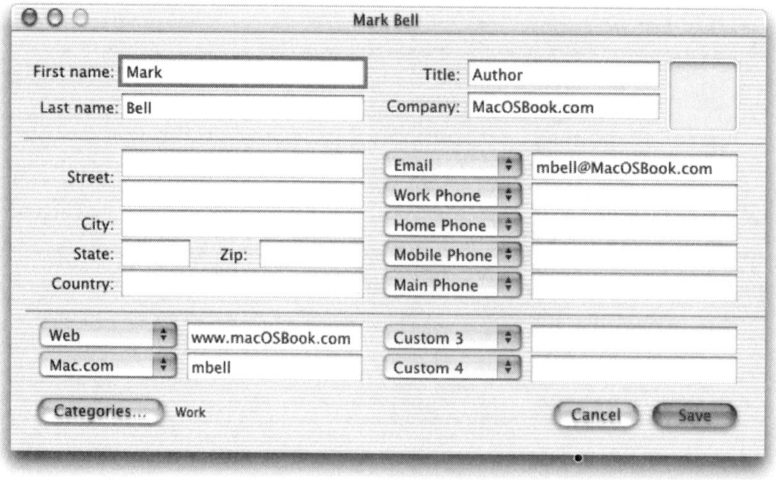

Figure 17.4
Use the Address Book to manage Internet contact information, including email address and home page, for friends, family, and colleagues.

Microsoft Internet Explorer

Mac OS X automatically installs a Carbonized version of Microsoft Internet Explorer. For the first time in recent memory, however, it doesn't install Netscape Navigator because Navigator is not yet compatible with Mac OS X. Internet Explorer is pretty comparable to most other Web browsers—URLs are entered and pages are loaded just as they are in Netscape Navigator. Figure 17.5 shows the Mactopia home page on the Microsoft Web site as viewed through Internet Explorer.

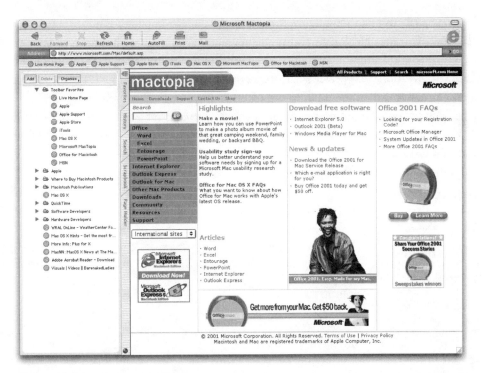

Figure 17.5
Browsing the Web with Microsoft Internet Explorer.

Explorer Bar

The Explorer Bar, visible in Figure 17.5 on the left side of the browser window, is a noticeable difference between Internet Explorer and other Web browsers. The Explorer Bar provides quick access to several useful resources:

- *Favorites*—A collection of bookmarks

- *History*—A log of the Web pages you've recently visited

- *Search*—One of several Internet search engines

- *Scrapbook*—A scrapbook for Web pages

- *Page Holder*—A temporary marker for a specific place in a Web page

You can expand or collapse the Explorer Bar by clicking once on any of the five tabs or by pressing Command+T. To further customize the appearance of browser windows, you can collapse the Explorer Bar and toolbars, thereby maximizing the space available for viewing HTML documents while retaining Internet Explorer's many navigational and shortcut buttons.

Printing Improvements

Microsoft Internet Explorer's ability to preview a Web page without the assistance of the Preview application is an outstanding advantage. Whereas many Carbon and Cocoa applications can preview a document by converting it into PDF format and opening it in the Preview application, Internet Explorer allows you to preview a Web page from within the browser itself. By choosing File|Print Preview when browsing a Web page, you can customize a few layout options and preview the changes before printing. Experiment with the following preview options to determine the best layout configuration for your Web pages:

- Headers And Footers

- Print Background

- Print Images

- Shrink Pages To Fit

- Crop Wide Pages

- Print Wide Pages

Once you've made your selections, choosing the Print button will open the Print dialog box instead of sending the page directly to the printer.

A Carbonized version of Netscape Navigator should be available soon. At least two other Web browsers for Mac OS X should be mentioned here in addition to Internet Explorer and Netscape Navigator:

- iCab (**www.icab.de**)

- OmniWeb (**www.omnigroup.com**)

These browsers have varying degrees of features—try them out to see if they work for you.

iTools

Because Apple wants to make using the free iTools services as easy as possible, access to your iTools account has been built into Mac OS X. An iTools account isn't required in order to use Mac OS X—but it's free and provides several valuable services, including:

- *iCards*—Customizable electronic greeting cards

- *iDisk*—20MB of free storage and Web space on Apple's servers

- *Email*—Your very own Mac.com email account

- *HomePage*—A Web site creation and storage tool

- *KidSafe*—A resource for kid-friendly Web sites

The main configuration options for iTools are discussed earlier in this chapter, and details on iTools services and how to use them are discussed in Chapter 15.

iTunes

iTunes, Apple's new MP3 player, is described in Chapter 10. iTunes is primarily used for playing MP3 audio files from your hard drive or a CD-ROM. I like to use iTunes to stream MP3s over the Internet from one of many Internet radio stations—with a fast Internet connection and a decent set of speakers on your computer, you'll be amazed at the quality of sound from an Internet radio station. Some stations broadcast at a higher bit rate than others, as illustrated in Figure 17.6. With hundreds of free stations to choose from, why not broaden your musical tastes?

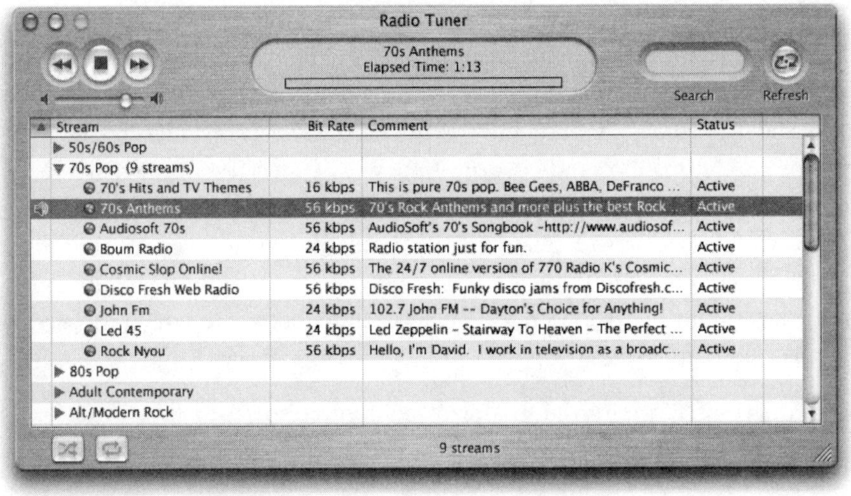

Figure 17.6
Use iTunes to listen to hundreds of free Internet radio stations.

Mail

The most striking addition to Mac OS X's Internet feature set is the Mail application. Mail is a feature-rich application that supports dozens of features you'd expect to find in other popular email clients such as Netscape Messenger, Microsoft Outlook

Express, and Eudora Pro. Mail hooks into the Address Book application for managing contact information and email addresses of your friends and coworkers; you can send mail from within the Address Book, or you can send mail to someone in your Address Book from within Mail. You can quickly add the address of someone from whom you have received a message by opening the message and choosing Add Sender To Address Book from the Message menu (or by pressing Command+Y).

Like Internet Explorer, Mail has about a zillion features and I can only mention the highlights here. Some of the more interesting features and capabilities of Mail include:

- Drag and drop attachments

- Keyword indexing and searching of messages

- A built-in spelling checker with a contextual menu for quick access to suggested spellings

- Formatted text, including HTML

- Rules for filtering messages

- Customizable toolbar

And this doesn't even begin to scratch the surface. If I had to pick a favorite feature, however, it would be the rules feature. I receive upwards of a hundred messages per day from friends, coworkers, family, and publishers, and I rely on rules to sort messages into the correct mailbox and even alert me with a special sound when a really important message comes in. For example, I belong to a discussion list about BBEdit, the HTML and text editor, so I created a rule that looks for messages containing "bbedit-talk@barebones.com" in the To: field and reroute them to the mailbox named "BBEdit-Talk." Figure 17.7 shows the BBEdit-Talk mailbox into which messages are routed by the rule I created.

If you have an iTools account, Mail is already configured to access your iTools email account using Mail. Why not give it a try? If you try it and don't like it, I suggest Eudora Pro (**www.eudora.com**) as an alternative email client. Eudora has been around forever and should be familiar to many Mac OS X users. Eudora operates in three modes: light mode (fewer features, but no advertising), sponsored mode (full features, but with onscreen advertising), and paid mode (full features, no advertising).

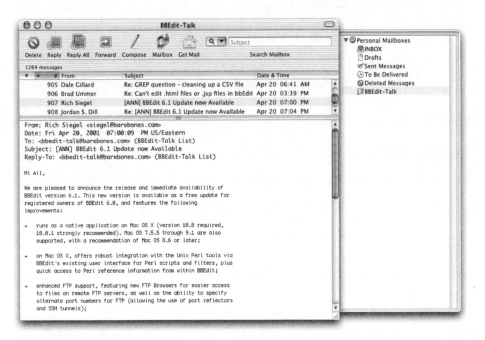

Figure 17.7
Use the Rules feature in the Mail application to automatically route messages to the appropriate mailbox.

Sherlock

Sherlock can find people and information on the Internet as effectively as it finds files on your computer (all of these search functions are discussed in Chapter 6). Apple was perhaps the first operating-system vendor to incorporate Internet searching capabilities as a core feature. Because Sherlock is extensible, more search sites and resources can be added to make Sherlock even more Internet-savvy.

Terminal

Advanced users and Unix geeks will recognize the Terminal application as more than a window to the local file system and a method of executing commands. Terminal is also a gateway to many of the most frequently used commands for Internet activities by system administrators, including:

- Telnet

- SSH

- FTP

- Ping

- Traceroute

Although experienced users will appreciate the command-line interface to these applications, most users would rather use an application with a graphical interface, such as the Network Utility application discussed a little later in the chapter.

URL Clippings

Mac OS X is able to create Internet *URL clippings*, URLs that have been selected with the mouse and dropped onto the Desktop from applications like Internet Explorer or Eudora. It does this by parsing (translating) clippings for tell-tale information such as "http://" and "mailto:" before creating the Desktop clipping. When double-clicked, the appropriate application is opened and the URL contained in the clipping will automatically be entered into the application. In Mac OS X, all URL clippings have the same Finder icon, whereas in Mac OS 9.1 the icons are visually differentiated to indicate the various types of URLs, such as http, FTP, and mailto.

Must-Have Utilities

In addition to the major Internet applications mentioned in the previous sections, Mac OS X installs several utilities to make communicating and working over the Internet easier than ever. Hundreds of third-party utilities—too many, in fact, to list in this chapter—are also available for Mac OS X even though the OS was only released in March 2001. The following Mac OS X and third-party utilities are essential to ensure that your Internet toolkit is complete.

Network Utility

The Network Utility is an essential tool for network system administrators. Located in the Utilities folder, the Network Utility is used to track, trace, troubleshoot, and identify other computers on a network or over the Internet. It has several advanced features, a few of which are mentioned in Chapter 14. The main features of this utility include:

- *Info*—Provides general information on your computer's network connection.

- *Netstat*—Displays information on the routing and protocols used by your computer.

- *Ping*—Sends tiny "pings" to another computer to help verify that the computer is accessible over a network.

- *Lookup*—Performs a DNS lookup on a host to determine what DNS servers are authoritative for that computer.

- *Traceroute*—Traces the connection from your computer to another computer on a network or the Internet, as illustrated in Figure 17.8.

- *Whois*—Provides a type of Internet directory query for looking up people with accounts on other computers.

- *Finger*—Displays information about one or more people logged into a computer; similar to Whois.

- *Port Scan*—Scans a computer for ports in use. Don't attempt to use this command if you are connected to a cable or DSL modem because your ISP could mistake you for a hacker!

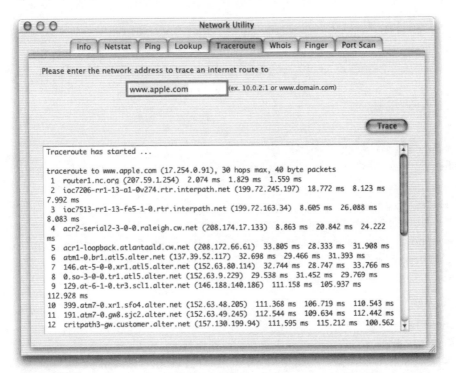

Figure 17.8
Use the Traceroute feature to trace a connection from your computer to another one.

Internet Connect

The Internet Connect application, discussed in Chapter 16, replaces the old Remote Access Control Panel as the means of dialing into an ISP. The specific configuration options for Internet Connect are configured through the Network System Preferences. Its only job is to connect and disconnect a dial-up connection. If you want detailed and graphed information about a PPP connection, as well as to be able to connect and disconnect from the ISP, check out PPP Monitor by Guy Meyer (**http://homepage. mac.com/rominar/monitor.html**).

Keychain Access

Mac OS X supports the storing of username and password information for a variety of Internet services in the Keychain, which is discussed in Chapter 15. This feature only works with Keychain-aware applications, however. The default keychain is automatically unlocked when you log in to Mac OS X; you can manually lock and copy the keychain to another computer to access Internet passwords from that computer.

Print Center

The Print Center is where you go to configure a printer in Mac OS X, including printers on the Internet or on a LAN that have an IP address. The Line Printer (LPR) protocol is supported by Mac OS X as a means of connecting to distant printers, as detailed in Chapter 9.

Adobe Acrobat Reader

Transferring files between two computers is the essence of the Internet; unfortunately, it can also be a real pain in the neck. This is especially true for documents created by word processing and page layout programs because no two computers are the same, and a file that looks great on one system may look like garbage—or may not even work—when transferred to another system. Even if a file is transferred between two identical computers with all the same fonts and programs, there's no guarantee that the document will look the same when it gets to its destination.

In Mac OS X, Apple has tackled this problem with native support for the Portable Document Format (PDF). Adobe Acrobat is a cross-platform (Mac, Unix, and Windows) program that creates and reads platform- and application-independent PDF files. Acrobat can also translate documents created in other programs— PageMaker, QuarkXPress, Microsoft Word—into PDF files. The new files include all the fonts, graphics, and other visual items of the original files. This feature allows users to share complex documents without worrying about losing their original look and feel.

Acrobat Reader, the free version of this application, allows you to read PDF documents but not create them. But if Mac OS X includes the Preview application for reading PDF documents, what good is Acrobat Reader, you ask? For starters, Preview is only a basic PDF reading application and contains only the most basic features, as does Acrobat Reader. Acrobat Reader, however, allows you to zoom in and out, find text, embed hyperlinks, and display information as either a continuous scroll, one page at a time, or as facing pages. Because PDF is a flexible file format, users have a great deal of control over how the document is displayed.

 Adobe has more information about Reader and the full version of Acrobat at its Web site, **www.adobe.com/products/acrobat/**.

It's also a good idea to download Acrobat Reader because it installs a plug-in for most Web browsers that allows PDF documents to be viewed within a browser window (although this particular feature has yet to be updated for Internet Explorer 5.1 for Mac OS X). Acrobat Reader has two other plug-ins that connect to the Web to access Web services and to embed hyperlinks into PDF documents.

BBEdit

BBEdit from Bare Bones Software (**www.barebones.com**) is the consummate tool for HTML authoring and text editing. It has powerful search-and-replace features, tools for making HTML authoring a snap, and can be extended to include new functions through a plug-in architecture. I use BBEdit to edit all my Web pages, which is made even easier because of BBEdit's built-in FTP client, which allows documents to be opened from an FTP server directly in BBEdit, as in Figure 17.9. Bare Bones provides the Lite version free of charge on their Web site, but it lacks many of the important features found in the commercial version, such as a Web-safe color palette, spelling checker, and HTML tools, that make BBEdit such an indispensable tool for Web developers.

Figure 17.9 shows an example FTP connection using BBEdit.

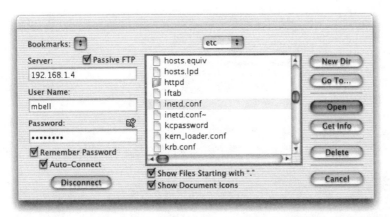

Figure 17.9
The commercial version of BBEdit is an essential application for accessing HTML and text files via FTP.

Transmit

The sole purpose of Transmit from Panic (**www.panic.com**) is to transfer files to and from FTP servers. It performs this task using an efficient, Mac OS-like interface backed by a multithreaded and Carbonized code base. According to tests performed by Panic, Transmit is the fastest FTP client available for the Mac OS. To see how Transmit works, refer to Chapter 15. Out of the many FTP clients for Mac OS X, Transmit is my favorite.

URL Manager Pro

URL Manager Pro from Alco Blom (**www.url-manager.com**) is to managing URLs as the Address Book is to managing names and addresses. It consists of a powerful URL organization window as well as a small floating window, the Helper Dock, that provides shortcuts to your frequently used Internet applications, such as your Web browser, email client, and news client. The URL Manager Pro organization and floating windows are shown in Figure 17.10.

Figure 17.10
Use URL Manager Pro to organize URLs and access to Internet applications.

A Word (or Several) about Shareware

Although the Macintosh platform hasn't traditionally enjoyed the same volume of commercial software as Wintel machines, Macs have a long and proud tradition of shareware—software uploaded to public sites and available on a use-before-you-buy basis. Generally, these programs are small, simple applications and utilities that enhance larger commercial products and add functionality to the Mac OS. Or sometimes they're simply silly, fun activities.

The deal with shareware is simple: If, after using it for a while, you decide you can't live without it, then send payment to the author. Generally, most shareware is available for a nominal fee; some programs, called freeware, are available at no cost.

Shareware is a long-standing custom on the Internet. Many of the most popular programs began life as shareware, and some of the best still are. In fact, two of the programs discussed in this chapter, Thoth and URL Manager Pro, are shareware. StuffIt Expander and Acrobat Reader are freeware.

Please remember that if you use shareware you have to pay for it. These programs are available on the honor system, so don't mess up a good thing by not paying.

URL Manager Pro supports drag and drop, works with several Mac OS X–enabled Web browsers, is very well documented, and is fairly inexpensive ($25).

VNC Server/Client

As demonstrated in Chapter 15, the ability to see another user's screen is essential when it comes to supporting and troubleshooting. Freeware Virtual Network Client (VNC) clients and servers are available for numerous platforms, including Mac OS X. Timbuktu (**www.netopia.com**) is the consummate screen and file sharing application, but my freeware picks for VNC are OSXvnc (**www.osxvnc.com**) for the server and VNCThing (**www.webthing.net**) for the VNC client.

Usenet News

The last Internet application I want to recommend is called Thoth, from Thoth Software (**www.thothsw.com**). Usenet News is a collection of discussion lists on a wide variety of topics broken down into *groups*. Each group can contain thousands of postings that typically expire after a certain amount of time, depending on how each news server is configured. Usenet News began as a means of communicating between Duke University and the University of North Carolina at Chapel Hill, two great basketball (and academic) rivals that are about a dozen miles apart. Most ISPs have a news server that you're entitled to access for free. If not, several public news servers are available as well, but they usually don't carry all the newsgroups found on an ISP's news server because of the cost of maintaining such a system. For example, over 50,000 groups currently exist!

To use Thoth, launch the application and choose File|New News Server to enter the address of the news server, and then choose Special|Check For New Groups. Depending on how many groups are carried by your news server, it could take a minute or two to obtain the listing. Subsequent launches of Thoth are much quicker because it only needs to update the newsgroup list. To browse groups, scroll through the Full Newsgroup List window, or to make it easier on yourself, type in the name or partial name of a group you are looking for. For example, I've filtered all the groups that contain the word Macintosh in Figure 17.11.

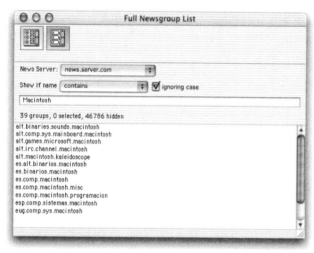

Figure 17.11
The Thoth newsreader can easily filter out unwanted newsgroups.

To access a group, just double-click on the name of the group, such as **seattle.users. macintosh,** and browse the message headings or create additional filters. In Figure 17.12, for example, I've narrowed down the postings from over 300 to just 6 that contain the word *advice* in the subject field. If you're researching a product or looking for an answer to a technical problem about the Mac OS or a particular model of computer, Thoth's filtering is an excellent way to get the job done.

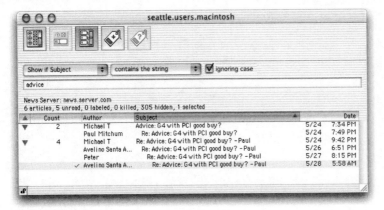

Figure 17.12
Create additional layers of filters to get the right answers from the thousands of groups and posts.

Wrapping Up

Apple invented the first commercial personal computer over 25 years ago, and today, Mac OS X continues to improve on the basic principle of Apple's first operating system: Make it simple, make it powerful, and most importantly, make it fun! Mac OS X implements many improvements and several new features to help you harness the power of the Internet and the Web, as well as the personal computer itself. I hope you find that Mac OS X meets your expectations.

Part  IV

Appendixes

Getting Help

With Mac OS X, virtually every facet of the Macintosh operating system, including the methods for getting help, has changed. Getting help with the operating system and your favorite applications is still easy, however, thanks to several powerful features provided by Mac OS X. The Help Viewer application, context-sensitive help, and the **man** command are the most useful methods of getting help.

Help Viewer

Getting help with a particular task can sometimes be difficult when you're not sure what terms to use in a search for help. (Of course, it's nothing like the frustration of thumbing through the index of the software manual in the days prior to online help.) Apple's Help Viewer application gives you the very best tools to search for help regarding all aspects of Mac OS X. Software developers can incorporate Help Viewer–style assistance into their applications, as they did in years past with tool tips, Balloon Help, and Apple Guide (the last two of which are no longer available in Mac OS X). The Help Viewer enables you to:

■ Browse documents

■ Search for one or more terms

■ Launch AppleScripts

To try it out, go to the Finder and choose Help|Mac Help, which launches the Help Viewer similar to the one shown in Figure A.1.

Let's look at each of the main functions of the Help Viewer.

Figure A.1
The Mac OS X Help.

Browse Help Documents

The Help Viewer allows application programmers to create help documents that can be categorized and viewed. The main view, depicted in Figure A.1, shows several subcategories of information that you can browse for detailed information. Clicking on any of the categories in the left-hand side of the window brings up even more information in a new browser window, as illustrated by the section entitled "Can I Send Email?," shown in Figure A.2.

Typically, each of the main categories of topics has one subcategory in which individual topics may be selected for viewing. Figure A.3, for example, shows the result of clicking on the topic entitled Sending Email.

To pilot your way around the Help Viewer, click on the buttons shown at the bottom of Figure A.3: The left-arrow button returns you to the previous page; the right-arrow button takes you to the next page (assuming that you've already visited it); and the question button links you back to the Help Center home page.

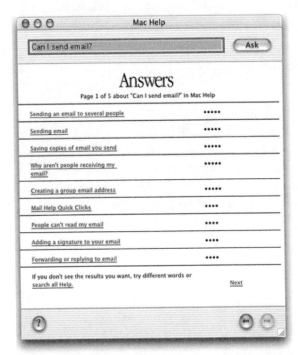

Figure A.2
A top-level heading of the Mac Help section of the Help Center.

Figure A.3
An individual topic as seen through the Help Viewer.

Search Help Documents

In addition to browsing documents, the Help Viewer also allows you to search for help topics using two search methods:

- Keyword searches

- Boolean searches

Depending on what components you have installed on your computer, the contents of the Help Viewer may differ. For example, applications you install after Mac OS X may contribute additional Help documents, and when you perform a search you may end up with results relating to more than one relevant application. To perform a simple keyword search, just type a phrase into the search field (paying no attention to case), as shown in Figure A.4. Then click the Ask button.

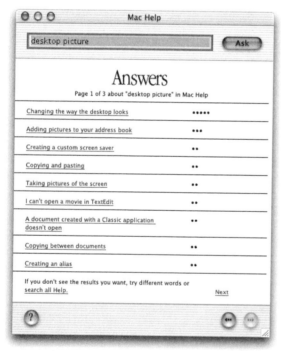

Figure A.4
The results of a simple keyword search.

As Figure A.4 illustrates, the Help Viewer window displays the search results in much the same way you would expect to see results of a Web search. For example, results are ranked according to how closely your term matches the contents of the Help Viewer's indices, and are displayed nine results (or *hits*) at a time. In this example, the search returned three pages of results that you can browse using the navigational buttons.

Table A.1 Symbolic Boolean operators used for searches in the Help Viewer.

Character	Meaning	Example
+	and	finder + icons + size
|	or	DVD | CD-ROM
!	not	desktop ! finder
( )	group	(AppleTalk + printer) ! Chooser

A

In addition to keyword searches, you can also execute Boolean searches in the Help Viewer. Use the criteria listed in Table A.1 to further refine your Boolean searches.

 It isn't necessary to insert spaces between search terms and the Boolean operators, as the Help Viewer will ignore gratuitous spaces.

For example, suppose you want to search for help on changing the size of the icons on your Desktop. Results of a search for the term "Desktop" may be so numerous that you'll be confused instead of helped. A more effective approach is to create a Boolean search using the terms and operators "finder + icons + size"; the results of this search are shown in Figure A.5.

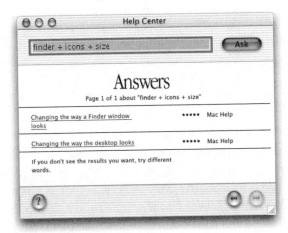

Figure A.5
The results of a Boolean search.

Finally, whenever you see the "Tell me more" option (see Figure A.3), you can command the Help Viewer to search further for terms related to the initial results of your search. The Help Viewer responds by summarizing the keywords of the result summaries and adding these terms to a new search. This feature is one of the first and best applications of the summarizing technology that Apple developed and patented a few years ago. Figure A.6 shows the results of a broadened search resulting from clicking Tell Me More.

If the expanded search doesn't yield the answer for which you are seeking, click the link at the bottom of the window entitled Search All Help. This link well execute the search again, but include every document available to the Help Viewer instead of the slightly broadened search performed by the Tell Me More link.

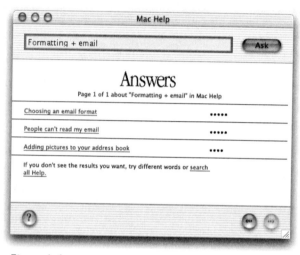

Figure A.6
The results of a broadened search.

Launch AppleScripts

In addition to enabling you to browse and search Help documents, the Help Viewer also allows you to launch AppleScripts from within Help documents. This capability makes it possible to create interactive examples that lead you through the help process, rather than just explaining it to you in a document. Under Mac OS X, of course, AppleScripts can do just about anything, including launching applications and accepting user input. For example, if you search for the term *Sherlock*, you'll come across a link within a Help document that says *Open Sherlock For Me* that, in turn, links to a compiled AppleScript. When you click on the final link, the AppleScript launches Sherlock.

Context-Sensitive Help

Context-sensitive help is a feature of Mac OS X that senses where you're working in the Finder and offers immediate help on a selected item. For example, you can Control+click a folder, such as the Applications folder, and select Help from the resulting contextual menu. The Mac OS then launches the Help Viewer. At this printing, context-sensitive help is limited in Mac OS X itself, although it functions very well in the Classic environment. As updates to Mac OS X are released, context-sensitive help should improve. Ideally, you will be able to immediately access information relevant to the item you are using. For example, you could Control+click the Utilities folder and find information relevant to the Utilities included with Mac OS X.

The **man** Command

To learn more about the Unix underpinnings of Mac OS X, you'll need to get acquainted with a command-line prompt. You can access this prompt by launching the Terminal program located in the Utilities folder. A window will open showing your Mac OS X log-in at a command line. You can now see your computer in a whole new light. You can explore folders, launch programs, and manage files without ever touching your mouse. In fact, the command line holds tremendous power, so getting help—which will help you master the command line—is one of the first skills you should learn. Thankfully, Terminal features its own context-sensitive help. It's called the **man** command, derived from the word "manual." The **man** command does not execute on its own, however. It is paired with the name of the command that you need help with.

For example, to see the contents of a folder, type "ls" and press Return in a Terminal window. The results would look something like this:

```
[localhost:~] mbell% ls
Applications    Documents    Movies    Pictures    Sites
Desktop         Library      Music     Public
[localhost:~] mbell% clear
```

Notice that you can only see the folder's contents listed as names. You probably can't distinguish folders from files and applications. Don't worry—the ls command has many options that will enhance the results. To find out more about these options, enter "man ls" in a Terminal window. You will see man pages like the one shown in Figure A.7. Press the space bar to read through each page in the man document or type "q" to quit. By reading the entire pages on this topic, you will learn that ls -l will list the folder contents in long format. The results of this command, pictured in Figure A.8, now provide much more information including rights, creator, and size.

Now you can brave the world of shell commands knowing that help is only a few keystrokes away. You can learn more commands in Appendix C, "Learning Unix Shell Commands."

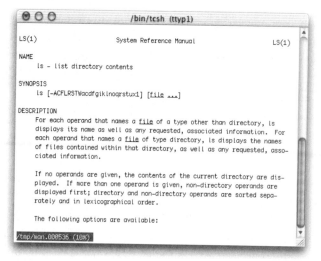

Figure A.7
The man page for the **ls** command.

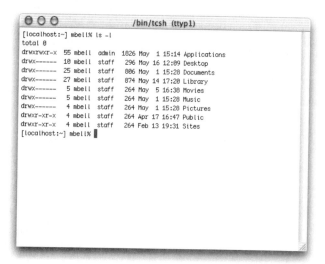

Figure A.8
An expanded file listing, the result of using the **ls -l** command in a Terminal window.

Proprietary Help

You can also get help from proprietary online help systems provided by applications. However, most Carbon and Cocoa applications for Mac OS X include built-in support for the Help Viewer application. Other programs may include a completely different style of help interface or have supplemental forms of help, such as tool tips, two examples of which are shown in Figure A.9. Only the programmers' imaginations limit the inclusion of new and unique ways to provide help in their applications.

Figure A.9
Tool tips are a supplemental form of help in many versions of the Mac OS, including Mac OS X.

A

Shortcuts

The Mac OS has always been easy to use—but some people (and you know who you are) just can't get enough of the many shortcuts that are available to help navigate applications and the Finder and start up and shut down the computer. Keyboard shortcuts can be more efficient than using the mouse to activate menu options and manipulate Finder objects. For example, it's much more efficient for me to use the Command+P shortcut to print a document than to take my hand from the keyboard, grasp the mouse, select a menu, choose Print, and return to the keyboard. And for those of us with repetitive-motion injuries, keyboard shortcuts are lifesavers!

If the dozens of shortcuts provided by the Mac OS aren't enough for you, at least one product that's currently in development for Mac OS X will create shortcuts for virtually anything you can imagine. QuicKeys from CE Software (**www.cesoft.com**) is a hybrid macro/scripting language that allows you to write, record, and edit strings of tasks and then execute these tasks with a click of the mouse or a tap of the keyboard. I've been using QuicKeys for several years to create simple keyboard shortcuts to my favorite applications, as well as highly complex macros to export data from one application, reformat the data, and then import the data to another application, for example. Programs like QuicKeys can make a huge difference in your computing life.

Common Shortcuts

Table B.1 lists the most common shortcuts involving starting up, shutting down, working with applications, and other miscellaneous actions. When using these or any other shortcuts, be sure to press the key combination only once and release the keys as soon as the shortcut has been activated. In the case of zapping the PRAM, release the keys as soon as the startup chime has sounded for the second time. Some CPU and monitor combinations, such as the Cube connected to the 15-inch Apple Studio Display LCD monitor (with an ADC connector), may not support all of the short-cuts. Also, some PowerBook and iBook keyboards may abbreviate the names of the keys, so choose your keystrokes carefully.

Table B.1   Common keyboard shortcuts.

Action	Keystroke(s)
Startup, shutdown, restart, or sleep	Power key
Start Classic environment without Extensions or Startup Items	Shift key (while starting up)
Zap PRAM	Command+Option+P+R (while starting up)
Close all open Finder windows	Shift (after logging in)
Boot from CD-ROM (must be bootable format)	C (while starting up)
Bypass startup disk	Option
Force quit an application	Command+Option+Escape
Force a restart (older models)	Command+Control+Power key
Stop processing (some applications)	Command+period
Stop processing (some applications)	Command+Escape
Switching between running applications	Command+Tab
Take a screenshot of the entire screen (Classic only)	Command+Shift+3
Take a screenshot of a region of the screen (Classic only)	Command+Shift+4
Take a screenshot of a specific window (Classic only)	Command+Shift+Caps Lock+4
Rotate to the default keyboard layout	Command+space
Rotate to the next keyboard layout	Command+Option+space
Log out	Shift+Command+Q
Empty Trash	Shift+Command+Delete
Hide Dock	Option+Command+D
Save a file	Command+S
Save as (some applications)	Shift+Command+S
Hide Application	Command+H
Print	Command+P
Quit	Command+Q
Cut	Command+X
Copy	Command+C
Paste	Command+V
Undo	Command+Z
Show Info	Command+I

Finder Shortcuts

Many people use Finder shortcuts without really thinking of them as shortcuts, and you may be surprised by how many shortcuts exist for navigating around the Finder. Table B.2 lists the Finder shortcuts available in Mac OS X and the extended keyboard. PowerBook, iBook, and the standard USB keyboards lack as many as 13 of the keys that are found on the extended keyboard. However, Function key combinations that compensate for the missing keys may be available; check your computer's documentation for details.

Table B.2   Finder shortcuts.

Action	Keystroke(s)
Close active window	Command+W or click close button
Close all open windows	Command+Option+O or Option+click close button
Open selected item and close the parent window	Command+Option+O or Option+ double-click
Expand closed subfolders one level in a list view	Click (on a closed folder's triangle) or Command+right arrow (on a closed folder)
Collapse open subfolders one level in a list view	Click (on an open folder's triangle) or Command+left arrow (on a closed folder)
Expand all closed subfolders in a list view	Command+Option+right arrow
Collapse all open subfolders in a list view	Command+Option+left arrow
Open a window to its largest possible size	Click (on zoom button)
Minimize window to Dock	Double-click (on title bar) or click minimize button or Command+M
Collapse all windows to Dock	Option+Double-click (on title bar) or Option+click minimize button or Option+Command+M
Move down to the next item in a list view	Down arrow
Move up to the next item in a list view	Up arrow
Select an item in a list view	(Type the first letters in that item's title in quick succession)
Scroll up one page in a list view	Page up
Scroll down one page in a list view	Page down
Move up one folder level	Command+up arrow
Open the selected item	Command+O

(continued)

Table B.2   Finder shortcuts *(continued)*.

Action	Keystroke(s)
Open the selected application or document	Command+down arrow
Locate the original of an alias	Command+R
Activate icon proxy pop-up	Command+click (on proxy icon)
Activate icon proxy	Click (on proxy icon)
Scroll left, right, up, or down	Option+drag mouse in window
Move an inactive window by its title bar	Command+drag title bar
Select an item in an icon view	Left, right, up, or down arrow
Select next item, alphabetically	Tab
Select the previous item, alphabetically	Shift+Tab
Select multiple, noncontiguous items	Command+click
Select multiple items	Click+drag mouse
Select everything in a window	Command+A
Copy all the file names of a window's contents to the Clipboard	Command+A, then Command+C
Create a new folder	Shift+Command+N
Create a new Finder window	Command+N
Show Info for selected item(s)	Command+I
Rename	Return
Create an alias	Command+M
Create an alias	Command+Option+drag
Copy (duplicate a file)	Command+D or Option+drag
Eject removable media	Command+E
Move to Trash	Command+Delete
Hide window toolbar	Command+B
Go to Computer window	Option+Command+C
Go to Home window	Option+Command+H
Connect to or open iDisk window	Option+Command+I
Go to Favorites window	Option+Command+F
Go to Applications window	Option+Command+A
Go to Folder	Command+~
Connect to Server	Command+K
Launch Help	Command+?

Open and Save Shortcuts

The attached sheets in Mac OS X (the Open and Save dialog boxes, also referred to simply as *sheets*) have many shortcuts that are similar to the Finder window shortcuts described in the previous section. These shortcuts may also work in the Open and Save window in Mac OS X that are not attached sheets, as well as the Classic environment if the application you are using supports Navigational Services. However, not all the listings in Table B.3 will work for all applications.

B

Table B.3   Navigational window shortcuts.

Action	Keystroke(s)
Move down one item	Down arrow
Move up one item	Up arrow
Select an item	Type the first letters in that item's title in quick succession
Scroll up one screen	Page up
Scroll down one screen	Page down
Move up one folder level	Up arrow
Open the selected folder	Right arrow
Expand closed subfolders one level	Right arrow
Collapse open subfolders one level	Left arrow
Open selected item	Return
Go to Home folder	Command+Option+H
Go to the Desktop	Command+D
Close the dialog box	Esc
Close the dialog box	Command+Period
Select all items that can be opened	Command+A

Learning Unix Shell Commands

Early personal computers often had an operating system with a prompt from which you entered commands to navigate the file system and execute programs. Then Apple released a revolutionary operating system that used icons and mouse actions, rather than a command prompt, to control the computer. The Mac OS continued to eschew the command-line interface until the introduction of Mac OS X, which includes a utility called Terminal that gives you the option of navigating the file system of your computer and executing commands by typing them.

Before you delve into the world of shell commands, however, you need to be aware that misuse of shell commands can seriously damage your operating system. Most users will never need to launch Terminal, but if you choose to run it, exercise caution.

The Terminal Application

Although many applications developed for Mac OS X can be configured in the Finder, some of the interesting Unix-based programs and utilities that are being ported to Mac OS X often require that you configure them manually. Terminal, an application for executing commands, provides an interface that allows you to perform these tasks.

Terminal is located in the Utilities folder and is launched like any other application by double-clicking on the Finder icon. When launched, a Terminal window similar to the one shown in Figure C.1 is created, which displays your login name for Mac OS X (or Short Name, as defined in the Users System Preferences) followed by a % symbol. Your home folder is the "current working folder" for each Terminal window.

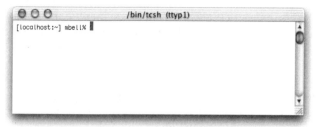

Figure C.1
A Terminal shell window, including the prompt.

Terminal Preferences

Before you begin working in Terminal, you may wish to modify the preferences for the shell window. Perhaps the text is too small, or you would like more lines of text to appear in a window. To make these changes, access Terminal|Preferences; the window shown in Figure C.2 will appear. Note that the toolbar at the top of the window contains icons for several different categories of preferences.

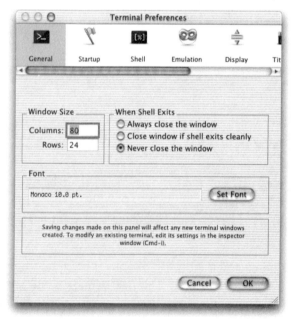

Figure C.2
The Terminal Preferences window.

As with many other programs, Terminal preferences are organized in categories. The categories are described in the following list for your information; I discourage you from changing any of these settings unless you're an experienced Unix user. The categories include:

■ *General*—This panel sets the size, font, and behavior of all shell windows. You can enlarge the default height and width of a shell window and specify the font and font size, as well as enable options that control whether a shell window closes automatically.

■ *Startup*—These settings control what happens when Terminal is launched. You can configure Terminal to launch automatically when you log in to Mac OS X, and enable options such as hiding or showing shell windows. The most useful setting here is the Always Prompt To Quit option, which allows you to disable the warning that appears if you quit Terminal while a shell window is still open.

■ *Shell*—This panel controls which shell program you use. The default is tcsh, a modified version of the C shell, and the path is listed in this panel. You can reveal the technical details about C shell by entering "man tcsh" at the prompt. Do not change this preference unless you're a highly experienced Unix user.

■ *Emulation*—The Emulation settings control how your keyboard input interacts with the shell. For example, you can set the Option key to act as the Escape key, which is useful for the emacs editor discussed later in this appendix.

■ *Display*—When you're working in a shell window, you may need to view previous text by paging up the window. The Display settings allow you to set a limit (including no limit) on the amount of text stored in a window. You can also control word-wrapping and the window's behavior when new data is entered at the prompt.

■ *Title Bar*—These settings control the text displayed in the title bar of the shell window. As you modify the settings, you can see the results in the preview title bar. By default, the shell path and the device name are displayed; you can also include the window size, file name, or a custom title for the window.

■ *Colors*—The shell window default is a gray world. However, if you'd like a little color, you can modify the background, the text and its different styles, and even choose different cursors.

■ *Activity*—When the Activity Monitor Enabled option is checked, Terminal monitors your active processes and will warn you if you attempt to close the window while a process is running. The list of commands in the Activity pane indicates exceptions to this rule. You can add additional commands or remove some of the existing ones.

Be aware that changes you make in Terminal Preferences only affect windows opened after the preferences are saved. For existing windows, select Shell|Inspector to select the different categories such as Window, Buffer, or Colors to modify individual window settings without modifying the Terminal defaults.

C

Additional Terminal Options

Now that you've configured Terminal, you can begin using the utility. Although you can still use the point-and-click method of selecting options from various menus, you'll most likely begin typing commands in the shell window.

If, during your Web ramblings, you've found an interesting command to run in the shell, you can copy the command and select Shell|Run Command to paste and run it. The results of the command will appear in a new window without a prompt.

To save the window to a file, select Shell|Save. You may want to save a command that you use to connect to another server on a regular basis, for example. You can then have Terminal open this file upon startup, or you can manually open the file from the Shell menu. You can also save the window contents to a text file or save selected text. Both options are found under the Shell menu.

Example Commands

Now that you know how to configure Terminal, you can begin entering commands. Because the Darwin environment in Mac OS X is derived from BSD (refer to Chapter 1 for more details), a wide array of commands are available through Terminal. In fact, these commands often work on any Unix-derived platform such as Linux or Solaris.

This appendix includes only a fraction of the commands and utilities available to you in Terminal. In fact, whole books have been written about these commands and all the things you can do with them. If you're serious about learning the Darwin environment and want to be productive in Terminal, you'll need additional documentation. Books for users of all levels are available. And, of course, you can find information and assistance on the Web. You will find several useful URLs listed in Appendix F.

For now, I'll review some of the most common and useful commands in the Terminal shell. The Terminal shell can be intimidating at first, so keep this information handy—especially if you are a beginner. Soon you'll be typing away. You may even discover that you're really a Unix geek at heart. The following shell commands are listed according to how often you will use them—the most frequently used commands are listed first.

ls

The **ls** (*list*) command is one of the easiest commands to remember. Typing "ls" alone simply lists the names of the files or folders in the current folder. For more information, add options to the command. Type "ls -a" to see all files and folders, including hidden ones. Type "ls -l" to view the long listing of folder content information, including whether an item is a file or folder and who created it.

pwd

The **pwd** (*print working directory*) command shows your current path. As you begin navigating your hard drive via Terminal, you can find yourself nested deeply. The **pwd** command will show the path to your current location. You can also find this information by typing a period.

cd

The **cd** (*change directory*) command allows you to change folders. Typing "cd .." will put you into the previous directory; typing "cd /" will place you at the root. If you know the path, you can enter "cd *pathname*" to change to that location. For example, "cd /Library" will place you in the Library folder located just off the root of the Mac OS X hard drive. If you want to return to your home directory, type "cd".

cat

The **cat** (*concatenate and print*) command displays the contents of a file in the Terminal window. Type "cat *filename*" to show the file contents. If the file is large, you'll need to modify the command by adding the **more** option. For example, type "cat *filename* |more" to display the contents one screen at a time. To continue through the screens, press the space bar.

more

The **more** command displays the contents of a file, screen by screen, when you type "more *filename*" at the prompt. A status bar at the bottom of the screen indicates what percentage of the file is currently displayed in that screen. To proceed to the next screen, press the space bar. To quit without viewing the entire contents, type "q".

The **more** command can also be used as an option in conjunction with other commands to produce a screen-by-screen display of the results of the command. For example, the **ls -l |more** command results in a screen-by-screen display of the same results that would fly by if you entered just the **ls -l** command.

ps

The **ps** (*process status*) command informs you about the processes running on your computer. Type "ps -aux" to see a complete listing of processes. You can also access this information in the Process Viewer utility.

history

The **history** command is pretty straightforward—it lists all the commands you've executed while working in the shell window.

clear

If the neat freak in you is bothered by the clutter in your shell window, type "clear" to clean up the mess. The **clear** command places the prompt at the top of a clear window.

man

The **man** (*manual*) command, which displays online help documents for commands, is one of the best tools for learning your way around Terminal. Pair **man** with the command for which you need assistance. Fox example, if you're using the **ls** command but can't remember the option to display all file information, type "man ls" to display manual pages that describe every option available with the **ls** command. Pages are displayed screen by screen; you can progress to the next screen by pressing the space bar, or access previous screens by typing "b". Type "q" to exit.

exit

The **exit** command exits the Terminal session. Depending on your Terminal settings, the window will close automatically or stay open with a message indicating that processes have been stopped.

 All previous commands that I've discussed are passive—the results do not make changes to the file system and are therefore considered "safe." However, the active commands that follow do make changes to the system. A simple typographical error in the command could have devastating results. If you are new to the command line interface, practice with passive commands and *always* double-check your text before pressing Return.

cp

The **cp** (*copy*) command allows you to copy files. To copy a file to a new location, type "cp *filename directory*". For example, the command **cp apples.txt /Users/Shared** copies the apples.txt file from my personal folder to the Shared folder.

To duplicate a file and assign a new name to the duplicate, type "cp *oldfilename newfilename*". For example, the command **cp apples.txt oranges.txt** duplicates the apples.txt file and gives it a new name.

The danger of the **cp** command lies in the possibility of accidentally overwriting a file. You will not receive a warning that you are overwriting an existing file, so use the **cp** command with caution. Also, a file's resource fork may not be copied when using the **cp** command. To ensure that both the data fork and the resource fork are copied, use the Finder to copy files.

mv

The **mv** (*move*) command is used to rename a file or move it to a new location. To rename a file, type "mv *oldfilename newfilename*". For example, **mv apples.txt oranges.txt** changes the name of the apples.txt file to oranges.txt.

To move a file to another location, type "mv *filename directory*". For example, **mv apples.txt /Users/Shared** moves the mbell.txt file from my personal folder to the Shared folder.

As with the **cp** command, use the **mv** command with caution—if you're not careful you may accidentally overwrite a file. You will not receive a warning that you are about to do so.

rm

Like all active commands, the **rm** (*remove*) command can be dangerous because it is used to delete files. Type "rm *filename*" to delete a particular file. You can also delete multiple files at once by using the * wildcard character. For example, typing "rm *.txt" removes all files with the extension of .txt in the current folder only; **rm *.*** removes all files, no matter what the extension, from that folder. Be very careful with the **rm** command.

mkdir

The **mkdir** (*make directory*) command creates a new folder within the current folder. Type "mkdir *foldername*" to create the new folder. For example, to create a folder called WebDocs, I would type "mkdir WebDocs".

rmdir

Like the **rm** command, the **rmdir** (*remove directory*) command can be dangerous because it removes empty folders. For example, to remove the apples folder, I would type "rmdir apples" once the folder has been emptied using the **rm** command.

tar

Tar files, denoted by the file extension .gz, are recognized as compressed Unix files. Although StuffIt Expander (located in the Utilities folder) can decompress tar files, the results are not always clean. To get the best results, try decompressing these files using the **tar** (*tape archive*) command. For example, to decompress the neatapp.gz file, I would type "tar xvf neatapp.gz". In most cases, you should move the tar file to an empty directory before expanding because the decompressed archive may contain several files that can become confused with other files in the folder.

Editors

After installing some of the Unix programs that have been ported to Mac OS X, you may find that configuration files must be edited to reflect your personal settings. The fact that in many cases these files are hidden can be a real handicap unless you use Terminal, which gives you access to the entire file system.

Mac OS X includes several command-line text editors for use with shell environments. These editors allow you to make changes to files that you may not be able to see in Finder. In the following section, I'll briefly discuss the most commonly used editors and include only the most basic commands. For more complete directions, you can browse the man pages for each editor or purchase a Unix manual that suits your needs.

vi

The vi editor, shown in Figure C.3, has many devotees in the Unix world. In fact, many of the instructions that are included with Unix-based software tell you to use vi to edit configuration files. But to be honest, I find vi difficult to use.

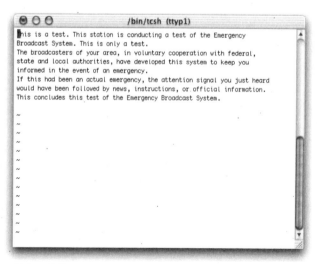

Figure C.3
The vi editor.

vi operates in two modes: edit and command. If you are in command mode, you cannot edit, and vice versa. This concept is difficult for first-time users to grasp. When you open a file using vi, it is opened in command mode. You must use certain commands to place the file in edit mode before you can begin modifying the text. And while in edit mode, you must press Escape to switch to command mode, where you can then save the file or exit the editor.

To edit a file in vi, type "vi *filename*". If the file does not exist, vi will open a new document and use *filename* as the name for the new file when you write the file to disk. When a new file is opened, you will see the ~ character on blank lines—note that these characters are not actually in the file. Now that you've opened the file, you can begin working with it. Table C.1 includes some useful vi commands. Keep in mind that you must be in command mode to use them. Most commands involve single keystrokes.

Because vi is case sensitive, a lowercase x does not execute the same function as an uppercase X.

Table C.1   Common vi commands.

Keystroke	Command
Escape	Switch to command mode
Control+f	Next page
Control+b	Previous page
a	Switch to edit mode and add text after the cursor
i	Switch to edit mode and insert text before the cursor
x	Delete a single character
dw	Delete the next word
dd	Delete entire line
/	When followed by a word or phrase, search the document for the word or phrase
:w	Save the file
:q	Exit vi
:q!	Exit vi without saving the file

emacs

Although the emacs editor is not as cryptic as vi, it is not as easy to use as pico (discussed next). Unlike vi, emacs does not have different edit and command modes. You can begin typing text and you can delete text using the Delete key. Figure C.4 shows emacs in action.

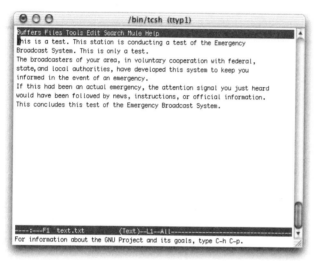

Figure C.4
The emacs editor.

In many of its commands, emacs uses the Meta key, a special key that is not available on a Macintosh keyboard—or on a PC keyboard, for that matter. If a command calls for the Meta key, press Escape followed by the other key in the command.

You can configure Terminal so that the Option key becomes the Meta key in emacs. Open the Terminal preferences and select the Emulation pane. Enable the Alternate Key Generates Escape Sequences option and click OK to save the preferences. In all subsequent shell windows, you can press Option instead of Escape. You may find that it feels more "natural" than using the Escape key.

To edit a file using emacs, type "emacs *filename*". If the file doesn't already exist, the file name you specify will be used when you save the file. Table C.2 lists some useful emacs commands.

As with vi, emacs is case sensitive. A lowercase x does not execute the same function as an uppercase X.

Table C.2 Common emacs commands.

Keystroke	Command
Control+v	Next page
Meta+v	Previous page
Control+g	Cancel the command
Control+s	Search the document for a word or phrase
Control+h	Get Help
Control+x then Control+u	Undo
Control+x then Control+s	Save
Control+x then Control+c	Exit

pico

The pico editor has one benefit that the emacs and vi editors don't have—it lists some of its commands at the bottom of the screen (see Figure C.5). If you're new to shell editors, you may want to start with pico so you don't give yourself whiplash jerking your head from the screen to consult a manual on how to save your file.

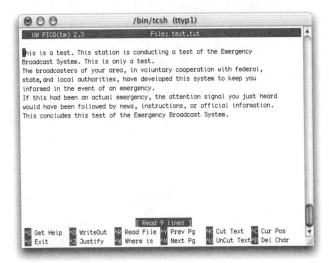

Figure C.5
The pico editor.

To edit a file using pico, type "pico *filename*". If the file doesn't already exist, the file name you specify will be used when you save the file. Because a file opened in the pico editor is always in edit mode, you can begin typing at the cursor to insert new text or press the Delete key to remove text. Table C.3 includes some common pico commands.

Pico is also case sensitive. A lowercase x does not execute the same function as an uppercase X.

Table C.3   Common pico commands.

Keystroke	Command
Control+v	Next page
Control+y	Previous page
Control+c	Set cursor position
Control+w	Search the document for a word or phrase
Control+g	Get help
Control+x	Exit the file with a prompt to save the document

Mac OS 9.1 and Mac OS X Feature Comparison

Mac OS 9.1 and Mac OS X are two different operating systems. But that doesn't mean each is alien to the other. As a user, you just have to find the similarities. Do you need to select a printer? If you're a seasoned Mac user, you may automatically reach for Chooser only to find it gone. It may be disconcerting at first, but soon Mac OS X Printer Center will be as familiar as the venerable Chooser. If you think in terms of "tasks" rather than mouse movements or keystrokes, you will soon be able to function in the Mac OS X environment and take advantage of the improvements. Use this appendix to learn which application is appropriate for your needs in Mac OS X when compared to Mac OS 9.1.

Fundamental System Components

The Aqua interface in Mac OS X is certainly eye-catching, but the really fundamental components are "under the hood." The stability of Unix, for example, has become the foundation for Mac OS X; in the past, when an application became unstable it could render the entire system unusable. In Mac OS X, however, an application that becomes unstable doesn't bring down the operating system itself thanks to the sophistication of Mac OS X's core foundation.

Table D.1 compares some of the major differences between Mac OS 9.1 and Mac OS X. Many of these differences are not seen, but are experienced instead.

Table D.1   Mac OS 9.1 and Mac OS X fundamental differences.

Feature	Mac OS 9.1	Mac OS X
Multitasking	Cooperative	Preemptive
Memory	Unprotected	Protected
User Interface	Platinum	Aqua

(continued)

Table D.1 Mac OS 9.1 and Mac OS X fundamental differences *(continued).*

Feature	Mac OS 9.1	Mac OS X
Open and Save windows	Navigational Services	Attached Sheets or Navigational Services
System Extensibility	Extensions and Control Panels	Frameworks
Graphics and Windowing	QuickDraw	Quartz and/or QuickDraw
Multiprocessing	Asymmetric	Symmetric

System Functions

The System Folder in Mac OS 9.1 contains the components necessary to boot the system. Some files in the System Folder are enhancements to the operating system and some are essential (without them, the computer will be unable to boot). However, in Mac OS X most of those components are, in fact, hidden from view. Although you can access these folders using the Terminal utility, keep in mind that Apple has hidden the system components for a reason. In the past, you could easily damage your System Folder because it was visible in the Finder, and therefore easily modified. In Mac OS X these vital folders are hidden, which reduces your chances of mangling the system.

Table D.2 lists several programs or tasks that are handled by the System Folder in Mac OS 9.1 and shows how they are handled in Mac OS X.

Table D.2 System functions.

Feature	Mac OS 9.1	Mac OS X
Desktop picture	Appearance Control Panel	Finder Preferences
System color scheme	Appearance Control Panel	System Preferences|General
AppleTalk	AppleTalk Control Panel	System Preferences|Network
Date & Time	Date & Time Control Panel	System Preferences|Date & Time
Monitor settings	Monitors Control Panel	System Preferences|Display
Sleep settings	Energy Saver Control Panel	System Preferences|Energy Saver
Keyboard layout	Keyboard Control Panel	System Preferences|International
Internet access settings	TCP/IP Control Panel	System Preferences|Network
Dial-up settings	Remote Access Control Panel	System Preferences|Network
Multimedia settings	QuickTime Control Panel	System Preferences|QuickTime
File Sharing	File Sharing Control Panel	System Preferences|Sharing
Sound	Sound Control Panel	System Preferences|Sound

(continued)

Table D.2   System functions (*continued*).

Feature	Mac OS 9.1	Mac OS X
Speakable settings	Speech Control Panel	System Preferences|Speech
Boot disk	Startup Disk Control Panel	System Preferences|Startup Disk
Computer accounts	Multiple Users Control Panel	System Preferences|Users
Select printer	Chooser	Print Center
Connect to servers	Chooser or Network Browser	Network or Connect To Server in Finder

Applications and Common Tasks

Mac OS 9.1 and Mac OS X include a limited number of applications that may meet your needs, especially if you're interested in the Internet. In Mac OS 9.1, most applications are stored in the Applications folder. In Mac OS X, you can access the Applications folder from the toolbar. Table D.3 lists several tasks and the application you would use to perform it in each environment.

Table D.3   Applications comparison.

Task	Mac OS 9.1	Mac OS X
Internet browsing	Internet Explorer 5	Internet Explorer 5.1
Multimedia viewing	QuickTime	QuickTime
Image viewing	PictureViewer	Preview
Editing text	SimpleText	TextEdit
Email access	Outlook Express	Mail
Search	Sherlock 2	Sherlock
Taskbar	Application Switcher	Dock
Printing	Desktop printing	Print Center

Utilities

Both Mac OS 9.1 and Mac OS X provide utilities that help you and your computer function. They can diagnose and repair your computer and provide information about settings and devices. Table D.4 provides a list that compares these utilities and their functions. Note that all utilities for Mac OS X are found in the Applications\|Utilities folder.

Table D.4   Utilities comparison.

Task	Mac OS 9.1	Mac OS X
Computer information	Apple System Profiler	Apple System Profiler
Color settings	Colorsync Control Panel	Colorsync Utility
Mount and create disk images	Disk Copy	Disk Copy
Disk repair	Disk First Aid	Disk Utility
Screen capture	Command+Shift+3	Grab
Font preview	Key Caps	Key Caps
Password management	Keychain Access Control Panel	Keychain Access
Configure computer settings	Mac OS Setup Assistant	SetupAssistant

Installing and Updating Mac OS 9.1 and Mac OS X

Rarely does an operating system release remain static. In the world of software, static usually means "no longer under development." Instead, updates are released and developers tweak the software to improve performance, fix problems, and add new features. Of course, the tweaking and new features often lead to more bugs that must be fixed in a later release. Unfortunately, many users don't take the time to install these updates and thus continue to use bug-ridden programs. Updates to the operating system are the most important updates to apply. In most cases, you must purchase the software to install the updates; some system updates are free, however. This appendix will discuss installing and updating Mac OS 9.1 and Mac OS X.

If you've recently purchased a new Macintosh computer, Mac OS 9.1 and Mac OS X may already be installed. However, if you purchased your computer in the spring of 2001 or earlier, it's likely that only Mac OS 9.1 was preinstalled. Or perhaps you purchased Mac OS 9.1 or Mac OS X to install on an older computer. Whatever your situation, this appendix will help you with the following:

- Performing a new installation of Mac OS 9.1

- Reinstalling Mac OS 9.1

- Preparing for Mac OS X

- Performing a new installation of Mac OS X

- Configuring Mac OS X

- Updating Mac OS 9.1 and Mac OS X

If you've never installed system software or components before, don't worry. After all, it's the Mac OS we're talking about here!

I'll discuss installing Mac OS 9.1 first. If you purchased Mac OS X, you probably already know that it includes Mac OS 9.1. To run versions of software that are not written for Mac OS X, you'll need the Classic, or Mac OS 9.1, environment. After Mac OS 9.1 is installed or updated, you can tackle Mac OS X.

Can you install Mac OS X first and save Mac OS 9.1 for later? Yes, but you must boot from a Mac OS 9.1 installation CD-ROM to install the system. Think about it. The Mac OS 9.1 installer is a Classic application. You can't run the installer in Mac OS X because you don't have a Classic environment installed. Save yourself some trouble. Install Mac OS 9.1 before Mac OS X.

Performing a New Installation of Mac OS 9.1

With Mac OS 9.1, the mechanics of a new installation, reinstallation, custom installation, or deinstallation are all pretty much the same. Of these processes, performing a new installation poses the most significant risk of accidentally harming your existing system software. We'll get to that in a minute; first let's look at the steps involved in installing the software.

The first step to installing the Mac OS successfully is to reboot your Mac and quit any applications that were automatically launched on startup. Like most software installation programs, the Mac OS installer requires that you quit all applications prior to beginning the installation process because the files being installed could be corrupted if another program interferes with them during the installation process.

The next step is to insert the Mac OS 9.1 installer CD-ROM. Of course, you can also boot from the installation CD-ROM by restarting with the CD-ROM inserted and holding down the C key until bootup begins. Figure E.1 shows the disk containing all the files necessary to perform an installation, including the installation application and documentation.

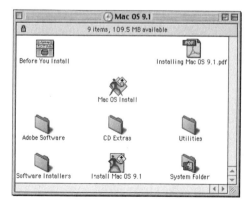

Figure E.1
A typical Mac OS 9.1 installation CD-ROM.

Once you have saved any open documents and quit your applications, or restarted the computer using the Mac OS 9.1 installation CD, launch the Mac OS Install application and be prepared to perform four main tasks:

1. Select the drive on which Mac OS 9.1 is to be installed.

2. Read the Important Information document that details known problems and incompatible hardware. This is a very important step, so don't skip it.

3. Complete the software license agreement.

4. Choose the software to be installed.

After you've completed these tasks, the installation program will ensure that your hard disk is capable of containing the installation of the software, check the integrity of the hard drive on which Mac OS 9.1 is being installed, and then begin the installation process. Mac OS 9.1 installs everything without requiring additional intervention on your part.

 You can also uninstall portions of the Mac OS using the Mac OS installer application.

Step 1: Select a Destination Disk

Selecting a destination disk is the first step. If you have multiple disk drives, the installer automatically evaluates each one to determine whether it has enough available space for an installation of Mac OS 9.1. In Figure E.2, for example, the hard drive named Starbuck has been selected for installation.

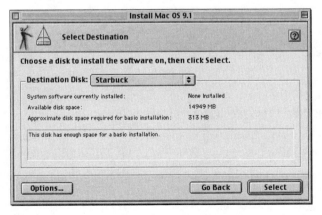

Figure E.2
Select a destination disk for Mac OS 9.1.

To perform a clean installation, which creates a new System Folder without deleting your existing System Folder, click the Options button at the bottom of the Select Destination window; in the resulting window, check the box entitled Perform Clean Installation, as illustrated in Figure E.3. If you've run into problems on previous attempts to install Mac OS 9.1, if you are doing a major upgrade from Mac OS 8.x, or if you're having persistent problems with system stability, check this box.

Figure E.3
Choose the Perform Clean Installation option to install an entirely new System Folder.

Step 2: Read the Installation Notes

No, I'm not kidding: You really should read every word of the installation notes to ensure that your hardware fully supports Mac OS 9.1. Because your ultimate goal is to install Mac OS X, be sure to confirm that your platform will run Mac OS X, not just Mac OS 9.1. Hardware requirements for Mac OS X are listed later in this appendix. Every version of the Mac OS has known problems in relation to certain hardware platforms; by reading the installation notes, you can find out what they are now rather than later—like when your system has deleted the report that's due at the end of the day!

Step 3: Complete the Software License Agreement

You will not be permitted to install Mac OS 9.1 unless you agree to the terms of the license agreement. After all, technically you don't own the software: Apple is selling you a license (subject to terms, conditions, and caveats) to use a copy of the software on your machine.

Step 4: Choose the Software to Install

The final step is to select the software you want to install. You can choose a basic installation of Mac OS 9.1 combined with certain applications and utilities, or perform a customized installation that includes all the software or just a single program.

At any time between Steps 1 through 4, you can click the Help icon for context-sensitive help. A window that addresses the issues presented in the current installation screen will be displayed. The Help window's contents should explain the function of each option and the consequences of each possible selection.

To perform a customized installation of Mac OS 9.1 or to remove any of its components, select the Customize button and click on the checkbox beside each component that you want to install or remove. To customize the selected component even further, click on the pop-up menu for each main component, such as Apple Remote Access or Internet Access. When you select a customized installation or removal, a window like the one shown in Figure E.4 appears. In this example, the Internet Utilities portion of Internet Access is selected as part of a custom installation.

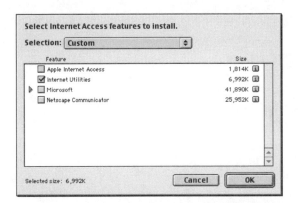

Figure E.4
A customized installation for the Internet Access component of Mac OS 9.1.

Last but not least, review the Options button at the bottom of the Mac OS Install window (see Figure E.2 for an example). It allows you to determine whether your hard disk drivers will be updated to the latest version. You can also request an installation report detailing what was added, removed, or replaced during the entire installation process.

Once you've selected the software to be installed, click the Start button to begin the process. It can take anywhere from just a few minutes to almost half an hour, depending on the software being installed and the speed of your computer and hard drive. Throughout the process, the installation program will display a progress bar.

Reinstalling Mac OS 9.1

If you need to reinstall Mac OS 9.1, go back to Steps 1 through 3. Pay careful attention to Step 1, in which you're asked whether you want to perform a clean installation. Provided that you have enough available disk space, you may want to consider performing a clean installation if your system is behaving strangely for any reason. If you're convinced you don't have enough disk space, proceed to Step 4 and install only the software that you think is needed. Note that you may not need to reinstall the entire operating system when only one component, such as Web Sharing, needs to be installed or reinstalled.

If you select a disk that already contains a previous installation of Mac OS 9.1, the window shown in Figure E.5 will appear. The Mac OS installer, after recognizing that Mac OS 9.1 is already installed, will ask whether you want to reinstall the OS or add or remove selected components. The remainder of the process is as described previously.

Figure E.5
The Mac OS installer, after detecting that Mac OS 9.1 is already installed on the selected drive, presents this window.

Preparing for Mac OS X

To use the Classic environment under Mac OS X, you must have Mac OS 9.1 or higher installed. If you purchased Mac OS X, you also received a Mac OS 9.1 installation CD-ROM. Go ahead and upgrade your operating system to Mac OS 9.1 before installing Mac OS X. Although you can install or upgrade Mac OS 9.1 at a later time, you won't be able to run Classic applications in Mac OS X until you do.

For those of you who have maintained the same System Folder through multiple system versions (in other words, for you long-time Mac users), be aware that your System Folder may contain software that is incompatible with Mac OS X. Although rare, this situation is certainly possible. You can detect such an incompatibility by restarting your Mac using Mac OS X; if the system can't finish booting, then you know you've got a problem. In case this happens to you, be prepared to do several things with your Mac OS 9.1 installation:

- Perform a clean installation of Mac OS 9.1 without adding third-party software.

- Boot successfully with Mac OS X and run the Classic environment so that Mac OS X can update it.

■ Install your third-party software, but don't attempt to manually combine the contents of a previous System Folder with the new System Folder.

■ Verify an application's compatibility with Mac OS X by restarting the Classic environment each time you install an application that modifies the System Folder by adding Extensions or Control Panels.

Most users can merrily install Mac OS X without a second thought; however, if you do run into problems, consider a clean installation.

Installing Mac OS X

Now you're ready to install Mac OS X. Although the installation process is quite simple—considering that you're installing a Unix-style operating system—it's also completely different from installing Mac OS 9.1.

If your hard drive has more than one partition, make sure that Mac OS X is installed on the primary partition. Refer to the Apple System Profiler to verify which partition is the primary one. You can also identify the primary partition as the first in the list of partitions in the Startup Disk Control Panel.

Mac OS 9.1 can be installed on another partition or hard drive, or both Mac OS 9.1 and Mac OS X can be installed on the same volume. You can also have Mac OS 9.1 on more than one partition, which is useful because it allows you to have a version of Mac OS 9.1 that has been modified by Mac OS X as well as one that has not. Although new software for Mac OS X is being released every day, you may find that some Mac OS 9.1 applications are unstable in the Classic environment. You can select either Mac OS 9.1 or Mac OS X as the operating system that boots the computer.

To install Mac OS X, insert the Mac OS X installation CD-ROM and double-click the Install Mac OS X icon. You will be prompted to restart the computer. Upon restarting, the computer will boot from the installation CD into Mac OS X. Alternatively, insert the installation CD-ROM, and restart the computer while holding down the C key to achieve the same results.

The Mac OS X installer launches automatically and you'll need to perform four main tasks:

1. Read the Important Information document that details known problems and incompatible hardware. This is a very important step, so don't skip it.

E

2. Complete the software license agreement.

3. Select the drive on which Mac OS X is to be installed.

4. Choose the software to be installed.

The Mac OS X installation process is simple but lengthy. Depending on the speed of your computer, even the booting process can take so long that you may think something is wrong. Have patience—the installer will eventually launch.

To install Mac OS X, your computer must meet the following requirements:

■ A G3 or higher processor, with these exceptions: The original G3 PowerBook with the multicolored Apple logo on the cover is not supported. Although processor upgrade cards are not supported, many users have reported that a wide variety of upgrade processor cards work just fine with Mac OS X.

■ A minimum of 128MB of physical RAM.

■ 1.5GB of free disk space.

If your computer meets these requirements, you are ready to install Mac OS X.

Step 1: Read the Installation Notes

Once the installer has launched, you'll see a Welcome screen, at which time you can click the Continue button to proceed to the Read Me window. Apple provides important information about what computers are supported by Max OS X, as well as known bugs in the operating system.

Common sense says that if you are able to boot from the Mac OS X CD, then you should be able to install Mac OS X, but this is not the case. Make sure that your computer meets all the system requirements, especially those related to memory and disk space. Once you've read the Read Me, click Continue. Note that all the steps in the installation process are listed on the left side of the window; past steps are denoted by a gray button, an active step is denoted by a blue bullet, and future steps are faint but visible. To access previous steps, click the Go Back button.

Step 2: Complete the Software License Agreement

The Software License agreement appears next. You can read the document in English, or choose from six additional languages. After you've read the agreement, click the Continue button. If you don't scroll to the bottom of the agreement, a window will ask whether you Disagree or Agree with the license; click Agree to continue. The Mac OS X installer will then survey your computer for hard drives in preparation for the next step.

Step 3: Select a Destination Disk

You now have an opportunity to select the destination volume. If you're in doubt, choose the volume listed first in the Select A Destination portion of the installation application.

Each volume icon indicates the volume name and available disk space, as in Figure E.6. Click an icon to select it; the volume's icon will then have a large, green arrow and be encircled. Once you've chosen a volume, you may see an option entitled Erase Destination And Format. If you select this, you can choose from two disk formats:

■ Mac OS Extended

■ Unix File System

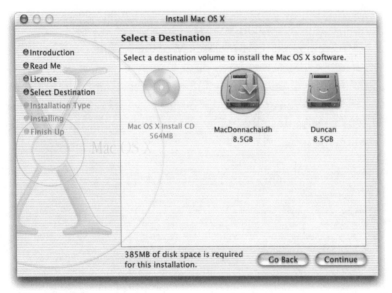

Figure E.6
The Mac OS X installation process allows you to select the destination drive on which Mac OS X will be installed.

Unless you're an experienced Unix user, select Mac OS Extended. Erasing the drive is not mandatory—in fact, you should only do this if it is necessary. For example, if you have the Mac OS X Public Beta installed but want to start with a clean slate, you could erase the disk and then proceed with a pristine installation of Mac OS X.

If you choose to erase the volume, a window confirming your decision will appear. If you aren't sure you want to erase the volume, click the Choose Another button and disable the Erase option. If you are sure, click Continue. (If you change your mind, you can click the Go Back button in the following window to disable the erase option.) If you did not enable the Erase option, click Continue to proceed to the next step.

Step 4: Choose the Software to Be Installed

The next window that appears is deceptively easy. If you want to accept the default installation of Mac OS X, then you're nearly finished—click the Install button to proceed. On the other hand, if you want to customize the installation, you can click the Customize button, the result of which is shown in Figure E.7. You'll be given a listing of the four packages that will be installed; if you haven't installed Mac OS X, then two of the packages, the Base System and the Essential System Software, cannot be unchecked. Two other options, BSD Subsystem and Additional Print Drivers, can be disabled. The BSD Subsystem option installs additional components for the core operating system, and is required if you install Mac OS X developer tools from the Mac OS X Developer Tools CD that accompanies Mac OS X. The Additional Print Drivers option installs additional drivers for popular Canon, Epson, and Hewlett-Packard printers, although the installer does not indicate what printer drivers are actually being installed. Unless you are very tight on space, you should probably leave all options enabled. The Custom Install window also reminds you of the size of the operating system about to be installed.

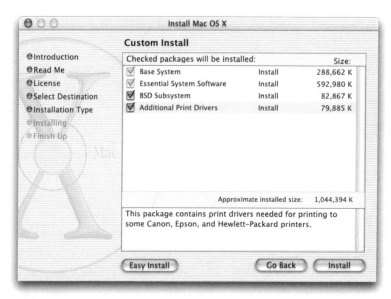

Figure E.7
The Custom Install options for Mac OS X.

If you decide not to customize the installation, you can click the Easy Install button or proceed to the next window by clicking the Install button. The installer will now begin examining your disk and installing the different components. To stop the installation, click the Pause button; the installer will not actually pause until it has finished the task at hand, however. This means you may not detect a pause until the installation is complete.

As the software is installed, messages are posted under the progress bar indicating what task is active. Actual system installation, the longest part of the process, can take 20 minutes or longer, depending on the speed of your computer. Once the process is finished, the computer will restart itself.

Configuring Mac OS X

Your computer is now ready to run Mac OS X—almost. You still need to answer some simple questions that will help configure Mac OS X for your personal use.

After restart, the computer will load Mac OS X. A progress bar depicting the loading of the different services will appear. (Soon a configuration program complete with musical soundtrack and soothing graphics will load.) You will be asked the name of your country; if it is not listed, click the Show All option. Then choose your country and click Continue.

You have the option of choosing a keyboard layout. The default layout matches your selected country of origin. If you need more layouts to choose from, click the Show All option.

At the next window, you will see that Apple wants to know more about you. You will see fields asking for your name, address, and telephone number. Supply the appropriate information. If you try to continue without doing so, a window reminding you to fill in the required fields as noted by the red-encircled arrows will appear. Apple is promising to protect your privacy, and if you want to view its privacy policy, click the Privacy button. After you have entered the required information, click Continue.

At the next window, you will see that Apple wants to know still more about you. It wants to know where you will be using the computer (home, work, school, and so on) and what you do for a living. You can also elect to receive information from Apple and other companies about your purchase. The option Yes is selected by default, but you can also click No, which conveys this message: "I never want to hear from you or anyone else in the foreseeable future." Click Continue twice to finish setting up the computer.

Now you've reached the important stuff; the time has come for you to create your user account. Mac OS X has been kind enough to fill in the Name field, based on the registration information you supplied. However, you can modify this field to reflect your personal taste.

The Short Name field may contain an entry based upon an interesting combination of your first and last name. You can change this if you like—just make sure the name is no longer than eight characters and contains no spaces.

Next, enter the password for this computer, and then enter it a second time in the Verify field. You can also optionally enter a Password Hint. Click Continue, and you'll see a progress bar indicating that the account is being created.

At the next window, you can enter your Internet access options, or choose the I'm Not Ready To Connect To The Internet option to defer this task until later. To configure your Internet settings, you'll need to specify which of the following you use for Internet access:

- Dial-up modem

- Local area network (LAN)

- Cable modem

- Digital Subscriber Line (DSL)

- Airport wireless

Make your choice and click Continue.

If you are using a dial-up modem to access the Internet, you'll be asked to provide your username and password. If you'd prefer to be prompted for your password, leave the field blank.

Next, enter the phone number you dial to access your Internet service provider. If you need to dial any special numbers for an outside line, enter that number in the next field. You can also alert Mac OS X to the fact that you have Call Waiting. Click Continue.

If you indicated Yes for Call Waiting, you can enter the key code to disable it. Apple has supplied the code *70, which works with most systems. Click Continue.

To configure the modem, specify how your modem is connected to your computer. Choose your modem model from the pop-up menu, and then click Continue. You can now skip to the "Finishing the Installation" section.

If you will connect to the Internet via an Ethernet port to a LAN, cable, or DSL modem, the next window will ask you to provide your TCP/IP connection method—Static IP, BootP server, or DHCP server. Depending on your selection, various fields will appear. For static IP, you'll need to enter your IP address, subnet mask, router address, and DNS hosts. For BootP and DHCP, most of these fields will be replaced with the phrase *Will Be Supplied By Server*. Optionally, you can supply the DNS host address as well as the domain name and proxy server settings. Enter your settings and click Continue. Your computer will be configured with the appropriate settings. See Chapter 16 for detailed information about choosing the correct network settings to connect to an ISP.

Finishing the Installation

A few more settings remain to be entered. You will be prompted to choose your time zone. You can use the map to graphically choose your location or select the time zone from the pop-up menu below the map. Choose your time zone and click Continue.

You will now be prompted to enter the correct date and time. You can use the calendar to select the date (if the month and year are incorrect, click the arrows until the current month and year appear). The current time will also be listed. You can manually enter the correct time (using military [24-hour] time) or use the arrow keys to adjust the time. If military time confuses you, try moving the hands on the clock. When your settings are correct, click the Save button and then the Continue button.

If your computer is configured to access the Internet, Mac OS X will attempt to connect and submit your registration. If you are not connected, Mac OS X will remind you that you can manually register at a later date by going to **www.apple.com/register**. Click Done. Now you're ready to use Mac OS X!

Updating Mac OS 9.1 and Mac OS X

Both Mac OS 9.1 and Mac OS X have the ability to update the operating system automatically over the Internet via the Software Update feature. In Mac OS 9.1, this feature is found in the Software Update Control Panel; in Mac OS X, it's found in the Software Update pane of the System Preferences. Because the Mac OS is modular, various components of the OS may be upgraded independently of the Mac OS as a whole. This is a real timesaver, considering how long it would take to upgrade the entire OS over the Internet! You don't have to update the Mac OS, but it's a good idea to check the Apple Web site (**www.apple.com**) often for a new version of the OS that may potentially add new features, increase the speed of the OS, or fix a bug or incompatibility.

You can manually check for software updates, or schedule the Software Update feature to look automatically for new software on a scheduled basis. To check manually for new versions of Mac OS components:

1. Open the Software Update Control Panel (Mac OS 9.1) or System Preferences (Mac OS X)—examples of both are shown in Figure E.8.

2. Click the Update Now button.

3. A status indicator will provide visual confirmation that a connection is being made to search for software updates.

4. Quit Software Update.

Figure E.8
The Software Update feature for Mac OS 9.1 (top) and Mac OS X (bottom).

If the Software Update feature finds no updates for your particular model of Macintosh or the versions of Mac OS components that are installed on it, you'll be informed that no updates are necessary.

You can also check for updates on a schedule that's convenient for you. This frees you from having to remember to do it manually. I prefer to check for updates on a weekly basis.

To configure an automated update in Mac OS 9.1:

1. Open the Software Update Control Panel.

2. Check the Update Software Automatically checkbox.

3. Click on the Schedule button and choose a schedule for the update, including the time of day and days of the week.

4. Click the OK button to close the Schedule window.

5. Indicate whether you want to be asked by the Mac OS before downloading the updates by checking (or not) the option entitled Ask Me Before Installing New Software.

6. Quit the Software Update Control Panel.

To configure an automated update in Mac OS X:

1. Open the Software Update System Preferences.

2. Select the Update Software Automatically button.

3. Choose to update software on a daily, weekly, or monthly basis in the Check For Updates pop-up menu.

4. Quit the System Preferences.

At the appointed time, the Software Update feature will automatically launch and start searching for updated versions of the Mac OS. If no updates are found, then it will not attempt to install anything. If an update is found, you'll be presented with an option similar to the ones shown in Figure E.9. In this example, multiple components for Mac OS 9.1 are available (top); only one component for Mac OS X is available for updating (bottom).

E

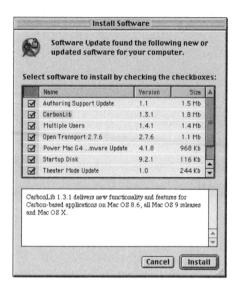

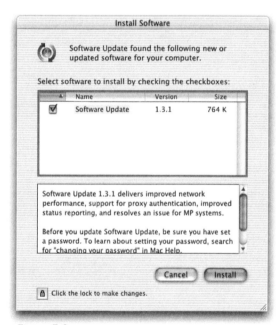

Figure E.9
Selecting software components to update in Mac OS 9.1 (top) and Mac OS X (bottom).

If you select a software package to update, you may have to restart your computer to complete the updating process (but not always). Some update packages may be several megabytes in size and could take more than an hour to download, depending on the speed of your Internet access. In the case of Mac OS X, you may be asked to enter an administrative username and password to make changes to the OS by selecting the Click The Lock To Make Changes option.

Additional Resources on the Web

Thousands of Web sites contain relevant information about the Mac OS, Apple Computer, Mac software and hardware, and news about computers in general. Too many, in fact, to be always sure where to go for the most accurate and up-to-date information. The following categories of Web sites contain the URLs of some of the best sites available at this time. Before you try any of these sites, please visit the two sites devoted to this book: my own site and the Coriolis Web site. You'll find the latest information about this book, including corrections and additions, as well as information about upcoming books about the Mac OS.

The Mac OS X Book

The Author's Home Page
www.macosbook.com

The Coriolis Group's Home Page
www.coriolis.com

Apple Computer

Apple Home Page
www.apple.com

Mac OS X Home Page
www.apple.com/macosx

Apple Products
www.apple.com/guide

Apple Support
www.apple.com/support

Apple Software Updates
www.apple.com/swupdates

Apple News
www.apple.com/hotnews

Apple Store
www.apple.com/store

Apple Developer
www.apple.com/developer

Apple Resource Locator
www.apple.com/buy

Apple iTools
http://itools.mac.com

Apple Open Source
http://publicsource.apple.com

Mac OS X–Related Sites

Macintosh News Network: Mac OS X News
http://osx.macnn.com

MacInTouch: Mac OS X Reader Reports
www.macintouch.com/mosxreaderreports.html

Mac OS X Hints
www.macosxhints.com

MacFixIt: Troubleshooting for Mac OS X
www.macfixit.com/macosx.shtml

Macworld: Mac OS X
www.macworld.com/subject/macosx/

Stepwise.com
www.stepwise.com

Mac OS X.org
www.macosx.org

Xappeal.org
www.xappeal.org

VersionTracker: Mac OS X
www.VersionTracker.com/vt_mac_osx.shtml

Mac OS X Server
www.macosxserver.com

Apple and Macintosh News

Macintosh News Network
www.macnn.com

MacInTouch
www.macintouch.com

Apple Insider
www.appleinsider.com

Mac OS Rumors
www.macosrumors.com

MacCentral Online
www.maccentral.com

Macinsites
www.macinsites.com

Apple and Macintosh Publications

Macworld
http://macworld.zdnet.com

MacAddict
www.macaddict.com

MacWEEK
www.macweek.com

Inside MacGames Magazine
www.imgmagazine.com

Mac Gamer's Ledge
www.macgamer.com

Mac Gaming
http://maccentral.macworld.com/games/

MacHome Interactive
www.machome.com

MacTech Magazine
www.mactech.com

Mac Design Magazine
www.macdesignonline.com

Macintosh Hardware and Software

Mac OS X Apps
www.macosxapps.com

Apple Mac OS X Downloads
www.apple.com/downloads/macosx

ClubMac
www.clubmac.com

Deal Mac
www.dealmac.com

Mac Trading Post
www.mactradingpost.com

MacMall
http://www.cc-inc.com/macmall/

MacWarehouse
www.warehouse.com/apple

MacConnection
www.macconnection.com

MacRes-Q
www.macresq.com

MacZone
www.maczone.com

Mostly Mac
www.mostlymac.com

FireWire Products
www.apple.com/firewire/firewireproducts.html

USB Stuff
www.usbstuff.com

Mac OS X Applications
www.macosxapps.com

F

Index

M

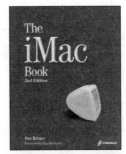

What's on the CD-ROM

The Mac OS X Book's companion CD-ROM contains elements specifically selected to enhance the usefulness of this book, including:

- *DragThing*—A powerful and flexible utility from James Thomson and TLA Systems for enhancing access to frequently used files, folders, applications, and other resources. The demo version displays a reminder to register and disables certain advanced features.

- *BBEdit*—The Lite version of the Bare Bones flagship HTML editing program, BBEdit, as well as a fully-functional but time-limited demo version of the commercial version of BBEdit.

- *GraphicConverter*—An essential shareware graphic editing application from Lemke Software that can open just about any graphic file format.

- *OmniWeb*—A demo version of the Mac OS X–native and award-winning Web browser.

- *iTools*—A 14-day unlimited demo version of the premier tool from Tenon Intersystems for providing Web browser–based configuration and management of Apache and other TCP/IP services.

- *AutoCompleter*—A shareware version of the award-winning utility for adding auto-completion capabilities to any Cocoa application.

- *Space.dock*—A freeware Dockling that creates virtual Desktops to increase workspace in Mac OS X.

- *MetamorphX*—A freeware utility for changing "themes" in Mac OS X.

- *Docking Maneuvers*—A freeware utility that unlocks hidden features allowing the Dock to be repositioned.

Note: *This book does not contain a copy of Mac OS X.*

System Requirements

Software

- Mac OS X.

- StuffIt Expander is needed to decompress the archived files included on the CD-ROM. StuffIt Expander is installed as part of Mac OS X and is located in the Utilities folder, or you can visit **www.aladdinsys.com** and download the latest version.

- Disk Utility is required to mount disk image files, and is also installed in the Utilities folder as part of Mac OS X.

Hardware

- Any Apple computer capable of running Mac OS X, including all G3- and G4-based computers except the original G3 PowerBook.